The extended self

MANCHESTER
1824

Manchester University Press

The extended self

Architecture, memes and minds

Chris Abel

Manchester University Press

Published by Manchester University Press
Altrincham Street, Manchester, M1 7JA, UK
www.manchesteruniversitypress.co.uk

British Library Cataloguing-in-Publication Data
A catalogue record for this book is available from the British Library

Library of Congress Cataloging-in-Publication Data applied for

ISBN 978 0 7190 9611 2   hardback

ISBN 978 0 7190 9612 9   paperback

First published 2015

Typeset in Bembo and Gill Sans by R. J. Footring Ltd, Derby
Printed in Great Britain
by Bell & Bain Ltd, Glasgow

For Margaret Perrin

Contents

List of figures   *page* ix
Preface   xv
Acknowledgments   xviii

Introduction   1

Part I: Identities

1 The common bond   7
   Place-identity · Place in architectural theory · Invisible landscapes · Disputed
   values · Cultural relativism · Proxemics · Narratives of the self · The politics
   of place

2 The body nucleus   26
   Architecture and the body · The persisting point · Theory of perception ·
   Tacit knowing · Spatial dynamic · Resolving the mind–body problem ·
   Indivisible reality

3 Embodied minds   39
   The enigma of the self · Body mapping and spatial extensions · Peripersonal
   space · Identifying with others · The aggregates of experience · Perpetual
   paradox · Extended cognition · Fields of being

Part I summary   55

Part II: Origins

4 Technics and the human   61
   The dynamics of technics · Epiphylogenesis · Debates and discrepancies ·
   Writing metaphors · Sociality and location

5 Rethinking evolution   73
   Nature's algorithm · A narrative science · The fourth dimension · Fatal
   flaw · Toward a natural history · Survival of the weakest · Brains and baby
   slings · Emergence · Autopoiesis and natural drift · More than a metaphor

6 From genes to memes   93
> *The replicators · The extended phenotype · Units of cultural transmission*
> *Abstract principles · Problems of definition · Memes and vehicles ·*
> *Meta-representation · Niche construction · Meme complexes ·*
> *Neurological composition · Beyond reductionism*

Part II summary   113

Part III: Combinations

7 Types and taxonomies   119
> *The roots of combinativity · Nature as model · Parts and wholes ·*
> *Classifying building types · Implicit and explicit meanings · Global types ·*
> *Urban typologies · Linked problem solutions · A question of logic ·*
> *Self-producing types*

8 Technical memes and assemblages   149
> *Form and content · The technical meme · Assemblage theory and the*
> *extended self · Contingent effects · Coevolutionary assemblages · Life on*
> *wheels · Symbol of mass consumption · The greatest public works project ·*
> *Urban impacts*

9 Combinatorial design   173
> *Cultural imperatives · Hybridization · Change and innovation · How*
> *technology evolves · Breaking surface · Mixed origins of radical design ·*
> *Evolution of the tower type... · ... and beyond*

Part III summary   213

Part IV: Transformations

10 Recasting the extended self   219
> *Creatures of habit · The illusion of free will · Waking up from the suburban*
> *dream · Obstacles to change · Adaptation or addiction? · Reducing*
> *automobile dependency · New urban structures*

11 Appropriating cyberspace   236
> *The topology of cyberspace · Cyberspace as movement space · Ghosts of*
> *Cartesian dualism · Gender inflections · Virtual selves · Customized*
> *automation · Design by artificial selection · Electronic ecologies*

Part IV summary   259

Postscript   262

Notes   272

Bibliography   329

Index   345

Figures

1.1 House on the outskirts of Sydney, by Glenn Murcutt, 1983.
Courtesy: Glenn Murcutt   *page* 8
1.2 Irwin House, Pasadena, Los Angeles, by Greene & Greene, 1906.
Photo and copyright: author   9
1.3 Idealized image of conventional suburban home. Fotosearch, Standard
License   10
1.4 A typical California bungalow in the suburbs of Wollongong, New
South Wales, Australia. Photo and copyright: author   11
1.5 A typical California bungalow in the suburbs of Los Angeles.
Photo and copyright: author   11
1.6 The streets and squares of Valletta, Malta. Photo and copyright: author   14
1.7 The Strip, Las Vegas, c. 1980. Photo and copyright: author   18
2.1 Vitruvian Man, by Leonardo da Vinci, c. 1492. Google Images   27
2.2 Le Corbusier's Modulor system of proportion. Copyright: Design &
Artists Copyright Society   27
2.3 Schematic plan of a Dogon village, Mali, by Douglas Fraser.
Copyright: George Braziller, Inc.   28
2.4 Diagram of upright human body, space and time, by Yi Fu Tuan,
Space and Place: The Perspective of Experience, Edward Arnold, 1977.
Courtesy: Hodder Education   29
2.5 British tennis champion Andy Murray in action. Photo by Clive
Brunskill. Copyright: Getty Images   35
5.1 Speculative drawings by Daniel Dennett of alternative ways of filling
upper corners in square rooms roofed by domes. Dennett, *Darwin's
Dangerous Idea*, Penguin, 1995. Courtesy: Penguin Books   79
5.2 Plans of the Coban Mustafa Pasa Mosque, Gebze, and the Haseki
Sultan Mosque, Istanbul, by Sinan, 1538. Aptulla Kuran, *Sinan*, ADA
Press, 1987. Copyright: Institute of Turkish Studies   80
5.3 Baby in sling on mother's back in Wangdue Phodrang, Bhutan.
Fotosearch: Rights Managed   84
5.4 Diagram of relations between an organism, its world, and the observer's
environment, after Humberto Maturana and Francisco Varela. Mingers,

Self-Producing Systems, Plenum Press, 1995. Courtesy: Springer Science and Business Media   90

7.1   Replicated hominid hand-axe forms. Gibson and Ingold, *Tools, Language and Cognition in Human Evolution*, Cambridge University Press, 1993. Courtesy: CUP   120

7.2   Schematic plan of a Bororo village, after Claude Lévi-Strauss. Choay, 'Urbanism and Semiology,' *Meaning in Architecture*, George Braziller, 1969. Courtesy: George Braziller, Inc.   122

7.3   Drawing by A. Bartholomew comparing the counter-abutments of gothic vaulting with the human skeleton. Steadman, *Evolution of Designs*, Routledge, 2008. Copyright: Taylor & Francis   125

7.4   New York Life Building, Chicago, 1894, by Jenney and Mundie. Huxtable, *The Tall Building Artistically Reconsidered*, Pantheon Books, 1982. Copyright: Georges Borchardt, Inc.   126

7.5   Le Corbusier's Domino House, 1914. *Le Corbusier 1910–60*, Editions Girsberger, 1960. Copyright: Design & Artists Copyright Society   127

7.6   Skulls of two species of primitive rhinoceros compared by the method of Cartesian deformation. Thompson, *On Growth and Form*, Cambridge University Press, 1966. Courtesy: CUP   128

7.7   Comparative plans of major eighteenth-century European theaters. Pevsner, *A History of Building Types*, Thames & Hudson, 1976. Courtesy: Penguin Books   131

7.8   Design of Pentonville Prison, 1842. Markus, *Buildings and Power*, Routledge, 1993. Copyright: Taylor & Francis   134

7.9   Aerial view of design for a model workhouse for 300 persons, 1835. Markus, *Buildings and Power*, Routledge, 1993. Copyright: Taylor & Francis   134

7.10   Rouse Hill town center, northwest Sydney. Photo and copyright: author   137

7.11   Figure-ground study of part of Le Corbusier's Plan Voisin, Paris, 1925, graphic by Stuart Cohen and Steven Hurtt. Rowe and Koetter, *Collage City*, MIT Press, 1978. Courtesy: Stuart Cohen and Steven Hurtt   140

7.12   Dining chair and side chair, 1958, by Charles Eames. Drexler, *Charles Eames: Furniture*, Museum of Modern Art, New York, 1973. Photo and copyright: Charles Eames/MOMA   146

8.1   Plan and elevation of Villa Malcontenta, 1560, by Andrea Palladio. Palladio, *The Four Books of Architecture*, Dover Publications, 1965   152

8.2   Front of Villa Stein, 1927, by Le Corbusier. *Le Corbusier 1910–60*, Editions Girsberger, 1960. Copyright: Design & Artists Copyright Society   153

8.3   Analytical diagrams comparing plan of Palladio's Villa Malcontenta with Le Corbusier's Villa Stein. Rowe, *The Mathematics of the Ideal Villa*, MIT Press, 1976. Copyright: MIT Press   154

8.4 Egyptian rendering of a battle with chariots, c. 2000 BC.
    Samuel Lilley, *Men, Machines and History*, International Publishers,
    1966   163
8.5 A waterwheel being used to draw heavy iron wire, c. 1540. Lilly, *Men,*
    Machines and History, International Publishers, 1966   165
8.6 Ford Model T tourer, Mk 1, 1913. Courtesy: Ford Motor Company   167
8.7 Interstate freeway, Westchester County, New York State, c. 1965.
    Photo: Fairchild Aerial Surveys. Copyright: New York State Archives   170
8.8 Traditional mid-twentieth-century suburban house with a front porch,
    in Lubbock, Texas. Photo and copyright: author   171
8.9 Typical large suburban houses in America, nicknamed 'MacMansions.'
    Fotosearch: Standard License   171
9.1 Painting of the interior of a Japanese house and its occupants by an
    unknown artist, 1849. Copyright: author   175
9.2 Schematic plan of a Bawamataluo village, South Nias, Indonesia, by
    Douglas Fraser. Fraser, *Village Planning in the Primitive World*, George
    Braziller, 1967. Courtesy: George Braziller, Inc.   178
9.3 Sectional drawing of the old Kampung Laut Mosque at Nilam Puri,
    Kota Bharu, Kelantan, Malaysia. Abdul Halim Nasir, *Mosques of*
    Peninsula Malaysia, Berita Publishing, 1984   179
9.4 View across the central public open space, called the Padang, in Kuala
    Lumpur, Malaysia. Photo and copyright: author   180
9.5 Ye Olde Smokehouse Inn, Cameron highlands, near Kuala Lumpur.
    Photo and copyright: author   180
9.6 High Court building, Kuala Lumpur, by A. C. Norman, 1909. Photo
    and copyright: author   181
9.7 Regional variations of the traditional Malay house type in the Malay
    peninsula. Yuan, *The Malay House*, Institute Masyarakat, 1987.
    Courtesy: Lim Jee Yuan   182
9.8 Characteristic Malay house in Penang with an 'A'-type roof form and
    atap covering. Photo and copyright: author   182
9.9 Colonial-era villa in Georgetown, Penang, Malaysia. Photo and
    copyright: author   183
9.10 Villa Cornaro, Piombino Dese, near Padua, Italy, 1570, by Andrea
    Palladio. Photo and copyright: author   184
9.11 Characteristic deep plan forms of terraced Chinese shop-houses
    found in Southeast Asia. Gurstein, 'Traditional Chinese Shophouses
    of Peninsula Malaysia,' *UIA International Architect*, no. 6, 1984.
    Courtesy: Penny Gurstein   185
9.12 Shop-houses in Georgetown with a 'Palladian motif' repeated at first-
    floor windows. Photo and copyright: author   186
9.13 Detail of the main façade of the Basilica, Vicenza, 1550, by
    Andrea Palladio, showing original Palladian motif at an upper level.
    Photo and copyright: author   186

List of figures

9.14 Sketches showing the evolution of the 'Queensland house' type from earlier colonial typologies in Ipswich, 1800–1920. Saini and Joyce, *The Australian House*, Lansdowne, 1982. Copyright: Balwant Saini   187

9.15 Schematic drawing of timber roof structure for a typical seventeenth-century adobe church in New Mexico. Kubler, *The Religious Architecture of New Mexico*, University of New Mexico Press, 1972. Courtesy: UNMP   190

9.16 Schwandbach Bridge, Canton Berne, Switzerland, 1933, by Robert Maillart. Gideon, *Space, Time and Architecture*, Harvard University Press, 1954. Copyright: Paul & Peter Fritz AG   196

9.17 The first safe mechanical elevator, invented by Elisha Grave Otis, 1853. Gidion, *Space, Time and Architecture*, Harvard University Press, 1954. Courtesy: Otis   198

9.18 St Paul Building, New York, 1890, by George B. Post. Shepherd, *Skyscraper*, McGraw-Hill, 2003. Copyright (drawing only): McGraw-Hill. Copyright (photo only): Museum of the City of New York   200

9.19 Woolworth Building, New York, 1913, by Cass Gilbert. Nash, *Manhattan Skyscrapers*, Princeton Architectural Press, 1999. Photo and copyright: Norman McGrath   201

9.20 Chrysler Building, New York, 1930, by William Van Alen. Sheppard, *Skyscrapers: Masterpieces of Architecture*, Todtri, 1996. Photo and copyright: Patti McConville   201

9.21 Larkin Building, Buffalo, 1903, by Frank Lloyd Wright. Frampton, *Modern Architecture 1851–1945*, Rizzoli, 1983. Copyright: Frank Lloyd Wright Foundation   202

9.22 Model of glass skyscraper project, Berlin, 1921, by Mies van der Rohe. Spaeth, *Mies van der Rohe*, Architectural Press, 1985. Courtesy: Architectural Press   203

9.23 Lever House, New York, 1952, by Skidmore, Owings & Merrill (SOM). Photo: Ezra Stoller. Copyright: Esto Photographics   203

9.24 Hongkong and Shanghai Bank Corporation (HSBC) headquarters, Hong Kong, 1986, by Foster & Partners. Photo and copyright: Ian Lambot   204

9.25 National Commercial Bank, Jeddah, Saudi Arabia, 1982, by SOM. Courtesy: Skidmore Owens and Merrill/Aga Khan Trust for Culture   205

9.26 Capita Centre, Sydney, 1989, by Harry Seidler. Courtesy: Harry Seidler   206

9.27 Sectional drawing of Commerzbank, Frankfurt, 1997, by Foster & Partners. Courtesy: Foster & Partners   206

9.28 Menara Mesiniaga, Kuala Lumpur, 1992, by T. R. Hamzah and K. Yeang. Courtesy: Ken Yeang   207

9.29 Swiss Re, London, 2003, by Foster & Partners. Copyright: Nigel Young/Foster & Partners   207

9.30 Competition entry for World Trade Center towers, 2002, by United
      Architects. Courtesy: Greg Lynn FORM and United Architects   208
9.31 Competition entry for World Trade Center towers, 2002, by Foreign
      Office Architects (FOA). Copyright: Alejandro Polo   209
9.32 Vertical Architecture STudio (VAST), 2006. Project for central Sydney,
      by Renn, Waterman and Wrightson, University of Sydney. Copyright:
      Chris Abel/University of Sydney   210
9.33 VAST, 2009. Project for a Vertical Garden City, Mark III, Barangaroo,
      Sydney, by Nor, Turner and Wang, University of New South Wales.
      Copyright: Chris Abel/University of New South Wales   211
10.1 Typical jumbo-sized American SUVs seen in Lincoln, Nebraska. Photo
      and copyright: author   222
10.2 A row of stone statues on Easter Island. Photo by Peter Marble.
      Copyright: Fotosearch, Standard License   229
10.3 Project by Alfie Arcuri, University of New South Wales, 2010,
      for an integrated, mixed-use town center and lower-level railway
      station for Leppington, Sydney. Copyright: Chris Abel/University
      of New South Wales   234
10.4 Rendering from the masterplan of Masdar City, Abu Dhabi, 2007,
      by Foster & Partners. Courtesy: Foster & Partners   234
11.1 The Boulevard Richard-Lenoir, 1861–63, part of Eugène
      Haussmann's plan for Paris. Gideon, *Space, Time and Architecture*,
      Harvard University Press. Copyright: HUP   237
11.2 Miletos, Greece, 466 BC. Plan, after Hippodamus.
      Courtesy: George Braziller, Inc.   238
11.3 Plan for Chicago, USA, 1909, by Daniel Burnham.
      Courtesy: George Braziller, Inc.   238
11.4 Front cover for special issue on cyberspace of *Time* magazine, spring,
      1995. Copyright: TIME Inc.   240
11.5 Part of map of Rome, Italy, 1748, by Giambattista Nolli. Bacon,
      Design of Cities, Penguin Books, 1976   241
11.6 Forbidden City, seventeenth-century Peking, China. Plan, after
      Chuta Ito. Mitsuo Inoue, *Space in Japanese Architecture*,
      Weatherhill Publishers, 1985. Copyright: Mitsuo Inoue and
      Hiroshi Watanabe   242
11.7 Eighteenth-century Karlsruhe, Germany. Plan. *Diercke International
      Atlas*. Copyright: Diercke Weltatlas   242
11.8 Hommaru Palace compound, Edo Castle, Japan, 1640. Plan, after
      Akira Naito. Mitsuo Inoue, *Space in Japanese Architecture*, Weatherhill
      Publishers, 1985. Copyright: Mitsuo Inoue and Hiroshi Watana   243
11.9 Diagrams of movement space (a) with orthogonal geometry and
      (b) with irregular geometry. After Mitsuo Inoue. Mitsuo Inoue,
      Space in Japanese Architecture, Weatherhill Publishers, 1985.
      Copyright: Mitsuo Inoue and Hiroshi Watanabe   244

11.10 Model of the System 24, Molins Machine Company, c. 1965.
Williamson, *Mollins Machine Company*, c. 1965. Courtesy: Mollins
Machine Company   252

11.11 Guggenheim Museum Bilbao, 1997, by Frank Gehry. Photo and
copyright: author   253

11.12 (a) Molteni Arc table. Courtesy: Molteni. (b) Parametric modeling
techniques. Courtesy: Foster & Partners   255

11.13 Prototype for a combined wall and seating unit, by Foster & Partners.
Courtesy: Foster & Partners   255

Preface

Nobody knows how long we have, under the present system, before some disaster strikes us, more serious than the destruction of any group of nations. The most important task today is, perhaps, to learn to think in the new way.

Gregory Bateson, 1970[1]

The theory of the extended self that is presented in this book was conceived, researched and written over the past eight years. However, the full period of its gestation goes back as far as the late 1960s, beginning with my earliest efforts in applying cybernetic concepts and systems thinking to architectural and urban planning theory, as listed in the bibliography. Those first tentative steps outside conventional architectural discourses were followed by continuous explorations over the ensuing years into the impacts of the built environment on personal and cultural identities – researches that were also invariably influenced by other disciplines – together with studies of the technological aspects of architectural production and their related effects. Summarizing that early work in a 1980 conference paper partly inspired by Gregory Bateson, the American cybernetician and polymath whose prescient words are quoted above, I wrote: 'A theory of mind which disperses the processes of human mentation among the group must also take into account the role of the physical environment in the evolution of mind.'[2]

That it has taken this long to elucidate the idea crystalized in that single sentence testifies not only to the complexity of the subject, but also to the need to make a strong enough case to overcome prevailing prejudices. Following the widespread rejection of orthodox modernism's optimistic but ill-fated assumptions of universal progress, it has been fashionable among architectural theorists as well as certain philosophers for a long time now to decry and debase any grand narratives or global perspectives. Despite these trends, however, unencumbered by the deterministic thinking that misled modernists, the more enduring principles of self-organization and related concepts established by the founders of systems theory and cybernetics have since been much elaborated, providing a healthy antidote and counter-movement to the narrower and nihilistic aspects of postmodernism.

Beyond any theoretical interests or academic commitments, the urge to attempt a book of this scope has been strongly motivated by the gathering warnings of runaway climate change and environmental degradation, for which the energy-hungry homes, automobiles and other things we typically make and use are much to blame. Whichever way postmodernists of the narrow school may like to interpret it, a grand, planetary-scale narrative with perilous consequences is unfolding in real time and urgently needs to be met by equally broad explanatory theories and alternative visions for the future. In this respect, the more than seven years I spent living in Australia – the latter five as an Australian citizen – where the great majority of people live in some of the most automobile-dependent cities in the world, have had a profound influence on my thinking, and on the direction and purpose of this book. Coming as that experience has after having also spent several years living in the USA in the late 1970s and early '80s, I was particularly struck by the similarities between Australian and American urban cultures and the spatial characteristics of their cities, as well as by the building types common to both, much of which is generated by a shared obsession with automobiles as personal possessions, beyond their utilitarian functions. The lessons I have learnt about the failures of modern dispersed cities to provide sustainable forms of habitation therefore have equal relevance on both sides of the Pacific, as well as anywhere else where similar patterns of urban life predominate.

However, while the problems of urban dispersal and automobile dependency are well known, as are the practical solutions to those problems, the reasons for the tragic failure to implement those solutions effectively are much less understood. It is the purpose of this book to shed some light on the origins of the personal and collective addiction to a technological culture that is rapidly spinning out of control. In so doing, we may be better prepared to take more effective action to cure our ills.

In addition to the guiding principles and basic concepts set out in the Introduction, the structure of the book itself is designed to help readers navigate this challenging and many-sided discourse. Broadly speaking, the first two parts offer a critical overview of the main schools of thought related to our theme, and highlight the key theoretical issues and problems to be resolved. Building on the preceding researches, the latter two parts of the book posit constructive and viable approaches and solutions to those problems, supported by numerous examples. A summary of the main ideas and conclusions presented in each group of chapters is also included at the end of that group, while each chapter also begins with a short introduction to help link the key arguments together. The Postscript further clarifies the philosophical principles underlying the approach and its relation to postmodern debates. If they wish, readers can therefore choose to run through the summaries first in order to get a quick idea of the main points before delving into each chapter.

Finally, while, as mentioned, some of the key theoretical foundations for this work were laid down many years ago, repetition of previously published texts has generally been minimized. The main exception is the final chapter, 'Appropriating Cyberspace,' passages of which are drawn from 'Cyberspace in Mind,' which was published as a chapter in an edited collection of my essays, *Architecture, Technology and Process*, by Architectural Press in 2004, and was in turn based on an earlier paper presented at a 1996 symposium, 'A Meeting of Metaphors,' by the Design

Research Society in London. Some passages in Chapters 1–3 are also abstracted from an essay of mine on the same subject, 'The Extended Self: Tacit Knowing and Place-Identity.' Originally written in 2009–10 at the request of editor Ritu Bhatt for her book *Rethinking Aesthetics: The Role of Body in Design*, the essay was published in that book by Routledge in 2013. A few passages from my 1979 essay 'Rationality and Meaning in Design,' explaining George Herbert Mead's concepts of mind and self-consciousness and their relevance to understanding architectural symbolism, are also included in the Postscript. The latter essay, together with a number of the other writings that I have described as building blocks for this book, has been republished in the first edition of my earlier collection of essays, *Architecture and Identity*, also by Architectural Press, in 1997 (the second edition, 2000, omits that essay, which was also republished elsewhere, but includes more recent works).

However, while the research covered in this book draws upon these and many accredited works written by others, the full theory of the extended self as set out in the following pages is entirely the fruit of my own recent labors.

Carrickfergus, February 2014

Acknowledgments

If the trail of the foundations for this book mentioned in the Preface were to be followed all the way back, the potential list of acknowledgments would be endless. However, most of those helpful persons concerned in those formative years have in any case already been named in the two collections of essays cited in there. I shall therefore confine myself here firstly to thanking a far smaller group of people who have had a direct impact on this particular work during the period in which it was actually written, and then latterly thank those key individuals in the more distant past who supported my previous forays into other disciplines and discourses.

Foremost among those persons to whom I am lately indebted is Professor Chris Smith at the University of Sydney, who supervised the doctoral thesis I completed in Australia in 2011 on which this book is largely based. His constructive advice and constant support were vital to the successful completion of the thesis, which bears the same title as the book. Dr John Wilkins at the University of Melbourne also lent valuable advice on speciation, which greatly helped to sharpen my own understanding of that subject and its various interpretations. I am also especially grateful to my old friend Alexander Cuthbert, emeritus professor of planning and urban development at the University of New South Wales, where I taught for several years, for his steadfast support and encouragement during some of the more difficult periods of the whole process. John Zerby, a mutual friend and former professor of urban economics still teaching at UNSW, also had many useful comments and suggestions to make, and, like Alex, understood and appreciated the scope and ambition of the exercise. Beyond Australia's shores, the invitation by Professor Bhatt at the University of Minnesota, who had read a 1981 essay I had published on the relevance of Michael Polanyi's theory of tacit knowing to architecture, to elaborate on those ideas for the edited collection cited in the Preface, greatly helped to focus my thoughts at an early stage in this work.

Loosening the timeframe, I must also express my deep gratitude for the late Harry Seidler's official and unofficial support for my migration to Australia in 2004, the environmental challenges of which loom large in these pages, and for my introduction to Tom Heneghan, then Chair of Architecture at Sydney University and still a good friend. Tom left the University before I actually began this project but was there to support my first Vertical Architecture STudio (VAST), which is briefly mentioned among the case studies in the evolution of the tower type described in this book. Thanks to Tom and others mentioned here – not forgetting my hard-working and creative students – the years I spent in Australia were among the most productive of my career.

Going further back, aside from my earlier researches into customized automation and other advanced methods of architectural production – also documented in my book *Architecture and Identity* – I owe my qualifications to write about technological matters in good part to my close studies of the work of Norman Foster and his practice over more than a quarter of a century, both as an independent critic and as a collaborator on the practice's own monographs. Covering literally dozens of projects of every sort and scale around the world, three major examples of which are briefly mentioned in this book, the experience has afforded me the kind of detailed knowledge and insights into how buildings are conceived and made at every stage of the process that are rarely given to any academic or professional critic, for which I owe Lord Foster and his partners special thanks. Not least, their commitment to reducing the carbon footprint of buildings and cities as a whole, culminating in the experimental Masdar City project in Abu Dhabi, reinforced my own concerns with climate change and with its causes and consequences, of which this book is a direct outcome. Similarly, my early interest in the tower type and further investigations with my students in the VAST program have been inspired by the pioneering work on 'green skyscrapers' and vertical urban design by Ken Yeang, an old friend from when I was teaching in Malaysia and Singapore in the 1980s.

However, it is not possible to offer an evolutionary theory of the extended self solely based on modern technologies. As the reader will find, the discussions and examples in this book also range from the ancient history of the spoked wheel to vernacular architecture and settlement patterns in different parts of the world, as well as architecture dating from different colonial periods, in both the American Southwest and Southeast Asia. While, as with my other earlier researches, there are too many individuals and institutions involved to name here who made it possible for me to work in so many places and cultures, the scope of this book owes as much if not more to those personal experiences in teaching and researching architecture in many of the actual regions described in the following chapters as it does to the relevant studies by others that I have drawn upon in support of my own observations.

Lastly, an interdisciplinary project of this kind requires at least enough knowledge of science and its methods to afford insights into the way its practitioners think and work, and to appreciate the value of that work. In addition to those many authorities I have cited in the book, I am especially indebted for those insights to the late British cybernetician Gordon Pask. While I am no professional scientist or philosopher myself, as both my tutor and mentor during my final year as an architecture student in London when I was writing my thesis on self-organizing cities, and in the following first few years of my academic career when I was researching environmental psychology among other disciplines, Gordon encouraged me to explore what the new sciences had to offer. My subsequent studies, which involved my own experiments in computer-aided instruction (CAI) simulating architect–client dialogues at

MIT during 1973–74, were generously supported by Nicholas Negroponte and his Architecture Machine Group – the forerunner of the Media Lab – with whom I spent a semester as Visiting Scholar, also at Gordon's instigation.[1] In addition to what I gained from Gordon's own seminal researches in cybernetics and learning theory, the experience of working with these ideas and techniques opened up a whole world of scientific and philosophical debate on the conscious and unconscious aspects of human cognition and communication, without which this book would truly not have been conceivable.

Acknowledgments

Introduction

For all the countless studies and measures promoting sustainable development and design, or the many related projects around the globe, little progress has been made in reducing the world's dependency on fossil fuels and averting catastrophic climate change.[1] We know what needs to be done, while the dire consequences of not changing course have been clearly spelt out to us in the mountain of scientific reports and other researches on the subject – now substantiated by the growing frequency and ferocity of extreme weather events.[2] Yet we continue to flounder on, apparently incapable of confronting the harsh realities of a way of life that can lead only to disaster.

This book takes a fresh look at the root causes of that dependency and their origins from the joint perspectives of embodied minds and extended cognition. It traces those roots to the coevolution of *Homo sapiens* and technology, from the first use of tools as extensions of the human body to the motorized urban culture sweeping the globe, the environmental effects of which are fast changing the planet itself.[3] Refuting popular concepts of the self and free will as autonomous realms of being, it proposes a new theory of the 'extended self' as a complex and diffuse product of that coevolution, comprising both social and material elements, including built habitations and artifacts in general.

Given the nature and complexity of the subject matter, in researching this book it has been taken from the outset that no single discipline or school of thought, whether it be within the humanities or any of the sciences, would yield the requisite insights and answers to the range of issues and problems in question, all of which are related to each other in complicated ways. That consideration alone has presented manifold challenges in completing a work of this kind. Despite a growing acceptance of the need for interdisciplinary approaches to complex subjects, with notable exceptions – some of which are cited in the following chapters – the vast majority of academic research remains the province of specialists and specialized disciplines and methodologies, as embedded in university structures and programs everywhere, together with their associated jargons.[4] All too often, territorial imperatives and obedience to a particular discipline and paradigm trump objectivity and critical thought. As a result, it is generally the chosen discipline and approach that determine the questions that need to be resolved, rather than the other way around.[5]

As explained in this book, the habit of classifying things, including forms of information, is a universal human trait, as reflected in taxonomies of every sort, by which we seek to impose some kind of order on life. Unfortunately for us, the world we actually live in is a great deal more complex and opaque than most disciplines and research methods allow for, as we constantly discover and rediscover through the yawning gaps in our knowledge of it. Even the most fruitful schools of thought have their blind spots, having usually developed along specific lines of inquiry. Among the prominent approaches documented in the following chapters, for example, there is a well established interest in applying phenomenological methods and concepts to issues of place-identity and other environmental topics, not only among new generations of philosophers themselves, but also among architectural theorists.[6] However, regardless of the valuable insights phenomenology provides into human experience and the existential role of the human body, it remains intentionally focused on describing the world as directly experienced in the here and now – phenomenology in itself has little to offer that might explain how we got to be the way we are, or what there might have been in our past to influence present perceptions.

Likewise, while evolutionary theory promises to fill those gaps, it too is hobbled in its own manner by neo-Darwinian concepts of natural selection that provide little help in understanding the modern condition, and how we came to shape the world in our own image to the extent that the phrase 'natural environment' has little meaning anymore; not the least outcome being the urbanization of half the global population, along with possibly irreversible changes to the climate and biosphere. Following Bernard Stiegler,[7] the philosopher of human technics whose work is discussed at length in this book, and Timothy Taylor,[8] an archaeologist who arrived at much the same conclusion from his own studies, it is argued that the discovery and use of tools and other devices by *Homo sapiens* and our hominid predecessors to modify their environment in favor of their survival not only marks the beginning of the long trek of human evolution and cultural development, but actually defines us *as* human.[9] It follows that either the concepts of natural selection and inherited traits need revising to accommodate such factors, or some other, broader theory of evolution is required that can better integrate both natural and artificial phenomena – issues that are further discussed in this book in the sections on emergent and autopoietic or self-producing systems in Chapters 5 and 7.[10]

However, notwithstanding the originality of both Stiegler's and Taylor's work in expounding the coevolution of humans and technology, both stop short of clarifying the cognitive processes involved in technological assimilation and diffusion. In turn, though Richard Dawkins' inspired concept of the 'meme' as a cultural equivalent of the biological gene proffers a fertile approach to cultural evolution,[11] it also has been hampered by confusions of meaning and a general failure by its proponents to clarify what precisely constitutes a meme and how memes actually 'travel' between people, spreading their contents as they do.

Similarly, the very idea of a human self is a highly controversial subject with its own history of debates, raising the most problematic philosophical and scientific questions concerning the human mind, its nature and location and how it works.

In search of answers to those questions, the book explores some of the most recent theories and discoveries in the neurosciences regarding the symbiotic relations between mind and body – findings that strongly support both Maurice Merleau-Ponty's and Michael Polanyi's thoughts on the subject,[12] while also challenging lingering traces of Cartesian dualism elsewhere.[13] Significantly, related discoveries also confirm both philosophers' theories that embodied cognition reaches outwards beyond the physical boundaries of the human body to take in spaces and objects and even other people's thoughts within the personal domain.

Moreover, while the extended self is impacted by the bodily experience of inhabited spaces, it is not limited by those spatial dimensions but only by the technologies that enable people to absorb a more extensive social and cultural realm – technologies, as recounted in the final chapter, that now include the Internet and virtual selves. Conceived here as a continuous loop beginning and ending with the mind–body synthesis, the extended self reaches outward to embrace a complex world of many kinds of experiences involving both interpersonal and cultural transfusions, but which nevertheless depends upon that same mind–body synthesis to make sense of everything. All of which has major implications for understanding the nature of the self as the outcome of an interaction between many different elements, including the material environment, rather than the independent spiritual or mental entity of much religion and popular mythology.

However, while the various different theories and schools of thought referred to above may be found wanting in this or that respect, this by no means implies any lack of relevance. On the contrary, the approach adopted throughout the present volume has been to incorporate the most useful ideas on offer, whether from recent or earlier studies, while discarding any less helpful or erroneous points and positing new concepts as necessary. Based as the approach is, therefore, on many different fields of research and varied sources, the arguments deployed may seem at times to resemble a jigsaw puzzle rather than a strictly linear progression from one logical proposition to another. Nevertheless, a few key principles will assist readers in putting the whole picture together. Among these, the principle of *combinativity* and the cognitive skills that underlie it run throughout the book, bridging different scales of thought and classification systems in biology and architecture, together with related concepts of species and types. The same linking idea of combinativity is equally pertinent to assemblage theory and the theories of innovation and design covered in the later chapters.

Likewise, in keeping with the relational approach adopted by many of the leading thinkers cited here, an emphasis on both *process* and the *interactions* between different elements, whether they are organic or non-organic, biological or cultural, is generally favored over detailed examination of the elements themselves, with some exceptions for selected architectural and technological case studies. All three principles are key to understanding how types of buildings and other artifacts evolve and propagate through human populations. The jigsaw-like methodology of the research is itself therefore an analogue for the principles of combinativity and interaction underlying much of what follows.

Beyond these general principles, the related concepts of 'self-producing types' and 'technical memes and assemblages' proposed in the second half of the book proffer viable modes of cognitive extension and reproduction, answering many of the outstanding theoretical questions and problems described in the first half, as outlined above. Rather than relying on viral metaphors, as has been fashionable, more concrete evidence for the way memes are propagated and may become entrenched in people's minds is also available in the growing literature on 'tribal thinking' and its psychological and social variants – climate change denial being just one expression of the common resistance to any information that challenges preconceptions or customary ways of life. Contrary to popular beliefs in free will, the conclusion is that, barring external invasions and other upheavals, human societies and their members are inherently *conservative* and that internal change and innovation proceed in mostly incremental steps, often despite collective and individual resistance.

The theory of the extended self that is expounded in this book therefore has dual aspects of a bright and darker character. On the one hand, the extension or 'exteriorization' of human capacities by technical means and artifice as it is described here is largely responsible for all the wondrous achievements of human creativity and culture, of which architecture of both the vernacular and professional kind is among the most visible and enduring. Those achievements in turn depend upon the unique human ability to interpret and record what we do by various technical methods and thereby pass them on to future generations to build upon, in what are effectively culture's own evolutionary procedures, the precise nature of which are a major focus of this book.

On the other hand, it is now frighteningly clear that those same extraordinary gifts of extension into and control over the natural environment, in which architecture and urbanization again play major roles, have taken us to the point where they are threatening to destroy that environment and the civilization responsible for its deterioration along with it.[14] The final outcome of the present global conflict with nature remains uncertain. However, just as it is common knowledge that the first essential step toward curing an addiction is to recognize it, so is it necessary to search for and to comprehend as best we can the reasons for humanity's stubborn adherence to a technological culture that, if left unchecked, endangers the survival of our species, together with that of countless others on the planet.[15]

Part I: Identities

1 The common bond

The merging of personal and group identities with specific places, whether they are family homes, neighborhoods or cities, is one of the most commonly accepted yet profoundly significant expressions of the extended self. Yet for all the attention it has received over the years from both design professionals and academic researchers of diverse backgrounds, the source of these ties remains a mystery, only partially resolved according to the interests of whichever profession or discipline is concerned.

The chapter begins with an examination of the meaning of place-identity as interpreted from different viewpoints, including those of ordinary home-dwellers, academics, literary figures and architectural critics and theorists. The marked differences in the meanings attached to spaces and places by both inhabitants and observers lead in turn to a discussion of cultural relativism, as argued by prominent linguists and anthropologists. The early influence of Martin Heidegger's phenomenology on the idea of place in architectural theory is also discussed, paving the way for an overview of related approaches by later theorists. Other recurring subjects described in the research on the cognition of place are the mental 'images' or 'maps' revealing the way individuals and groups assimilate the spaces they inhabit, including whole districts – concepts that are further developed in the writings and researches reported in the following two chapters. The anthropologist Edward Hall's theory of 'proxemics'[1] is also outlined, pointing toward later developments on the subject of mind–body extensions. The chapter concludes with a summary overview of recent studies aimed at reassessing the meaning and significance of place in philosophical and cultural discourses, together with some current debates on identity formation in the modern world as seen by human geographers.

Place-identity

There are as many interpretations of place-identity as there are approaches to the subject. 'Sense of place,' '*genius loci*,' and 'spirit of the place' are commonly used terms that describe much the same idea, though the meaning varies according to context and profession. For environmental psychologists like Maxine Wolfe and Harold Proshansky,[2] place-identity is inextricably linked with personal identity:

1.1 *House on the outskirts of Sydney, by Glenn Murcutt, 1983*

The self-identity of every individual has elements of place in it – or as we have said elsewhere, all individuals have a 'place-identity.' They remember, are familiar with, like, and indeed achieve recognition, status, or occupational satisfactions from certain places. Whether we are talking about 'the family home,' 'the old hangout,' 'my town,' or some other place, it should be obvious that physical settings are also internalized elements of human self-identity.[3]

Award-winning designers like the Australian architect Glenn Murcutt have also captured people's imagination with iconic houses carefully set into the landscape (fig. 1.1).[4] In such cases, as with the earlier houses by Greene & Greene in the suburbs of Los Angeles (fig. 1.2),[5] the work of some specially gifted architects may come to represent, if only for a limited period, not only an idealized form of dwelling, but a sense of place and preferred way of life for a whole country: the 'Great Australian Dream' as it is known in the former case, or the 'Great American Dream' in the latter. In either case, the dwelling type and the dream are basically alike, which says much for the similarity between the two cultures.

Even the most ordinary suburban home can evoke strong responses in its present or former occupants, whatever the building looks like, so long as it has the requisite features of the type: functional and comfortable rooms sufficient for all the family; a substantial garden or backyard, a garage and so on (fig. 1.3). In her essay 'The House as Symbol of the Self,' Clare Cooper[6] finds a deeper explanation in Carl Jung's

1.2 *Irwin House, Pasadena, Los Angeles, by Greene & Greene, 1906, set the style for the popular California bungalow*

concept of archetypes for the importance people attach to their homes and their consequent resistance to any change of customary habitats:

> If there is some validity to the notion of house-as-self, it goes part of the way to explain why for most people their house is so sacred and why they so strongly resist a change in the basic form which they and their fathers and their father's fathers have lived in since the dawn of time. Jung recognised that the more archaic and universal the archetype made manifest in the symbol, the more universal and unchanging the symbol itself. Since self must be an archetype as universal and almost as archaic as man himself, this may explain the universality of its symbolic form, the house, *and the extreme resistance of most people to any change in its basic form* [added emphasis].[7]

Quoting a touching poem about a suburban family home written by a 12-year-old, Cooper also ventures that children, not having yet been socialized into thinking of themselves as individual beings separate from their physical habitat, are generally more sensitive than adults to its value in their lives:

O JOYOUS HOUSE

When I walk home from school,
I see many houses
Many houses down many streets.

The common bond

1.3 *Idealized image of conventional suburban home*

They are warm comfortable houses
But other people's houses
I pass without much notice
Then as I walk farther, farther
I see a house, the house.
It springs up with a jerk
That speeds my pace;
I lurch forward
Longing makes me happy,
I bubble inside.
It's my house.[8]

As common as such bonds are, except for a few writers like Cooper,[9] architectural critics have generally been slow to acknowledge their strength or meaning. Typically, the Australian architect and polemicist Robin Boyd[10] lampooned suburban aesthetic styles and tastes in Australia in the 1950s and '60s, including the imported and much admired 'California bungalow' (figs 1.4, 1.5).[11] Nevertheless, Boyd, a pioneering modernist and inventive designer, never actually challenged the detached family dwelling type itself or the suburban pattern it generated, recognizing how deeply rooted they were in Australian culture. 'Australia is the small house,' he wrote,[12] and he designed many such dwellings himself in the modernist manner he propagated.

Other critics, especially in Europe, launched their own attacks on suburban aesthetics during the same period,[13] but like Boyd had no effect whatsoever on the popularity or appearance of suburban homes. Dismissing such reactions as irrelevant to the people who actually live in suburbia, the American sociologist Herbert Gans[14] argued that, far from suburbia being the social and cultural wasteland depicted by its detractors, suburbanites enjoy a full social life with their neighbors, who share

1.4 A typical California bungalow in the suburbs of Wollongong, New South Wales, Australia

1.5 A typical California bungalow in the suburbs of Los Angeles

the same family-centered values and lifestyles. Postmodern critics like Charles Jencks[15] and artists like the Australian painter Howard Arkley[16] have also accepted and even celebrated suburban aesthetics. From *I Love Lucy* onwards, countless television sit-coms confirmed the continuing popularity and deep cultural roots of the suburban lifestyle, inviting viewers into their studio-sized but otherwise ordinary-looking living rooms to share the tastes and day-to-day antics and problems of their favorite families on-screen.

Cities often exert a similar hold on individuals, both in fiction and in real life. James Joyce, a voluntary exile in continental Europe for most of his life, evokes a powerful sense of place in his novel *Ulysses*, which follows Leopold Bloom and other characters through the real streets and alleyways of the Dublin of his time.[17] The novel testifies to the enduring impression Joyce's early years in the city had on his consciousness, despite his rejection of the conservative culture of his native land and his later decision to move to Paris, where he found equally memorable surroundings. While *Ulysses* was a unique achievement in many other respects, Joyce was not alone in capturing the essence of a city between the pages of a novel. In her study of the city in literature, Diana Festa-McCormick[18] analyses the pivotal role played by major cities in 10 novels by different authors, including Honoré de Balzac and Émile Zola (Paris), Marcel Proust (Venice), Lawrence Durrell (Alexandria) and John Dos Passos (Manhattan). Most authors, she explains, express ambivalent attitudes toward the cities in their novels, acknowledging their darker aspects, including ubiquitous poverty, corruption and injustice, as well as their capacity to inspire. In every case, however, the city is presented as an enduring, dynamic force – a protagonist in itself – shaping and directing the lives of the characters in their novels as much as, if not more than, the other characters around them:

> The city often is a catalyst, or a springboard, from which visions emerge that delve into existences unimaginable elsewhere. The city there acts as a force in man's universe; it is a constant element, immutable in its way while constantly renewing itself. It serves as a repository for miseries, hardships, and frustrations, but also for ever-renascent hopes.[19]

Joseph Luzzi, a devoted scholar and teacher of the work of Dante, offers a brief but still more eloquent example in literature of the sway a city can have on an individual life. Following the sudden death of his wife in a car accident, Luzzi found echoes of his personal grief in Dante's epic poem *Divine Comedy*, where the author describes his own profound grief at having been exiled for the rest of his life from his beloved Florence: 'You will leave behind everything you love / most dearly, and this is the arrow / the bow of exile first lets fly.'[20]

Place in architectural theory

Among architectural theorists, Christian Norberg-Schulz has done much to focus attention on the nature of place-identity and its psychic roots. In *Genius Loci*,[21] he attributes his phenomenological approach to the philosophy of Martin Heidegger and to the 1971 collection of essays on language and aesthetics, *Poetry, Language, Thought*[22] in particular. In a widely quoted essay from that collection, 'Building Dwelling Thinking,' Heidegger argues that 'building' and 'dwelling' have an older and far deeper significance beyond their common meanings as activities or a form of habitable shelter:

> What then, does *Bauen*, building, *mean*? The Old English and High German word for building, *buan*, means to dwell. This signifies, to remain, to stay in a place. The real meaning of the verb, *bauen*, namely, to dwell, has been lost to us [...]. The way in which you are and I am, the manner in which we humans *are* on the earth, is *Buan*, dwelling. To be a human being means to be on earth as a mortal. It means to dwell.[23]

Accordingly, for Heidegger, to build or to dwell implies a fundamental *act of engagement* with the land we live upon. While habitable buildings as we commonly know them are included within the scope of Heidegger's meaning, he also includes any form of human activity or construction, like a bridge, that modifies the landscape and reflects our presence within it:

> [The bridge] does not just connect banks that are already there [...]. It brings stream and bank and land into each other's neighbourhood. The bridge *gathers* the earth as landscape around the stream.[24]

Elaborating on Heidegger's concept of dwelling, Norberg-Schulz argues for a broader appreciation of architecture, not just as a practical art fulfilling various social and cultural functions, but as 'a means to give man an "existential foothold."'[25] Thus, 'dwelling above all presupposes *identification* with the environment.'[26] Similarly, a 'place' implies more than a simple spatial or geographical designation and describes somewhere with a distinct *character* of its own. This can include ambient qualities related to different activities, such as 'protective' for dwellings, 'practical' for offices, 'solemn' for churches and so forth. Character may also be a function of time and the changing seasons, together with the different conditions of light that go with them. More generally, it 'is determined by the material and formal constitution of the place.'[27] The purpose of architecture is thus defined as understanding 'the "vocation" of the place,'[28] as bringing forth and expressing the *genius loci*.

However, having made the case for an existential understanding of architecture and place, Norberg-Schulz devotes most of his treatise to describing the physical and spatial properties of places that generate the kind of character he suggests people readily identify with, which he illustrates with numerous examples drawn from widely different cultures around the world. For instance, he notes that a common feature of such places is a strong 'inside–outside' relationship; buildings and settlements are tightly grouped and provide a tangible sense of enclosure, differentiating them sharply from the extended spaces and landscapes beyond (fig. 1.6). Notably, except for a handful of exceptions – he includes the skyscrapers of Chicago among them[29] – all his exemplars are of a historical or traditional nature, including indigenous settlements.[30] Only in a closing section titled 'The loss of place' does he turn

1.6 *The streets and squares of Valletta, Malta, are typical of the well defined urban forms and spaces described by Norberg-Schulz*

his attention to more recent architectural and urban developments. Bemoaning the widespread lack of any clear distinction between town and country, he writes: 'Spatially, the new settlements do not anymore possess enclosure and density.'[31] Buildings, he notes, are separately scattered about in open spaces or spill out into the countryside, while streets and squares as we know them from older towns and cities no longer exist: 'the continuity of the landscape is interrupted and the buildings do not form clusters or groups.'[32]

Invisible landscapes

Notwithstanding Norberg-Schulz's attempts to explain the meaning of place-identity to us or the undoubted attractions of his exemplars, the criteria he sets out for what makes a place worth identifying with exclude a large proportion – possibly the majority – of humanity, who do not necessarily share the same values or live the same way, but who may nevertheless be equally attached to their environments. And not only Western suburbanites. To take an extreme counter-example, according to Amos Rapoport,[33] an anthropologist who has focused his work on the relations between built form and culture, buildings play no significant role in the way Australian Aborigines identify with the land they inhabit. Aboriginal tribes in different parts of the country make use of a number of forms of basic shelter, including windbreaks and several varieties of huts made from bark and simple wooden frames. A few dwellings with low walls of stone and arched roofs of saplings covered with bark and grass are also known. However, none of these shelters offers any substantial protection against the climate, which varies from one extreme to another across the continent, or compares with the more elaborate dwelling forms of indigenous cultures elsewhere.[34]

Neither, as Rapoport explains, do Aboriginal dwellings fulfill any discernable symbolic function, as might be expected from studies of other cultures.[35] To understand what is important to Aboriginal culture, Rapoport goes on, we have to look elsewhere, to the land itself. Instead of imbuing dwellings or any other form of human construction with symbolic values as other peoples do, Aborigines invest the *whole landscape* with meaning derived from a highly complex cosmology and cosmogony:

> Many Europeans have spoken of the uniformity and featurelessness of the Australian landscape. The aborigines, however, see the landscape in a totally different way. Every feature of the landscape is known and has meaning – they then perceive differences which Europeans cannot see. These differences may be in terms of detail or in terms of a magical or invisible landscape, the symbolic space being even more varied than the perceived physical space [...]. It is thus a likely hypothesis that aborigines *humanize* their landscape, that is take possession of it conceptually, through symbols – as we do. But whereas our symbols are material – buildings, cities, fences, and monuments – aboriginal symbols are largely non-material.[36]

There are, therefore, good reasons for the insubstantial nature of Aboriginal dwellings, but we can understand them only by inversing 'normal' Western perceptions and values. For Aborigines, the landscape is all. Where we conventionally build to *separate* ourselves from nature, both symbolically and materially, or to *take possession* of some part of it, Aborigines eschew any form of shelter or construction that might possibly *get in the way* of their complete identification with the land in which they live. As difficult as it is for most other people to grasp, making buildings – so central to other cultures, both technologically primitive as well as advanced – hardly counts for anything in Aboriginal culture:

> Other cultures create a new physical landscape in keeping with their creation myths. Aborigines structure their *existing* physical landscape mentally, mythically and symbolically *without building it* [added emphasis].[37]

In a sense, therefore, the flimsy constructions that pass for dwellings in Aboriginal culture *do* have a symbolic value, if only of a negative kind, insofar as they indicate that the full symbolic weight of the culture has been firmly placed elsewhere.

The significance of Aboriginal rock-art and its unique relation to the landscape supports this view. While examples of early rock-art are also found in other parts of the world, the most famous being the cave paintings in France and Spain, Josephine Flood[38] argues that the special relation of Aboriginal peoples to the land in Australia adds another dimension to the art form: 'where rock-art serves to explain and map the landscape'[39] as it was created by Ancestral Beings before humans or any other creatures inhabited the earth. For example, a typical motif found in rock-art in the Northern Territories of Australia consists of linked concentric circles tracing the epic journeys of these spiritual beings across the landscape during the time of creation, known as the Dreamtime or Dreaming. Others depict where water and other resources may be found, or record similar mythologies allocating the inhabitants to specific locations within the landscape itself, the stories of which comprise an inscribed as well as a vocal history of the people. In sum, Australian rock-art is intrinsically place related and carries substantially more meaning for Aborigines than any shelter they ever built was intended to. Like Rapoport, Flood concludes: 'it is less a case that people own land, more a case that land shapes and defines people.'[40]

Disputed values

From the 1960s onward, various professional students of the built environment have attempted to resolve such issues by adopting a more empirical approach, often borrowing their ideas and methods from the human sciences. Much of this work revolves around the concept of a mental 'image' by which individuals anticipate events and actions and generally find their way about in the world. As used by Kenneth Boulding in his influential study *The Image*,[41] the term denotes the integration of discrete mental 'schemata,'[42] including social, economic and political issues, into a coherent whole – a kind of subjective model or picture of the world that helps a person to make sense of it. David Canter,[43] who helped to establish environmental psychology as a new discipline in the UK, traces the concept still further back, to the work of Sir Henry Head,[44] a pioneering neurologist:

> As a neurologist, Head was concerned with how we are able to take into account changes in bodily posture and movement in order to carry out effective motor actions, *how we know where our limbs are* [added emphasis] To explain our abilities Head proposed that we must carry in our brains a model of our body which is being continually modified on the basis of information received about each action.[45]

Taking the idea a significant step further, Kevin Lynch[46] applied both psychological theory and empirical methods of analysis to the study of urban form. Hitherto, judgments on the merits of one urban form over another had been the exclusive province of city planners and urban designers, according to whichever theoretical or historical model they favored. Seeking a more objective basis for decision making using field surveys and interview techniques that were familiar to sociologists and psychologists but new to the planning and design professions, Lynch elicited the impressions of city dwellers themselves. Though based on only a small sample, he interpreted the results as confirming the value of 'imageability' or 'legibility' of urban form, which he associated with the presence of 'landmarks,' 'nodes' and other 'image elements' garnered from his surveys.[47]

However, despite Lynch's efforts to establish the objectivity of his ideas and methods, like Norberg-Schulz, who frequently quotes Lynch's work in support of his own approach, he reveals a strong personal preference in his writings for familiar historic urban models like Venice and a disdainful, even condescending view of American cities and their inhabitants' aesthetic tastes:

> A beautiful and delightful city environment is an oddity; some would say an impossibility [in America]. Not one American city larger than a village is of consistently fine quality, although a few towns have some pleasant fragments. It is hardly surprising, then, that most Americans have little idea of what it can mean to live in such an environment.[48]

Lynch's urban values and aesthetic preferences, which he shared at the time with many of his peers, including Lewis Mumford,[49] the urban historian, were subsequently challenged by other leading American urban theorists like Melvin Webber,[50] a planner, and Robert Venturi, Denise Scott Brown and Steven Izenour,[51] an influential group of postmodern architects and critics. Just as Gans had argued for an understanding of suburbia on its own terms, so Webber and Venturi and his co-authors argued that criticism of American cities was Eurocentric and out of touch with popular culture. American cities, they maintained, are fundamentally different from historic European cities. The latter, with their compact spatial patterns and pedestrian-friendly streets and squares, had mostly evolved before the invention of the automobile. By contrast, since the early twentieth century, modern American cities and their low-density suburbs, freeways and commercial 'strips' have grown around the almost exclusive use of private transportation. Venturi et al. went so far as to urge architects to stop looking to Rome for inspiration and look to the commercial aesthetics and colorful roadway signs of Las Vegas instead for appropriate models of design for the contemporary American city (fig. 1.7).

Despite such criticisms, Lynch's ideas and methods had a considerable impact, not only on architectural theorists like Norberg-Schulz, but on workers within other fields as well, stimulating whole new areas of interdisciplinary research.[52] In an essay on cognitive mapping titled 'Architecture in the Head,' David Stea[53] explains that, much like the graphical maps we use to find our way around a city or transport system, the maps we hold in our heads of the places we live in tell us what to expect around the corner: 'To be useful, a cognitive map must "predict" something – it is not enough to have a network of images; images of our present surroundings must be associated with images of those objects and events likely to come next.'[54]

However, not all the work that followed supported Lynch's findings. Aside from advances in survey and interview techniques, Stea points to a contrary outcome in

1.7 *The Strip, Las Vegas, c. 1980*

the research since Lynch's pioneering work, namely the 'recognition of a simple fact with which architects have become quite concerned: the responses of various subgroups of our population to a given environment are different; that is, *there seems to be no "universal aesthetic"* [added emphasis].'[55] Lynch himself had stressed that he was less interested in the psychology of personal differences in perception than in the shared perceptions that constituted what he claimed as the *public* image of the cities he studied. However, according to Stea's observations, subsequent research would appear to undermine Lynch's conclusions, suggesting that either Lynch's small sample, most of whom were selected from the professional classes, or his interview techniques may have prejudiced the outcome.

The complicated picture of the nature of place-identity that emerges thus far from all these debates and researches is that the qualities associated with particular places that people identify with – including but not confined to aesthetic issues – may vary significantly according to an individual's cultural background. To use Lynch's terms, what is 'legible' and attractive about a place to one group or culture may be totally obscure and unattractive to another. While Lynch and Norberg-Schulz might find ideal models for places that many people can identify with in historical architecture and urban form, other people can and do identify strongly with buildings and cities – and even just landscapes – in ways that do not conform to the same criteria or cultural values.

Cultural relativism

While architects and planners have often struggled to accept the evident diversity of environmental values among the populations within which they live and work, as the above findings indicate, other research professionals have adopted a more open approach to the expression of cultural differences. Linguists have played an especially important role in showing us how different peoples view the world. Of these, Edward Sapir and Benjamin Lee Whorf[56] are responsible for what is known as the 'Sapir–Whorf hypothesis': the belief that every culture has its own worldview, or what is generally referred to as cultural relativism.[57] According to the hypothesis, a major part of that shared experience is embodied in the language of that culture:

> It is quite an illusion to imagine that one adjusts to reality essentially without the use of language and that language is merely an incidental means of solving specific problems of communication or reflection. The fact of the matter is that the 'real world' is to a large extent unconsciously built up on the language habits of the group [...]. We see and hear and otherwise experience very largely as we do because the language habits of our community predispose certain choices of interpretation.[58]

Whorf himself, who was a former pupil of Sapir, spent much of his time researching the language and culture of the Hopi, a tribe of Pueblo Indians in the American Southwest. Like other Pueblo tribes, the Hopi were among the earliest settlers on the continent and have lived as sedentary agriculturalists in permanent villages and dwellings for thousands of years.[59] As Whorf discovered, the Hopi language not only differs from other Pueblo dialects, but also embodies a radically different worldview to that of Western languages and cultures, including the way people perceive the spaces they inhabit.

Paul Oliver, a world authority on vernacular architecture, was later impressed enough to record his own observations of Whorf's discoveries.[60] Constructed of adobe, or sun-dried mud bricks, Hopi dwellings are technically much like the mud-brick dwellings of other rural cultures in different parts of the world.[61] However, while, as Whorf notes, the Hopi have recognizable terms for specific architectural details, such as 'shelf' and 'partition,' Oliver points out they have no terms at all for classifying interior spaces and their functions, such as the kind of common names of rooms modern Americans and Europeans are familiar with. Neither is it possible to say 'my room' in Hopi. It might be assumed accordingly that Hopi architecture was spatially undifferentiated, either for specific uses or for personal occupation. However, as Whorf explains, Hopi buildings in fact comprise many different sorts of rooms used for quite different purposes. They even have what Westerners would recognize as building types, such as schools and storehouses. Despite this, they only have one word, *ki hi*, for 'house' or 'building.'

Summarizing Whorf's work, Oliver suggests that, while Hopi architecture might include rectangular rooms similar to Western dwellings, the Hopi conceptual-ize the use of space in quite different ways. Whereas Western names for different building types and rooms generally conflate both spatial form and function, the Hopi identify spaces in a system of *relational concepts*, whereby other things and activities are *located* in one place or spot on the ground rather than another. Drawing his own conclusions, Oliver writes:

> The values attached to the building or settlement [by the Hopi] may be such as to perceive relationships between built form and environment, or meanings in the built structure which fall outside the conceptual framework within which we ourselves structure the world in the West.[62]

Subconscious cultural motivations of a mythological nature may also play their part in modern times, as in the durability of the Great Australian Dream. Whether incarnated in the romanticized form set in the Australian bush as created by Murcutt, or in its humbler suburban variations, the detached house situated in the forested fringes of Australian cities both conforms with and gives built expression to prevailing mythologies and preferred self-images. In his dissection of the Australian soul, *The Australian Legend*, Russel Ward[63] argues that Australians trace their national character and cultural identity, or their 'legend' as he calls it, back to the bush and the hardy early settlers who learnt to live in it. According to Ward, in contrast to the settlers in the cities, whose manners, dress and values mimicked city dwellers in Britain, from whence most of the early settlers came, the tough bushmen who raised cattle or sheep or otherwise made a living from the land were a race apart:

> Up to about 1900 the prestige of the bushman seems to have been greater than that of the townsman. In life as in folklore the man from 'up the country' was usually regarded as a romantic and admirable figure. The attitude towards him was reminiscent, in some interesting ways, of that towards the 'noble savage' in the eighteenth century.[64]

Subsequently idealized by Australian writers and artists, the figure survives to this day in popular fictional and real-life male personalities, such as 'Crocodile Dundee' of cinematic fame[65] and the late Steve Irwin, the naturalist equally famous for his exploits with crocodiles and other native creatures. As Graeme Turner writes:

> Enthusiastically discredited within Australian history and literary studies, the social conditions which sustained it long since gone, the 'Australian Legend' was revived in our movies, prolonging its mythological life well beyond probability.[66]

Proxemics

Inspired by Sapir and Whorf, in *The Hidden Dimension* Edward Hall[67] coined the term 'proxemics' for 'the interrelated observations and theories of man's use of space as a specialized elaboration of culture.'[68] Extending the Sapir–Whorf hypothesis, Hall argues that the evidence of cultural relativism goes far beyond any specific relations of language and built form. Summarizing his approach, he writes: 'The thesis of this book and of *The Silent Language* which preceded it, is that the principles laid down by Whorf and his fellow linguists in relation to language apply to the rest of human behaviour as well – in fact, *to all culture* [added emphasis].'[69]

Hall cites the importance of 'territoriality' in animal behavior, describing it as 'a system that evolved in very much the same way as anatomical systems evolved.'[70] Similar factors, he argues, influence human spatial behavior. Hall is particularly struck by the differences between the body language and spatial behavior of Americans and Arabs, who 'live in different sensory worlds much of the time,'[71] which they express in various ways, from what is regarded as the correct distance between people conversing together according to status and familiarity, to the relations between the ego and the body. He notes, for example, that American women married to Arabs frequently remark on the way their husbands' behavior changes when they travel in the West but immediately reverts back to 'normal' when they return home: 'They become in every sense of the word quite different people.'[72]

More to the point, while Hall does not comment on Whorf's specific studies of Hopi architecture, he also has much to say about the way spaces in buildings are generally organized and the impact that has on human behavior, particularly those interior spaces people associate with specific activities and functions. Architects, he suggests, are usually more interested in the *visual* qualities of spaces and underestimate the way people become habituated to their form and use. He concludes that territorial behavior of this kind 'is quite fixed and rigid,'[73] as reflected in the constant spatial and physical boundaries that have evolved in different cultures for regular activities, for which he coined the term 'fixed-feature space.' Such culturally induced constraints, he argues, extend beyond individual buildings and govern the way they are grouped together: 'The layout of villages, towns, cities, and the intervening countryside is not haphazard but follows a plan which changes with time and culture.'[74]

However, Hall goes much further, to suggest that proxemics is only part of a far broader and deeper pattern of behavior peculiar to humankind. As will become apparent later in this book, Hall was remarkably clear sighted in anticipating later thinking on related issues, particularly the role of technology in human evolution:

> In spite of the fact that cultural systems pattern behaviour in radically different ways, they are deeply rooted in biology and physiology. Man is an organism with a wonderful and extraordinary past. He is distinguished from the other animals by virtue of the fact that he has elaborated what I have termed *extensions* of his organism. By developing his extensions, man has been able to improve or specialize various functions. The computer is an extension of part of the brain, the telephone extends the voice, the wheel extends the legs and feet. Language extends experience in time and space while writing extends language. *Man has elaborated his extensions to such a degree that we are apt to forget that his humanness is rooted in his animal nature* [added emphasis].[75]

Narratives of the self

Since Norberg-Schulz's elaboration on Heidegger's thought, a new generation of scholars is also now reassessing the idea of place-identity. Reaffirming the wider significance of place in human development, prominent philosophers of the new school include Edward S. Casey and J. E. Malpas, who have each written extensively on the subject.[76] In his definitive philosophical history of the concept, Casey asserts the existential role of place:

> To be at all — to exist in any way — is to be somewhere, and to be somewhere is to be in some kind of place. Place is as requisite as the air we breathe, the ground on which we stand, the bodies we have. We are surrounded by places. We walk over and through them. We live in places, relate to others in them, die in them. Nothing we do is unplaced. How could it be otherwise? How could we fail to recognize this primal fact?[77]

Casey contests that, while with notable exceptions place has generally been passed over by modern philosophers, there is plentiful evidence that it has pre-occupied numerous prominent thinkers since the ancients. While his main aim is to present an intellectual history of the idea, he also briefly covers the relatively recent mutual exchanges in thought between the French philosopher Jacques Derrida and prominent architects of the 'deconstructionist' school like Bernard Tschumi and Peter Eisenman.[78] For the most part, however, Casey is more concerned with reinvigorating philosophical debate on the subject and refocusing attention on those key thinkers who have contributed most to its development, some of whom will figure later in these pages, if they have not done so already.

Malpas is equally concerned to redress recent neglects and to give proper due to place as a legitimate topic for philosophical discourse. However, rather than concentrating on the principal players and periods in the history of the idea as Casey does, Malpas structures his investigations and chapters around key aspects of place and its relation to human experience, which he argues are still little understood. Significantly, Malpas also stresses the two-way nature of that relationship:

> the human relation to the land, and to the environing world in general, is clearly not a relation characterized by an influence running in just one direction. There are obvious ways, of course, in which the environment determines our activities and thoughts — we build here rather than there because of the greater suitability of the site; the presence of a river forces us to construct a bridge to carry the road across; we plant apples rather than mangoes because the climate is too cold — but there are other much less straightforward and perhaps more pervasive ways in which our relation to the landscape and environment is indeed one of our own *affectivity* as much as of our ability to *effect*.[79]

Malpas, who is a professor of philosophy at the University of Tasmania in Australia, illustrates his case with examples drawn from a wide range of literary and other sources, from the poetry of William Wordsworth, who extols the identity of a shepherd with the landscape through which his flock roams, to the intimate relationship of Australian Aborigines with their own land. Like Rapoport before him, he is particularly impressed by the indivisibility of the latter relationship, as exemplified in Aboriginal myths of conception:

> The mother does not contribute to the ontological substance of the child, but rather 'carries' a life whose essence belongs alone, to a site. The child's core identity is determined by his or her place of derivation [...]. *Life is annexation of place* [added emphasis].[80]

Among his primary themes, Malpas also tackles the difficult issue of the self as it relates to place. 'What exactly,' he asks, 'is the relation between the concept of self or of subjectivity that is involved in a creature's grasp of subjective space and the idea of spatiality?'[81] Exploring but eventually rejecting the notion of a pre-existing self or 'primitive subjectivity' that somehow expands into and connects with the surrounding world, Malpas comes down on the side of 'the unity of life'[82] and invokes the analogy of a narrative in which all the multiple strands of life and experience are being constantly knitted together:

> Often coming to understand how and what we believe, who and what we are, is just a matter of coming to configure and reconfigure our lives in ways that enable those lives to be integrated in an interconnected and comprehensive fashion. And this suggests a central role for narrative in the sort of life of which humans are capable – the interconnectedness that makes for mental content and for self-identity would seem to be the sort of interconnection achieved, in a certain paradigmatic fashion (though it is certainly not the only form in which such interconnection may obtain), by means of narrative and story.[83]

According to Malpas's interpretation, therefore, human agents, mental states, actions and spatial locations are all intertwined as different aspects of the same narrative: 'The ordering of subjective spatiality, then, is an ordering in relation to action, and, inasmuch as mental states are also ordered in this way, so the ordering of subjective space and the ordering of an agent's thoughts and experiences are closely interconnected.'[84] However, subjective space in turn cannot be grasped independently of the objective qualities of space and location, that is, those qualities that do not originate solely from personal experience, but which are ultimately the product of an interaction between the two: 'What is thus starting to appear is a structure in which subjective and objective elements [of place] are interconnected and interdependent.'[85]

The politics of place

Among the new generation of architectural writers on the subject, in his essay 'Belonging' Neil Leach[86] faults proponents of the 'critical regionalism' school for focusing too much of their attention on the formal attributes of their architectural subjects at the expense of other cultural factors.[87] While, as the preceding discussion affirms, the same criticism does not apply to the work of many other researchers and critics, particularly those engaged with anthropological, linguistic and related perspectives,[88] Leach points to contemporary cultural theory as an underused source of inspiration and insights into the relations between architecture and regional or national identity. Drawing upon the work of Homi Bhabha and his concept of identity as a form of discourse, Leach locates architecture within 'a language of forms not only embedded within various cultural discourses but also given meaning by those discourses.'[89] In focusing on matters of form only and neglecting those cultural discourses that give architecture meaning, Leach suggests that critical regionalism also misses a vital aspect of architecture, namely that:

> the same form will take on radically different connotations in different cultural milieus. The same concrete tower replicated in, say, America, China, Latin America and Eastern Europe – will effectively appear different, as it is treated and used differently in each context. Furthermore, in standard architectural theory there is no accepted framework for exploring how people make sense of place, and identify with it. Without this, the relation of architecture to cultural identity can hardly be addressed. In order for architecture to be understood in terms of cultural identity, some kind of identification with architecture must have taken place. But how exactly does this identification occur?[90]

In itself the comment on differences in cultural interpretation adds nothing to what has already been the subject of much published debate, as noted in this and later chapters.[91] However, Leach finds fresh support in Judith Butler's interpretation of identity based upon the concept of 'performativity,'[92] which he suggests offers a 'far more fluid and dynamic way than traditional methods permit.'[93] Based upon identity politics, and gender politics in particular, Butler's aim as Leach describes it is to dissociate the idea of gender from its conventional physical association with the human body and to reinterpret it instead in behavioral terms: 'Gender, she argues, is not a given ontological condition, but is performatively produced.'[94] Neither does it arise from any singular act or behavior, 'but through the accumulative iteration of certain practices.'[95] Thus identity is not so much a 'given' but is an acquired, *externally demonstrated* set of attributes arising out of those repeated practices. Extending Butler's approach to culture in general, Leach writes: 'Imitation lies at the heart of all cultural practices. It is that which reinforces them, but – equally – that which potentially destabilizes them.'[96]

This leads Leach in turn to an interpretation of 'belonging' to and sense of identification with a place as the outcome, not of any deterministic or fixed association between specific architectural forms and specific meanings, but of potentially changeable relations between customary habits, rituals and other personal and social factors and the actual spaces those habits and rituals are enacted in. Framed in terms of the contemporary condition of 'placenessness' arising out of cultural and economic globalization, for Leach the ambiguous possibilities inherent in a more dynamic concept of belonging allows for a dialectic of place-identity more in keeping with our own uncertain times, where both 'place' and 'non-place' are defined in terms of each other within a constantly changing local and global context.

Nevertheless, while the concept of performativity accords with much of what has been written here and elsewhere about cultural relativism, in denying any significant role for the body in gender and identity formation in their interpretation of the concept, Butler and Leach are both in danger of throwing out the baby with the bathwater, so to speak – a position that can be supported only by ignoring the research in the neurosciences and other fields reported in this book and other published sources confirming the reality and significance of mind–body relations.[97]

Lastly, human geographers are also now increasingly making their own contribution to the field. As Tim Creswell[98] defines it: 'When humans invest meaning in a portion of space and then become attached to it in some way (naming is one such way) it becomes a place [...] place is not just a thing in the world but *a way of understanding the world* [added emphasis].'[99] However, as we have seen, while most of the research and literature in other disciplines has centered on the *rootedness* of place, geographers have put their own spin on the subject: 'Place, at a basic level, is space invested with meaning in the context of power.'[100] Consequently, much of the current research in human geography is concerned with what is best described as the politics of place, as evidenced in the spatial expression and differentiation of power, whether it is between one gender and another or between social elites and other groups, or even as it is expressed in such common terms as being 'in place' or 'out of place.'

Similarly, globalization and related political and economic factors and their impact on place are all regarded as fair game. For example, Creswell discusses at length a paper by Doreen Massey, 'A Global Sense of Place,'[101] in which the author proposes a new and more open conception of place more in keeping with the world we now live in, based upon what Massey describes as 'interconnecting flows – of routes rather than roots,'[102] not unlike Leach's plea for a more flexible conception of place. In either case, the question arises as to what extent any lessons learnt from the peripatetic lifestyle of the business, political and academic elites shaping Leach's and Massey's thinking can be applied to the great majority of humankind, who still spend most of their lives in the same place or region, whether from choice or from necessity. Knowingly or not, both Leach and Massey also overlook what remains of any individual or collective power linked to place, such as the right to vote and combine political forces with others, in favor of a boundless and dysfunctional world dominated by remote and unaccountable systems of economic and technological power.

2 The body nucleus

The preceding chapter spotlighted differences in the kinds of homes and other places people of diverse backgrounds and cultures commonly identify with. However, one inescapable factor that every human being shares with every other human being on the planet in his or her everyday experience of the world – regardless of background or culture – but which is generally taken for granted, is the human body, the existential role of which we now turn to.

The chapter opens with a brief look at the perception of the human body in architectural design and theory. It then moves to a more detailed look at the writings of Maurice Merleau-Ponty and Michael Polanyi[1] on the body as the nucleus or fulcrum of human experience. Though neither author wrote directly about architecture or urban form, their work has significant implications for understanding the way people relate to their environment.[2] Of the two, Merleau-Ponty is the better-known author and a philosopher in the same school of thought as Martin Heidegger, both of whom in turn acknowledge Edmund Husserl[3] as the intellectual father of phenomenology. Together with Polanyi's writings on 'tacit knowing' of the same period, Merleau-Ponty's work offers the most illuminating insights of the last century on the interrelations between consciousness, bodily experience and spatial awareness.

Architecture and the body

Though most architects may have been tardy in acknowledging any aesthetic tastes different from their own, they have long recognized the importance of the human body in their work. From the 'symbolic expression of Christ crucified'[4] in the Latin cross plan of Christian churches, through the familiar images by Leonardo da Vinci and others[5] of a naked 'Vitruvian Man' with outstretched arms encased within a circle and a square (fig. 2.1), to Le Corbusier's Modulor,[6] a proportional scale of measurements based on the human body (fig. 2.2), architects have been fascinated by the relations and tensions between abstract geometric form and the human figure. Anthropomorphic symbolism and other references have also shaped architectural form and history in non-Western cultures, both directly, as in the layouts of Dogon

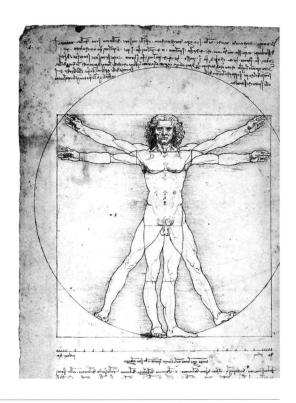

2.1 *Vitruvian Man, by Leonardo da Vinci, c. 1492*

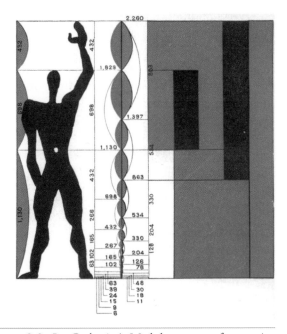

2.2 *Le Corbusier's Modulor system of proportion*

The body nucleus

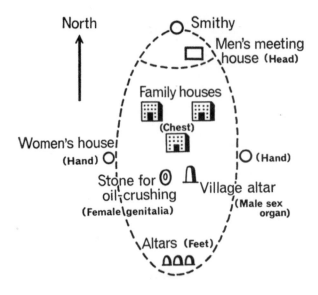

2.3 *Schematic plan of a Dogon village, Mali, by Douglas Fraser. The layout represents parts of the human figure, including male and female sexual organs*

villages (fig. 2.3) in Mali,[7] Africa, or indirectly, as in the Japanese concept of 'movement space' – that is, space as experienced from the viewpoint of a moving observer – an important concept covered in the final chapter of this book. Yi-Fu Tuan,[8] a prominent geographer, also presents numerous examples from different peoples, both in their language and in their buildings, where the body image has influenced the way they relate to and shape their environment. Generally speaking, the upright, forward-facing human body itself (fig. 2.4), Tuan argues, is the basic source of all our spatial coordinates:

> Upright, man is ready to act. Space opens out before him and is immediately differentiable into front–back and right–left axes in conformity with the structure of his body. Vertical–horizontal, top–bottom, front–back and right–left are positions and coordinates of the body that are extrapolated onto space [...]. What does it mean to be in command of space, to feel at home in it? It means that the objective reference points in space, such as landmarks and the cardinal positions, conform with the intention and the coordinates of the human body.[9]

A frequent criticism directed at orthodox modernist architects in the last century was that they had forgotten the fundamental relations between architecture and the body and had consequently lost the ability to create engaging and memorable places. Despite the humanistic motivations behind the idea, Le Corbusier's Modulor had little if any impact on the general perception of his urban schemes and has been

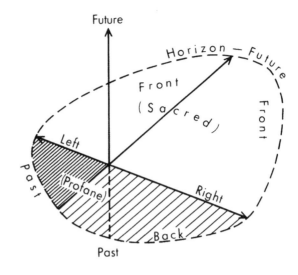

2.4 *Diagram of upright human body, space and time, by Yi Fu Tuan*

ignored by architects at large. Later, as one of the more substantial postmodern designers and theorists, Charles Moore was a leading voice in the movement to restore the body to center stage in architectural theory and practice. In *The Place of Houses*, he and his co-authors[10] attempt to show how designers can restore a sense of place to residential architecture, not only through careful attention to the relations between building and landscape, but also by creating intimate spaces within the houses themselves that people can identify with and feel they belong to. In another co-authored study, *Body, Memory and Architecture*,[11] he writes: 'We believe that the most essential and memorable sense of three-dimensionality originates in the body experience and that this sense may constitute a basis for understanding spatial feeling in our buildings.'[12]

More recent studies of traditional or indigenous habitats have also yielded new perspectives on the subject. Contrary to Amos Rapoport's view of climate as a secondary factor in shaping building form (as reported in Chapter 1), in his essay 'Body, Settlement, Landscape,' Robert Mugerauer[13] claims that comparative studies between human habitats in hot and cold humid climates reveal significant relations between bodily posture, climate and settlement patterns within each climate zone, while also pointing to differences in those relations between the two kinds of climate. Whereas bodily posture and settlements in hot humid climates have a more 'open' character intended to dissipate heat, he writes, the reverse is true for cold humid climates, where both posture and settlement patterns have a more 'huddled' appear-ance conducive to conserving heat. While such findings do not necessarily negate Rapoport's claim for the general priority of cultural factors over all else in shaping human habitations, they do serve as a healthy corrective and a reminder that denying or downplaying the influence of climate on the way people live may carry its own price, as Rapoport himself acknowledges elsewhere with respect to the low comfort level of traditional Japanese dwellings.[14]

The subject continues to exercise architectural theorists and historians. Most of the authors in a collection of essays published in honor of the distinguished critic Joseph Rykwert,[15] who wrote extensively on the subject himself,[16] explore different aspects of the relation between the human body and architecture, while others examine its impact in the related arts. Typifying the wide range of thought, in 'The Architectonics of Embodiment' Dalibor Vesely[17] disputes the significance of the literal Vitruvian interpretation of the human body's impact on architecture – a tradition to which Le Corbusier's Modulor also belongs. Arguing for a different view that takes in the broader relation between the body and the structure of human reality closer to the approach adopted in this book, Vesely draws attention to 'the deep reciprocity that exists between the human body and the world and, by implication, between the human body and architecture.'[18] By contrast, sticking to the Vitruvian tradition, in 'Body, Diagram, and Geometry in the Renaissance Fortress,' Simon Pepper[19] suggests that the image of the human body was a major factor in shaping the plans of military structures and settlements, which he illustrates with examples of fortifications throughout the Mediterranean and references to the texts of their designers.

Juhani Pallasmaa[20] also makes the case that modern architecture has been dominated by the visual sense at the expense of other sensory and bodily experiences, particularly the tactile sense, but additionally the acoustic and oral senses. Pallasmaa traces the problem in Western culture back to antiquity and the association of vision with thought and certainty – seeing things clearly, so to speak. However, he argues that the bias toward the visual sense, or 'ocularcentrism' as he calls it, has been greatly exacerbated in modern times with the invention of photography and the exponential growth in the printed and televised images that now permeate all aspects of our lives. Similarly, he sees dangers in the growth of computerized design techniques, which nourish the visual sense with glossy and seductive images.[21] The loss of human scale in modern architecture is likewise attributed to a lack of understanding of the role of the body in spatial experience:

> Understanding architectural scale implies the unconscious measuring of the object or the building with one's body, and of projecting one's body scheme into the space in question. We feel pleasure and protection when the body discovers its resonance in space.[22]

The persisting point

While the influence of Merleau-Ponty's thought[23] is evident in some of the above works, they do not of themselves provide a more general basis for a theory of the extended self. For that it is necessary to go directly to Merleau-Ponty's own work, followed by that of Polanyi, who between them furnish the foundations for some of the principal ideas in this book.

Like Husserl, Merleau-Ponty is careful to distinguish phenomenology from the explanatory sciences as a purely 'descriptive psychology': '[It] tries to give a direct description of our experience *as it is* [added emphasis] without taking account of its psychological origin and the causal explanations which the scientist, the historian or the sociologist may be able to provide.'[24] Merleau-Ponty was also particularly influenced by Husserl's assertion of what the latter called 'the privileged position' of the human body. According to Husserl, the human body is the one thing that is never experienced independently or at a distance, but is always 'the persisting point to which all spatial relations appear to be connected.'[25] Likewise, for Merleau-Ponty the body is the very center and origin of human existence:

> Our body is not merely one expressive space amongst the rest, for that is merely the constituted body. It is the origin of the rest, [of] expressive movement itself, that which causes them to begin to exist as things, under our hands and eyes [...]. *The body is our general medium for having a world* [added emphasis].[26]

Spatial awareness, and the awareness of objects in space, he explains, is possible only by virtue of our having a body at all. When a person circulates a room or an apartment, for example, the different aspects of the scene are not experienced separately or as the mere conjunction of different views, but as a *sequence* of views, the totality of which originates in the moving body from which each view is experienced, and which retains its own identity throughout the sequence. Similarly, an object on a table may have an abstract description attached to it, but our actual experience of it *as an object* will depend upon our own position in relation to it in space and our ability to move around it. If the object on the table is, say, a cube, we know from its geometric description that all the faces are equal. However, as we move around it and above it, the faces of the cube present themselves to us differently according to the angle at which they are viewed. But our personal awareness of it as a cube is an outcome of our having a stable reference point in our bodies, from which we are able to integrate the different facets into a whole. In the same way, our awareness of time itself derives from our being able to experience one thing *before* or *after* another, in some kind of sequence, whether we ourselves are moving about, or events are changing *around* us. In either case, the stable reference point and ultimate origin of the experience is again our own body.

Theory of perception

For Merleau-Ponty, the conventional Cartesian treatment of the body, as simply yet another physical object in space viewed dispassionately by detached minds, denies the unity of consciousness and bodily experience:

The body nucleus

Consciousness is being towards the thing through the intermediary of the body [...]. We must therefore avoid saying that our body is *in* space, or *in* time. It *inhabits* space and time.[27]

In the same way, he contends, we also inhabit our own bodies. We do not experience our body objectively as a collection of adjacent limbs and organs – we are in unique *possession* of our body and are aware of the relation of one part or limb to another 'through a *body image* in which all are included.'[28] Here, though, while assimilating the term for his own purposes, Merleau-Ponty takes issue with psychologists' interpretation of the idea as a simple compendium of mental images of different body parts, or even the Gestalt 'whole' favored during his lifetime. Crucially, for Merleau-Ponty the body image is *purposeful*. It has intentional and situational aspects:

My body appears to me as an attitude directed towards a certain existing or possible task [...]. In the last analysis, if my body can be a 'form' and if there can be, in front of it, important figures against indifferent backgrounds, this occurs in virtue of its being polarized by its tasks, of its *existence towards* them, of its collecting together of itself in its pursuit of its aims; the body image is finally a way of stating that my body is in-the-world.[29]

Perception is defined accordingly: 'The theory of the body image is, implicitly, a theory of perception.'[30] Finding support for once in empirical psychology, Merleau-Ponty cites the now familiar responses of subjects to the perception of different colors. Red and yellow, for instance, evoke 'an experience of being torn away, of a movement away from the center,' while blue and green commonly evoke feelings of 'repose and concentration.'[31] In both these and other similar cases, some kind of bodily association is directly involved in the perception of the color itself, in this instance with either a body in motion or a body at rest. In a manner remarkably similar to some of Polanyi's examples of tacit knowing described in the following section, Merleau-Ponty also suggests that getting accustomed to an item of clothing or a tool or any other personal possession involves a virtual *extension* of the body image to encompass the thing itself: 'To get used to a hat, a car or a stick is to be transplanted into them, or conversely, *to incorporate them into the bulk of our own body* [added emphasis].'[32]

Neither is the role of the body confined to gathering in various sensory experiences; it is also the unique and indispensable vehicle through which one person relates to another and to any other people or objects within a shared field of vision: 'To say that I have a visual field is to say that by reason of my position I have access to and an opening upon a system of beings, visible beings.'[33] Sharing the same basic physiological and sensory apparatus, Merleau-Ponty suggests, allows us to *identify with others*, by analogical extension of our own bodies and the way they shape our experience of the world in a fashion that is inconceivable if we were all built differently. Thus, for all the obvious variations of race and culture that may and often do get in the way of that process, the shared universal fact of the human body acts as a natural if fragile impediment to seeing others as mere objects. Moreover, the same process of identification extends beyond the individual or group of persons concerned to take in any physical and cultural objects within the same field:

No sooner has my gaze fallen upon a living body in process of acting than the objects surrounding it immediately take on a fresh layer of significance: they are no longer simply what I myself could make of them, they are what this other pattern of behaviour is about to make of them.[34]

Tacit knowing

While Polanyi's own background in science – he was a notable organic chemist before turning to philosophy and epistemology – sets him apart from Merleau-Ponty and other philosophers, the work of both thinkers overlaps in key respects, most obviously in their related treatments of the body as the nucleus of experience. Significantly, while Polanyi had the advantage of understanding the work of scientists as an insider, he was also driven to philosophy by his own dissatisfaction with the assumed detachment of scientists from their work, and the consequent denial of any personal commitments in the way they conducted their researches or approached their subjects, whether human, organic or otherwise. Like Merleau-Ponty, he also firmly rejected the Cartesian split between mind and body and the stereotypical thinking – objectivity versus subjectivity, rationality versus irrationality and suchlike – that goes with it.[35]

Seeking a new cognitive synthesis Polanyi found it in his theory of tacit knowing. Polanyi's argument commences with the acknowledgment of a simple but fundamental principle of human knowledge: 'We can know more than we can tell.'[36] Even such a common task as the recognition of a human face involves a complex process of cognitive extension or 'indwelling,' as Polanyi calls it, only part of which manifests itself at a conscious level. Asked to describe a person's features from memory, for example, most people would fail to provide a convincing picture. However, provided with an 'identikit' they can usually reconstruct the face from a selection of drawings of eyes, noses, jaws and other features to a fairly accurate degree, sufficient to identify a police suspect. As with any complex task, Polanyi explains, the recognition of the face involves not one but two sorts of cognition: 'subsidiary awareness' and 'focal awareness,' the former being just as much a vital part of cognition as the latter. However, as its name implies, subsidiary awareness is constantly out of focus – a subliminal backdrop and source of assimilated knowledge that is only *activated indirectly* by an act of concentrated attention on the point of focal awareness. The term 'tacit knowing' therefore refers not just to the unconscious parts of cognition but also to the complementary relations between both conscious and unconscious processes. The key is in understanding how the two work together. In the following example, Polanyi explains how the use of a simple tool comes to feel, without our being fully aware of it, like an extension of our selves:

When I use a hammer to drive a nail, I attend to both, but quite differently. I *watch* the effects of my strokes on the nail as I wield the hammer. I do not feel that its handle has struck my palm but that its head has struck the nail. In another sense, of course, I am highly alert to the feelings in my palm and fingers holding the hammer. They guide my handling of it effectively, and the degree of attention that I give to the nail is given to these feelings to the same extent, but in a different way. The difference may be stated by saying that these feelings are not watched *in themselves* but that I watch something else by keeping aware of them. I know the feelings in the palm of my hand *by relying on them for attending to the hammer hitting the nail.* I may say that I have *a subsidiary* awareness of the feelings in my hand which is merged into my *focal awareness* of my driving the nail.[37]

Spatial dynamic

The above example illustrates a critical feature of tacit knowing, namely that it has a *spatial dynamic*, or, as Polanyi describes it, the two forms of cognition have an intrinsic 'from-to-relation.' The first, subsidiary awareness, or the 'proximal term,' as he also calls it, feels close to us while the second, the point of focal awareness or the 'distal term,' is at a distance from us. Only by relying tacitly on the specific details or 'particulars' of the proximal term as we keep our attention firmly fixed on the distal term are we able to draw upon all the subsidiary knowledge we need to accomplish a task, no matter what it is. In the same manner, Polanyi also restores the body to its central place in human experience and cognition:

> Whenever we use certain things for attending *from* them to other things, in the way in which we always use our own body, these things change their appearance. They appear to us now in terms of the entities to which we are attending *from* them, just as we feel our own body in terms of the things outside to which we are attending *from* our body. In this sense we can say that when we make a thing function as the proximal term of tacit knowing, we incorporate it in our body – or *extend our body to include it* [added emphasis] – so that we come to dwell in it.[38]

Or again:

> While we rely on a tool or a probe, these instruments are not handled or scrutinized as external objects. Instead, *we pour ourselves into them* [added emphasis] and assimilate them as part of ourselves.[39]

Put another way, tacit knowing involves an unconscious process of *immersion* in whatever we are doing. Whether it is hammering in a nail, hitting a ball in a game of tennis or any other sport (fig. 2.5), driving a car down the road ahead or communicating with another person, all of which require special skills we rely upon totally to perform well but which we are only ever partly aware of at any time, we *extend ourselves to absorb the objects or subjects we need in order to complete a task or action.* Thus we absorb the racket or bat in order to hit the ball; absorb the car in order to drive down the road; absorb the other person in order to communicate with him or her, and so forth.[40]

In her perceptive essay on Polanyi's thought, Marjorie Grene[41] also clearly expresses the spatial character of tacit knowing:

2.5 *British tennis champion Andy Murray in action*

I attend from a proximal pole, which is an aspect of my being, to a distal pole, which, by attending to it, I place myself at a distance from myself. *All knowing, we could say, in other words, is orientation* [added emphasis]. The organism's placing of itself in its environment, the dinoflagellate in the plankton, the salmon in its stream, or the fox in its lair, prefigures the process by which we both shape and are shaped by our world, reaching out from what we have assimilated to what we seek.[42]

The same subliminal processes apply to learning even the most complex forms of knowledge. While both Merleau-Ponty and Polanyi shared the same disdain for the prevalent scientific culture of their time, as a former scientist himself Polanyi was better positioned to identify the commonalities as well as the differences, which he believed to be largely unfounded, between science and other fields. Anticipating Thomas Kuhn's own landmark study of the modes and mores of science,[43] Polanyi argues that personal beliefs and a commitment to a particular vision of reality, together with a consensus among a community of workers on the value and moral purpose of their endeavor, are just as important to scientists as they are to anyone else. Like Kuhn, Polanyi also stresses the importance of *learning by example* against being taught by explicit rules alone, in which *inference* takes precedence over deduction.[44] Translated into the terms of tacit knowing, the novice scientist immerses himself or herself in the exemplary experiment or project as the proximal term of tacit knowing, by which he or she 'enters into' a whole body of knowledge (the very phrase itself has suggestive connotations), that is, the distal term, which would otherwise be inaccessible.[45]

Resolving the mind–body problem

For Polanyi, there is no form of knowledge that does not have its origins in the same mind–body fusion. In a passage that echoes the primacy of bodily experience in both Husserl and Merleau-Ponty's thought, he states:

> Our body is the ultimate instrument of all our external knowledge, whether intellectual or practical. In all our waking moments we are *relying* on our awareness of contacts of our body with things outside for *attending* to these things. Our own body is the only thing which we never normally experience as an object, but experience always in terms of the world to which we are attending from our body.[46]

However, whereas both Husserl and Merleau-Ponty mostly highlight the differences between science and everyday experience, Polanyi, as with his theory of how knowledge is acquired, is more concerned about building bridges between science and other familiar ways of engaging with the world, a view substantiated by other writers on Polanyi's work. C. P. Daly,[47] for example, finds parallels between Polanyi's approach to scientific rationality and the later work of Ludwig Wittgenstein and his concept of a 'form of life':

> Polanyi pursues his relentless critique of positivism by showing that science cannot be isolated from other forms of human knowing, living, loving, valuing. He shows that science cannot be understood apart from the 'form of life' of the scientific community, and indeed of the rational human community in general [...]. Rationality in science is not unique. It is akin to rationality in ethics. It is akin to rationality in politics, in jurisprudence and law. Creative thinking in science is not dissimilar to intuition in art and literature. Formal intellectual beauty is a criterion of truth in science, as it is of excellence in aesthetics.[48]

Polanyi does not therefore deny the rationality of science, but rather seeks to remind us that, notwithstanding other differences between culture-forms and belief systems, scientists are not alone in deferring to some shared concept of reality, as expressed in both a shared language and criteria of evaluation. Moreover, quoting

Polanyi, Grene suggests that the common roots of rationality and rational behavior may be found in the purposeful nature of tacit knowing itself:

> We can assimilate an object as a tool if we believe it to be actually useful to our purposes and the same holds for the relation of meaning to what is meant and the relation of the parts to the whole. The act of personal knowing can sustain these relations only because the acting person believes that they are apposite: that he has not *made them* but *discovered them*. The effort of knowing is thus guided by a sense of obligation towards the truth: by an effort to submit to reality.[49]

The ambiguity of being part of reality and yet somehow distanced from it, so we always move 'toward the truth,' extending ourselves *outward*, Grene argues, is inherent in the from–to relation between the two terms of tacit knowing. For Grene, Polanyi's from–to dynamic offers:

> the resolution, indeed, the dissolution of the mind–body problem [...] to comprehend is to rely on myself as *bodily* in order to envisage a coherent, intelligible spectacle *beyond* myself [...]. The dichotomy, or, more truly, the complementarity of self and world, inner and outer, is not that between a secret, inner, significance-conferring consciousness and a public, outer, meaningless 'reality.' *It is the polarity of a bodily self and an intelligible world* [added emphasis].[50]

Indivisible reality

Summarizing current research in the coevolution of mind, body and tools in a manner similar to Polanyi's theory of tacit knowing, but which he attributes to Wittgenstein, Tim Ingold[51] writes:

> For example, I am presently writing with a pen, I am wearing spectacles which help me to see, I carry a watch which tells me the time, a chair and table provide supports respectively for my body and my work, and I am surrounded by innumerable other bits and pieces that come in handy for one thing and another. I incorporate these diverse objects into the current of my activity without attending to them *as such*: I concentrate on my writing, not the pen; I see the time, not my watch. Indeed it could be said that these and other instruments become truly available to me, as things I can use without difficulty or interruption, at the point at which they effectively vanish as objects of my attention. And if anything links them together, it is only that they are brought into the same current, that of my work. Drawing an explicit parallel with tool-use, Wittgenstein made much the same point about the use of words in speech – different words have different uses, just as do the pen, watch and spectacles; one normally attends not to the words themselves but to what the speaker is telling us with them, and they are bound together solely by virtue of the fact that the various situations of use are all embedded within a total pattern of verbal and non-verbal activity, a form of life.[52]

We do not therefore enter into this world biologically and genetically pre-equipped with all the know-how and skills we need 'ready to be topped up from the environment,'[53] as Ingold puts it. Rather, the specific languages we speak, what we learn and the skills we acquire in using the tools we need to make our way in the world, all emerge out of an indivisible reality:

> In short, the acquisition of culturally specific skills is part and parcel of the overall developmental process of the human organism, and through this process they come to be literally *embodied* in the organism, in its neurology, its musculature, even in features of its anatomy [...]. And by the same token, what are commonly designated as cultural processes *are* biological, and historical processes *are* evolutionary.[54]

3 Embodied minds

Since Maurice Merleau-Ponty and Michael Polanyi recorded their thoughts on extended cognition, advances in the neurosciences have not only shed new light on the subject but have also generated a fruitful exchange with other disciplines, sometimes involving close collaboration between philosophers and scientists. This has led in turn to radically new approaches and potential answers to the perennial mystery of the self: what a self is, how it relates to issues of consciousness and, if such a thing really exists, how it might have evolved.

This chapter follows the new thinking and discoveries of leading researchers in the field, some of whom have been motivated by the belief that a full understanding of the self and consciousness will come about only from a broadening of the cognitive and neurosciences to encompass the phenomenology of human experience. From an exploration of current concepts of the self and embodied minds, the discussion then moves on to some of the more specific and important discoveries in the latter field, many of which lend empirical support to Merleau-Ponty and Polanyi's speculations, particularly those concerning the spatial and social extensions of the self. There follows a section dealing with aspects of Buddhist thought on the fragmentation of the self that have influenced one major group of researchers, along with Merleau-Ponty's works. Some unresolved issues are pointed out concerning the 'illusion' and instability of the self as it is described by some of these writers, and what qualifies for a subjective or objective experience or not. The chapter concludes by positing an alternative and psychologically more realistic concept of the self expressed as a 'field of being,' centered upon the human body, but also capable of extension into the physical and cultural environment as it evolves.

The enigma of the self

In addressing the subject of what a self is or is generally presumed to be, the German philosopher Thomas Metzinger, author of *The Ego Tunnel: The Science of the Mind and the Myth of the Self*,[1] suggests that we are only now beginning to catch up with Buddhist philosophy of 2,500 years ago. Introducing his book, Metzinger, who has worked closely with scientists on the subject for many years, offers an uncompromising approach:

In this book, I shall try to convince you that *there is no such thing as the self* [added emphasis]. Contrary to what most people believe, nobody has ever *been* or *had* a self. But it is not just that the modern philosophy of mind and cognitive neuroscience together are about to shatter the myth of the self. It has now become clear that we will never solve the philosophical puzzle of consciousness – that is, how it can arise in the brain, which is a purely physical object – if we don't come to terms with this simple proposition: that to the best of our current knowledge there is no thing, no indivisible entity, that is *us*, neither in the brain nor in some metaphysical realm beyond this world. So when we speak of conscious experience as a *subjective* phenomenon, what is the entity *having* these experiences?[2]

As a philosopher, Metzinger believes that cognitive scientists have generally neglected the phenomenological experience of consciousness in their explorations into the workings of the human brain. However, adopting an open attitude toward the sciences closer to Polanyi's viewpoint than Merleau-Ponty's, Metzinger also strongly believes that the value of empirical data has been likewise ignored by philosophers themselves, to the detriment of both sides of the debate. As an example of what he describes as 'the purely experiential nature of the self,'[3] Metzinger cites a 1998 experiment by Matthew Botvinick and Jonathan Cohen, two psychiatrists at the University of Pittsburgh. The now famous experiment involved normal, two-handed patients' imagined experience of an artificial hand in place of one of their real hands as part of their bodies. The artificial rubber hand was placed in front of the patient about the same distance from the shoulder as the corresponding real hand, which was hidden from the patient's view behind a screen. Both real and fake hands were then stroked simultaneously while the patient fixed his or her gaze on the fake hand. After about a minute or more the patient not only perceived the stroking sensation as emanating from the rubber hand, but the fake limb also felt as though it were joined to the shoulder by an arm just like a normal hand, effectively displacing the real arm with a 'virtual' one. Electrodes attached to patients' brains monitoring activity in the premotor cortex – a part of the brain critical to bodily movement and control – confirmed patients' subjective experience. Summarizing the experiment, which Metzinger himself also underwent, he writes:

> What you feel in the rubber-hand illusion is what I call the content of the *phenomenal self-model* (PSM) – the conscious model of the organism as a whole that is activated by the brain [...]. The content of the PSM is the Ego.[4]

As Metzinger explains, while most animals exhibit some degree of consciousness, *Homo sapiens* has developed a unique consciousness, or, to be more accurate, *self-consciousness* about the forms of representation involved:

> We mentally represent ourselves *as* representational systems, in phenomenological real-time. This ability turned us into thinkers of thoughts and readers of minds, and it allowed biological evolution to explode into cultural evolution.[5]

However, Metzinger is at pains to stress that, no matter how 'real' the self-model or ego appears to be to us, it is just as he describes it – a representational system that enables us to pull together all our other representational systems into a more or less coherent whole. There is no actual self beyond the representational system that simulates it. Moreover, the representations that make up the self-model only ever comprise a miniscule fraction of all the possible representations of the world about us, or what Metzinger describes as the 'Ego Tunnel.' Humans have only so much capacity to represent the world (which they need to do in order to function at all), he argues, so representations are necessarily selective: 'Therefore, the ongoing process of conscious experience is not so much an image of reality as a tunnel *through* reality.'[6] However, the creation of this narrow tunnel that everyone normally thinks of as the 'I' is no random process but the outcome of *directed action*. Using language similar to Merleau-Ponty's to describe the purposeful and rooted nature of conscious experience, Metzinger writes: 'In ordinary states of consciousness, there is always someone *having* the experience – someone consciously experiencing himself as directed toward the world, as a self in the act of attending, knowing, desiring, willing, and acting.'[7]

Thus, having a self-model implies not only an 'integrated inner image' of ourselves but experiencing the world from a *viewpoint* 'that is firmly anchored in our feelings and bodily sensations.'[8] Nevertheless, for all our self-consciousness we are never aware of the actual neurological mechanisms and other complex processes creating the self-model: 'We do not see neurons firing away in our brain but only what they represent for us.'[9] In this sense, Metzinger explains, self-models are always *transparent*; they provide us with a window *onto* the world, but we do not ever see the window itself – except perhaps, one might add, whatever neuroscientists can reveal of it to us through their brain scanners and other devices. However, pouring cold water on any lingering delusions anyone might still cherish about self-identities as more concrete phenomena, Metzinger reminds us again that:

> although our brains create the Ego Tunnel, *no one lives in this tunnel* [added emphasis]. We live with it and through it, but there is no little man running things inside our head […]. Ultimately, subjective experience is a biological data format, a highly specific mode of presenting information about the world by letting it appear as if it were an Ego's knowledge. But no such things as selves exist in the world.[10]

Body mapping and spatial extensions

Metzinger offers other equally intriguing examples of the experiential nature of the self-model in his work, including cases of 'phantom limbs' hallucinated by injured patients who have lost an arm or a leg – an experience similar in essence to the case of the displaced hand and arm described above. He also investigates the mysterious 'out of body experiences' (OBEs) many people have recounted after surviving a major operation or other near-death event, during which they recall floating above their physical bodies, from which they seem to have become detached. Interpreted by people of a religious inclination as evidence of a 'soul,' Metzinger offers the more rational if less entrancing explanation that they, too, are simply manifestations of temporarily modified self-models.

Against the conscious manifestations of the self-model described above, he also draws our attention to the mostly unconscious *spatial* dimensions of self-models, or what is now generally called 'body mapping' by neuroscientists. As Metzinger observes, the idea of a unified 'body schema' was hypothesized by neurologists early in the history of their science as 'an unconscious but constantly updated brain map of limb positions, body shape, and posture.'[11] However, unlike any conventional maps we normally think of, it appears that body maps exhibit some remarkably flexible spatial properties. For example, recent experiments with species of monkeys normally unaccustomed to using tools in the wild have shown that, when trained to use tools to perform acts like raking in a morsel of food to within easy reach or some other simple task:

> changes occur in specific neural networks in their brains, a finding suggesting that *the tools are temporarily integrated into their body schemata* [added emphasis]. When a food pellet is dispensed beyond their reach and they use a rake to bring it closer, a change is observed in their bodily self-model in the brain. In fact, it looks as though their model of their hand and the space around it is extended to the tip of the tool.[12]

In sum, Metzinger writes: 'The brain constructs an internalized image of the tool by assimilating it into the existing body image.'[13] Polanyi himself could hardly have designed a better experiment to demonstrate his theory of indwelling.[14] Moreover, while such experiments have so far been confined to primate behavior, given how close humans and primates are in genetic and evolutionary terms,[15] it seems reasonable, as Metzinger and others have done, to extrapolate the same findings to human behavior. However, it is Metzinger's observations on the broader implications of such experiments for human evolution that are most striking, the full significance of which will become more apparent as this book unfolds:

> One exciting aspect of these new data is that they shed light on the evolution of tool use. A necessary precondition of expanding your space of action and your capabilities by using tools clearly seems to be the ability to integrate them into a pre-existing self-model. You can engage in goal-directed and intelligent tool use only if your brain temporarily represents the tools as part of your self. Intelligent tool use was a major achievement in human evolution. One can plausibly assume that some of the elementary building blocks of human tool-use abilities existed in the brains of our ancestors, 25 million years ago. Then, due to some not-yet-understood evolutionary pressure, they exploded into what we see in humans today [...]. The decisive step in human evolution might well have been making a larger part of the body model globally available – that is, accessible to conscious experience. As soon as you can consciously experience a tool as integrated into your bodily self, you can also attend to this process, optimize it, form concepts about it, and control it in a more fine-grained manner – performing what we today call *acts of will*.[16]

Peripersonal space

In their own wide-ranging and engaging study of embodied minds, *The Body Has a Mind of Its Own*, Sandra and Matthew Blakeslee,[17] like Metzinger, reject conventional ideas of the self as having some kind of mental center or 'little man' in the head:

> The illusion of the self is that self is a kernel, rather than a distributed, emergent system [...]. [However,] the mind has no kernel, no 'little man' sitting at the center of the fray directing the action. But it is teeming with noncentral 'little men,' the brain's motley team of homunculi, who form the backbone of the whole production.[18]

Explaining how body mapping works, they add several more key discoveries and experiments to Metzinger's list. Crucially, the body schema not only assimilates the tools we use, but extends *beyond* the human body itself to embrace the clothes we wear, other objects in the surrounding space we touch or interact with and even those we have intimate relations with, in a harmonious blending of individual body maps.[19] Neuroscientists call this extended and flexible spatial domain the 'peripersonal space,' every part of which is also mapped by our brain cells: 'When you observe or otherwise sense objects entering that space, these cells start firing.'[20] There is also evidence, some of it gleaned from patients suffering from heart stroke, that the brain distinguishes between peripersonal space and the space farther out, called 'extrapersonal space.' For example, asked to perform a simple task with a laser pointer within their personal space, the stroke patients have no problem, but fail the same task if it involves reaching out too far.

However, it seems the dividing line between personal space and the space beyond is neither fixed nor even always close to the body. On the contrary, as with Polanyi's claims for the power of tacit knowing, peripersonal space is *highly elastic* and can be stretched at will to embrace tools or baseball bats, objects coming our way, and even the actions of other people in the vicinity. More like an expandable 'bubble' of space as the Blakeslees describe it than a stable aura, peripersonal space behaves much like an invisible and highly sensitive muscle, flexing with our every movement. No less significant, the neurological structures responsible for body maps and personal spaces are equally plastic, and are forever evolving throughout our life-spans:

> The old picture was of body maps settling into a fixed configuration like fired clay. *The new picture is one of dynamic stability* [added emphasis]. Neuroplasticity continually reshapes your brain in response to experience; the fact that it seems static merely reflects the consistency of your experiences throughout most of your adult life.[21]

The Blakeslees recount another series of experiments with monkeys' body maps, in 1994, by Michael Graziano and Charles Gross, two Princeton University neuro-scientists, demonstrating their flexibility. Exploring the body maps located in the monkeys' premotor cortex – the same part of the brain monitored in the Pittsburgh University experiment with humans – the researchers found that moving an object to within a few inches of a spot on the monkey's hand while the monkey watched the action fired exactly the same brain cells that fired when the hand had been previously touched. Alone, one might suspect the response was simply connected with the monkey's recent memory of the touch. However, moving the object closer or further away from the monkey's hand also produced corresponding changes in the *speed* at which the cells fired: the closer the object was moved in, the faster the cells fired. When the object was withdrawn, the cells fired more slowly. The authors conclude: 'In other words, these cells were mapping not just touch, but the nearby bubble of space around the body.'[22]

However, extraordinary as these findings are, current research described by the Blakeslees into space-mapping neurons called 'place cells' and 'grid cells' located in the hippocampus, where memories are formed, points to further likely revelations of a complete mind–body synthesis.[23] The former are 'context dependent' and respond to specific features and objects in our immediate environment, mapping the actual space around us at any one time and everything of any significance to us within it. The latter cells, however, are 'context independent.' As the name suggests, they provide a constant reference space around the body, independently of the changing contents of that space, so we can always accurately locate ourselves and anything else within the same measurable framework. The former were first discovered in 1971 by two neuroscientists, John O'Keefe and John Dostrovsky, while they were monitoring the hippocampus in the brains of mice to find out how the memory functions. As the mice moved around their enclosure, the researchers noticed that different brain cells in the hippocampus fired according to which part of their enclosure the mice moved into. Moreover, the same cells fired up again if the mice moved back to the same place. Each mouse, it seems, had formed its own accurate mental map of the enclosure, which it had previously memorized when it was familiarizing itself with its new home: 'In fact, it was possible to tell where an animal was inside its enclosure simply by looking at which cells were active.'[24]

Searching the neurosciences for a physiological basis for spatial behavior, grid cells were discovered only in the last few years, by Edvard and May-Britt Moser, a married couple of Norwegian psychologists at the University of Science and Technology at Trondheim. Operating at a higher level in the brain than place cells, grid cells function as though every fraction of the space around us is marked out with a regular triangulated grid, stretching far beyond us. Only firing up as the body moves into the vertex of one of the triangles in front, they remain inactive for any locations in between the vertices. No matter where we are, it seems, our brains are always carefully pacing out the space around us in the same measured steps.

Initially surprised at their findings, the Mosers concluded that the invariant spatial environment mapped out by grid cells necessarily complements the variable spaces mapped by place cells. Though the subjects of their experiments have been restricted to date to laboratory rats, they believe all animals, including humans, possess similar neural systems. Anticipating further research, they speculate that gifted sportsmen and sportswomen possess highly developed versions of both place cells and grid cells, enabling them to strike a speeding ball with repeated accuracy or to track the movements of numerous other players on the field. Venturing further, the researchers suggest the two cell functions may be interconnected in other, still more significant ways: 'There are many reasons to believe that *place cells are sums of grid cells.*'[25] It would seem that spatial awareness may have something like its own subconscious formal logic underpinning the infinite variety of mental maps we all create and use in our everyday lives.

Identifying with others

Whatever support new research provides for the Mosers' speculations about place cells and grid cells, the neurosciences have thus already yielded promising empirical evidence of a tacit mind–body synthesis to substantiate many of Polanyi's fundamental ideas, as well as those of Merleau-Ponty and other prominent writers discussed in this book, if sometimes only in part. The basic idea that we all create internal models of the world about us that help us to find our way around, integrate different aspects of that world, anticipate what lies ahead, make decisions and identify with specific places is broadly sustained. However, our knowledge of how those internal models are created has dramatically changed as a result of the research described above. From an understanding of images and maps as a product of purely mental processes, as presented by Boulding and Lynch et al. in Chapter 1, we have moved closer to the more complex picture painted by Polanyi and Merleau-Ponty, whereby the human body itself plays an integral role in those processes, without which we would literally have no place at all in the world or, indeed, any sense of our own selves. In particular, as the above experiments have shown, the inherent spatial character of tacit knowing is strongly supported by the research on body mapping and peripersonal space, much like Polanyi's account of the way we incorporate a tool or anything else into our own bodies, by extending ourselves outwards, 'so that we come to dwell in it.'[26]

Giacomo Rizzolatti and his research team at the University of Parma, Italy, have also revealed that much the same thing goes on when people identify with others.[27] Initially focused on a series of experiments with primates in the 1980s, the research has since also included human subjects. For Metzinger, the discoveries, which he includes with the new 'social neurosciences,' have considerable significance for what they reveal about how the human ego graduates from the 'I' to the 'we.' The ego tunnel, he suggests, not only comprises selected information about all kinds of other aspects of the world of importance to the ego, both material and immaterial, it also includes selected information about the ego tunnels of *other* persons with whom people interact. Regarding the earlier experiments with primates, Metzinger explains they involved two related groups of neurons located in part of the premotor region of the monkey brain called F5. Part of the monkey's unconscious self-model, the first set of neurons, Metzinger recounts, 'code body movements in a highly abstract way.'[28] Rizzolatti describes these as the monkey's 'motor vocabulary' and it includes whole integrated actions such as 'reach,' 'tear,' or 'hold,' and so on, involving relations between the agent's goals and the time-governed sequence of related actions required to reach the objective.

It is now known that human beings, Metzinger writes, have similar neurological systems. Significantly, the same 'canonical neurons,' as they are called, are also involved in the recognition of common objects in the environment: 'Our brain does not just register a chair, a teacup, an apple; it immediately represents a seen object as what I could do with it – as an affordance, a set of possible behaviors.'[29] The consequences of these discoveries for understanding the perception of things and related matters, Metzinger asserts, are far reaching:

> As it turns out, *the traditional philosophical distinction between perception and action is an artificial one* [added emphasis]. In reality, our brains employ a common coding: Everything we perceive is automatically portrayed as a factor in a possible interaction between the world and ourselves. A new medium is created, blending action and perception into a novel, unified representational format.[30]

The other group of related neurons located in the F5 region of the brain were discovered by the same team in Parma in the 1990s and are no less remarkable for the role they play in the way we interact with the world – and more specifically, with others. Appropriately called 'mirror neurons,' they not only fired up when monkeys grasped things or performed other purposeful actions themselves, but they also fired up when they observed another agent using an object in a similar purposeful way. Though Metzinger does not mention the experiment himself, significantly, the first recorded observation of mirror neurons involved both a monkey and a human agent. As recounted by the Blakeslees,[31] who also devote much attention in their own study to the same corresponding experiments and developments, the discovery came about almost by accident. Set up with electrodes attached to the monkey's brain in preparation for an experiment into the premotor cortex – again, the same part of the brain involved with planning and movement as in the earlier experiments – the waiting animal was observed to be following the actions of a research student with rapt attention. The student had just entered the room eating an ice cream cone, and the monkey was jealously eyeing the hand holding the cone. Normally, previous experiments had shown that the relevant brain cells of the monkey would fire up whenever it grasped or moved an object itself. But now the monitor was showing the identical brain cells firing up, though the monkey itself remained perfectly still. What it was actually doing, Rizzolatti concluded, was mimicking the actions of the student – not by any movements of its own, but by *mentally simulating the same movements* it had visually observed the student making.[32]

Later, similar experiments with human subjects using modern neuroimaging techniques confirmed Rizzolatti's hypothesis across a broad range of common experiences, including empathizing with the pain and emotions of others. Translating these discoveries into the terms of his own theory of the ego, Metzinger writes:

> We use our own unconscious self-model *to put ourselves in the shoes of others, as it were* [added emphasis]. We use our own 'motor ideas' to understand someone else's actions by directly mapping them onto our inner repertoire, by automatically triggering an inner image of what *our* goal would be if our body also moved that way [...]. The conscious self is thus not only a window into the internal workings of one's own Ego but also a

window into the social world. It is a two-way window: It elevates to the level of global availability the unconscious and automatic processes that organisms constantly use to represent one another's behaviour.[33]

Critically, as Merleau-Ponty intimated in his own writings on the subject, the capacity for identifying with others depends upon *already having an equivalent sensory schema*, that is, a body image, or at least the same kind of image, as the other agent.[34] The monkey in the laboratory in Parma could not have simulated the student's movements in its own brain so accurately if it did not *also* have arms and hands and body maps of those limbs, much like all humans. Likewise, the more developed those similar maps are, the more sensitive a human subject will be to another's actions and concerns.

According to the Blakeslees, the importance of the discovery of mirror neurons cannot be overestimated. For example, V. S. Ramachandran, a neurologist at the University of California, has argued that mirror neurons not only account for how infants acquire language, by mimicking the sounds and lip movements of their parents and others,[35] but also how we acquire any kind of cultural trait:

> Mirror neurons provide an alternative explanation for human brain design. Your brain is unique not because it has evolved highly specialized modules, but because it is parasitic with culture [...]. Mirror neurons absorb culture the way a sponge sucks up water.[36]

However, it appears that mirror neurons are not the only part of the neurological apparatus involved in identifying with others. As recounted by Caroline Williams,[37] recent research on so-called von Economo neurons, or VENs, may provide the most important evidence yet of the deeper processes underlying empathy and related aspects of social consciousness. Named after Constantin von Economo, a little-known neuroscientist who first discovered them in the late 1920s, they were mostly ignored on account of their rarity but were rediscovered 80 years later by Esther Nimchinsky and Patrick Hof at Mount Sinai University in New York. Concentrated in two small areas of the brain known as the anterior cingulate cortex (ACC) and the fronto-insular (FI) cortex, though much larger than more common neurons, they comprise just 1% of those found in both areas. Also shaped and linked together quite differently from most neurons, VENs and the two areas of the cortex they are located in are now thought to be responsible for many of the defining behaviors we associate with consciousness and the self:

> Their location in those regions suggests that VENs may be a central part of our mental machinery, since the ACC and FI are heavily involved in many of the more advanced aspects of our inner lives. Both areas kick into action when we see socially relevant cues, be it a frowning face, a grimace of pain or simply the voice of someone we love. When a mother hears a baby crying, both regions respond strongly. They also light up when we experience emotions such as love, lust, anger and grief. For John Allman, a neuroanatomist at the California Institute of Technology at Pasadena, this adds up to a kind of 'social monitoring network' that keeps track of social cues and allows us to alter our behaviour accordingly.[38]

Moreover, both the ACC and FI are activated when a person recognizes his or her reflection in a mirror. Hof hypothesizes that such reactions point to a neurological basis for the self and, with it, mind:

> It is the sense of self at every possible level – so the sense of identity, this is me, and the sense of identity of others and how you understand others. That goes to the concept of empathy and theory of mind.[39]

While, as with mirror neurons, *Homo sapiens* may be especially blessed with VENs, neither are they exclusive to our species. Experiments conducted with various other highly social species of mammals, including chimpanzees, gorillas, elephants and some whales and dolphins, have identified VEN-like clusters of neurons located in similar areas of the brain, together with related patterns of social behavior similar to our own. Allman suggests that, extrapolating back in evolutionary time, VENs may have evolved along with a refinement of the olfactory senses (taste and smell) as a by-product of sharing food and the need to recognize what could make others in a group healthy or sick as well as oneself – basic empathetic skills that might then have been generalized to cover other interpersonal situations. Taking the argument further, Bud Craig, another neuroanatomist, at Barrow Neurological Institute in Phoenix, Arizona, reasons that the fusion of bodily senses, mind and sense of self involved in such interactions was driven by the high-energy requirements of large brains and the need to react quickly and efficiently to any situation that might arise: 'Evolution produced a very efficient moment-by-moment calculation of energy utilization and that had an epiphenomenon, *a by-product that provided a subjective representation of my feelings*.'[40]

Summarizing the implications, Williams observes: 'If he's right – and there is a long way to go before we can be sure – it raises a very humbling possibility: that far from being the pinnacle of brain evolution, consciousness might have been a big, and very successful accident.'[41]

The aggregates of experience

Though Francisco J. Varela, Evan Thompson and Eleanor Rosch, authors of *The Embodied Mind*,[42] make few direct references to the findings of neuroscientists on the subject, like Metzinger they firmly believe in an interdisciplinary approach to cognitive science inspired by Merleau-Ponty's phenomenology. Asserting a symbiotic view of mind and body, they write:

> We hold with Merleau-Ponty that Western scientific culture requires that we see our bodies both as physical structures and as lived, experiential structures – in short, as both 'outer' and 'inner,' biological and phenomenological. These two sides of embodiment are obviously not opposed. Instead, we continuously circulate back and forth between them. Merleau-Ponty recognized that we couldn't understand this circulation without

a detailed investigation of its fundamental axis, namely, the embodiment of knowledge, cognition, and experience. For Merleau-Ponty, as for us, *embodiment* has this double sense: it encompasses both the body as a lived, experiential structure and the body as the context or milieu of cognitive mechanisms.[43]

However, they also acknowledge that, while this 'double sense' of the embodied mind has been mostly absent from the cognitive sciences in the last century, which were then divisively split between psychiatry, behavioral psychology and neurology, there is a gathering momentum, as we have seen in the previous sections in this chapter, toward a merging of hitherto separate disciplines and fields of thought, both inside and outside the sciences. As a consequence of their work within this new, heterogeneous field, the authors maintain 'that the self or cognizing subject is fundamentally fragmented, divided and non-unified.'[44] Like Metzinger, the authors boldly state their position at the outset regarding the non-existence of the self as it is generally conceived:

> We wish to make a sweeping claim: all of the reflective traditions in human history – philosophy, science, psychoanalysis, religion, meditation – have challenged the naïve sense of self. No tradition has ever claimed to discover an independent, fixed, or unitary self within the world of experience.[45]

Nevertheless, they concede that everyone behaves *as if* such a self does indeed exist; that is, they jealously guard it and, as we all tend to do, they project what they think is their very best self-image onto the world at large. The task for the new breed of cognitive scientists, they suggest, therefore boils down to explaining the origins of the *illusion* of the self, if that is indeed all there is to it, together with the cognitive mechanisms involved in maintaining that illusion.

In addition to Merleau-Ponty, Varela et al. also acknowledge the influence of Buddhist conceptions of a fragmented or 'decentered' self. Whereas Metzinger only briefly mentions the relevance of Buddhist traditions of thought to the subject, the authors go to some length to explain why those traditions merit closer attention and what they have to offer the new sciences of cognition. For Buddhists, they explain, this common human insistence upon an ego-centered self is the source of all suffering, a condition that can be overcome only by uncovering the true workings of the mind through meditation: 'The search for how the self arises is thus a way of asking, "What and where is mind?" in a direct and personal way.'[46] The Buddhist answer to that question is an elliptical one, comprised of different categories of experience, the most common to all Buddhist schools of thought being the 'five aggregates,' which they list as follows:

1. Forms
2. Feelings/sensations
3. Perceptions/discernments/impulses
4. Dispositional formations
5. Consciousnesses[47]

The first of these, they explain, has a physical and material basis while the rest all have a mental basis: 'All five together constitute the psychophysical complex that makes up a person and that makes up each moment of experience.'[48] Each aggregate in turn contains the preceding aggregates so that the last, 'consciousnesses,' contains all the other four. The authors search each aggregate in turn for evidence of the existence of a core self that we all normally respond to, but while each can be said to contribute something of importance to the illusion of a self, they can find no convincing evidence of anything more concrete than that. Even consciousness in the Buddhist account, while it *includes* all the other aggregates, fails the test and remains little more than the sum of its parts: 'The combination of mental factors that are present make up the character – the color and taste – of a particular moment of consciousness.'[49] Moreover, the most important aspect of consciousness is that the illusion of the 'totality and continuity of experience of consciousness masks the discontinuity of momentary consciousness.'[50] Nevertheless, they argue, terrified at the thought of death we persist in hanging on to our belief in that continuity. 'Yet when mindfulness-awareness reveals the disunity of this experience – a sight, a sound, a thought, another thought, and so on – it becomes obvious that *consciousness cannot be taken as that self we so treasure* [added emphasis] and for which we are now searching.'[51]

Perhaps, they hint, 'all the aggregates combine in some way to form the self.'[52] That seems like a good idea to them except that they cannot see how it might actually work.[53] If consciousness cannot provide the requisite holistic and continuous properties of the imagined self, then nothing can. The feelings, sensations, perceptions, dispositions and so on that are associated with all the different aggregates are all real enough, they conclude: 'Indeed, we entered the very eye of the storm of experience, we just simply could discern there no self, no "I."'[54] In the end, the authors are compelled to accept the idea, as Buddhism teaches, that *there is no self beyond the aggregates of experience*. The insights and 'calm mindfulness' which come with meditation, they suggest, unveil the ephemeral nature of experience, which, the more you try to pin it down, the more it slips away. However, fond as we are of our ego-selves and unwilling to give them up, the authors argue that, if there were such a thing as a concrete, ever-stable self, the fluidity of actual experience would be threatened:

> If there were a solid, really existing self hidden in or behind the aggregates, its unchangeableness would prevent any experience from occurring; its static nature would make the constant arising and subsiding of experience come to a screeching halt [...]. But that circle of arising and decay of experience turns continuously, and *it can do so only because it is empty of a self* [added emphasis].[55]

Perpetual paradox

If the above authors' conclusion concerning the existence or non-existence of the self is therefore ultimately negative, it hardly resolves the question as to why the vast majority of human beings all persist in maintaining the illusion. Nor, aside from registering the not inconsequential fear of death, do they begin to explain what evolutionary purpose or history, if any, might account for that persistence. Not least, there is an evident discrepancy between the authors' declared allegiance to Merleau-Ponty's phenomenology and the apparent separation in the school of Buddhist thought described above of physical and bodily matters, constituting the first aggregate of experience from the other four aggregates. While the distinction is partly resolved by the incorporation of the first aggregate into all the rest, there is an implicit *downgrading* of the physical elements of experience in the order of incorporation which ill fits with Merleau-Ponty's philosophy of the centrality of bodily experience, and with much else that is written in this book.

Exploring other schools of Buddhist thought, Varela et al. point to closer parallels between neuroscientists' concepts of embodiment and the Madhyamika Buddhist tradition, sometimes called the 'middle way.' Stressing the 'co-dependence' of subject and object, neither of which exists without the other, as the authors describe it Madhyamika avoids the extremes or 'two truths' of objectivism and subjectivism but ultimately only reinforces the 'groundlessness' of existence:

> nothing can be found that has an ultimate or independent existence. Or to use Buddhist language, everything is 'empty' of an independent existence, for it is codependently originated.[56]

There remains, therefore, a perpetual paradox underlying the whole question of the 'reality' of experience in rejecting the ego-self as an illusion, and what should be regarded as a legitimate experience and what should not. If, as Merleau-Ponty urges us, we take everyday experience as the fundamental grist of life, then why should the imagined self, if that is what it is, *not* be counted at least as one of those experiences, if not perhaps the most important of them all? Whether or not it can ever be pinned down, if the self still appears 'real' to us, then, phenomenologically speaking, it *is* real. Not only that, as all the writers discussed here agree, daily experience confirms the impact of the ego-self, real or not, on practically everything else we do. In particular, when dealing with others we are more likely, as Metzinger suggests, to be dealing with their own ego tunnels than with any of their discrete emotions or thoughts. The very fact that it takes years of disciplined training for individuals even to begin to penetrate through or shake off this tenacious thing called an ego-self or tunnel should also give pause for thought about its experiential status and possible evolutionary value.

Moreover, it should be patently obvious that, while one might well believe in the advantages of a fluid being-in-the-world, people often *do* fiercely resist change, especially when it threatens the ego and the way of life in which it has become embedded. It is arguable, therefore, that, while accepting we will probably never isolate or pin down the imagined self beyond the multiple representational systems which comprise it, if we want to understand the *reasons* for the self's persistence, then we also need to treat it as though it exists as a key part of the experiential world – fragmentary, decentered and impermanent though it may be.

Extended cognition

Andy Clark and David Chalmers take an important, if hesitant, step in this direction in their 1998 essay 'The Extended Mind.'[57] Addressing the question as to where the boundary lies between the mind and the rest of the world, the authors propose 'an *active externalism*, based on the active role of the environment in driving cognitive processes.'[58] To illustrate their argument, they consider various common cases where people perform problem-solving operations on a computer screen, supplemented with a neural implant in one hypothetical but likely case in the not so distant future. In all cases the authors suggest the basic cognitive process is the same:

> We cannot point to the skin/skull boundary as justification [for distinguishing between cognitions], since the legitimacy of that boundary is precisely what is at issue. But nothing else seems different.[59]

The authors argue that much the same applies to the common use of any external tools or media, whether it involves a simple pen and paper, a slide rule, books or diagrams. Citing a work by David Kirsh and Paul Maglio,[60] they describe such cases as examples of 'epistemic action,' or actions that:

> alter the world so as to aid and augment cognitive processes such as recognition and search. Merely *pragmatic* actions, by contrast, alter the world because some physical change is desirable for its own sake (e.g., putting cement into a hole in a dam).[61]

They also distinguish active externalism, which concerns cognitive processes taking place in the here-and-now, from more distant or 'passive' events or beliefs, which do not involve any *current* external features affecting the cognition. By contrast, in the cases of active externalism they describe, 'the relevant parts of the world are *in the loop*, not dangling at the other end of a long causal chain.'[62] As a simple if extreme example they offer the hypothetical case of Otto, a person suffering from Alzheimer's disease, who, like many such people similarly affected, relies upon externally recorded notes of names, places and other information to fill in for the growing failures of his memory. New information gets recorded and old information can be looked up when needed. Effectively, the notebook plays the role of an external memory bank, just as it does with healthy people, except the role is probably not as constant or as vital to their daily lives as it is to Otto's. The important thing is that Otto believes the information in his notebook to be *just as true* and reliable as if it were in his head:

> The moral is that when it comes to belief, there is nothing sacred about skull and skin. What makes some information count as a belief is the role it plays, and there is no reason why the relevant role can be played only inside the body.[63]

Pushing the argument further into the realm of social relations, or what they call 'socially extended cognition,' the authors see no reason why the mental states of one person might not be constituted in part by those of another closely related person:

'In an unusually interdependent couple, it is entirely possible that one partner's beliefs will play the same sort of role for the other as the notebook plays for Otto.'[64] In such cases, they argue, the sharing or coupling of mental states is greatly enhanced by language, which allows us to 'spread the burden' (the verb 'outsource' might also apply here) of cognition into the wider world:

> Language, thus construed, is not a mirror of our inner states but a complement to them. *It serves as a tool whose role is to extend cognition in ways that on-board services cannot.* Indeed, it may be that the intellectual explosion in recent evolutionary time is due as much to this linguistically enabled extension of cognition as to any independent development in our inner cognitive resources.[65]

In conclusion, the authors ask whether the concept of an extended mind might not also imply an extended *self*, which they answer in the affirmative:

> The information in Otto's notebook, for example, is a central part of his identity as a cognitive agent. What this comes to is that Otto *himself* is best regarded as an extended system, a coupling of biological and external resources. To consistently resist this conclusion, we would have to shrink the self into a mere bundle of occurrent states, severely threatening its deep psychological continuity. *Far better to take the broader view, and see agents themselves as spread into the world.*[66]

Fields of being

The difference between Clark and Chalmers' attitudes toward the self and that of Varela et al. and, to a lesser extent, Metzinger could not be more striking. Where the other writers almost make the ego-self disappear before readers' eyes without so much as a fond farewell, Clark and Chalmers are evidently concerned that, in explaining the self away, as they put it, as 'a mere bundle of occurrent states' – which is pretty much as the other writers describe it – something of great psychological and social value might be getting lost. Initially, they describe their concept of active externalism in deterministic terms, in which the environment plays an active role 'in driving cognitive processes.' However, their concluding description of the self might be better likened to dropping a stone into a pool, setting off ripples across the water.[67] Some other aspects of their conception do not hold up very well, as we shall see in subsequent chapters. For example, the distinction between 'active' and 'passive' externalism is hard to maintain, given that even the use of language between interdependent partners involves a system of communication that has evolved over many thousands of years. They also generally treat the use of external aids to cognition as convenient 'add-on' or supplementary devices – basically separate tools that extend or enhance the capacity of the human agent. As we shall see in the following chapter on technics, the relationship between humans and their tools, whether of the simple or complex variety, is a great deal more subtle and complex than the two authors suggest.

If anything, therefore, while it usefully broadens the scope of human cognition, Clark and Chalmers' conception of active externalism does not go far enough to capture the full depth of the interrelations between people and the artifacts and related technological cultures that have shaped the course of human evolution. Closer to the mark, in describing the elusive fusion of mind, self and world, William Barrett[68] proffers a more promising metaphor when he likens Heidegger's theory of man to a 'Field Theory of Being' analogous to Einstein's field theory of matter or a magnetic field, except that, unlike the latter, it has no center: 'Think of a magnetic field without the solid body of the magnet at its center; man's Being is such a field, but there is no soul substance at the center from which that field radiates.'[69]

However, the metaphor is incomplete as it stands. Magnets set up patterns in the surrounding field of elements about them. Take away the magnet and you may have a field of some kind but no pattern and maybe even no field at all. Yet patterns are plentiful in human behavior, good and bad, clear-cut or fuzzy. Happily, Merleau-Ponty and Polanyi provide us with a ready candidate to fill the void. While there may be no single origin of the self, it *does* have an identifiable working nucleus and focal point in the human body, through which all our experience and self-models are mediated: a field of being, therefore, held together, not by any physical force, but by an *existential force*, with the body at its center. Unlike the fixed magnetic field, this latter field is also very much a living thing, constantly evolving throughout its lifetime, overlapping and interacting with other fields of being in unpredictable ways, creating the miraculously complex but now dangerously unstable world we inhabit.

Part I summary

The purpose of this summary of the previous three chapters, as it is of each summary of the other three parts of this book, is not to cover all of the points or arguments presented in these chapters, but to focus on whatever ideas and conclusions may be drawn from them that contribute most to a viable theory of the extended self, and to an understanding of the environmental implications.

Thus, the first lesson to be drawn from Chapter 1 is that, while there is widespread agreement across disciplines that the identities of individuals, groups and places are significantly interrelated, there are equally divergent views as to the nature and origins of those relationships. Architectural theorists like Christian Norberg-Schulz and Kevin Lynch (Paul Oliver is a marked exception to the rule) are especially prone to making value judgments about different forms of habitats on the assumption that some are inherently easier to identify with than others, severely limiting the generality and usefulness of their ideas. Researchers in other disciplines like Amos Rapoport and Edward Hall, on the other hand, stress the importance of cultural factors in determining how different people respond to different environments – a position strongly supported by the examples presented in this book.

By contrast, among the first and most important points of agreement to emerge, the related ideas of mental or body 'images,' 'schemas' or 'maps' reappear in all three chapters, as well as in later chapters, though, as with the idea of place-identity, their precise meanings vary according to whichever writer is employing them. Expanding on his theory of proxemics, as quoted in Chapter 1, Hall also points directly to the driving theme in this book, stating that 'Man [...] is distinguished from the other animals by virtue of the fact that he has elaborated what I have termed *extensions* of his organism.' In turn, Edward Casey and J. E. Malpas have also both reinvigorated the subject of place, especially the interdependence between the subjective and objective elements of place experience, as being worthy of renewed philosophical attention.

The prime importance of the human body in spatial cognition and human perception generally is also firmly established in the second chapter, as propounded by both Maurice Merleau-Ponty and Michael Polanyi, whose philosophical speculations antedate many of the more recent theories of embodied minds and related findings of neuroscientists. Arriving independently at the same conclusion as Hall, both also present detailed and convincing arguments for regarding tools and other artifacts in use as virtual extensions of the human body. Moreover, having a body with the same basic outline as other people, no matter what their color or creed, also provides a cognitive springboard enabling one person to empathize with another, thus opening the way for the sharing of minds and cultures beyond individual perceptions – possibly even preceding the use of common languages.

In stressing the fundamental role of the body as the medium of all personal experience, the concept of the self that emerges thus far retains a strong unitary core. Taking a radically different turn, Chapter 3 opens with Thomas Metzinger's claim that there is no such thing as a self, only a collection of *representations* of the self that can be easily manipulated to reveal their fragility, for which he provides evidence from numerous experiments. At the same time, he also suggests that we need to take the way we actually experience the world more seriously, offering his concept of the ego tunnel as a purpose-directed *selection* of representations of the self and others from a potentially endless range of other possible representations.

Like Metzinger, Francisco Varela and his co-authors portray themselves as dedicated phenomenologists as well as being respectful of what science has to offer, specifically citing the work of Merleau-Ponty as their inspiration and guide. Also like Metzinger, they present the self as an essentially ephemeral and fragmentary construction originating in multiple sources, for which they find strong parallels within Buddhist traditions of thought, which they analyze in some detail. However, as with Metzinger's approach, serious contradictions arise between Merleau-Ponty's conception of the body as the indispensable fulcrum of personal experience and the picture Varela et al. present of the self as a 'non-unified,' or decentered phenomenon, particularly as portrayed in Buddhism, which by their own account treats bodily experience as the lowest order of human existence.

Other related discoveries by neuroscientists of the complex workings of the mind, such as 'body mapping,' 'peripersonal space' and 'mirror neurons,' are also described which verify Merleau-Ponty's and Polanyi's earlier theories of embodied cognition. The flexibility of peripersonal space and its ability to absorb personal objects especially supports Polanyi's theory of tacit knowing. As with mirror neurons, recent experiments with von Economo neurons also provide convincing evidence of the neurological basis for empathy, an essential precondition, as indicated above, for the sharing of cultures and any socially based activities, including the making of shelters and settlements and other human artifacts. The same discoveries also confirm the *distributed* nature of the neurological processes involved, suggesting that neither conventional unitary concepts of the self nor opposing non-unified, or decentered theories provide satisfactory models for an extended self.

Arguing that extreme theories of fragmented or non-existent selves ignore the psychological and social value of having a continuous focal point for the self of some kind, however fragile its foundations might be, Andy Clark and David Chalmers offer an alternative theory of extended minds which retains the integrity of individual human agents while also embracing the extension of personal powers by external devices – that is, external to the human body. Significantly, while they do not elaborate on the idea, they suggest their approach might allow for a concept of the extended self as 'a coupling of biological and external resources.'

In conclusion, searching for a new and appropriate metaphor consistent with such an approach, the extended self was likened to a magnetic 'field of being,' comprised of objects and places as well as others, with the body at its center, the origins and properties of which we are only now beginning to comprehend.

Part II of the book will explore some other key outstanding issues, including the causal sequence of humankind's technological and material extensions, such as it may be; how they are in turn raising basic questions about evolutionary theory itself; whether cultural ideas can have an evolutionary life of their own, and if so, what the possible processes of reproduction and transmission involved are.

Part II: Origins

4 Technics and the human

Though some of the writers discussed in the last two chapters offer examples of the use of tools and other artifacts in their theories of cognitive extension, none of them pursues the wider implications for the technological development of human culture, or the possible role of the extended self in that development.

For a more comprehensive view of the impacts of technology on human behavior and evolution, or technics as it is known in the broadest sense, the discussion now turns to Bernard Stiegler, one of the current generation of leading thinkers grappling with a world increasingly shaped by technological innovation.[1] While, as his critics point out, Stiegler himself makes no attempt to identify any more specific cognitive or evolutionary agents involved, the philosophy he expounds of the coevolution of humanity and technology in his trilogy, *Technics and Time*,[2] and, most importantly, the *exteriorization* of that coevolution, provides a substantial framework within which to explore those agents and their role in the formation of the extended self.

Following an overview of Stiegler's main ideas, the debate then shifts to the writings of a selection of the many researchers affected by his radical thought, and to some of the more important ramifications and possible limitations of his approach. Several key issues and criticisms arising out of these debates are examined more closely, including the relevance of animal tool use to Stiegler's claims for the uniqueness of humans as tool makers, the significance of writing and writing metaphors in the conception of technics and, lastly, the impact of location and geography on its development.

The dynamics of technics

While Stiegler is one of the more important contemporary thinkers on the subject of technics, he is far from being the first to question its meaning or impacts. In his seminal essay 'The Question Concerning Technology,'[3] Martin Heidegger contests the instrumental definition of technology as a mere means to an end, according to which the main challenge for humanity is that of mastering those means:

Everything depends on our manipulating technology in the proper manner as a means. We will, as we say, 'get' technology 'spiritually in hand.' We will master it. The will to mastery becomes all the more urgent the more technology threatens to slip from human control.[4]

Moreover, Heidegger equates the conception of instrumentality itself with causation: 'Wherever ends are pursued and means are employed, wherever instrumentality reigns, there reigns causality.'[5] Thus all forms of technology are generally interpreted as the *cause of*, that is to say, the *means* by which some desired material or social ends or *effects* are achieved. All of which, Heidegger suggests, may be perfectly correct as far as it goes but it also gets in the way of understanding the real meaning of technology and what it might actually tell us about who we are as human beings on this earth:

> Technology is therefore no mere means. *Technology is a way of revealing* [added emphasis]. If we give heed to this, then another whole realm for the essence of technology will open up to us. It is the realm of revealing, i.e., of truth.[6]

Prominent later thinkers voiced other, more direct concerns about the impact of technology on human life. In a series of lectures published in the aftermath of the Second World War, *Art and Technics*, Lewis Mumford[7] expressed his view that humankind's obsession with modern technology was threatening the very civilization it had made possible: 'Man has become an exile in this mechanical world: or rather, even worse, he has become a displaced person.'[8] Gregory Bateson,[9] who, like Michael Polanyi, was one of the first to argue the case for mind as a distributed phenomenon,[10] also warned of the dangers of becoming so attached to a particular technological culture and way of life that it might prevent people from seeing the threat it presented to their survival. Describing addiction as a class of evolutionary changes 'that are not adaptive and do not confer survival value,'[11] Bateson reminds us that nature is as indifferent to the human race as most humans are to it: 'Even professional biologists have not seen that, in the larger view, evolution is as value-free and as beautiful as the dance of Shiva, where all of beauty and ugliness, creation and destruction are expressed or compressed into one complex symmetrical pathway.'[12]

For Mumford, who viewed art and technics as representing two opposite sides of the human character, the solution lay in re-evaluating and restoring the symbolic life of humans over the technical life.[13] However, for Stiegler, the duality inherent in Mumford's analysis and proposed solution is itself the root cause of common misunderstandings about what it means to be human. In *Technics and Time, 1: The Fault of Epimetheus*,[14] the first of his trilogy, Stiegler traces the problem to the Aristotelian duality between organic life and what is artificial, or made by humans:

> To these two regions of beings correspond two dynamics: mechanics and biology. Lodged between them, technical beings are nothing but a hybrid, enjoying no more ontological status than they did in ancient philosophy. Since matter receives accidentally the mark of a vital activity, a series of objects that are manufactured over a period of time

does nothing but report an evolution: a technical being belongs essentially to mechanics, doing little more than conveying the vital behaviour of which it is but a thin trace.[15]

While Stiegler acknowledges Heidegger's contribution in opening up another and deeper way of looking at technology beyond the instrumental, he argues that Heidegger does not go far enough himself in pursuing the hinted line of alternative thought, and is not very clear about where it might lead.[16] For Stiegler, it is not sufficient to suggest that technics might comprise another, little-understood dimension of being – it is *the* dimension by which we define ourselves as distinctly human and which more than any other factor accounts for the manner and sheer *speed* of human evolution. Taking up Bertrand Gille's claim that modern societies are chiefly characterized by 'permanent innovation,'[17] Stiegler observes that it is no longer possible for anyone to control or even comprehend all the possible effects and implications of constantly introducing so many new technologies into society on the one hand, and removing the obsolescent technologies they replace on the other. Simply put: 'Technics evolves *more quickly* than culture.'[18] Moreover, technological change has more to do with the logic and momentum governing what Gille describes as 'technical systems' – complexes of related technological, social and material factors dominant at any one time, all of which create their own constraints and opportunities – rather than any simple addition of individual inventions.[19] The outcome, Stiegler writes, is 'a divorce, if not between culture and technics, at least between the rhythms of cultural evolution and the rhythms of technical evolution.'[20]

To comprehend how this situation could have come about, Stiegler argues that we have to rethink the scope and dynamics of technics itself. In so doing, he suggests that underlying the persistent duality in thinking about technology is a more fundamental distinction, due to the ancients, between pure thought (*episteme*) and technology (*tekhne*), 'whereby all technical knowledge is devalued.'[21] For Stiegler, beginning with the first tools and language, and especially writing, *any* extension of the biological individual into the wider world has a technical dimension. While distinguishing modern technics from that of earlier periods by the speed of its development, Stiegler therefore makes the case for understanding technics in *all* its manifestations as an exteriorization and enhancement of biological capacities – what he aptly describes as 'the evolution of the prosthesis.'[22] Adapting Carl von Clausewitz's description of war as politics 'by other means,'[23] Stiegler writes: 'As a "process of exteriorization," technics is the pursuit of life by means other than life.'[24] Along with that same process of technical emancipation comes the potential for technics to outrun its human originators and users and to create its own dynamic. Accordingly, between the hitherto separate realms of the organic and inorganic, Stiegler posits an intermediate form of life bridging the former two realms, or what he calls:

a third genre of 'being': 'inorganic organized beings,' or technical objects. These non-organic organizations of matter *have their own dynamic* [added emphasis] when compared with that of either physical or biological beings, a dynamic, moreover, that cannot be reduced to the 'aggregate' or 'product' of these beings.[25]

Technics and the human

Epiphylogenesis

Stiegler devotes most of his first volume to tracing the historical roots of this third genre and how it might have evolved, amounting to an ambitious search for an evolutionary theory of human technics: 'Technical evolution results from a coupling of the human and matter, a coupling that must be elucidated.'[26] Drawing on the work of the paleontologist André Leroi-Gourhan,[27] Stiegler finds parallels between the durability of biologists' and zoologists' early classification systems of different species, all of which were created while most species had not yet been identified, and what he describes as 'universal technical tendencies.'[28] As Leroi-Gourhan writes:

> Everything seems to happen as if an ideal prototype of fish or of knapped flint developed along preconceivable lines from the fish to the amphibian, to the reptile, to the mammal, or to the bird, from form-undifferentiated flint to the polished knapped tool, to the brass knife, to the steel sword. This should not lead us into error: these lines render only an aspect of life, *that of the inevitable and limited choice that the milieu proposes to living matter* [added emphasis].[29]

From the outset, therefore, like Gille, Stiegler downplays the role of individual creativity in the evolution of technics. In both Gille's and Leroi-Gourhan's perspectives, the possibilities for human invention and development are always constrained by current historical circumstances, both material and non-material, driving technical evolution in some directions rather than others. Thus, in earlier periods when communications were more restricted, the same or similar technical solutions or archetypes might spontaneously appear in widely separated cultures with no known contact between them, for which, Leroi-Gourhan suggests, there is no other adequate explanation. Conversely, similar archetypes found in neighboring lands enjoying frequent contact develop their own characteristic features unique to each location, suggesting forms of ethnic technical diversification equivalent to species diversification.[30]

However, the problem with Leroi-Gouhan's analogy of human technical development with biological or zoological approaches, Stiegler argues, is that it is just that, an analogy: 'the whole question being *up to what point* the analogy holds.'[31] While it has its biological and zoological aspects, the basic issue of human technicity, that is to say, the intrinsic coupling of the human and matter that Stiegler claims defines us, cannot be explained, he suggests, by reference to those aspects alone. Significantly, as Leroi-Gouhan points out, whereas interbreeding between different animal species is limited by genetic factors, ensuring the relative unity and stability of each species within its own milieu, 'all human races can be crossbred, all peoples are fusible, and all civilizations are unstable.'[32] Stiegler adds: 'The problem is then to know how these "cross-breedings" work.'[33] Agreeing with Leroi-Gouhan that there is no logical difference in such cases between invention and borrowing, in so far as either resolves or fulfills some kind of need for a given group or society, Stiegler writes: 'What is essential is that an invention, borrowed from the exterior or produced locally, becomes acceptable and necessary.'[34]

Diffusion from different sources among different peoples, then, is as much an integral part of technics as the universal tendencies described by Leroi-Gouhan. The origins of human technicity itself, however, lie much further back in time, when the first hominids to make and use tools appeared on the scene. Elaborating on Leroi-Gouhan's concept of 'exteriorization,' the 'invention of the human,' writes Stiegler,[35] involved the simultaneous development of both the cortex in the human brain and the use of tools:

> From the Zinjanthropian to the Neanderthal, cortex and tools are differentiated together, in one and the same movement. It is a question of a singular process of structural coupling in 'exteriorization,' an instrumental maieutics, a mirror 'proto-stage' in which *the differentiation of the cortex is determined by the tool as much as that of the tool by the cortex* [added emphasis], a mirror effect in which one, informing itself of the other, is both seen and deformed in the process, and is thus transformed. It is straightaway this couple that forms the original dynamic in a transductive relation.[36]

While *Homo sapiens* has been commonly distinguished in the past from other species as a tool maker, Stiegler goes much further, to suggest that the reciprocal development of brain and tools marks the beginning of what he calls *epiphylogenesis*, a higher level of evolution unique to humankind involving the *externalized accumulation of experience*. As distinct from epigenetic memory, which, while not involving genetic information, like genetic memory is restricted to the individual carriers in each generation,[37] epiphylogenetic memory conserves and passes on the sum of previous events to future generations as external traces of one kind or another, thus having a profound impact on the course of future developments:

> Epiphylogenesis, a recapitulating, dynamic, and morphogenetic (*phylogenetic*) accumulation of individual experience (*epi*), designates the appearance of a new relation between the organism and its environment, which is also a new state of matter. If the individual is organic organized matter, then its relation to its environment (to matter in general, organic and inorganic), when it is a question of a *who*, is mediated by the organized but inorganic matter of the organon, the tool with its instructive role (its role qua instrument), the *what*. It is in this sense that the *what* invents the *who* just as much as it is invented by it.[38]

On this basis, Stiegler asserts that, at least as far as how historical time is measured or understood, technics itself, 'far from being merely in time, properly constitutes time.'[39] For without those external traces of its experience humanity has left on this earth, we would simply not be able to comprehend our passage through it, or to anticipate the possible consequences of our actions: 'A tool is, before anything else, memory: if this were not the case, it could never function as a reference of significance.'[40]

For Stiegler, as for French philosophers of earlier generations, notably Jacques Derrida and Maurice Blanchot, writing, as one of the earliest and most direct forms of externalizing and recording human experience, therefore occupies a special place in the history of technics, or what might be better described from his own perspective as 'the technics of history.' Quoting from Blanchot, who, like himself, betrays not a little self-regard in this respect, Stiegler claims:

> What is true of the person who writes is true of humanity in general *qua* an organism that invents and produces. *This* question of writing is nothing but a radicalization of that of the memory of the human. It is the reason why [Blanchot writes] 'if we see work as the force of history, the force that transforms man while it transforms the world, *then a writer's activity must be the highest form of work.*'[41]

Debates and discrepancies

Expanding on Stiegler's debt to Derrida's work in privileging writing as a fundamental technics – a debt the philosopher freely acknowledges[42] – Michael Gallope,[43] one of the growing school of Stiegler's followers, traces the argument through to the evolutionary process itself. According to Derrida, writing *as* technics was preceded by biology's own method of inscribing itself in time. As Gallope explains, the issue revolves around Derrida's interpretation of life as *differance*,[44] a concept that recurs repeatedly in Stiegler's work:

> Life *defers in time* and *differentiates itself spatially* from the entropy around it with the beginning of genetic memory – the first form of writing. Amidst the disorder of the universe, genes are the first thing that remains, that stays fixed for some time. Derrida calls this the first form of writing, the beginning of the *gramme*, constituting a coup of the universe's own temporality by holding genetic code, or the first information, constant through time. *Life, which is usually considered to be absolute dynamism, is in fact, the beginning of writing, of permanence* [added emphasis].[45]

In addition to genetic memory, the evolution of epigenetic memory as embodied in the central nervous system created the possibility, while also being physically identified with its owners, of recognizing or 'reading' the traces of past events during a creature's life-span and thus the possibility of anticipating and responding to similar events should they recur. According to Derrida's liberal conception of 'writing,' therefore, while epiphylogenetic or external memory may be unique to humanity, as Stiegler suggests it is, the conditions for its emergence *as a means of marking time* were already well established by the two more primitive forms of memory.

Over and above such issues, Gallope's personal interest in Stiegler's work lies in understanding music as a particular variety of technics with its own characteristic means of transmission, an investigation that has its own broader cultural implications:

> For technics, music is merely technical sound, a sonic exteriorization of creatures. It emerges when sound is anticipated and repeated, and in turn when instruments concretize this anticipation, and future generations inherit the instrument and technique as a tradition.[46]

Gallope's aim is to go beyond generalized conceptions of musical technics of this kind and to explore its relations to other cultural aspects, such as 'social use, aesthetic construction, religion,'[47] and so forth. While an investigation into musical technics itself lies outside the scope of this book, it is worth noting for what Gallope sees in its potential for explaining an important dimension of human culture not normally associated with technological development, except in the manner of its recording: 'Perhaps music and consciousness are subject to continual revision and evolution, in the way that technology is seen to be continuously evolving.'[48]

Others have focused on different aspects of Stiegler's thought according to their own interests. For Nathan Van Camp, writing in a collection of essays on Stiegler's work and technics,[49] it is the ambiguity in Stiegler's conception of human technicity exemplified in the above quoted passage, 'the *what* invents the *who* just as much as it is invented by it,' that drives the discussion. Drawing on the work of the Italian philosopher Giorgio Agamben, Van Camp finds metaphorical parallels in Agamben's explanation of *homo sacer*,[50] a term originating in Roman law designating a person who may not have committed homicide but who could, in given circumstances, still be condemned to death. Yet ritual practices normally reserved for executions, whether sanctioned by law or by religious custom, do not apply in the case of *homo sacer*, making it difficult to work out: 'The reason why the conceptual structure of this figure is so hard to understand for both ancient and modern scholars is that it can be situated neither inside or outside of profane and divine law and, thus, *seems to be pending between these two realms* [added emphasis].'[51]

The case interests Agamben himself for what it suggests of the problems in getting to grips with the uncertain evolutionary passage from the animal to the human. Historically, he argues, the debate has been dominated by what he describes as the 'anthropological machine,' by which the human is always distinguished in *opposition* to the animal, with insidious social and political effects, leading, for example, to the denigration of some groups as *less* than human, thereby legitimizing their treatment as 'animals.'[52] As Van Camp explains, Agamben challenges the simplistic anthropological stance, but fails to offer a convincing alternative account of the same evolutionary passage, leaving the field open to the usual explanations of an exceptional or transcendental nature – essentially little different from arguing that humans simply won the lottery.

While Stiegler's theory of human technicity also sets *Homo sapiens* apart from other animals in so far as he explicitly claims technics as the exclusive province of humans, Van Camp argues that his account of the reciprocal relations between the human and matter opens up a more subtle interpretation of what makes us unique. Retracing his theory of the exteriorization of human memory through tools to Leroi-Gourhan's work, Van Camp detects a significant qualification in the importance Stiegler assigns to cortical development in his theory. In Stiegler's view, the upright posture of early hominoids played an equally vital part in the evolution of human technicity by liberating the upper limbs for other uses, along with other important physiological changes:

The 'freeing' of the hand during locomotion is also that of the face from its grasping functions. The hand will necessarily call for tools, movable organs; the tools of the hand

Technics and the human

will necessarily call for the language of the face. The brain obviously plays a role, *but it is no longer directive: it is but a partial element of a total apparatus* [added emphasis], even if the evolution of the apparatus tends towards the development of the cerebral cortex.[53]

While Leroi-Gourhan comes close to identifying the specifically human with technicity, unlike Stiegler, who steadfastly maintains the ambiguity between cortical and technical development, he ultimately gives the main credit for technical evolution to the cortex. The implication, as Van Camp explains, is that 'the genuine origin of the human is the acquisition of a faculty for symbolization.'[54] Stiegler, however, begs to differ:

> There is no such [second] origin because technical differentiation presupposes full-fledged anticipation, at once operative and dynamic, from the Australanthropian onwards, and such anticipation can only be a relation to death, which means that symbolic intellectuality must equally be already there. Reflective intellectuality is not added to technical intelligence. It was already its ground.[55]

There remains the contrary evidence – predating Stiegler's works by many years but apparently ignored by him – that, gifted as they are at it, humans are not the *only* creatures on the planet to make and use tools.[56] Since Jane Goodall's first momentous observation in 1960 of a chimpanzee in the wild purposefully stripping off the leaves of a twig and using it to poke into a termite's nest, 'fishing' for food,[57] the number of similar observations of various species at work with tools of one kind or another has grown, changing perceptions of what other creatures are capable of.[58] Responding by letter to Goodall's own discovery, her then employer, the renowned Kenyan paleontologist Louis Leakey, wrote: 'We must now redefine man, redefine tool, or accept chimpanzees as human.'[59]

Other writers, including Van Camp, have seized on the discrepancy in Stiegler's thought, suggesting it points to a 'residual form of anthropocentrism.'[60] Despite such reservations, Van Camp concludes that, for all Stiegler's unsupportable claims for humankind as the sole tool maker and user, the alternative position of ignoring any differences between humans and other species altogether is, if anything, equally untenable. At the very least, Stiegler's equation of anthropogenesis with techno-genesis refutes any notions that the human is some kind of miraculous quality grafted onto the animal. Nevertheless, as Van Camp writes: 'Whether this will silence the anthropological machine once and for all or rather generate new border skirmishes will however remain open to question.'[61]

Writing metaphors

In the same collection of essays as Van Camp's, Andrés Vaccari[62] likewise suggests that, rather than challenging oppositional distinctions between the organic and non-organic, or the genetic and non-genetic and nature and culture in general, in many ways Stiegler actually consolidates those distinctions. While Vaccari, like the former writers, acknowledges Stiegler's influence on current thinking on technics, his essay stands out for offering a wide-ranging critique of Stiegler's thought, clearly intended to prepare the way for an alternative approach, which he tentatively outlines in a second paper.[63] Overriding any specific issues, Vaccari also displays a more general impatience with what he describes in the title of his paper as 'the hegemony of technics,' which, he implies, has the effect of suppressing or diverting attention away from other aspects of the human condition. Worse, in Vaccari's view, 'Stiegler's framework also comes to underpin a historical narrative of epochal ruptures leading to a final crisis in which technology comes to play an apocalyptic role, threatening "us" with cultural dissolution, biotechnological takeover, and phenomenological collapse.'[64]

However, while many of Vaccari's criticisms are valid, some do not quite match Stiegler's stated position. For example, early in his essay, Vaccari questions Stiegler's wisdom in following Leroi-Gourhan's lead in placing so much emphasis on the early use of flint tools as the beginnings of external or non-organic memory and, with it, the coevolution of the human mind and matter: 'Can this flint–cortex dynamic be a viable way to approach the genesis of the human and technology?'[65] Continuing the same line of questioning, Vaccari points to other possible early developments in human evolution with potentially equally significant effects on human technicity:

> Although stone tools are the most predominant type of evidence in the archaeological record, they were not the first technical invention. Stonecutting most likely developed alongside a range of other innovations in food preparation, shelter, storage, transportation, and tracking and hunting. Early tools were probably made of bone and wood; if animal technics are any guide, the first tools were found objects, instances of 'natural' technics. The human body itself could be considered the first mirror or surface of inscription, as technical developments required new techniques, and practices of incorporation, transmission, and enculturation.[66]

Vaccari has similar issues with the liberal writing metaphors Stiegler borrows from Derrida, according to which the essence of all technics is inscription and its various forms: 'One of the targets of this paper is this tendency to shrink the history of technology into a logical trajectory that thinks technics in terms of writing and related metaphors.'[67] This leads in turn, Vaccari argues, to Stiegler's skewed focus on the mass media and related technologies like photography and cinema in the later volumes, which lend themselves to similar interpretations: 'Thus the Stieglerian framework has some difficulty addressing aspects relating to the body, matter, and the material configurations of technologies; and how these are articulated outside and beyond inscription.'[68] The stress on inscription, Vaccari further argues, also comes at the cost of neglecting questions of *transmission*, which in turn are tied up with fundamental issues of *sociality* and all that that implies in building and maintaining technical traditions.

Vaccari's second target is the *programmatic character* of human technicity in Stiegler's approach, with its deterministic undertones, most clearly expressed in the earlier quotation from Leroi-Gourhan regarding the development of 'ideal' prototypes of fish and knapped flint. As Stiegler explains, while both fish and flint appear to follow similar trajectories, the appearance of external memory in the form of tools and other human traces creates a new kind of program: 'namely, exteriorized programs no longer inscribed in the organism itself.'[69]

The problem here, Vaccari argues, is with the idea of the program itself, which is inspired by informatic models and is applied indiscriminately across all three stages in the evolution of memory, from the genetic to the epigenetic and finally to the epiphylogenetic:

> The model of the extragenetic program is the genetic program. Stiegler places these three forms of memory along a conceptual continuum that projects onto the genetic level a model of 'program' and 'memory' that erodes the purity of life at the foundation of epiphylogenesis.[70]

As Vaccari points out, current research within molecular biology on related programmatic models, while still hotly debated, suggests 'a much more complex picture than the one [Stiegler] takes for granted.'[71] Moreover, 'Stiegler assumes genetic programs are determinate in their structure and operations, whereas cultural programs are open to indeterminacy.'[72] Similarly, Vaccari notes that the latter are only vaguely defined by Stiegler, who, as he quotes below, broadens the idea to include almost any cultural activity:

> The very idea of the 'program' must be expanded, in fact, to include many differing kinds of activities: academic and scholarly programs, political programs, programs for work, all must be applied to everything that formalizes rhythms, repetitions, habits, and customs, including the most complex.[73]

A consequence of this kind of thinking, according to Ben Roberts,[74] another critic of Stiegler quoted by Vaccari, is that 'the opposition between epigenesis and epiphylogenesis only reproduces in a different form the more traditional opposition between nature and culture.'[75] Calling again for a broader approach, Vaccari writes, 'The question of the "program" must give way to the much more pressing issue of transmission, reproduction, exhumation, repetition, reactivation, and restitution into the present-future.'[76]

Sociality and location

It is not entirely clear how many of the above contradictions and confusions are due to Stiegler or to Vaccari himself, who on occasion overstates his case. For example, while Vaccari's criticism concerning the bias of Stiegler's technics toward a limited range of technologies is a valid one, as Van Camp points out Stiegler was well aware of the part played by the changing physiology of the human body in the evolution of human technicity and expresses his own reservations about the dominant role of the cortex in that process. Neither does it help much to clarify the meaning of technics when Vaccari throws in ill thought out ideas like 'natural' technics to describe the use of found objects like unshaped stones as tools, either for cracking open nuts or for any other purpose by animal or human. What clearly counts in such cases is not so much that the stone was used in its natural state, but that a *particular* stone – not all stones would fit the required task[77] – was *recognized* as potentially useful for such purposes, implying the capacity both for anticipation and for purposeful behavior.

Regarding the issue of inscription and related metaphors, while Stiegler, like Derrida, may be guilty of stretching the idea beyond its useful limits – a common weakness of analogical thinking but which does not negate its value[78] – there can be no questioning the significance of writing itself in human evolution or its elevated status in human technics generally, albeit relatively late in coming compared with tools and other basic forms of technicity, or even spoken language.[79] In her perceptive account of the role of writing and its flipside, reading, in the evolution of the human mind, Maryanne Wolf[80] leaves little room for doubting its importance: 'Reading is one of the most remarkable inventions in history: the ability to record history is one of its consequences.'[81] Inspired by Marcel Proust's insights into the author's craft, she also stresses the vital function of reading in developing the capacity to empathize with other people and other worlds, both real and imaginary, beyond direct experience, which may in turn have an impact on the reader's own life:

> Proust saw reading as a kind of intellectual 'sanctuary,' where humans have access to thousands of different realities they might never encounter or understand otherwise. Each of these new realities is capable of transforming readers' intellectual lives without ever requiring them to leave the comfort of their armchairs.[82]

Viewed in this light, contrary to Vaccari's assertion that Stiegler's stress on writing metaphors comes at the cost of neglecting issues of sociality, Wolf makes it clear that the act of reading, and therefore of writing, at least as far as novels and other literary forms go,[83] is *intrinsically* social, involving role playing and the development of related skills as well as communication: 'While reading, we can leave our own consciousness, and pass over into the consciousness of another person, another age, another culture.'[84]

As for the status and implications of the program concept in Stiegler's thought, on the one hand Vaccari argues that the imposition of the programmatic or informational model across all three stages of memory diminishes any differences between each stage, and on the other that the shift from genetic to cultural programs revives traditional oppositional thinking between the organic and non-organic. It may also be noted that while Vaccari accuses Stiegler of stressing inscription at the cost of transmission and related factors of socialization, Stiegler actually includes some of the supposedly 'missing' social concepts and issues, such as 'repetition, habits and customs,' in his own broad definition of cultural programs, as quoted by Vaccari himself above.

Nevertheless, regarding the more specific mechanics of transmission, Vaccari makes a good point. Aside from the brief description of cultural programs, Stiegler makes no serious attempt to investigate the issue any further, leaving open the whole question of how the coevolution of humanity and technology actually works or why some forms of technics prosper while others do not. In the same way, while Stiegler has no qualms in asserting the unique position and character of *Homo sapiens* among other species, he notably fails to perceive that such claims might have serious implications for evolutionary theory generally, the established principles of which he appears to take for granted.

Less convincingly, in tying the idea of program to that of inscription, Vaccari questions the significance of *location* in technics:

> If we take inscription as the program's material substratum, or at least its material dimension, we should first ask about its location. *But cultural knowledges cannot be located in any specific place or reduced to any material organization* [added emphasis].[85]

Given that Vaccari includes 'shelter' in his list of basic technologies ignored by Stiegler, which, unless one is talking of caravans and other mobile homes, is historically both culture and place related, this is an odd statement to make, to put it mildly. While, as Vaccari suggests, other factors of a cultural nature may undoubtedly be involved, the issue of location, which was a key subject of debate in the first part of this book, cannot be so easily dismissed. Aside from the primary example of human shelter, a strong case might also be readily made for treating agriculture – which for obvious reasons evolved within quite specific geographical and climatic contexts – along with language as among the most basic of all transformative technics.[86] The change from *Homo sapiens* as hunter-gatherers to settled farmers between 8,000 and 10,000 years ago (estimates vary) had multiple enduring and catalytic effects, with both positive and negative outcomes for the evolution of humankind, as well as for that of many other animal and organic species.[87] Not the least of those effects was the later emergence of cities – the most complex of all who–what complexes – for which, as Mumford relates in his own epic study of urban civilization,[88] we owe the advanced development of architecture as well as literate society, together with most of the technologies that have shaped our world, for better or worse.

More generally speaking, though Vaccari may find Stiegler's stress on the apocalyptic aspects of modern technics to be exaggerated, given the mounting evidence of destructive climate change, the causes of which originate in the uncontrolled acceleration of human technicity that he writes of, Stiegler is both empirically and morally correct to sound the alarm. It is in truth hard to exaggerate the dire consequences for humanity of continuing down this path.[89] What is more, as Jared Diamond reminds us in his sobering study of the failure of previous civilizations,[90] humans have journeyed down the same dead end many times before, though never on the same planetary scale of self-destruction. While, as Stiegler argues, there are many other negative aspects to runaway technics, including severe psychological and cultural disorientation – the subjects of his second and third volumes – they are overshadowed by the growing environmental crisis. It is therefore all the more important to understand what it is about human technicity that could have brought us to this impasse.

The extended self

5 Rethinking evolution

Most readers of a work of this kind will have at least a rudimentary knowledge of Charles Darwin's theory of natural selection, sufficient up till this point to appreciate why architectural theorists and others should take such a strong interest in the kind of issues discussed in this book.

However, if, as Edward Hall suggested and Bernard Stiegler has since argued at great length, technology has played a major role in the evolution of *Homo sapiens*, distinguishing it from all other species, the question arises as to whether our species is subject to the same evolutionary laws and principles as every other form of life, and if not, then what laws and principles? While differences between schools of evolutionary thought are nothing new, these have gathered pace in recent years, challenging the basic tenets of orthodox Darwinism, including natural selection, whether applied to humans or the evolution of life in general. For all these and other good reasons that will become apparent as these new approaches unfold, evolutionary theory requires a fresh examination if we are to understand just how the coevolution of humans and technology has shaped the extended self in the past, and the impacts it now has on the self in the uncertain present.

The chapter opens with a brief explanation of Darwin's original theory and subsequent key developments that laid the foundations for neo-Darwinism and the related theories that followed. It then proceeds to outline several alternative approaches that help to fill in some of the gaps in Stiegler's account of the evolution of technics itself. These range from new biological perspectives on the different factors influencing hereditary characteristics, to more general theories of evolution applicable to both organic and social systems.

Nature's algorithm

The theory of evolution Darwin set out in *On the Origin of Species*[1] is now so much a part of contemporary culture and mythology that the elegance and power of its central principles can be easily overlooked. At the core of Darwin's theory lies the idea of natural selection, which came to him from studying the selective breeding techniques of farmers – in essence a form of *artificial* selection. Now common knowledge but little understood in Darwin's time except by those who practiced it, the process involves the repeated breeding of the most promising animals and their offspring, until the desired characteristics of the breed have been achieved. As Darwin explains:

> The key is man's power of accumulative selection: nature gives successive variations; man adds them up in certain directions useful to him. In this sense he may be said to make for himself useful breeds.[2]

What if, Darwin speculated, in the absence of any human or other external agents, a similar process of selection in nature was working in favor of some organisms and against others? In such a case, what would be the criteria for selection? Drawing upon T. R. Malthus's[3] theory of growing populations competing for limited resources, Darwin deduced that, given limited resources in the natural world, a similar competitive struggle for existence between organisms must be at work in nature, sifting out the weaker specimens and selecting those better equipped to survive. The winning characteristics of those organisms would then be inherited by the next generation to undergo yet another round of selection, and so on, resulting in ever more elaborate and stronger features along the way, each better suited or adapted to its own environment than previous generations:

> This is the doctrine of Malthus, applied to the whole animal and vegetable kingdoms. As many more individuals of each species are born than can possibly survive; and as, consequently, there is a frequently recurring struggle for existence, it follows that any being, if it vary however slightly in any manner profitable to itself, under the complex and varying conditions of life, will have a better chance of surviving, and thus be *naturally selected*.[4]

The second major plank in Darwin's theory addressed the *source* of the variations that natural selection acts upon. In his history of evolutionary theory, David Young[5] recounts how Darwin's view on the subject changed following his extensive studies of variations in such relatively simple creatures as barnacles:

> As long as each species was regarded as a fixed and permanent entity, little attention was paid to variability. Individuals of a species were thought to be a little like toy soldiers produced from a mould, which are identical except for occasional variations due to minor disturbances in the casting process. So it was widely believed that variation was in some way accidental or unnatural, in that it was due to disturbances outside the reproductive system. Hence variability was thought to be comparatively rare and unimportant, and not to affect the essential character of a species.
>
> In his [early work] Darwin had largely adhered to this view, and supposed that variation was triggered from time to time by disturbances such as geological change. However, his long study of barnacles showed him that *variability is a normal feature of animal species* [added emphasis]. This first-hand study taught him, as no amount of reading or reasoning could have done, that plenty of variation occurs in natural populations. Moreover, the variation was found in all parts of the body, and was not limited to trifling structures of little importance to classification.[6]

The extended self

Abstracting the essence of Darwin's theory, Daniel Dennett,[7] a philosopher and passionate defender and propagator of neo-Darwinism, boils it all down to a set of simple rules, the nature of which will be familiar to any computer programmer: first, generate a number of solutions to a given (environmental) problem; subject them all to the same test (of fitness); see which one performs best (survives); pick that one, then generate a number of variations from the winner and subject all those to a new test (of fitness); pick the winner again; and so on, *ad infinitum*. In sum, Dennett writes:

> The theoretical power of Darwin's abstract scheme was due to several features that Darwin firmly identified, and appreciated, and appreciated better than many of his supporters, but lacked the terminology to describe explicitly. Today we would capture these features under a single term. Darwin had discovered the power of an *algorithm*.[8]

A narrative science

Darwin was not the first to challenge the then prevailing belief that all the species of the earth are fixed in time as the product of some supernatural design, the idea having already been advanced by earlier naturalists in their work on classification systems, whose contributions are related in Chapters 7 and 8. Nor was he the only naturalist to conceive of the process of natural selection, that insight being shared by his contemporary and fellow naturalist Alfred Wallace.[9] But Darwin was the first to argue the case convincingly and to present sufficient empirical evidence of both variation and selection to persuade the scientific community of his time of the verity of the theory.

Further, Young writes that, in claiming that a species has a different past life as well as a possibly different future, Darwin also set biology clearly apart from chemistry and physics as a special kind of science, with aims and methods of its own: 'What makes the difference is that the complex structures studied in biology *are the products of history* [added emphasis].'[10] Without doubt, a major reason for the appeal of Darwin's theory to non-biologists is precisely in the time-related perspective it provides, making it a narrative science that scholars and researchers in the humanities, including the architectural theorists discussed in this book, can readily identify with and draw inspiration from in their attempts to explain how the subjects of their own studies got to be the way they are now. However, aware as he was of the potential storm of controversy his theory might instigate within a culture then dominated by religious beliefs and anthropocentrism, Darwin himself initially avoided any applications of his theory to human evolution, restricting himself to just one short sentence in his concluding chapter: 'Light will be thrown on the origin of man and his history.'[11] That was all it took. Just as Darwin feared, the popular press of the period quickly dubbed natural selection 'ape theory,' sparking a fierce debate on humankind's place in the world that continues in our own time.

However, for all the fertility of Darwin's theory, it was only much later, in the early twentieth century, that the actual biological mechanisms required for the reliable transmission of inherited characteristics were hypothetically located in 'genes' by Wilhelm Ludwig Johannsen,[12] a Danish botanist. Appropriately, Johannsen named his concept after the Greek for 'to give birth to.' Johannsen also distinguished between the 'genotype,' which is the total make-up of genes in each organism, and the 'phenotype,' or sum total of the various hereditary characteristics of the organism, the effects of which are the *product* of the information carried by the genes, both terms being now part of biologists' standard lexicon.[13] And it took yet another half century before the ground-breaking discoveries by Francis Crick, James Watson and others finally identified the precise molecular structure responsible for the transmission of genetic information in the spiraling chains of deoxyribonucleic acid, known as DNA, thus completing Darwin's theory.[14] Likewise, mutations – those spontaneous variations generated within species that natural selection seizes upon – are now better understood, Young writes, as 'copying errors that occur from time to time when the DNA is replicating within a cell.'[15]

The fourth dimension

One of the earliest and best-known figures to offer an alternative theory of evolution was Jean-Baptiste de la Marck, better known as Lamarck, who originally coined the word 'biology' as the science of life.[16] Lamarck had argued that favorable biological traits could be acquired *during the lifetime* of an organism and passed on to the next generation, thus breaching the basic law of natural selection, which lays down that favorable variations evolve only by a process of elimination of the weaker species. In other words, unless a species is *already* possessed of such traits, as a result of either previous selection or random mutations, those traits will not be carried forth.

Rejected as heresy by neo-Darwinists, Lamarck's theory is being taken increasingly seriously by critics of orthodox evolutionary theory, if mostly at other levels of human evolution. For example, in their comprehensive review of current research, Eva Jablonka and Marion Lamb[17] examine the claims of biologists for the priority of genes in the transmission of inherited characteristics, against contesting claims for each of the three other main kinds of variation – *epigenetic* (the transmission of information from cell to cell by non-genetic means of inheritance); *behavioral* (the transmission of learned behavior) and *symbolic* (linguistic and cultural change) – each of which provides grist for the evolutionary mill. Arguing that there has been altogether too much focus in evolutionary theory on genetic variation at the cost of the other forms, they conclude that, whatever the final balance of accounts between the different modes of transmission might be, 'It is therefore quite wrong to think about heredity and evolution solely in terms of the genetic system.'[18]

Among the many insights Jablonka and Lamb offer into the complex workings of evolution, they stress the importance of the interactions *between* the four different levels, as well as the methods of transmitting inherited characteristics specific to each dimension. The two authors also provide evidence that epigenetic variations can and do lead to genetic assimilation in a Lamarckian-like process by 'unveiling' hitherto hidden genetic variations *already* in the population, which then become available for selection through their own effects. In the other direction, they argue for the ability of some animals as well as humans to construct cultures, pointing to the 'growing evidence that animals have traditions,'[19] suggesting that the genetic roots of such ability go back further in evolutionary time than is commonly supposed.

However, it is the authors' observations on the fourth dimension – at the symbolic level of human evolution – that are most relevant to the discussion at this juncture. Quoting from the German philosopher Ernst Cassirer,[20] they stress the uniqueness of human culture as a way of organizing, transferring and acquiring information through the use of symbols. The 'symbolic animal,' as Cassirer describes humans, is like no other:

> this world [the human world] forms no exception to those biological rules which govern the life of all the other organisms. Yet in the human world we find a new characteristic which appears to be a distinctive mark of human life. The functional circle of man is not only quantitatively enlarged; it has also undergone a qualitative change. Man has, as it were, discovered a new method of adapting himself to his environment. Between the receptor system and the effector system, which are to be found in all animal species, we find in man a third link which we may describe as the *symbolic system*. This new acquisition transforms the whole of human life. As compared with the other animals man lives not merely in a broader reality; he lives, so to speak, in a new *dimension* of reality.[21]

Similarly, what differentiates the human use of symbols like words or pictures from the use of signs or signals in communication between animals, Jablonka and Lamb explain, is that from a very early age humans are able to *generalize* from the use of a word or image in one situation to its use in another situation, and to link it to related symbols. In so doing, they come to see each word or image as part of a larger and comprehensible organization of symbols: 'where there are symbols there is, by definition, a *symbolic system*.'[22]

Fatal flaw

In their audacious work *What Darwin Got Wrong*, Jerry Fodor and Massimo Piattelli-Palmarini[23] go even further than the previous co-authors and refute the fundamental principle of natural selection itself, upon which Darwin's original theory of evolution and most subsequent developments rest. While they accept the basic idea of the genealogy of species and their common origins and subsequent differentiation, for the two authors the concept of natural selection itself 'is fatally flawed.'[24] At the heart of the problem lies the question of how phenotypic traits are stabilized. Though they suggest that the precise degree of correspondence between a species' phenotype and its natural environment might be exaggerated sometimes, the authors do not doubt that such relations do indeed exist, as verified by countless empirical studies, including Darwin's own – that, they say, is the part that Darwin got *right*. However, they cannot agree that natural selection offers a convincing explanation of those relations. Gracefully conceding that neither they nor anyone else they can think of knows just how evolution really works, the authors, one of whom is a biologist and the other a philosopher, and who have joint interests in cognitive science as well as evolutionary theory, question the assumptive logic of adaptation to the environment underlying Darwin's theory:

> there is at the heart of adaptationist theories of evolution, a confusion between (1) the claim that evolution is a process in which *creatures with adaptive traits are selected* and (2) the claim that evolution is a process *in which creatures are selected for their adaptive traits*.[25]

Darwinism, so the authors argue, incorrectly infers the second proposition from the first – an example of what philosophers of logic call the 'intensional fallacy,' whereby the *content* of one idea automatically (and usually unconsciously) invokes another.[26] Behind the same error of logic in turn, they hold, lies another common problem, namely the incorrect, exaggerated or otherwise mistaken use of analogical thinking,[27] in this case Darwin's analogy with the breeding of animals and plants as a demonstration of how selection might produce similar results in nature. While Darwin substitutes Malthus's theory of the survival of the fittest for the breeders' process of artificial selection, the authors contend that the basic idea of 'selection *for*' some preferred end result (i.e., 'fitness') underpins *both* natural and artificial selection. They further argue that while the logic works perfectly well for artificial selection – because breeders have minds and can therefore distinguish between desirable and undesirable characteristics, which may often be bundled together as 'coextensive traits' – there is no parallel mechanism in nature for distinguishing between or separating out traits for fitness from what they call 'free-riders,' that is, traits that have no special relevance to any criteria of fitness:

> when phenotypic traits are (locally or otherwise) coextensive, selection theory cannot distinguish the trait upon which fitness is contingent from the trait that has no effect on fitness (and is merely a free-rider). Advertising to the contrary notwithstanding, natural selection can't be a general mechanism that connects phenotypic variation with variation in fitness. *So natural selection can't be the mechanism of evolution* [added emphasis].[28]

While the authors offer a number of instances of phenotypic free-riders in nature, they place by far the greater weight of their argument on a single analogical case study in architecture taken from an essay by Jay Gould, a renowned biologist and critic of neo-Darwinism and adaptationism, and Richard Lewontin,[29] another leading biologist and critic of the same school. While, architecturally speaking, the matter involves a simple misunderstanding of engineering principles by non-architects, the impact of the essay on subsequent debates on evolutionary theory is such that it merits closer examination.

Titled 'The Spandrels of San Marco and the Panglossian Paradigm: A Critique of the Adaptationist Programme,' Gould and Lewontin point to the use of spandrels under the dome of St Mark's Cathedral in Venice as indisputable evidence of an architectural 'necessity,' which was only later 'adapted' for use as a decorative surface.

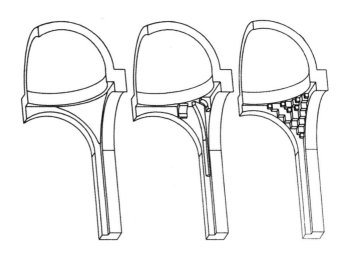

5.1 *Speculative drawings by Daniel Dennett of alternative ways of filling upper corners in square rooms roofed by domes*

According to the authors of the essay, it would be obviously mistaken to imagine that the adaptation of the surface led to or preceded the architectural purpose: 'Yet evolutionary biologists, in their tendency to focus exclusively on immediate adaptation to local conditions, do tend to ignore architectural constraints and perform just such an inversion of explanation.'[30]

As Dennett – from whose writings on Darwin the above quote from the paper is taken – scathingly points out, Gould and Lewontin's critique is based solely on the premise that neo-Darwinists would in reality invert the sequence of development as they suggest they would do, or otherwise ignore the role of significant constraints in the selection process, for which, Dennett argues, there is no supporting evidence in the literature. Gould's real problem with neo-Darwinism, Dennett suggests, is that he is basically uncomfortable with the algorithmic model of evolution, that is, the iterative process of replication, variation and selection as he characterizes it, or the idea that even relatively modest innovations like the spandrel might be explained by the same process. As we shall see, there are genuine concerns about the validity of this picture. However, Gould and Lewontin's notion of what an architectural 'necessity' might mean is itself based on questionable grounds. As the authors interpret it, the smooth triangular surface we call a spandrel is a necessary outcome – meaning the only conceivable result – of the architectural combination of a dome mounted on rounded arches arranged in a square plan. Not so, counters Dennett, and he invites us to imagine some alternative variations where the smooth area of the triangle is replaced by stacks of masonry projections (fig. 5.1). They may not look as good as the smooth version, Dennett suggests, but they do the same job just as efficiently.[31]

More importantly, Gould and Lewontin's whole case, as is that of Fodor's and Piattelli-Palmarini's borrowed example, is based on a misunderstanding of the nature and purpose of spandrels, in all their forms. As far as Gould and Lewontin

Rethinking evolution

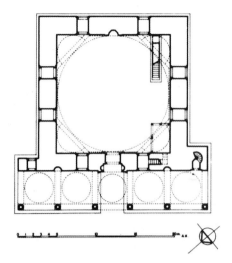
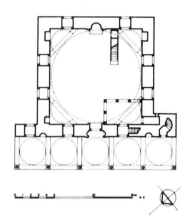

5.2 *Plans of the Coban Mustafa Pasa Mosque, Gebze (left), and the Haseki Sultan Mosque, Istanbul (right), by Sinan, 1538*

are concerned, the sole purpose of the spandrel is to close the two spatial geometries formed by the dome above and the four arches below. From their viewpoint, therefore, the architectural necessity is *one of form only*, and is directly associated with the problem of resolving the two geometries. Likewise, while Dennett correctly points out that smooth spandrels are not the only possible solution to bridging both geometries, he too subscribes to a form-based rationale.

Pushing the same argument to what they clearly but mistakenly regard as its logical conclusion, Fodor and Piattelli-Palmarini repeatedly describe the spandrel as an example of a coextensive feature or free-rider having no special function or purpose of its own, for which various adaptationist explanations – they provide useful surfaces for decoration and so forth – are offered in retrospect:

> Gould and Lewontin's point is that, as a matter of fact, all such adaptationist theories of spandrels are false; they are 'just so' stories, elaborated post hoc, to license teleological explanations of what are, in reality, functionless facts. *Spandrels don't actually do anything, they are merely 'free-riders'* [added emphasis]: geometry guarantees that if [architects] choose arches, you get spandrels willy–nilly as a by-product. It's the arches that architects select for. The spandrels just come along for the ride.[32]

However, as any competent engineer would explain, just the opposite is true: domes *cannot* be placed on top of arches or square walls of any sort without the additional support of spandrels or something like them to *help spread the load of the dome onto the substructure*. Imagine a dome placed over four arches or square walls without any intermediate support. In this case the bottom rim of the dome would meet the tops of the arches or walls only at four narrow points, corresponding with each arch or wall. Unless the dome is supported around its rim by a massive circular beam or is otherwise reinforced, it will collapse. Today, with modern steel and other lightweight materials of construction, such an option is quite feasible. However, the masonry techniques available for the building of the Venice dome and countless earlier and later examples of the same typological series require spandrels or equivalent solutions as a matter of *structural* necessity. For example, the earliest mosques with masonry domes placed over square rooms built by the great Turkish architect Sinan, who was as much of an engineer as the master of Ottoman architecture in the sixteenth century, made use of a combination of semicircular squinches and diagonal masonry arches in the corners to support the dome, a solution which cannot be explained by anything other than structural logic (fig. 5.2).[33]

Toward a natural history

To their credit, Fodor and Piattelli-Palmarini point to a still little understood aspect of phenotypic traits: why some traits are correlated with others, and if so, whether those same traits are all *necessarily* correlated, or include some free-riders, as they suggest they often do. The issue is especially pertinent to extended phenotypes, where there may be no actual direct physical or biological relation between characteristic traits, and where correlations between different traits, whether necessary or otherwise, may be difficult to pin down. Ignoring their own warnings about the uses and misuses of analogical thinking, the authors speculate on a possible alternative to either natural or artificial selection as an explanation for the acquisition and persistence of traits, invoking the analogy of a virus:

> Here's a metaphor that we prefer to Darwin's [analogy with artificial selection]: organisms 'catch' their phenotypes from their ecologies in something like the way that they catch their colds from their ecologies. The aetiological process in virtue of which phenotypes are responsive to ecologies *is more like contagion than selection* [added emphasis]. There are at least two respects in which this is so: one is that what diseases a creature catches depends not just on what kind of world it inhabits but also, and probably ineliminably, on features in its endogenous structure: features which it may have innately, or may have acquired in consequence of its prior interactions with its ecology.[34]

In summarizing their conclusions Fodor and Piattelli-Palmarini venture to suggest a still more radical revision of evolutionary theory, breaking altogether with neo-Darwinist orthodoxy. Reflecting Jablonka and Lamb's observations on the limitations of biologists' perspectives, they suggest that 'natural selection badly underestimates the significance of endogenous factors in the determination of phenotypes.'[35] The problem with Darwin's theory, they argue, is that it attempts to explain the evolution of species at the one level of adaptation to the environment only, whereas in reality it is a lot more complicated than that. Given the uncertain and incredibly varied nature of species differentiation, it may be more accurate, they suggest, to think of evolution and phenotypic traits in terms of 'natural history' rather than natural selection. As was noted above in Young's appraisal of Darwin's approach, one of the original attractions of evolutionary theory was the built-in historical perspective. However, the authors have a different, more complex idea of natural history in mind:

> What's essential about adaptationism, as viewed from this [neo-Darwinist] perspective, is precisely its claim that there is a level of evolutionary explanation. We think this claim is just plain wrong. We think that successful explanations of the fixation of phenotypic traits by ecological variables typically belong *not to evolutionary theory but to natural history* [added emphasis], and that there is just no end to the sorts of things about a natural history that can contribute to explaining the fixation of some or other feature of a creature's phenotype. Natural history isn't a theory of evolution; it's a bundle of evolutionary scenarios. That's why the explanations it offers are so often post hoc and unsystematic.[36]

Survival of the weakest

Arriving at much the same conclusion as Stiegler regarding the impact of technology on human evolution, though from a different discipline,[37] in *The Artificial Ape* the archaeologist and prehistorian Timothy Taylor[38] offers an alternative critique of neo-Darwinism. While, like Stiegler, Taylor only briefly mentions human shelter in passing, the implications of his findings for the role of built forms and settlements as well as for any other kind of artifacts in shaping human evolution and, in turn, conceptions of the self, are considerable. Turning Darwinism on its head and characterizing the evolution of *Homo sapiens* as 'the survival of the weakest,'[39] Taylor argues that ever since its origins the species has relied upon its ability to make up for a relatively weak physique by supplementing its powers with the invention of useful objects. Like Stiegler, he is also circumspect about the prospects for the future of humankind's dependence upon technology:

> There is increasing evidence that we are no longer governed by natural selection. Technology can and does supersede biology and lead us into a new form of life, one not primarily governed by Darwinian process. The implications of being the first entity on our planet to escape natural selection are immense. We have never been wholly natural creatures, and we have evolved to being increasingly artificial. Even should we want it, escape from technology is no longer possible. *It may in fact be that technology has escaped from us: the inertia of the entire system of technological civilization is by now so immense that the sort of choices left for us to make in the future are essentially trivial* [added emphasis]. The ride we are now on may be unsustainable, or it may not; but there are many reasons for believing that we are incapable of getting off. Either we crash, or we continue our artificial ascent.[40]

As far as the big picture is concerned, at first glance Taylor's position on human and technological evolution therefore closely mirrors Stiegler's technics, raising much the same worrying questions as to where it is all leading us.[41] However, while both Stiegler and Taylor privilege *Homo sapiens* in possessing a unique capacity for technological development, Taylor's position also differs from Stiegler's in one crucial respect. Where Stiegler and his followers generally regard human and technological development as a *coevolutionary* process with two-way causal chains and reciprocal effects laden with ambiguities, Taylor makes the bold claim that it is the *objects themselves*, that is, the artifacts and other forms of technology unique to humankind, that take the lead:

> I aim to demonstrate by clear examples that rather than humans evolving to become intelligent enough to invent tools and weapons, shelters, monuments, art, and writing, *the objects, in the most critical instances, came first* [added emphasis]. Our changing biological capacities, physical and mental, positive and negative, followed.[42]

While Stiegler and his followers generally rely heavily upon other expert sources for evidence of tool use and suchlike, at least in prehistorical periods, Taylor works closer to the archaeological coal face, so to speak. This yields a great many examples of the way early humans gradually shed the physical attributes of strength and endurance they once shared with primates in favor of artificial substitutes, including tools and clothing, most of which, however, leave the question of causal sequence unanswered. Eventually, however, in a roundabout way, Taylor finally homes in on his main thesis. The first major piece of evidence suggesting that it was objects that came first rather than the intelligence to make those objects, Taylor argues, concerns the apparent gap of 190,000 years between the first known use of a chipped stone tool, around 2,520,000 years ago, and the earliest species of upright walking ape of the *Homo* genus known as *Homo habilis*, the earliest evidence for which dates it as no older than 2,330,000 years. As Taylor points out, while 190,000 years may not be a long time in the evolution of life on earth it is close to the total amount of time our own species, *Homo sapiens*, has existed. Since our predecessor, *Homo habilis*, was possessed of small, chimp-like brains, Taylor deduces that the first stone tools were one of perhaps a number of crucial objects that *preceded* and eventually gave rise to the rapid growth in brain size that typifies our own species, instead of the other way around, as is generally assumed.

Brains and baby slings

For Taylor, however, the clinching evidence lies in the use of another object, the origins of which lie deep in prehistory but which is still very much in use, the full significance of which he suggests has been partly if unconsciously suppressed till now by gender factors among his profession. That object is the simple baby sling (fig. 5.3). While most archaeologists and anthropologists – who until recently were mostly males themselves – have focused on the early male of our species as the primary hunter gatherer and tool maker and user, the use of artificial props and supports by females has been relatively neglected. Correcting the error of omission, Taylor links the use of the baby sling directly to the emergence of the *Homo* genus as an upright walking species, the reasons for which, he explains, still remain a subject of debate.

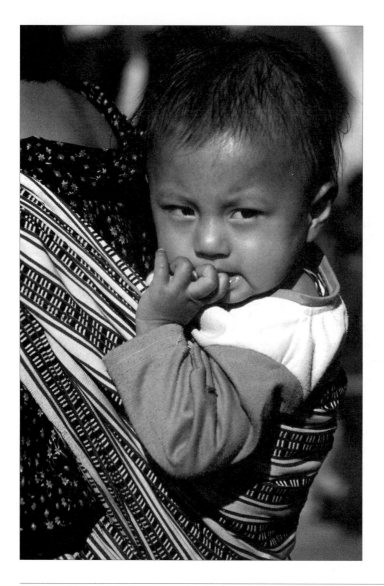

5.3 *Baby in sling on mother's back in Wangdue Phodrang, Bhutan*

Some point to the advantages gained in being able to see further by the increase in height, together with the cooling effects on the head that access to the breezes above ground level affords. More commonly, experts cite the increase in mobility that eventually came with the ability to walk and run on two legs for long distances, and even to outrun some prey or predators.

Whatever the initial reasons or advantages, the upright posture also came with major disadvantages that would be overcome only by artificial means. One of those drawbacks was the shrinking of the length of the intestines by some 60% relative to those of other primates, resulting in a drastically reduced capacity for digesting raw foods. This in turn created a yawning energy gap in the requirements to sustain survival in a hostile world, a gap which was resolved, Taylor argues, only by the discovery of fire and cooked food, especially protein-heavy meat, making it easier to digest and releasing huge amounts of extra energy in the process, thus negating the need for longer intestines.

Much of that extra energy was needed for the development of the outsized brain of *Homo sapiens*, which consumes as much as 20% of the total energy requirements of the human body, as well as for hunting the meat which was essential to sustain such high levels. The discovery of cooked food, therefore, also counts as one of those technological inventions that preceded, or at least, *enabled* the growth of the human brain to its present size of three to four times larger than the brains of any other ape.

However, before the human brain could grow to its full size, other physical obstacles created by the upright posture had to be overcome. As well as shrinking the length of the intestines, the size of the pelvic girdle was greatly reduced, creating severe limitations for females to accommodate and give birth to an infant with an enlarged brain. It seemed that, even with the discovery of cooked food, the upright posture might have prevented any significant further advance in the intelligence of the species. In addition, while other infant apes easily straddle their mothers' backs, hanging onto their fur, without greatly hindering the movement of their mothers' body or arms, upright female hominids could carry their infants only on their hips, secured by one arm, which was thus rendered useless for any other purpose, just as modern mothers and fathers do everywhere today.

Until, that is, the introduction of the baby sling. Just how the invention or discovery came about we will probably never know. Taylor speculates it might have involved the simple adaptation of a 'twisted loop of animal skin – perhaps some sun-toughened membrane at a scavenging site, or some scorched but not burnt pelt from the embers of a bush fire.'[43] However it happened, Taylor is in no doubt about the tremendous consequences of that discovery for the future evolution of humankind:

Although carrying slings do not in themselves drive brain-size increase, they certainly encourage it. Rather than having to fit a larger and larger cranium through a pelvic girdle that has contorted itself to support an upright frame, helpless babies can be catered for in a pouch. The time that they remain helpless – a week, a month, a year, several years – becomes less critical. Sling technology removed the glass ceiling on the degree of ontogenetic retardation (in primate terms, premature birth) that genus *Homo* could begin to accommodate. *And that, of course, is the solution to growing larger brains: you do it outside the womb* [added emphasis].

From the point of onset, our evolution was critically driven by technology. The sling, in particular, allowed the final australopithecines to become artificial marsupials and, by accommodating ever higher levels of helpless paedomorphism, took the lid off the pelvic limits to bipedal expansion. Increased intelligence, in turn, allowed the development of a more complex techno-cultural system, the evolution of a fully and habitually two-legged stance, and the possibility of colonizing all the continents of the world.[44]

While, like Fodor and Piattelli-Palmarini, Taylor places perhaps too much of the burden of his case on one example, it is a far more convincing one than the former authors' ill-researched architectural case study. If objects or artifacts can be shown to precede or create the conditions for human evolution in such an important case as the baby sling, then the belief that artifacts and the ideas they embody have dynamic properties of their own capable of outstripping human control – just as Stiegler and Taylor maintain they do – becomes a lot more plausible.

Emergence

Beginning in the latter half of the last century, theories of emergence and self-organization, or 'autopoiesis' as it is now known, meaning 'self-producing,' have also attracted increasing attention as offering alternative approaches to evolutionary theory, applicable to both natural and artificial phenomena. While both ideas are now closely interrelated in many minds, emergence has become a particularly hot topic in recent years among computer scientists simulating the behavior of living systems, as well as architectural researchers using related techniques – a subject we will come back to in the closing chapter of this book. The concept has also become closely associated with the work of Francisco J. Varela and his long-time research colleague and co-author Humberto Maturana, whose theories will be discussed shortly.

However, the credit for the original concept of emergence goes to Michael Polanyi, who first broached the idea in 1958 with the publication of *Personal Knowledge*.[45] Critical of the neo-Darwinist picture of evolution as 'the sum total of successive accidental hereditary changes which have offered reproductive advantages to their bearers,'[46] as he describes it, and of the principle of natural selection which is supposed to have brought those advantages about, Polanyi offers his own interpretation:

> My argument will be based on a different conception of life. *I shall regard living beings as instances of morphological types* [added emphasis] and of operational principles subordinated to a center of individuality and shall affirm at the same time that no types, no operational principles and no individualities can ever be defined in terms of physics and chemistry. From which it follows that the rise of *new* forms of life – as instances of *new* types and *new* operational principles centered on *new* individualities – is likewise undefinable in terms of physics and chemistry.[47]

In thus refuting the neo-Darwinian account of evolution, Polanyi not only subordinates the incremental or accumulative character of evolution to higher principles of order – as we shall see, he does not refute the idea that evolution generally proceeds in small steps, only that such steps can account for the more significant, longer-term phenomena of life – but he also firmly rejects any purely physical or chemical account of evolutionary processes.[48] Significantly, at the same time as he rejects reductionist theories of evolution, he also conflates the idea of species with that of types, and morphological types in particular, affirming their common origins in human cognition, a key subject we shall also return to in Part III of this book.

In place of the rejected physical and chemical, that is, genetic account of life, Polanyi turns instead to the theory of open systems, which at the time he wrote *Personal Knowledge* had only been recently defined.[49] While also inspired by biological models, for Polanyi, as for a growing number of other radical thinkers at the time, the open-systems concept represented an entirely new perspective on what kept living organisms going – in essence, what sustained their *identity* – which he likened to the dynamic relations between a gas flame and its environment. Once the flame has been lit, Polanyi explains, it will maintain its shape by a constant inflow of combustible material and outflow of waste products: 'To this extent, its identity is not defined by its physical or chemical topography, but by the *operational principles which sustain it* [added emphasis].'[50]

Noting that evolution works too slowly to observe any major functional changes at first hand, Polanyi stresses the larger perspective that systems theory affords: 'There is a cumulative trend of changes tending toward higher levels of organization, among which the deepening of sentience and the rise of thought are the most conspicuous.'[51] While Polanyi does not altogether reject the incremental side to evolution, he does therefore emphatically refute the idea that that is all there is to it, as he suggests neo-Darwinism assumes, or that genetics and natural selection provide adequate explanations in themselves. Changes of this order, he asserts, lie well outside the normal scope of biologists and geneticists, focused as they are on the short-term 'mechanisms' of inheritance: 'Hence the long-range operations of evolution will not be noticed by the experimental geneticist, nor even by the students of population genetics, and geneticists will have no difficulty in explaining all hereditary variations observed by them, without reference to the action of evolutionary trends.'[52]

For evidence of the tendency toward ever higher levels of organization, Polanyi suggests we can find no better proof than in the evolution of human consciousness:

> From a seed of submicroscopic living particles – and from inanimate beginnings lying beyond these – we see emerging a race of sentient, responsible and creative beings. The spontaneous rise of such incomparably higher forms of being testifies directly to the operations of an orderly innovating principle.[53]

However, Polanyi concedes we do not know precisely at what stage of human evolution consciousness made itself felt. Most likely, he suggests, it did so in very small ways at first, pretty much like everything else that has evolved; the first signs of consciousness showing up in an increasing polarity between subject and object, 'and with it, the fateful obligation to form expectations based on necessarily insufficient evidence.'[54] Whenever or however it first appeared, it marked the separation of *Homo sapiens* forever from the rest of the animal kingdom, not by virtue of possessing consciousness as such – as previously noted, animals, especially other primates, also show indications of conscious behavior and even self-consciousness – but by the sheer *complexity* of human consciousness, as evidenced in the self-conscious, self-searching cultural record it has left throughout the history of the species. As Polanyi

Rethinking evolution

puts it: 'This great spectacle, the spectacle of anthropogenesis, confronts us with a panorama of emergence; it offers massive examples of emergence in the gradual intensification of personal consciousness.'[55]

Autopoiesis and natural drift

Maturana and Varela's work on autopoiesis also springs originally from the same well of early systems theory as Polanyi's concept of emergence, except that, entering the field in the 1970s, they had the advantage of being able to draw upon more advanced concepts of self-organization, which by that time had already been well formulated.[56] Both have since written many papers elaborating their approach, separately as well as jointly, the key aspects of which are ably summarized by John Mingers[57] in his study of self-producing systems. Aside from explaining Maturana and Varela's thought on the subject, Mingers' work is especially useful for his insights into what has become a fertile field of research in its own right, covering human social systems as well as the biological organisms and other living systems the two theorists' original work was focused on. Part of the broader attraction of autopoiesis – despite, as Mingers notes, the opaque style of Maturana's and Varela's original writings – can be deduced from his own succinct definition of the idea, which stresses the relative autonomy of autopoietic systems from their environments, natural or otherwise:

> an autopoietic system has a circular organization, which closes in on itself, its outputs becoming its own inputs. *This gives it an important degree of independence or autonomy from its environment since its operations ensure, within limits, its future continuation* [added emphasis]. Maturana and Varela contend that all living systems are autopoietic and that autopoiesis explains their particular characteristics.[58]

However, rather than focusing, as most naturalists and biologists do, on either the species at one end of the scale or genes at the other end, like Polanyi, Maturana and Varella take the identity of the *individual* as the central entity of autopoietic systems. Secondly, according to their theory, all living systems are comprised of interactions between their components and their neighbors, both within the system itself and in its environment. While an observer might perceive interactions between wholes, the components of the system themselves cannot do this but only react to other components within the system. From this viewpoint, autopoietic systems are comprised of multiple interacting components, the outcome of which cannot be accurately predicted. Following on from the last two aspects of the theory, *there can be no teleological or purposeful explanation for the behavior of living systems*, except that which is gained in hindsight by an external observer.

The key to what makes and sustains an individual living entity *as an individual* out of all these interacting multiple components, as Polanyi correctly intimated, is the circular *operational principle* underlying the whole process.[59] Mingers offers the relatively simple case of a single cell, the chemical elements of which are in constant interplay with each other and with the cell's membrane, which comprises the boundary between it and the external world. Mingers asks what is it that qualifies the cell 'as an autonomous, dynamic, living whole?'[60] The answer, he explains, lies in the reciprocal relations between what the cell produces and what produces the cell:

> in essence, it produces many complex and simple substances which remain in the cell (because of the cell membrane) and participate in those very same production processes. Some molecules are excreted from the cell, through the membrane, as waste. What is it that produces the components of the cell? With the help of some basic chemicals imported from its medium, the cell produces its own constituents. So a cell produces its own components, which are therefore what produces it in a circular, ongoing process [...] that is what a cell does: it continually produces itself. Living systems are autopoietic – *they are organized in such a way that their processes produce the very components necessary for the continuation of these processes* [added emphasis].[61]

As systems continually exchanging materials and energy with their environments, autopoietic systems therefore still fulfill the definition of open systems. But the idea of self-production goes a vital step further in explaining just what holds living systems together as individuals.

At least two other concepts are essential to understanding how autopoietic systems work: 'organization' and 'structure.' While the meaning of these terms varies somewhat in the authors' original writings, Mingers offers the following broad definitions:

> The organization consists of the relations among components and the necessary properties of the components that characterize or define the unity in general *as belonging to a particular type or class* [added emphasis]. This determines its properties as a whole [...]. Structure, on the other hand, describes the actual components and actual real relations of a particular real example of any such entity, such as the Boeing 757 I board at the airport.[62]

While the central focus of autopoietic systems remains the identity of the individual and what holds it together, again, like Polanyi, Maturana and Varela also therefore explicitly embrace the idea of types and, by implication, also the idea of species. As with the relation between open and autopoietic systems, we see not a rejection of the other idea, but a *more comprehensive* explanatory theory that also accounts for what the earlier concept and approach does not, that is, the *individuality* of a species member. Elaborating on the key issue of organization, the two authors explain that, while many composite systems are also organized in some way, autopoietic systems are a special class of their own, in so far as they are 'organizationally closed.' As Mingers defines it: 'A system is organizationally closed if all its possible states of activity must always lead to or generate further activity within itself.'[63]

In his concluding chapter, Mingers also helpfully clarifies Varela's concept of the self and embodied cognition as related aspects of what he describes as the 'enactive paradigm' to which autopoietic systems belong. As opposed to conventional theories of cognition, which assume that individuals are constantly striving to match their own representations of the world to an objective world that is somehow already 'out

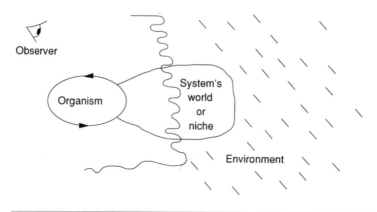

5.4 *Diagram of relations between an organism, its world, and the observer's environment, after Humberto Maturana and Francisco Varela*

there,' following Merleau-Ponty, Varela asserts there is no such thing as an environment completely independent of the organism that perceives it; all life forms decide for themselves what is meaningful and what is not:

> the organism itself specifies what, in its environment, is significant for itself. An organism exists within a niche of possible environmental interactions of relevance for its continued self-production. It embodies a particular perspective [...]. The structure of the organism determines the possible interactions that it could have and the subset of these that are important to it.[64]

Autopoietic systems therefore have no external goal or destiny beyond their own self-production. Similarly, the identity and character of an autopoietic system, including the elusive human self, are not so much a predetermined right as an *emergent* property, a never-ending process of interactions between an individual's internal constituents and its own self-selected environment (fig. 5.4).

This might be interpreted as a form of extreme relativism. However, while autopoietic systems select what they need for their own self-production from their environments, their survival still depends very much upon their selecting the *right* elements for their own needs from all the possible elements that might be available for other uses, in other words, doing what Varela et al. in their work on extended cognition describe as *satisfying the conditions for self-production*, as opposed to optimizing for fitness. Likewise, in place of natural selection, Varela and Maturana substitute the idea of 'natural drift,' a concept meant to evoke both the dynamic coupling of an organism and its changing environment and the open-ended nature of evolution as an emergent process:

> In moving toward evolution as natural drift [in contrast to natural selection] we recast selective pressures as broad constraints to be satisfied. The crucial point here is that we

The extended self

do not retain the notion of an independent, pregiven environment but let it fade into the background in favor of so-called intrinsic factors. Instead, we emphasize that the very notion of what an environment is cannot be separated from what organisms are and what they do.[65]

More than a metaphor

While, as Mingers explains, neither Maturana nor Varela believes that social systems can be accurately described as self-producing systems in the same precise terms that living systems can, that has not stopped numerous theorists and researchers in the social sciences and other fields mining their work for insights into their own chosen subjects. Mingers diligently trawls through the most fruitful of these applications, from legal systems to family therapy, information systems, cognitive science and artificial intelligence, pointing out the strengths and weaknesses of each approach, which he describes as varying from the 'simplistic' to the most convincing.[66] Addressing the problems involved in stretching what, like much of neo-Darwinian theory, was originally developed as a theory of biological evolution, to cover the evolution of human societies, Mingers writes:

> If the attribution of autopoiesis to social systems is to be more than a woolly generalization, then we must examine carefully its specific definition. There are three essential elements:
>
> 1. Centrally, autopoiesis is concerned with processes of production – the production of those components that themselves constitute the system.
> 2. It is constituted in temporal and spatial relations, and the components involved must create a boundary defining the entity as a unity – that is, a whole interacting with its environment.
> 3. The concept of an autopoietic organization specifies nothing beyond self-production. It does not specify particular structural properties and thus shouldn't need to be modified to deal with social systems.
>
> In applying these ideas strictly, there are obvious problems. Is it right to characterize social institutions as essentially processes of production and, if it is, *what exactly is it that they are producing* [added emphasis]? If human beings are taken as the components of social systems, then it is clear that they are not produced by such systems but by other physical, biological processes. If we do not take humans as components, then what are the components of social systems?[67]

Having found most attempts at applying the theory to human societies to be wanting, Mingers suggests that, rather than trying to apply it too literally beyond its original scope, it might be better to think of autopoiesis as a 'useful metaphor.'[68] Following the same line of thought, he adds:

> A more radical approach is to apply autopoiesis not to physical systems, *but to concepts and ideas* [added emphasis]. Such a system might consist of ideas, descriptions, or messages that interact and self-produce.[69]

Pursuing a similar approach, the next chapter examines some plausible agents of self-production in the cultural and technological realms, the search for which continues into Part III of the book. It will also be argued in later chapters that, more than a metaphor, provided the chosen analogy is an appropriate one, the process of abstracting ideas from one domain and applying them to another in this fashion is a legitimate and even common mode of innovation and an important key to understanding cultural evolution generally, including those human technics that Stiegler and others have described as having their own evolutionary dynamics.

6 From genes to memes

One of the more serious criticisms leveled at Bernard Stiegler's coevolutionary theory of technics was that, for all his keen insights into the human condition, he paid little attention to how technically inscribed forms of behavior and culture might actually be cognized and transmitted from person to person and thus diffused through the population. This becomes an especially important issue if one accepts that, aside from the impact of technology on human evolution generally, there is the possibility, as Stiegler himself writes and Taylor also argues, that many technologies and culture-forms have dynamics of their own. Any such autonomy or momentum would in turn have fundamental consequences for a theory of the extended self, raising vexing questions regarding an individual's control over his or her life and self-perceptions.

In search of answers to those questions the discussion now turns to the work of Richard Dawkins and his followers on the concept of the meme as a possible agent of cognitive extension, applicable to both interpersonal and cultural transfusions of the kind described in previous chapters. Though Dawkins originally provided no more than a sketchy outline of his concept, the meme has since attracted keen attention in various disciplines as well as from the wider public, sparking much debate as to the nature and function or even existence of such an entity. While there are many more contenders in the field, following an explication of Dawkins' original theory, for the sake of clarity this chapter focuses on the subsequent works of several writers who between them represent the main schools of thought, these being roughly divided between those who take the genetic analogy literally and those who adopt more open positions. Other writers will be given voice in later parts of the book as more specific themes are developed.

The replicators

Dawkins first arrived at the idea of the meme via his theory of what makes genes so special and how they function, which he set out in his well known work on biological evolution, *The Selfish Gene*.[1] As the fundamental units of evolutionary development, he explains, the peculiar power of genes lies in their ability, following their DNA codes, to make – occasional errors and mutations apart – exact copies of themselves: 'What, after all, is so special about genes? The answer is that they are *replicators*.'[2] As replicators, genes are thus able, by exploiting the bodies that house them through their reproductive processes, to pass themselves and their associated characteristics on to the next generation, and so outlive the individual organisms they helped to build. However, as explained in the previous chapter, natural selection only works *indirectly* on the genes themselves, favoring those genes whose phenotypic effects or hereditary characteristics give the organism some kind of advantage over organisms lacking those same attributes, or whose genes produce less robust effects. Although it is the genes, as efficient if not always perfect replicators, which are actually transmitted through the generations, it is therefore the effects or characteristics they produce in the organism itself that determine their survival.

Among the most radical ideas included in that work, Dawkins rejected biologists' conventional assumption that the primary targets of natural selection were the species or group, or that the successful transmission of genes from generation to generation was subordinate to the same goal: the survival of the species. On the contrary, following the pioneering works of W. D. Hamilton and G. C. Williams in the 1960s,[3] Dawkins asserted that biologists had got it the wrong way around. Impressive entities though they may be, bodily organisms as such are merely convenient 'vehicles' that genes assemble, through their phenotypic effects, for their *own* benefit and procreation. Moreover, genes will always behave 'selfishly,' as it were, and choose that form or configuration in nature that most favors their survival. Accordingly, he argued, natural selection is more accurately understood as a competition between genes themselves, rather than between species or between organisms. In the same spirit, Dawkins characterized the organisms that genes build for themselves, however complex they may be, including human beings, as genetic 'survival machines.'

The extended phenotype

Not content with reversing the conventional order of priorities in natural selection – a reversal his followers likened to a Copernican revolution in thought – Dawkins further complicated matters by questioning the assumed extent of a gene's effects:

> The phenotypic effects of a gene are normally seen as all the effects that it has on the body in which it sits. This is the conventional definition. But we shall now see that the phenotypic effects of a gene need to be thought of as *all the effects that it has on the world.*[4]

As examples, Dawkins points to artificial shelters and other artifacts that have been purposefully constructed by various creatures to better shape their environment to suit their own needs, such as beaver dams, bird nests and the less familiar but impressive homes of caddis larvae.[5] Caddis flies themselves spend their adult lives flying back and forth over rivers. However, it is their earlier lives as larvae on the river bottom that captivates Dawkins. Caddis larvae, he asserts, 'are among the most remarkable creatures on earth.'[6] By his account, they certainly qualify as being among nature's most gifted home builders. Using assorted materials gathered from the riverbed, together with 'cement' they manufacture and excrete from their own bodies, these tiny creatures construct tubular houses for themselves, which they drag about like mobile homes. Moreover, different species use different materials, including, in the case of one species, tiny fragments of stone, which the larvae diligently gather and assemble, looking for stones of the right size and hardness and even turning them around to find the best fit to each other.

As Dawkins observes, we accept without quibbling that a snail's shell is a natural extension of the organism, and is therefore just as much a product of the snail's genes as the rest of the creature. As such, the shell has evolved by natural selection, in the same way as the snail's remarkable eyes have evolved – because they gave it some kind of advantage over other variations of snail, and so ensured the survival of the particular genes responsible for those effects. Similarly, at some time in caddis history, argues Dawkins, natural selection favored those caddis genes whose effects included house-building behavior, because such behavior gave the caddis larvae that possessed it a clear advantage over those that did not – protecting them against predators and so forth. Similarly, Dawkins muses, at some point there must have been enough caddis genes around generating sufficient variations in caddis house-building techniques for natural selection to work, favoring those most suitable for different species and habitats: 'for selection cannot produce adaptations unless there are hereditary differences among which to select.'[7]

While biologists generally accept that an organism's genes can have an indirect influence, through the development of the nervous system, on behavioral patterns that affect its survival, Dawkins goes much further, to include the actual *materials themselves* used for caddis house building among the phenotypic effects of caddis genes: 'If it is legitimate to speak of a gene as affecting the wrinkliness of a pea or the nervous system of an animal (all geneticists think it is) then it must also be legitimate to speak of a gene affecting the hardness of the stones in a caddis house.'[8]

For Dawkins, the hardness of stones in caddis houses – we might also include the size of the twigs in a bird's nest or the logs in a beaver's dam, the quality of the soil in an ant hill, and so on – presents an example of what he calls the 'extended phenotype,' and it opens a veritable Pandora's box of questions and challenges to orthodox evolutionary thinking. Though the comparison might offend some, it does not take a great stretch of imagination to see the possible connections between the humble caddis larvae's creative building techniques and selection of materials – it is tempting to call them 'caddis technics' – and human constructions. An evolutionary biologist of a fundamentalist disposition might even go so far as to posit a similar chain of extended phenotypic effects from human genes to the evolution of human artifacts, including buildings. If it is reasonable to speak of caddis genes *for* material qualities like stone size and hardness, as Dawkins claims, why, one might ask, should there not also be human genes *for* selected qualities of building materials. In other words, should we not regard the great variety of houses and other buildings we construct as simply different *kinds* of vehicles for natural selection to work on, no less important in their own way to the survival of our genes than the frail human bodies they are designed to shelter?

Units of cultural transmission

Aside from any questions regarding the scope and verity of natural selection raised in the last chapter, while it might be interesting to go down that path, Dawkins gives us one very good reason why it would not take us very far in understanding how architecture, or indeed any other culture-form, evolves. The reason is that such a process would simply be far *too slow* to work effectively, and could never have produced such an incredible variety of culture-forms in the relatively brief period of human history. Adopting a line of argument not dissimilar to Stiegler's, Dawkins concludes that the sheer speed of cultural evolution sets it apart from strictly biological evolution: 'Fashions in dress and diet, ceremonies and customs, art and architecture, engineering and technology, all evolve in historical time in a way that looks like highly speeded up genetic evolution, but has really nothing to do with genetic evolution.'[9]

Working on the premise that Darwin's basic theory of evolution is too broad and fertile in its implications to be confined to biological organisms alone, Dawkins speculates that there might be *other* kinds of replicators in the universe aside from genes, manufacturing copies of themselves in much the same way, but composed of different things or materials: 'if I had to bet, I would put my money on one fundamental principle. This is the law that all life evolves by the differential survival of replicating entities.'[10]

Naming his concept after *mimeme*, the Greek root for 'mimic' – purposefully shortened to rhyme with gene to highlight the analogy with genetic transmission – Dawkins proposes 'the idea of a unit of cultural transmission, or a unit of *imitation*.'[11] He also specifies that, in order to function effectively as replicators, memes, like genes, should include at least three attributes: fidelity, fecundity and longevity. Building further on the analogy, he suggests that, while they evolve at vastly different rates of speed, memes multiply in much the same way as genes do:

> Examples of memes are tunes, ideas, catch-phrases, clothes fashions, ways of making pots or of building arches. Just as genes propagate themselves in the gene pool by leaping from body to body via sperms or eggs, so memes propagate themselves in the meme pool by leaping from brain to brain via a process which, in the broad sense, can be called imitation.[12]

Similarly, just as genes compete through their diverse survival machines with other genes for scarce resources, whether they be suitable mates or food supplies, so do memes also compete with other memes for human attention, that is, limited space in the human brain.[13] Thus an idea or tune that makes a greater impression or impact than another idea or tune will be more likely to be imitated and eventually passed on. A meme may also become linked with one or more memes for similar reasons, in the way that co-adapted gene complexes can arise in the same gene pool, because the linkage increases its competitive advantages over other memes. Selecting one of his own favorite topics, Dawkins asks:

> Has the god meme, say, become associated with any other particular memes, and does this association assist the survival of each of the participating memes? Perhaps we could regard an organized church, with its architecture, rituals, laws, music, art, and written tradition, as a co-adapted stable set of mutually-assisting memes.[14]

Equally provocative, Dawkins also asserts that, like genes, memes can exhibit basically selfish characteristics: 'a cultural trait may have evolved in the way it has simply because it is *advantageous to itself*.'[15] In such circumstances, even co-adaptation can have negative effects. Summarizing his theory, Dawkins pinpoints the dangers of a conservative culture comprised of selfish memes:

> Selection favours memes that exploit their cultural environment to their own advantage. This cultural environment consists of other memes which are also being selected. The meme pool therefore comes to have the attributes of an evolutionary stable set, *which new memes find it hard to invade* [added emphasis].[16]

What this means in actual practice is accepting the unwelcome notion that memes, like genes, exist primarily for *their* own benefit, and not the human populations they thrive in. To make the point, Dawkins offers the extreme negative example of the suicide meme – now all too familiar – which spreads when a well publicized martyrdom inspires others to die for the same cause. Dawkins was so concerned himself with the capacity of some memes to 'infect' people's minds and replicate themselves at humanity's expense that he likened their parasitic behavior to that of a virus, and their negative effects to that of an infectious disease. Like biological viruses, he argued, which 'hijack' the host genes' replicative mechanisms to make copies of themselves, what makes meme viruses so dangerous is their ability to piggyback surreptitiously on other, more benign memes, so spreading themselves along with those memes with the active support of their unwitting human vehicles.[17]

Abstract principles

Of the main schools of thought on Dawkins' idea of the meme, Daniel Dennett[18] and Susan Blackmore[19] argue separately for a broad interpretation of what memes are and how they work. A firm believer in Dawkins' basic concept of the meme, Dennett has also positioned himself as a fierce advocate for universal Darwinism, a term he prefers to neo-Darwinism as it suggests the possibility of wider applications. In like spirit, he refutes the apparent opposition to the application of Darwinian thinking to culture, which he sees as mostly emanating from the more conservative corners of the humanities: 'Some people, I have found, just hate the whole idea [...]. They want the human way of life to be radically different from the way of life of all other living things, and so it is, but, like life itself, and every other wonderful thing, *culture must have a Darwinian origin* [added emphasis].'[20]

His response is to draw out those more abstract principles of Darwinian theory which can be applied to evolution in *all* its forms, whether it has a material foundation in organic life or not. Thus, according to Dennett, evolution can be said to occur whenever the following conditions are satisfied:

(1) variation: there is a continuing abundance of different elements.
(2) heredity or replication: the elements have the capacity to create copies or replicas of themselves.
(3) differential 'fitness': the number of copies of an element that are created in a given time varies, depending on interactions between the features of that element and features of the environment in which it persists.[21]

Underlying all of these conditions is the recursive logic of natural selection described in the previous chapter. For Dennett, the abstract nature of Darwin's theory and the algorithmic process underlying natural selection are the foundations of universal Darwinism, and thus also offer a general theory for memetic evolution. However, he also concedes that, while the above general principles might hold for both genetic and cultural evolution, further parallels between the two are open to question. At one extreme, he suggests, lies the possibility that cultural evolution precisely mirrors all the key features of genetic evolution, including DNA, genotypes, phenotypes, sexual reproduction and selection, and so on. At the other lies the possibility that cultural evolution operates according to quite *different* principles and has little if anything in common with biological evolution, in which case even the above very general principles might not hold well in all cases.

Adopting a position somewhere in between these extremes and allowing for the broadest possible interpretation, Dennett tentatively defines memes as complex ideas that comprise '*distinct memorable units*,'[22] which may vary enormously in scope and purpose. Among a few randomly chosen examples he offers the ideas of: 'arch; wheel; wearing clothes; vendetta; right triangle; alphabet; calendar; the Odyssey; calculus; chess; perspective drawing; evolution by natural selection; impressionism; "Greensleeves"; deconstructionism.'[23] However, on the very same page he back-peddles and, echoing Dawkins' original specification for effective replicators, defines memes more narrowly as: 'the smallest elements [of culture] that can replicate themselves with reliability and fecundity.'[24] For example, the first four notes of Beethoven's Fifth Symphony count as a meme for Dennett because they have a musical identity and effect all of their own and are replicated – tediously, one might add – in situations Beethoven could never have imagined they would be.

Problems of definition

Like Dennett, Blackmore highlights the recursive form of natural selection, which she describes in similar fashion as a foolproof recipe for success:

As Darwin realized, *a simple reiterative process can create the most intricate and functional designs apparently out of nowhere* [added emphasis]. It works like this – start with something; make lots of copies of it with slight variations; select just one of these; and then repeat the process. That's all.

The power lies with the effect of selection [...] in a world with insufficient food, space, light, and air to go round, inevitably some creatures will do better than others, and whatever it was that helped them in the competition for survival will be passed on to their offspring, and so the process continues. As it does, characteristics such as eyes, wings, hair, and teeth all appear and evolve. These are the adaptations that helped the animals to survive, and will be passed on if they breed.[25]

However, given so much continuing debate in memetics over fundamentals, Blackmore also favors theoretical flexibility over possibly premature precision. Among the most contentious issues, she identifies three recurrent problems: specifying the unit of a meme; specifying the mechanism(s) for copying and storing memes; and resolving what Blackmore describes as the Lamarckian character of memes, that is, the possibility that cultural characteristics may be acquired during the lifetime of a person by learning and then passed on to succeeding generations in similar ways. Regarding the first problem, while genes have a relatively finite chemical structure and can be endlessly recombined as molecular strings of DNA, it is unclear just what constitutes a meme, or how large it might be. Should it be the minimum number of recognizable bars in a tune or piece of music, as Dennett suggests it should, or the whole piece? Likewise, should it be any of the key ideas or identifiable characters in a book, or the whole book? Or should it be something in between, like a musical movement or a story?

In addressing such questions Blackmore refers to Dennett's own definition of memes as 'the smallest elements' that replicate themselves reliably. However, Blackmore readily concedes that this still leaves the field pretty much wide open. Pointing out that similar problems plagued genetics in its early stages without prejudicing later achievements, she optimistically suggests that such questions probably will not hinder progress in memetics either in the long run.

Blackmore is equally relaxed in response to the second set of problems, regarding the nature of the copying and storage mechanisms involved, and candidly admits there is no clear answer yet to those questions either. Nevertheless, she argues, 'we may assume that, at least at some phase in their replication, memes have to be physically stored in brains.'[26] Looking to the future, she suggests that advances in the neurosciences may eventually offer more substantial insights, possibly in conjunction with progress in artificial neural networks and computer simulations of memory functions. In the meantime we can make some useful educated guesses. What counts most, she proffers, is the ability of memes to lodge themselves faithfully in the mind, and so to infect the carrier long enough to be accurately copied and passed on:

Effective memes will be those that cause high-fidelity, long-lasting memory. Memes may be successful at spreading largely because they are memorable rather than because they are important or useful.[27]

As for problems of transmission, Blackmore briefly surmises that the successful transmission of memes depends crucially on psychological factors, such as human emotions, desires and preferences. Here, as with storage issues, she suggests that related disciplines such as evolutionary psychology may provide guidance.

However, the third issue, the Lamarckian character of memes, presents a different order of problems, which cannot be deferred so easily. Most biologists would agree with Blackmore's claim that, at least between sexual organisms, the transmission of inherited characteristics is wholly restricted to the spread of genes, or the 'germ line' as it is known. The reason for this, argues Blackmore, is simply that, whatever changes might develop in the body or behavior of the organism, there is no way that these changes can affect the genes themselves, except indirectly, by selection. In other words, as explained in the previous chapter, if the change favors the survival of the organism, then natural selection will ensure that that organism will get the chance to pass on its genes, and not some other, less favored organism. However, it is always the genes that generate the behavior, rather than the behavior itself, which get passed on.

However, while the line of inherited characteristics might be relatively clear in genetics, Blackmore concludes that the issue is not so clear in memetics, where there is still much uncertainty about methods of cultural transmission. Cautioning us against taking the analogy between memes and genes too literally, Blackmore suggests that, while both are replicators, the processes of transmission of information involved in each case might differ: 'A more interesting way to use the analogy is to forget about phenotypes and biological generations and look at memes and memetic generations.'[28] In place of the biologist's concepts of genotype and phenotype, she proposes a more appropriate memetic distinction between two modes of cultural replication and transmission: 'copy-the-product' and 'copy-the-instructions.'[29] In the first method, a song, for example, might be copied by a talented person memorizing the words and music, and then passed on to other singers, as a folk song might be propagated in traditional societies. In such a case, any variations in the performance or changes in the words or music might also be transmitted from person to person and eventually from generation to generation, so that, for better or worse, later versions might differ considerably from earlier versions. However, if the song was to be written down as sheet music at some point in time, then the written version might act as a permanent set of instructions or template, ensuring that any excessive or un-popular variations in individual performances could always be corrected by reference back to the written version. In the biological world, Blackmore concludes, genes propagate solely by copying-the-instructions, whereas in the cultural world memes propagate by using both methods, and it would be overstretching the analogy with genes to try to restrict our understanding of cultural propagation to just the latter.

Memes and vehicles

Presenting her own interpretation of the concept in *The Selfish Meme*, Kate Distin[30] disagrees with Dennett and Blackmore on several key issues. However, where the writers differ most clearly is over the problem of where exactly memes are located and, consequently, in the role each writer assigns to artifacts and other vehicles in memetic development. The issue is crucial to understanding the nature of memes and their transmission, because their material location ultimately determines how, or even whether, they can be identified and described, or what form that description takes. For Blackmore, memes can be located both *internally*, within the brain and its workings, and *externally*, in any of the many recordable versions, whether books, recipes or music, in which they take shape: 'As long as that information can be copied by a process we may broadly call "imitation," then it counts as a meme.'[31] Much of Blackmore's subsequent exploration of memetics is likewise applied to its external manifestations, with frequently controversial results, whether it is sexual behavior, health fads, religions or the Internet.

By contrast, Distin prefers to focus on defining the basic attributes of memes more clearly before launching into any investigations of their cultural effects. The problem with Blackmore's inclusive definition of memes, she asserts, is that it conflates two quite different concepts, the idea of the meme itself as a cultural replicator, and its phenotypic effects, or vehicles. In genetics the two concepts are quite distinct: genes are the irreducible replicators, and the bodies or vehicles they build are there as protection systems to ensure their survival – hence Dawkins' so-called 'survival machines.' Neither is Blackmore alone in blurring the lines between genes, memes and their respective vehicles. Dennett goes further to claim that memes are *fundamentally* dependent upon their external carriers for their very existence:

> Genes are invisible; they are carried by gene vehicles (organisms) in which they tend to produce characteristic effects (phenotypic effects) by which their fates are, in the long run, determined. Memes are also invisible, and are carried by meme vehicles – pictures, books, sayings (in particular languages, oral or written, on paper or magnetically encoded, etc.). Tools and buildings and other inventions are also meme vehicles. A wagon with spoked wheels carries not only grain or freight from place to place; it carries the brilliant idea of a wagon with spoked wheels from mind to mind. A meme's existence depends on a physical embodiment in some medium; if all such physical embodiments are destroyed, that meme is extinguished [...]. Memes, like genes, are potentially immortal, but, like genes, *they depend on the existence of a continuous chain of physical vehicles, persisting in the face of the Second Law of Thermodynamics* [added emphasis].[32]

Distin argues that Blackmore's and Dennett's conflation of memes and their vehicles is just one of many current confusions in memetics. In this case, she explains, as the sum product of a meme's phenotypic effects, a vehicle, whatever physical shape or form it takes, cannot *also* be the source of the meme or memes that built it.[33] Further, the notion that any kind of idea at all or its physical embodiment can be called a meme is just far too vague. Distancing herself from Dennett and Blackmore's position and echoing Jablonka and Lamb's view on the importance of being able to generalize from particular words and images to different situations and symbols, Distin asserts that memes are in fact very special sorts of ideas:

Memes must be *generally applicable concepts* [added emphasis]: in mathematics, for example, when I acquire a new meme it endows me with the ability to solve any example of a given type of problem; I do not merely acquire the memory of how to solve those already encountered. When it comes to human artifacts, this distinction is crucial. *It is the design or blueprint for an artifact* [added emphasis] which contains generally applicable information about the construction of that *type* of object. The artifact itself does not contain any such information – and this is true of the artifacts that Dennett cites as examples of meme vehicles (tools and buildings), as of any other. That crucial information is represented in the blueprint or design from which artifacts result.[34]

Elaborating on her core belief in the vital role of blueprints in the production and replication of artifacts, Distin also ventures into the subject of engineering design, describing it as an evolving process combining both a conscious selection among alternative designs aimed at improving the product in some way, that is, increasing its suitability or fitness for a given market, and the impact of cultural factors – memes – outside the designers' awareness or control. Based on the four-stage engineering model for product design proposed by Ken Wallace,[35] Distin presents an idealized account of the design process similar to the systems engineering and 'problem solving' models of earlier decades.[36] According to this model, the first stage in designing any new product like an automobile is dominated by market research and analysis aimed at identifying appropriate gaps in the market to be filled: 'A solution–neutral statement of the problem can then be formulated, in order to identify the true needs without making assumptions about how they should be met.'[37] The second stage is focused on generating alternative design concepts to meet the needs identified in the first stage, which will be separated into essential (demands) or optional (wishes) requirements. Depending upon how each proposed design meets the required specification, the most promising will then be selected for further study in the third stage, called 'embodiment design.' This increasingly concrete procedure involves the production of physical models and whatever drawings and other media are required to visualize and assess the merits of the product – in essence, multiplying the different forms of representation. The final stage involves the detailed design and testing of the product, including the building of full-scale models, working prototypes and drawing up the blueprints for production.

The whole iterative process entails repeated feedback loops as each step is evaluated and the need for more research or detailed design becomes evident, until a satisfactory fit is found between the proposed design and the desired requirements. Distin concludes that, while we should not look for exact parallels: 'It is clear that there are analogies between this design process and biological evolution.'[38] Thus replication, variation and selection – the hallmarks of neo-Darwinism – characterize each step of the process, just as they characterize the evolution of any organism. Tried and tested solutions like engine configurations are replicated over and over again, while the open-ended nature of the design process and the exploration of alternatives will always ensure ample generation of variations: 'Each time it is replicated, an aspect of design runs the risk of embellishment, corruption or diminishment, but this is no different from the risk that each gene runs of mutation during replication.'[39] As for the vital process of selection itself, this too is apparent at every stage, in the weeding out of competing concepts as they fail one or another requirement or test and, last but not least, in the ultimate verdict of the public marketplace, where products are advertised and sold.

Meta-representation

In keeping with her theory of memes as generally applicable concepts or types, Distin also approaches the mind as an active organ with an 'innate capacity to represent – to abstract information from the environment and realize it in a different, more concrete form.'[40] The different forms of representation resulting from this process of abstraction, Distin submits, constitute the symbolic equivalent of cultural DNA, by which ideas are transmitted intact from person to person. However, unlike the genetic information shaping an organism's growth, which remains fixed during the lifetime of the organism, the human mind has the ability to acquire *new* information at any time. Moreover, while Distin accepts the importance of human language, she argues that: 'language itself is too narrow to play the role of cultural DNA. Rather, the answer lies in our *general capacity for representation*, of which language is merely a particular (if ubiquitous) example.'[41]

Significantly, human beings enjoy the additional flexibility of being able to *abstract* the essence of an idea from one representational system and translate it into another, quite different system. Distin argues that this special talent for 'meta-representation,' as she calls it, is crucial to the evolution of human culture and even thought itself because it enables us to compare different systems of representation. The same information or concept may also be represented in different ways: 'It is this, too, which accounts for the ways in which our non-innate concepts have increased so furiously, and our thought processes acquired such powerful machinery.'[42]

Selection can therefore occur *between* symbolic systems themselves as well as within any given system. Distin asserts that this ability to move between different forms of representation, and thus to choose the *way* an idea is represented, is 'hugely important for memes.'[43] The mind, she continues, cannot simply be reduced to the sum total of whatever memes govern a person's behavior, but is more like a 'muscle' with an innate capacity or *potential* shaped by genetic evolution for doing useful things – in this case, processing thought – but which, like any muscle, needs exercising in order to fulfill that potential. While Distin concedes that this *active* picture of the mind might seem to contradict the original concept of memes as autonomous units of culture, she argues that there is plenty of room for both mindless memes and intentional thought in evolutionary theory.

Niche construction

A clear distinction can therefore be drawn between the position taken by Distin and those taken by Blackmore and Dennett. For Distin, for all the differences between genes and memes, there remains a clear, one-way chain of cause and effect from memes to phenotypic effects or vehicles, just as there is from genes to their own phenotypic effects and organic manifestations through the germ line. Blackmore and Dennett, however, would probably both describe Distin's interpretation as a good example of overstretching the analogy between genes and memes. The relation between memes and their effects, they propose, is more like a two-way exchange, and can be understood only by accepting memes as evolutionary phenomena in their own right, related to, but nevertheless distinct from, the behavior of genes.

In their brief but important essay on the subject, Kevin Laland and John Odling-Smee[44] adopt a similar position to Blackmore and Dennett on the reciprocity of phenotypic effects. Pursuing Dawkins' theory of the extended phenotype, they suggest that the capacity of organisms to actively modify their environments to their own advantage, or 'niche construction' as they call it, has been neglected by evolutionary biologists in favor of a generally more passive picture of natural selection. Far from being unusual, this ability of organisms to alter their environment in some way is common to a vast range of species of all kinds:

> To varying degrees, organisms choose their own habitats, mates, and resources and construct important components of their own, and their offspring's local environments, such as nests, holes, burrows, pupal cases, paths, webs, dams, and chemical environments [...] we argue that *organisms not only adapt to environments, but in part also construct them* [added emphasis].[45]

In so doing, the authors claim, a gene, through its wider phenotypic effects, may modify environmental selection pressures *in favor of its survival*. A secondary recursive form of feedback is thus established in the evolutionary process between a gene's phenotypic effects and changes in the environment, leading in turn to modification of selection pressures favoring the gene's replication, leading to further changes in the environment favoring its descendants, and so on. Taking one of Dawkins' own earlier examples, the construction of the beaver dam creates a whole set of modified selection pressures feeding back to act not only on the genes that generate the dam-building behavior, but also on other genes underlying different hereditary characteristics in beavers, from their sharp teeth and broad tails to their social system and other phenotypic effects, which may be directly or indirectly related to their altered environments. Significantly, they write, when feedback of this kind occurs, 'adaptation ceases to be a one-way process, exclusively a response to environmentally imposed problems, and instead becomes a two-way process, with populations of organisms *setting as well as solving problems* [added emphasis].'[46]

Moreover, while they do not develop the idea any further, Laland and Odling-Smee suggest that the evolutionary roots of the cultural transmission of ideas and behaviors through memes may lie in such forms of niche construction. In effect, they submit, any modification of the environment by an organism that might impact on selection pressures constitutes an elementary form of cultural transmission in itself. If that same change in the environment were to be replicated by an organism's descendants, then, the authors conclude, the conditions for memetic evolution would be established. What applies to beavers and all the other countless organisms with a special talent for niche construction, it may be reasoned, therefore also applies to humans and the diverse environments they inhabit.

Meme complexes

Regarding the mystery of the human self, Blackmore suggests that, beyond helping us to understand how ideas and cultures may be transmitted, memetics also raises fundamental questions concerning the self's very nature and boundaries, with related implications for the role of artifacts and personal possessions.

Summarizing the various viewpoints, Blackmore groups theories of the self into two main streams, not unlike some of the theories discussed in earlier parts of this book: those, like members of the Cartesian school of thought and most people of a religious persuasion, who believe in the self as some kind of separate entity or center of consciousness, and those who believe the self is more like an elaborate illusion or story subconsciously constructed by individuals to explain or rationalize their actions after the event, as it were. Of the second group, which Blackmore personally favors, she includes Dennett, together with followers of the Buddhist religion, which, as we saw in Chapter 3, differs radically from most other religions in this respect. In *Consciousness Explained*, Dennett,[47] who disparages any variation of Cartesian dualism, offers a complex picture in which the brain produces 'multiple drafts' or versions of events. One of these – the 'benign user illusion' – creates the illusion, as the name implies, that we are the authors of our own stories, and use our brains the way we might use any computer or other flexible machine, directing it to do this or that. Moreover, not only does the self depend on the interactions of individuals with others, Dennett explains, but it also depends upon the uniquely complex environments and artifacts created by *Homo sapiens*, out of which the species has evolved – supporting both Clark and Chalmers' theory of extended cognition discussed in Chapter 3 and Laland and Odling-Smee's theory of niche construction. However, Dennett is more ambivalent about the potential reach of cognitive extension than Clark and Chalmers are:

> Do our selves, our nonminimal *selfy* selves, exhibit the same permeability and flexibility of boundaries as the simpler selves of other creatures? Do we expand our personal boundaries – the boundaries of our selves – to enclose any of our 'stuff'? In general, perhaps, no, but there are certainly times when this seems to be true, psychologically. For instance, while some people merely own cars and drive them, others are *motorists*; the inveterate motorist prefers being a four-wheeled gas-consuming agent to being a two-legged food-consuming agent.[48]

Blackmore, on the other hand, offers a less ambiguous, simpler memetic solution, though she also allows for the role of artifacts in her definition. The trouble with the self, she argues, is that we are too close to it:

so that we are unable to see it for what it is – *a bunch of memes* [added emphasis]. It comes about because our brains provide the ideal machinery on which to construct it, and our society provides the selective environment in which it thrives.[49]

The self, then, according to this interpretation, is neither more nor less than a highly elaborate meme complex, or, in Blackmore's own terminology, 'the ultimate memeplex,' which she dubs the 'selfplex.' What distinguishes a self from other elaborate meme complexes where memes gang together in collaborative ventures, she explains, is that memes attach themselves to the selfplex by taking the form of a personal belief: 'By acquiring the status of a personal belief a meme gets a big advantage. Ideas that can get inside a self – that is, become "my" ideas, or "my" opinions, are winners.'[50]

In this way, the self becomes a kind of 'safe haven' for memes that somehow bolster or reinforce a person's sense of identity in a literally self-perpetuating cycle. A meme that gains access to the self complex by reinforcing a person's existing beliefs will raise the barrier of admission to new memes, to the point where those memes that do not conform to a person's beliefs may be rejected as a potential threat to the other memes that make up the self. Darwinian selection, it seems, may operate within the self in ways that make natural selection in the jungle seem like child's play.

Notably, *personal possessions* are also an intimate part of this elaborate complex. Such things acquire significance far beyond any functional purpose they may serve, argues Blackmore, precisely because they are identified with the 'I' in each of us. Whatever they may consist of – and they will certainly change throughout our lifetimes – we are never quite free, especially in the developed world, of the material things we surround ourselves with:

> I realize, with some dismay, that I am partly defined by my house and garden, my bicycle, my thousands of books, my computer, and my favorite pictures. *I am not just a living creature, but all these things as well* [added emphasis]; and they are things that would not exist without my memes and would not matter without 'me'.[51]

Neurological composition

In *The Electric Meme*,[52] Robert Aunger, who organized the first academic conference on memetics,[53] also makes a strong bid to explain the precise constitution, location and function of memes. While advancing his own theory, in the course of the work he also provides backing for Dennett's claim for the importance of artifacts in the life and transmission of memes, though, as we shall see, the two differ significantly as to the nature of their role. Moreover, Aunger's theory supports Blackmore's contention that (as quoted above), 'at least at some phase in their replication, memes have to be physically stored in brains.'[54] However, perhaps inevitably, given the relatively short life of memetics, Aunger's concept of memes as the self-perpetuating, neurological entities expressed in the title of his book ultimately leaves many questions unanswered.

Introducing his work, Aunger confidently states: 'After considering alternative proposals, I conclude memes will be found only in the brain.'[55] For Aunger, while books and other artifacts provide the external *means* by which memes may escape individual brains and leapfrog into the brains of others, at the most they provide a *medium of transmission* but should not be confused with memes themselves. Only *ideas*, which reside physically in brains *as* memes, can legitimately be so described. The main task in memetics, as Aunger sees it, therefore, is explaining the neurological composition of memes, and the processes of transmission and reconstitution involved in the passing of a meme from one brain to another, via whatever external medium may be relevant.

Aunger finds support for his theory in recent research into other non-genetic replicators, like the newly discovered prion in biology, and computer viruses. Though vastly different in other respects — prions are chemically based organic elements that are able to replicate themselves with the same precision as genes, while computer viruses, as every computer user knows all too well, are an uninvited and unwelcome form of software — they share the ability to reproduce themselves accurately and so pass on whatever other properties they may have from host to host, whether biological or mechanical. Aunger claims that both cases show that, while employing quite different material processes of replication to genes, non-genetic replicators can reproduce themselves with comparable accuracy and efficiency.[56]

Aunger asserts that such evidence supports an interpretation of memes as clusters or 'nodes' of neurological activity capable of reproducing themselves with fidelity, which he describes in some detail. The key to understanding how memes live and work in the brain, he argues, lies in understanding the neurological processes involved in long-term and short-term memory. All brains, whether human or otherwise, are comprised of billions of special kinds of cells called 'neurons' linked together by thin fibers called 'axons.' What makes neurons so special is their ability to pass binary signals to each other along their axons in the form of electromagnetic pulses — the same basic mechanism employed by computers. These create a chemical reaction at the junction with the neuron at the receiving end, called a 'synapse,' either activating or inhibiting that neuron, which may in turn pass along its own signals and change the state of other neurons it is connected with, creating whole neural circuits or networks for specific functions.

Many of those circuits are comprised of sensory or motor neurons activated by external stimuli or links with other parts of the nervous system distributed around the human body. However, the vast majority of neurons in the brain are connected only with each other and are responsible for all the normal processes and features we associate with human cognition. As brains grow and their owners accumulate more experience and knowledge, so the level of connectivity between neurons and networks also increases. The extent of connectivity in a brain will therefore depend partly upon the age of the owner — young brains have fewer connections than older brains — and partly upon how much work an individual being or any environmental pressures put the brain to.[57] Beyond these familiar features, however, Aunger draws our attention to a crucial difference between long-term and short-term memory:

Everything we know about learning mechanisms suggest that short-term changes in neuronal states are not accompanied by the expression of genes. In fact, the concept of 'short-term' memory is defined by the lack of protein synthesis, which is the normal consequence of gene expression. *The primary difference between short-term and long-term memory is therefore the direct involvement of genes* [added emphasis].[58]

For Aunger, the difference is vital to any definition of what a meme is as a non-genetic cultural replicator. Like prions, memes must be able to replicate themselves independently of genes, otherwise they can have no separate identity or purpose. This is not to say that the basic neural mechanisms of memory are not affected by the expression of genes: 'But the *products* of those mechanisms – memetic information, potentially – is not subject to the same selection effects as it scoots around the brain.'[59] In sum, 'a meme must be an *aspect* of the neuronal network [...]. Memes, then, are just a class of memories that can copy themselves.'[60]

However, as he elaborates his theory Aunger struggles to reconcile his conception of the integrity of memes and their electrochemical form and location in the human brain with what he conceives as the *intermediate role* of artifacts in their transmission from one brain to another. Like Distin, Aunger strongly objects to any conflation of memes with their vehicles. Artifacts, he claims, as vehicles or phenotypes, ultimately exist only 'as the *embodiment* of an idea.'[61] As such, they should not be confused with the ideas that actually produced them: 'Hammers don't make hammers; people with hammer-making knowledge do.'[62] Memes themselves, he insists, never actually leave the security of their homes in the brain, protected as they are from the elements by the bony shells that evolved for just that purpose. Aunger even goes so far as to suggest that memes first evolved 'exclusively within individual brains,'[63] sealing their separateness. Only later, he speculates, did they apparently learn to move about from brain to brain using artifacts as stepping stones along the way.

Which leaves open the question of how memes actually travel from one brain to another if they themselves never leave the comfort of their cranial homes. Turning over the contrary theories of memetic diffusion posited by other writers, Aunger targets what may be called the 'extended phenotype theory' of memes advanced above by Dennett and by Laland and Odling-Smee, which effectively erodes biologists' conventional distinction between genotypes and phenotypes. This presents a conceptual bridge too far for Aunger. Not only does it threaten the basic notion of a meme as a separate, identifiable unit in its own right, but it also allows for Lamarkian-like processes of transmission from generation to generation, which Aunger, who firmly adheres to the genetic model, cannot or will not accept.

Aunger's own solution is to keep memes safely at home in the host brain and to place the burden of transmission onto communication signals, whether they be fragments of speech or some other medium, as 'instigators' in the process of rebirth in the brains of others. Drawing parallels with Noam Chomsky's original theory of innate linguistic skills, Aunger suggests that memetic signals do not actually *need* to communicate *all* the information contained within a particular meme, but simply act as a kind of 'trigger' in recipient minds:

What is new in this perspective is that signals are seen as rabble-rousers. They are projected into the environment, with which they must interact [...]. This implies there is no direct meme-to-meme contact during memetic replication: memes don't go flying through the air to meet up with their brethren in other brains but stay inside their original host. *Memes don't move: Signal instigators do* [added emphasis]. This means the idea of a meme may be a meme, but the spoken word 'meme' is not itself a meme; it is a signal. A meme can only be a state of matter coded in 'brain language.'[64]

As Aunger describes it, signals are thus *converted* into their full memetic selves rather than reconstructed. This not only avoids the necessity for any Lamarckian-like processes – 'Lamarck's folly,'[65] as he calls them – but also any possibility of deterioration of information in the original memes in the process of transmission, which might occur if they have to be reconstructed each time they are received by another brain.

Despite Aunger's evident conviction and strenuous attempts to give memetics a more rigorous foundation, which it badly needs, his theory therefore ultimately rests on an as yet incompletely explained and unverified process of *conversion* by which a complex idea can be somehow reborn in someone else's mind from a much simpler signal derived from the original meme, which stays firmly put in the sender's brain – the explanation for which Aunger can offer only the vaguest reference to Chomskian linguistics for support.[66] More seriously still, if, as Aunger suggests, memes started out as wholly separate entities in individual brains and only later reappear in other brains, then what of the social origins of cultural evolution, without which memes would never have propagated through populations at all?

Beyond reductionism

At the opposite end of the spectrum from Aunger's reductionist approach,[67] William Durham and Manuel De Landa both include memes within theories of evolution that bridge biological and cultural systems of inheritance, in tune with the broader approaches outlined in the preceding two chapters.

Beyond overcoming prevalent conflicts and distrust between workers in the social and biological sciences, Durham's major study, *Coevolution*,[68] on the inter-actions between genetic and cultural systems of human evolution, was motivated by what he perceived as the progressive decline in human diversity across the globe:

> the last few hundred years have successfully reversed the general trend of prior millennia toward increasing human diversity. Worse still, the process seems to be self-reinforcing. The remaining variation seems subject to ever greater depreciation and intolerance.[69]

Dissatisfied with earlier attempts to bridge gaps between the two sciences, Durham found sufficient encouragement in recent advances in anthropology and evolutionary biology to conclude that: 'The question was not *whether* genes and culture are related in their influences on human diversity, but *how*.'[70] In answer to that question, Durham finds common ground in neo-Darwinian evolutionary theory, as he sees it, in that both genes and culture are based on systems of reproduction, the phenotypic effects of which can be traced back through time to shared parenthoods, that is, more primitive forms of organic life in the former and more primitive forms of culture in the latter.[71] In the same way, stretching Darwinian concepts of natural selection and fitness across both phenomena, Durham argues that the products of each system are subject to their own kinds of selection pressures and criteria of fitness. These he illustrates with various examples, including an increased tolerance by humans for lactose (in milk and other foods) as an outcome of genetic changes, and the incest taboo and other social pressures in the evolution of cultures, both of which in turn had significant cross-over effects on human development – the growth of dairy farming in the evolution of settled agricultural societies in the first case and the powerful impact on genetic diversity in the latter. Building on such examples, Durham models the interactions between the two systems as a dynamic equilibrium between complementary systems:

> genes and culture exist in a symmetrical relationship with respect to both human phenotypes and the environment. In other words, they share the same basic properties of instructing phenotypes and of being transformed sequentially through replication in a given environment. My contention is that an adequate theory of gene–culture relations must build upon these symmetries.[72]

In keeping with his broader neo-Darwinian approach to cultural evolution, Durham was also strongly influenced by Dawkins' concept of the meme. After having considered various more familiar alternatives, such as 'ideas,' 'concepts' and 'symbols,' all of which he rejects as being either too vague or carrying too much semantic history, he presents the meme as the preferred 'unit' of cultural replication. In an innovative step, adapting the genetic concept of 'alleles,' which are the main source of variation within species,[73] Durham also introduces two further categories of memes:

> The first and more inclusive group consists of all variants of a given meme – its 'holomemes' – whether they are acted upon or not. Holomemes, in other words, represent the entire cultural repertory of variation for a given meme, including any latent or unexpressed forms. The second and more important group for our purposes, 'allomemes' (a deliberate parallel to the term 'allele' in genetic theory), refers to the subset of holomemes that are actually used as *guides to behavior* [added emphasis] by at least some members of the population in at least some circumstances.[74]

However, when Durham attempts to define the contents of either kind of meme, in rejecting the minimalist interpretation offered by some writers as described earlier in this chapter – memes are the smallest identifiable units of culture and so forth – he falls back upon something similar to Dawkins' original vague, catch-all interpretation of memes as any element or form of culture that can be replicated, no matter how simple or complex: 'I have suggested that meme should refer to any kind, amount, and configuration of information in culture that shows both variation and coherent transmission.'[75]

De Landa[76] in turn offers an interpretation of what memes are and how they function within a bold worldview of the material interactions between organic and non-organic forms, covering a whole millennium of what he describes in emergent terms as a 'nonlinear history' of events. Arguing for a historical philosophy of life on the planet – not unlike Fodor and Piattelli-Palmarini's call for a 'natural history' of evolution, only broader still – De Landa starts from the premise that 'all structures that surround us and form our reality (mountains, animals and plants, human languages, social institutions) are the product of specific historical processes.'[77] From there he works his way through an impressive series of geological, biological and linguistic developments over the past thousand years that have helped to shape life on this planet, including our own. Like some of the other radical thinkers discussed in previous chapters, De Landa also argues that the shape of any specific phenomenon is the outcome, not of any teleological processes, whether couched in historical or in evolutionary terms, nor of the mere accumulation of countless separate events, changes or decisions, but of the interactions between all those things, the emergent effects of which only ever become clear in hindsight.

However, while crediting Dawkins with the original concept of the meme as a cultural replicator,[78] like Durham, De Landa's agenda is focused more on understanding how the two kinds of replicators, genes and memes, interact and work *together* to create the great series of historical events, life forms and other material phenomena he describes in his panoramic study. For this he draws heavily on Durham's work. Contradicting the earlier position taken by anthropologists like Margaret Mead,[79] who argued that human culture evolved independently of any biological imperatives, De Landa writes:

> Fortunately, anthropologists seem to be moving away from dogmatic positions and developing a new *interactionist* approach, wherein both organic and cultural evolution are considered simultaneously. One version of this new approach (the one developed by William Durham) seems particularly close to the view we are exploring here: *that both organic and cultural change involve replicators and that new structures arise by selective retention of variants* [added emphasis].[80]

However, whereas Durham attempts to balance genetic and cultural replicators as different but equal units of reproduction, like Dawkins and Stiegler, De Landa points to the great speed of cultural evolution as a distinguishing factor in comparison with the leisurely pace of genetic evolution. For De Landa, this suggests that the effects of the latter on the former are *only marginal* and are best understood as 'the organic limitations imposed on us by our own bodies which can be called "human universals" as long as we do not attach any transcendental meaning to this term.'[81]

While this does not mean that De Landa discounts the significance of the human body in cultural evolution, compared with the treatment given to it by many of the other leading thinkers referred to in this book, the body thereafter recedes into the background of De Landa's otherwise all-encompassing perspective. Moreover,

From genes to memes

unlike Durham, who follows Dawkins and others in using the term 'meme' to cover all forms of cultural entities, no matter what their size or complexity might be, De Landa presents memes as *only one* of a number of different *kinds* of cultural replicators, among which he lists the kind of social norms and taboos included by Durham within the one concept. Both the 'flows,' as he describes them, of genetic and cultural replicators in turn are governed and constrained by the flows of matter and energy with which they interact and which make possible or limit the outcomes of that interaction, and vice versa: 'The role of genetic and cultural replicators (or, more accurately, of the phenotypic effects of those replicators) is to act as catalysts that facilitate or inhibit the self-organizing processes made possible by intense matter–energy flows.'[82] While De Landa thus accords the same importance to the phenotypic effects of cultural entities as Dawkins does to biological entities, memes themselves play a relatively limited role in his perspective: a cultural unit of imitation only, as he defines it,[83] no different from Dawkins' original definition but which, as we have seen, has since been the subject of much debate.

As important as Durham's broader theory of coevolution is, his interpretation of memes is weakened by a lack of any more precise definition than Dawkins' original interpretation. As a consequence, while consistently presenting genetic and cultural replicators as being different but more or less symmetrical dimensions of human evolution, he is unable to explain away the fundamental *asymmetry* between the relative precision of genes as replicators and the wide-open definition he offers of memes. The failure is all the more apparent when one considers that there is no *direct* means of cultural transmission from person to person and generation to generation equivalent to the sexual transmission of genes. For similar reasons, his proposed supplementary concepts, holomemes and allomemes, are limited by the same logic.[84]

The outcome is that, for all the daring scope and fertility of both Durham's and De Landa's theories, the issue of precisely how memes are assimilated and propagated among individuals and populations remains unresolved. In Durham's case, the problem is all the more pronounced since it means that, ultimately, his theory falls short of accounting for the rapid and self-perpetuating loss of human diversity that he was primarily concerned with in the first place. While all these writers have made valuable contributions to the field, the larger question of how the coevolution of humankind and technology actually works, and the nature and place of the self in that process, is at best therefore only partially settled at this point, leaving key pieces of the puzzle missing. The next part of the book will address these and other outstanding issues as we home in on a viable and comprehensive theory of the extended self.

The extended self

Part II summary

Commencing in Chapter 4 with an examination of Bernard Stiegler's theory of technics, the second part of this book opened up the scope of inquiry to take in the wider impact of technology on human evolution and the extended self. While Stiegler overlooks the making and use of tools by primates and other creatures, he argues convincingly that the accumulative effects of humankind's technical exteriorization, or what he crisply describes as the coevolution of the 'who and the what,' sets our species apart from any other. Selected writings from some of Stiegler's prominent followers and critics were also examined for what they contribute to our understanding of Stiegler's ideas and their possible further applications. Among the more telling criticisms, it was pointed out that Stiegler's stress on writing metaphors results in a biased emphasis on media at the expense of other culture-forms, the transmission and diffusion of which he leaves unexplained.

Similarly, though Stiegler's technics implicitly challenges natural selection as the primary mechanism of human evolution, both he and his followers continue to fall back upon neo-Darwinian concepts and terminologies in elaborating their ideas. In attempting to resolve these issues, Chapter 5 pursued the search for a coevolutionary theory of biology and matter for understanding evolution in general. Beginning with an account of Darwin's original theory, it progressed through an examination of some of the most recent critiques of neo-Darwinism, raising questions about some of its basic tenets. In particular, doubts were cast on the concept of natural selection itself, which the most radical critics like Jerry Fodor and Massimo Piattelli-Palmarini claim does not explain the evolution of organic life, let alone, as Timothy Taylor also argues, how humanity's unique powers of technology to change and dominate the natural environment might have evolved.

Theories of emergence and self-production, or autopoiesis as it is also called, were investigated in the same chapter as promising alternatives to orthodox evolutionary theory, proffering a concept of 'natural drift' in place of natural selection. The chapter concluded with a critical examination of applications of autopoiesis to human social systems, of which the most promising was the evolution of ideas themselves. During the course of the discussion, the concept of *types* also repeatedly surfaced as a key theme in the work of several writers, suggesting the basis for a general concept bridging both natural and artificial phenomena.

This led in turn to questions regarding the nature and definition of the principal agents involved in the evolution and proliferation of ideas, and their possible solution. In seeking answers to those questions, Chapter 6 explored Richard Dawkins' concept of the meme as the primary unit of cultural reproduction. Among other conclusions, several key lines of thought common to both Stiegler's theory of technics and discussions of the nature and function of memes came to the fore. Above all, both discourses revolve around the issue of exteriorization, whether it is the evolution of external memory, as described in Stiegler's work, or the location of memes within artifacts and other external sources. Just as important, both approaches are also equally inspired by evolutionary and genetic analogies and metaphors, with comparable debates in each case concerning their merits and limitations. Indicative of common weaknesses as well as strengths, Stiegler's assorted examples of what cultural programs consist of echo Dawkins' original and equally vague examples of what memes are, which had lasting and mostly confusing effects on subsequent debates on the subject, particularly regarding the issue of imitation or copying.

Not least, both memes and technics are frequently described as exhibiting evolutionary forces of their own, irrespective of the interests or well-being of their vehicles or users. Taylor's conclusion, as discussed in Chapter 5, that the discovery of simple technologies like the baby sling *precedes* cortical development rather than the other way around, lends powerful support to the same thesis, challenging the more ambiguous process of reciprocity described by Stiegler.

Among the more promising approaches in memetics was Kate Distin's interpretation of memes as generally applicable concepts such as types – an interpretation which, by definition, involves the ability to generalize. As the sole writer in Chapter 6 to address the subject of design, Distin also makes a brave attempt to interpret the design process in evolutionary and memetic terms. However, her chosen model of design as an objective process of research, invention and selection has been much criticized within the design professions as being unreflective of how designers really practice or how innovation actually works – subjects covered in Chapter 9 of this book. There also remains much confusion within the field as to the nature and function of memes and how they evolve. Most of this confusion arises from Dawkins' original definition of memes as being analogous to genes, and the resultant stress, as mentioned, on copying ideas and culture-forms rather than other less exact but more realistic forms of reproduction. The related insistence by some writers, including Distin and Robert Aunger, on a clear separation between memes and their vehicles creates another major stumbling block to further progress. Similarly, the attempts by most writers on the subject to isolate the meme and to break it down into its smallest possible components convey a reductionist perspective, of which Aunger's 'electric meme' is the most extreme example. Moreover, the same conception of memes as some kind of purified mental entity separate and distinct from the artifacts and techniques they are embodied in suggests a strong element of Cartesian dualism in both Distin's and Aunger's approach, all of which is at variance with the new thinking on evolutionary theory discussed in Chapter 5, pointing to serious weaknesses in the neo–Darwinian model and genetic metaphors underpinning memetic theory.

The last two writers covered in Chapter 6, William Durham and Manuel De Landa, both adopt a wider perspective and are more concerned with the *interactions* between genetic and cultural replicators than with either as separate entities. However, while Durham presents those interactions as a more or less symmetrical or balanced system of interrelations, De Landa, who quotes Durham's earlier work in his own writings as a positive approach, suggests that the relative speed of cultural change greatly diminishes the significance of those interactions. Unlike Durham, who accepts the concept of the meme as a basic cultural replicator of the kind described by Dawkins and his followers, De Landa also treats memes as only one among many different kinds of cultural replicators, encompassing language, taboos and other social constraints of the sort included by Durham within his own interpretation of memetic functions. However, while placing the meme firmly within a broader coevolutionary framework, both Durham's wide-open definition of memetic functions and De Landa's more limited interpretation of memes as copying mechanisms advance the concept of the meme itself little beyond Dawkins' original definition.

While Stiegler and the other key writers covered in the first two parts of this book therefore go a long way to clarifying the impacts of the coevolution of humankind and technology on the human mind and the self, the actual methods of extension and reproduction involved remain at best ill defined, leaving open the key question of just how the extended self actually evolves and functions. In answer to that question, the next few chapters posit several solutions revolving around a new and more rigorous concept of the meme, as a fusion of types and technics, the reproduction of which has its own defining characteristics.

Part III: Combinations

7 Types and taxonomies

Moving on from the work of clarifying which parts of the puzzle are missing, the remainder of this book is devoted to the main task of filling in those gaps, paramount among which is the problem of specifying the primary modes of cognition involved in creating and maintaining the extended self.

As the debates covered in Chapter 6 show, most of the confusion concerning the function and meaning of memes as agents of cultural evolution and diffusion arises from problems Richard Dawkins and his followers have in pinning down their cultural correlates, or explaining how they might be transmitted from person to person and spread through populations. However, while cultural replicators of the kind Dawkins posits may not be immediately recognized by the name or vague descriptions that have been given to them, it may be reasoned that sound evidence for their existence should nevertheless be detectable in everyday language and culture.

It will be argued in this and the following two chapters that such evidence is readily apparent in the ubiquitous naming and use of 'types,' whether of buildings, familiar artifacts or other technically inscribed culture-forms. Moreover, types, as manifest in taxonomies of all kinds, including species and building types as described in the following pages, indicate a *universal* process of diversification and reproduction common to all forms of evolution, whether they involve forms of life or cultural artifacts or their coevolution.[1] While the precise agents of reproduction may differ between life forms and material artifacts, therefore, they share common, time-dependent traits compatible with the more recent theories of evolution and self-producing systems outlined in Chapter 5. The idea of types therefore proffers an essential bridge between technics and a satisfactory reinterpretation of the meme, leading finally in the next chapter to the proposition of a universal agent of cultural evolution called the 'technical meme' as the vital link between the extended self of an individual and the broader culture in which that self is embedded.

Beginning with an examination of the cognitive basis and general significance of classification systems in human language and culture, the discussion in this chapter moves on to more detailed studies of the history and meaning of taxonomies in architecture, many of which have been influenced by biological analogies. There follows a summary of George Kubler's general theory of artifacts as 'linked problem solutions'[2] – a key source in this book for understanding how artifacts evolve. Some

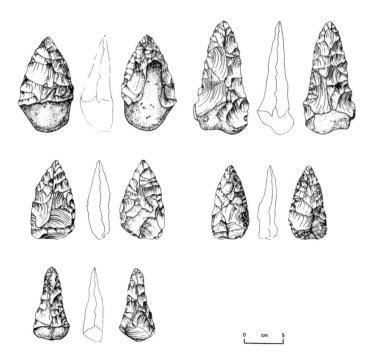

7.1 *Replicated hominid hand-axe forms indicating regional or tribal traditions of reproduction*

misunderstandings are also clarified concerning the narrow, logical interpretation of type and the more open interpretation used by naturalists and most other people when identifying things in the world around them. In conclusion, in line with Kubler's theory and John Minger's definition of an autopoietic system, a concept of types as self-producing systems is proposed, based on inferring relatively stable features from not one but a *series* of exemplars.

The roots of combinativity

A consistent theme in recent research into the origins and evolution of human language, as in the theories of human technics and evolution discussed in Chapters 4 and 5 and elsewhere in this book, is the reciprocity between the development of language and tool usage and other inventions. Evidence of the capacity for perceiving groups of tools as *types* of artifacts, and hence the ability to form classification systems and to reproduce useful features, can be seen in the earliest hand axes (fig. 7.1).[3] Thus, in discussing the emergence of symbolic thought, Henry de Lumley[4] argues that:

The extended self

The tool serves not only to dominate the exterior world *but also to understand it* [added emphasis]. The transmission of knowledge and skills indicates the appearance of the human communication system: the development of language structured from social experience.[5]

Other ideas and values of a very human sort emerged around the same time. The very earliest hand axes, writes de Lumley, 'show both lateral and bifacial symmetry, thus demonstrating early human acquisition of the notion of symmetry,'[6] while the Acheulean culture which followed soon after 'produced perfectly symmetrical and very regular tools, sometimes with the choice of rocks of a pleasing colour for their fabrication.'[7] None of which, de Lumley observes, served any functional purpose alone but which together suggest primitive aesthetic sensibilities: 'Hominisation thus passed a new threshold in the path towards greater complexity: the emergence of the sense of harmony.'[8]

In like fashion, beyond its purpose in cooking food and thus irrevocably changing the hominid diet and all that followed, the discovery of fire had other multiple effects, from providing light and warmth and facilitating migration to colder parts of the world, to the use of fire in hardening spear-points. However, de Lumley speculates there may have been still more to it than that:

> But fire was mainly a factor in inspiring conviviality. Group spirit was surely kindled around the hearth. This was the birth of the first myths. It is at this point that regional traditions emerged: the first cultural identities, showing styles and *designs* in the manufacture of some tools.[9]

No less significant, echoing the important discovery of canonical neurons noted in Chapter 3, Jonas Langer[10] contends that the propensity to group things together and give them names has deep roots in human cognition and the evolution of tool use and language. Asserting the universality of classification systems, he writes:

> Common general-purpose structures underlie logical cognition (e.g., classification, ordering, and quantifying), physical cognition (e.g., the causality involved in tool construction and use), and language. *A general-purpose structure that is central to both cognition and language is combinativity* [added emphasis]. Combinativity includes composing, decomposing, and recomposing operations. These operations construct fundamental elements, such as sets and series, without which cognition and language are not possible.[11]

All three cases of cognition and language, Langer argues, involve similar processes of discrimination: whether any given entities are identified as being different from each other or belonging to the same class (logical cognition); whether a given tool is intended to be used for a given purpose or end (physical cognition); and lastly which two or more symbols are conjoined to form a grammatical expression (language). Moreover, the same combinatorial skills are experimentally evident not only in human infants at an early stage in their lives, but also in at least two primates, cebus and macaques, tracing general powers of discrimination even further back in evolutionary time. However, when given more advanced tests in composing objects

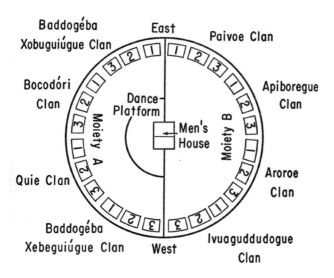

7.2 *Schematic plan of a Bororo village indicating main east–west axis, distribution of clans and other key elements symbolizing social and cosmological structure, after Claude Lévi-Strauss*

into sets at later ages, both primates hit apparently insurmountable cognitive barriers, while human infants forge ahead.[12]

In his ground-breaking studies of the taxonomies of indigenous tribes in central Brazil, Claude Lévi-Strauss[13] also provides ample evidence of the universal character of combinativity. Rejecting the commonly held beliefs of his time in the developed world regarding such cultures, Lévi-Strauss argued that the manner in which these so-called 'primitive' peoples named and differentiated one thing or form of life from another and related them together was indicative of systems of thought at least as sophisticated as those of modern human societies:

> Native classifications are not only methodical and based on carefully built up theoretical knowledge. They are also at times comparable from a formal point of view, to those still in use in zoology and botany [...]. It was a professional biologist who pointed out how many errors and misunderstandings, some of which have only been recently rectified, could have been avoided, had the older travellers been content to rely on native taxonomies instead of improvising entirely new ones.[14]

In his related studies of the villages of the Bororo and other South American tribes (fig. 7.2), Lévi-Strauss also showed how similar classification systems were interwoven into the actual spatial pattern and distribution of the dwellings and other elements of villages, examples which later made a considerable impression on

The extended self

architectural theorists searching for systems of meaning beyond the surface features of their subjects, leading to a whole new sub-discipline of semiotics.[15]

Such evidence not only points to the most fundamental cognitive and classificatory skills dating far back in human history, it also confirms what makes *Homo sapiens* so very different from other species, as those formative skills have been pursued to such extraordinary ends, not only in the sciences and in other culture-forms, but also in the everyday life of peoples at all stages of development.

Nature as model

The history of architectural theory and practice offers especially rich grounds for the study of combinatorial thinking, not only in the fundamental role the idea of types has played in the evolution of buildings of all kinds, but also from the frequent mixing over time with ideas derived from biological taxonomies, generally expressed in the form of organic analogies of one kind or another. In his brief but illuminating history of biological analogies in architecture, Peter Collins[16] traces their source back to the first half of the eighteenth century and the publication of the *System of Nature* by Carl Von Linnaeus[17] – the very first systematic attempt to classify different members of the vegetable and animal kingdoms. Believing, like most people of religious conviction at that time, that all forms of life had a divine origin, Linnaeus argued that every species has its own distinctive and *unchanging* structural features or 'style.'[18]

Linnaeus's pioneering work was followed by the first clearly enunciated theory of evolution, set out in the middle of the eighteenth century by Georges-Louis Leclerc, Comte de Buffon, in his *Natural History*.[19] Buffon strongly disagreed with the whole idea of immutable species advanced by Linnaeus, together with what he described as his 'arbitrary' selection of characteristics for classification.[20] Anticipating some of Darwin's principal ideas and methods by a full century, Buffon argued that 'all species must have derived from a single type,'[21] which he supported by empirical evidence gleaned from fossil shells and the recent discovery in his time of mammoth remains in Siberia. However, Buffon's theory was handicapped by his own religious beliefs – beliefs Darwin would also struggle with and eventually overcome – which caused him to exclude humans from the same evolutionary processes he applied to other species.

Nevertheless, for all the early stumbles, both men's works had a lasting impact on architectural theorists as well as the scientific world. Buffon was the first scientist to view both plants and animals within the same evolutionary framework, as variations of organic life, and therefore possessed of certain common properties as well as different characteristics – a view that was embraced by architects searching for a more harmonious relationship with nature. While Collins quickly dismisses Linnaeus as not being relevant to his own, more focused inquiry, the basic idea that different species might be classified by their primary characteristics (note also the reference to 'style' in Linnaeus's work, a topic he later lectured on) outlived the scientist's own flawed interpretation and has since been embraced by biologists everywhere.

Parts and wholes

Together with Linnaeus and Buffon, Baron Georges Cuvier[22] and D'Arcy Went-worth Thompson[23] also loom large in the pantheon of naturalists whose work has influenced architectural thought, directly or indirectly, the first for his observations on the relations of animal parts to their wholes and the second for revealing the structural principles underlying similarities of form between different species.

By David Young's account, Cuvier was particularly inspired by Aristotle's concept of 'final causes,' which stressed that each part of an animal or plant ultimately served a *specific purpose* in the life of that organism. Taking the idea a major step further, Cuvier argued that a creature could not be understood solely from inspection of its separate parts and their functions, but only by apprehending how they all related to and interacted in harmony with one another. As Young puts it, Cuvier deduced that: 'The life of an animal depends not only on the performance of certain functions *but on their coordination* [added emphasis].'[24]

In the first volume of his *Lectures in Comparative Anatomy*,[25] Cuvier set out the two rules guiding his methodology. The first, the 'correlation of parts,' expressed the idea of coordination. Thus 'an animal must have all parts of its body correlated with one another so as to fit it for a given way of life.'[26] The second, the 'subordination of character,' stressed that 'the most important parts of the body for classification are those that are least modified by adaptations to different ways of life.'[27] Thus a genus is identified by its relatively stable or invariant features, while individual species are identified by the *differences* in their parts, produced as a result of adaptation.

Cuvier applied his two rules to the study of a large range of animals in much detail, comparing the same parts across genera and species, so as to ascertain the reason for their differences. For example, Young writes, he found significant differences between the common parts of flesh-eating and plant-eating animals, which he deduced could be explained only by different diets and foraging habits:

> A flesh-eating animal must be able to see its prey, to catch it and to tear it apart. Hence it possesses legs adapted both for fast running and for grasping, as well as jaws with cutting teeth for tearing flesh. Cutting teeth are never found in the same species as a foot cased in horn that cannot be used for grasping. For hooves on the feet are correlated with a jaw bearing flat-crowned molar teeth for grinding food. All hooved animals are plant-eaters.[28]

For Cuvier, each part of an animal therefore embodied the whole, an insight he eventually extended to the study of animal fossils: 'Consequently, by looking at one single bone […] the appearance of the whole skeleton can be deduced up to a certain point.'[29] Cuvier concluded that by applying the same two rules of correlation and subordination to the reconstruction of skeletons from partial remains, he could arrive at a reasonable approximation of the whole, even when the remains of more than one species were mixed together in the same site, as frequently happens.

In his own comprehensive account of the biological analogy in design, while refraining from commenting on any similarities and differences between them,

7.3 *Drawing by A. Bartholomew comparing the counter-abutments of gothic vaulting with the human skeleton, an image popular with gothic rationalists*

Philip Steadman[30] devotes a whole chapter to classification systems in both the natural sciences and architecture. Steadman focuses particular attention on the impact of Cuvier's work on anatomical analogies in architecture, tracing it from Eugène Emmanuel Viollet-le-Duc's 'gothic rationalism' through the first skyscrapers in Chicago to the early modern movement. In its simplest interpretation, he writes, 'the anatomical analogy as applied to buildings takes the form of a simple metaphorical comparison of the skeleton of the animal with the supporting structural framework of columns and beams or piers and vaults.'[31] In particular, Viollet-le-Duc saw in the pared down, expressed elements of gothic architecture the structurally efficient frames of animal skeletons (fig. 7.3). He was also inspired by Cuvier to believe that the same method the founder of paleontology used to infer the whole of an animal's skeleton from its parts could also be applied to gothic structures: 'Just as when seeing the leaf of a plant, one deduces from it the whole plant; from the bone of an animal, the whole animal; so from seeing a cross-section one deduces the architectural members; and from the members, the whole monument.'[32]

7.4 *New York Life Building, Chicago, 1894, by Jenney and Mundie. Drawing showing 'skeleton' construction*

Anatomical thinking in architecture took another leap forward in the first skyscrapers with the separation of the load–bearing functions of the structural frame, or 'skeleton' (fig. 7.4), from the walls or 'skin' of the building, the weight of which, once relieved of their previous structural role, could be reduced to the minimum required to protect the building from the elements – a story that will be picked up again in Chapter 9. Le Corbusier's schematic 'Domino House' of 1914 completed the conceptual separation of structural skeleton from skin (fig. 7.5), further reduced by advances in glazing technology to a transparent film, except where the requirements of privacy or thermal insulation dictated otherwise.

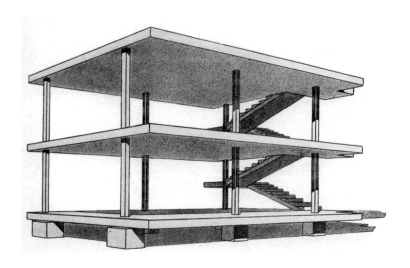

7.5 *Le Corbusier's Domino House, 1914*

In addition to Cuvier, Steadman makes repeated references to Thompson's classic study of morphology, *On Growth and Form*, first published in 1917, which, of all relevant biological studies, he suggests 'has most directly stimulated architects.'[33] Even a cursory look through Thompson's book, which is sprinkled with stress diagrams of bridges and other engineering structures compared with similar diagrams of the skeletons of animals and other creatures, will quickly reveal why it should have impressed architects so much, among other circles. The most influential part of the book though is Thompson's concluding chapter, 'On the Theory of Transformations, or the Comparison of Related Forms.'[34] Using a simple technique of grid deformation based on the method of coordinates devised by Descartes, Thompson uncovers startling similarities of surface form or skeletal structure between different species of the same genus, from fish to the skulls of primates and humans. While the coordinates of the grid stay in the same relationship to each other in each figure in the series as they do on the first example overlaid with a regular grid, the distances between the coordinates and the geometrical proportions of the grid are dramatically distorted in the other figures (fig. 7.6). Tracing the source of these transformations back to Galileo's original 'principle of similitude,' which governs the size and proportion of everything, be it living or non-living, according to the effects of gravity pulling on its weight, Thompson writes:

> [Galileo] said that if we tried building ships, palaces or temples of enormous size, yards, beams and bolts would cease to hold altogether; nor can Nature grow a tree nor construct an animal beyond a certain size, while retaining the proportions and employing the materials which suffice in the case of a smaller structure. The thing will fall to pieces of its own weight unless we either change its relative proportions, which will at length cause it to become clumsy, monstrous and inefficient, or else we must find new material, harder and stronger than was used before.[35]

Types and taxonomies

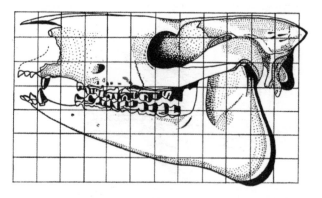

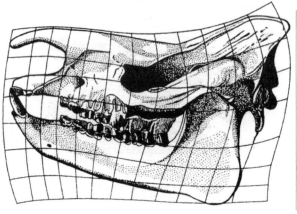

7.6 *Skulls of two species of primitive rhinoceros compared by the method of Cartesian deformation; by D'Arcy Thompson*

While Galileo could not have anticipated the invention of steel and reinforced concrete and its consequent liberating effects on the limitations of gravity on man-made constructions, now dramatically visible in the ever taller buildings springing up around the world, the principle of similitude still holds firm for explaining the relations between the growth and form of nature's creatures: why, for example, elephants have short necks to carry their large heads and great, stumpy legs to support their enormous body weight; why whales can grow to such a great size because they live in a medium which negates gravity's effects, and so on. Similarly, Steadman finds parallels in the application of the same principle in architecture, from neo-classical designs through to the modern period.

However, the most significant aspect of Steadman's work regarding the main theme of this book concerns his discussion of the influence of Lamarck's theories on the perception of tools and other cultural artifacts as embodied extensions of human evolution, in some respects not far removed from the theories outlined in earlier

The extended self

chapters. In a chapter titled 'Tools as Organs or Extensions of the Physical Body,'[36] Steadman suggests that, whereas social Darwinists applied neo-Darwinian metaphors to the evolution of human societies, in proposing that a species' characteristics might be partially acquired by non-genetic means during the lifetime of an organism by exposure to the environment, Lamarck was in effect unconsciously applying a metaphor of cultural evolution to nature, thus reversing the analogy. While, as previously noted, Lamark's theory of natural evolution has been rejected by most, if not all biologists, Steadman asserts that, as an explanation of *cultural* evolution, his theory was perfectly correct. Similarly, citing the distinction originally made by Alfred Lotka,[37] a theoretical biologist and demographer, between 'endosomatic' and 'exosomatic' hereditary systems, that is, between genetic evolutionary processes that take place 'within the body' as against cultural evolutionary processes that take place 'outside the body,' Steadman writes:

> The word 'exosomatic' hints at the notion of artifacts constituting a kind of shell or skin around a man's body, interposed by him between his naked self and the environment around. As P. B. Medawar puts it, tools are 'appendages, exosomatic organs if you like, that evolve with us.'[38]

Steadman goes on to recount similar metaphors used by other writers, including the famous analogies with the evolution of types of artifacts by Le Corbusier and Amédée Ozenfant.[39] However, adopting a typically cautious position he stops short of positing any kind of systemic reciprocity between the two hereditary methods, such as that suggested by Kevin Laland and John Odling-Smee in their theory of niche construction, or by William Durham and Manuel De Landa in their related theories of coevolution, and falls back instead upon the conventional hard line drawn between Lamarckian and Darwinian theories:

> Lamarkism was essentially an 'instructive' theory of evolution. An organism, so the theory suggested, somehow received instructions from its environment (acquired characters), and the information gained from these instructions could be passed on, genetically, to the next generation. But this is not a true picture, and instead the environment is now known to act in an 'elective' way, to bring out or choose genetic potentialities offered by the organism. In Medawar's words: 'So far as we know, the relationship between organism and environment in the evolutionary process is an elective relationship. The environment does *not* imprint genetical instructions upon living things.'[40]

Classifying building types

Given the prime importance of speciation in the development of biology and evolutionary theory, it is reasonable to expect a discussion of types as a comparable agent of development in biological models of design. While there was scant discussion of this kind in Collins' own account, aside from Steadman's more recent study there is plentiful evidence of the significance of building types in architectural history and theory from other sources, amounting to a tacit, if not wholly conscious, acknowledgment of their role in the evolution of human culture.[41]

Surprisingly, though, while human structures serving distinct, if not necessarily exclusive functions, such as dwellings, palaces, temples, tombs, arenas and markets, have been recorded from the earliest civilizations, prior to the late twentieth century, systematic studies of building types as such were few and far between. Significantly, the earliest, such as J. N. L. Durand's work in the early nineteenth century,[42] mainly focused on morphological types and their formal and spatial compositions, rather than their functional or social origins. In Steadman's view, this led to some basic contradictions in Durand's interpretation of types:

> What is paradoxical about Durand's system is that, despite the fact that the original classification of historical buildings is a functional one, at least at the level of the building's function as a whole, and despite the necessity for new building types being occasioned by the appearance of new functional demands – industrial, social and so on – *his compositional procedure is essentially a formal, geometric one, and not in a certain sense functional at all* [added emphasis]. The elements of composition are discrete structural units – columns, arches, domes – which are set together according to combinatorial rules and governed overall by geometrical constraints of symmetry.[43]

It was not until Nikolaus Pevsner published *A History of Building Types* in 1976[44] that social functions were treated as the primary generator of types. Even so, Pevsner's history goes no further back than the late twelfth century, and then only to cover government buildings of that time – the subject of the second chapter in his book, following monuments. Before then, Pevsner argues, the same governmental functions could be performed in a variety of different locations:

> Differentiation is a theme which will run through many of the chapters in this book. Nowhere is the development from multiple functions to single, rigidly special functions more patent than in medieval government buildings. Before the late twelfth century administration in general and the administration of law took place in the palace of emperor, king, prince, bishop, and if for some purpose extra space was needed, the churches and of course any public square where available.[45]

While Pevsner makes no explicit attempt to relate building types to biological species, there are clear allusions in the above passage to some kind of developmental process, whereby the emergence of more specific building types is closely linked to the differentiation of social functions – not greatly unlike the differentiation of species through time by adaptation to particular environments. Similarly, Pevsner's restricted focus on building types in the Western world, most of which also date back to the Industrial Revolution and related social and technological developments, can be explained by the earlier proliferation in the West of building types for specialized functions, including factories, offices, railway stations, banks, exhibition buildings, theatres (fig. 7.7) and department stores (Pevsner includes offices in the same chapter as warehouses – an idea office workers might not find flattering). Notably, he underlines the social origins of his types by distinguishing between the functional types

The extended self

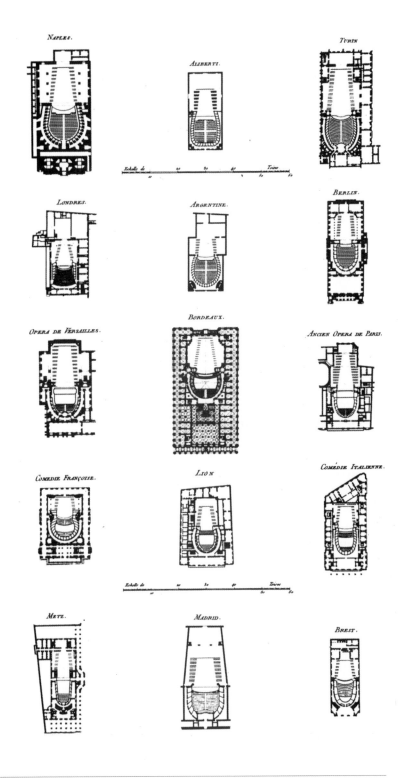

7.7 *Comparative plans of major eighteenth-century European theaters*

Types and taxonomies

themselves and the impact of architects on their design and form: 'The history of building types had fascinated me for many years, because this treatment of buildings allows for a demonstration of development both by style and by function, *style being a matter of architectural history, function of social history* [added emphasis].'[46]

For Pevsner, therefore, unlike Durand, who was totally absorbed in the dominant neo-classical culture of architecture in Paris, social function has a clear *a priori* role in shaping building types over stylistic approaches, which, he implies, are applied only *after* the basic form and spaces have already been resolved. At the same time, the distinction between types and styles allows for an inherent ambiguity in the relations between form and function already present, by his own account, in the flexible use of building forms in early architectural history, before more specialized types appeared.

Implicit and explicit meanings

More recently, following the example of Michel Foucault's[47] work on the relation between building types and structures of social power and control, both Thomas Markus[48] and Kim Dovey[49] have broadened the scope of Foucault's research, which concentrated mainly on penal institutions, to embrace a wider range of familiar building types from different historical periods.[50] Both authors also use a variation of the 'space syntax' method of analysis developed by Bill Hillier,[51] a graphical method of expressing the relations between spaces based on their usage and connectivity.

Like Pevsner, Markus and Dovey generally focus on relatively static models of building form and usage relating to specific periods of time and social conditions. Also like Pevsner, Markus concentrates his researches on the Enlightenment and Industrial Revolution, during which time most of the common building types of the modern world were created and which are most amenable to classification and social analysis. However, Markus not only rejects conventional art-historical and stylistic systems of classification, he also rejects any simplistic physical or visual equation of types and functions with specific activities or spaces, which rarely rises above the level of formal description. Strongly influenced by Umberto Eco[52] as well as by Foucault, Markus instead proffers a deeper, explanatory theory of social relations and the meanings those relations convey – what he calls the 'invisible structures' of buildings – the empirical evidence for which lies in various kinds of documented 'texts':

> Language is at the core of making, using and understanding buildings. Through it a community is able to articulate its feelings and thoughts about them, to share its experience of meaning. Much of what we think and feel is the direct outcome of descriptive texts – scholarly works, educational material, media productions, travel literature and exhibition catalogues. There is a host of prescriptive ones too such as competition conditions, briefs, legislation, building regulations, feasibility reports and design guides. These texts exist before a building is designed and yet in many ways 'design' it.[53]

Seen in this light, every building is a 'social object' and carries implicit and explicit meanings, both to the occupants and to others in the same society. Applying

The extended self

his own criteria, Markus identifies three main groupings of building types from his chosen era, not all of which have survived, at least not under the same names:

> those which control relations between people directly – schools, institutions of various kinds, buildings for cleansing and hygiene, clubs, assembly rooms and hotels; those which reproduce knowledge – museums, art galleries, libraries, exhibitions, panoramas and dioramas, learned institutions and mechanics' institutes; and those used for production and exchange – mills, production utopias, markets, shops and exchanges.[54]

Employing the documented evidence from the period, as well as Hillier's techniques of spatial analysis, Markus traces the power structures underlying the choice, organization and control of spaces and functions. For Markus, as with the new thinking on the politics of place in geographical circles noted in Chapter 1, the classification of types itself is inextricably associated with those same power structures – a way of putting things and people into their proper place, so to speak, and thus making them more amenable to social control:

> That buildings can be regarded as classifying devices is obvious in libraries where classification is overt and governs the location of books in space and the very structure of that space. *But all buildings classify something* [added emphasis].[55]

Markus thus effectively upturns the way we normally think about building types and systems of classification, and the relationship between classifier and classified. In Pevsner's schema, as in all conventional studies of building types, whether identified by function, morphology or style, the building is the passive object being classified by an external and presumably detached observer. But in Markus's schema, classification systems work both ways: the building itself is not only the initial object of classification but, once occupied, it also acquires the status of subject, and it is the *occupants and users themselves* and their social relations that are the objects being classified (figs 7.8 and 7.9).

The drawback to this approach, as Markus readily concedes at the beginning of his book, is that, while it opens up new dimensions of social understanding, it generally works best when the correspondence between building types and the strict social divisions they were designed to preserve and represent are relatively fixed, as they were during his chosen period in history. Striking an oddly nostalgic note of regret for the lost certainties of what was, by his own description, a rigid social order expressed in bricks and mortar, Markus observes that such matters are no longer as clear-cut as they once were:

> When the ordinary world is obscure and confused, digging beneath its surface is that much harder. This seems to have happened to towns and buildings as a result of an erosion which started some two hundred years ago, a period which, paradoxically, defined itself in terms of making the world clear through reason. Designers, scholars, critics and users now no longer seem to inhabit the same world. Many places no longer distinguish between public and private [...]. Ambiguity in forms, confusion about function, or labyrinthine space deprive towns and buildings of clarity. *Forms have become difficult to decode* [added emphasis].[56]

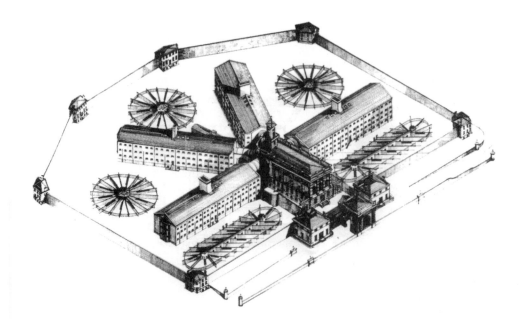

7.8 *Design (aerial view) of Pentonville Prison, 1842, showing similar radial configuration to the workhouse shown in fig. 7.9, indicating similar control regimes*

7.9 *Aerial view of design for a model workhouse for 300 persons, 1835*

The extended self

As Markus admits, as thorough as his theory and methodology are, they offer little guidance to more recent developments.[57] More problematic still, his reliance on the empirical evidence of texts offers no help at all in understanding how vernacular architecture in non-literate or pre-literate societies could have possibly evolved.

Global types

While both Markus and Dovey adopt similar approaches and methodologies, where Markus confines his analyses of building types to the early period of the Industrial Revolution, a significant part of Dovey's thesis on the creation of architectural and urban space is devoted to contemporary types. In turn, each of the three main types Dovey selects – office towers, shopping malls and suburban houses – can now be found in most parts of the world, including developing as well as developed countries, earning Dovey's classification of 'global types.'

However, as promising as the subjects of Dovey's researches are, the value of his observations, like that of Markus's own work, is ultimately limited by the relative narrowness of his approach – particularly his chosen sources of evidence. Commencing with his study of commercial office towers, Dovey's initial statements expose the author's ideological agenda and restricted methodology:

> I shall not discuss the intentions of the architects, nor the experiences of the users. This is not because these intentions and experiences are less important, *but in order to focus on the source of profit – the decision to lease* [added emphasis].[58]

Having excluded any other possible criteria or sources of information about the objects of his study, like Markus, Dovey bases his analysis on a selection of available texts written about several projects for office towers either completed or under construction in Melbourne – the author's home city – at the time of writing. However, whereas Markus draws upon a wide range of texts, including project briefs and communications between clients and designers, Dovey restricts his sources solely to the commercial advertisements commissioned for each project by developers to attract potential corporate investors and leaseholders. Like most such advertisements, these are all heavily focused on whatever distinctive *image* the design has that makes it stand out from its neighbors and competitors, thus supposedly enhancing its relative status and financial value as a preferred corporate location. Expressions of power and dominance in the skyline – and yes, phallic symbolism – proliferate in Dovey's analyses of these advertisements and, though obviously true as far as they go, they quickly become repetitive, adding little to common knowledge and cliché. While, as Dovey correctly points out, the competition to be the tallest among the tall and to offer the best views and therefore the most prestigious office spaces is self-defeating when one tower after another loses out to its taller and intrusive new neighbors, the same tight clusters are also responsible for what, in his only positive comment on the type, Dovey describes as the 'intoxicating effect' of the downtown skyline.[59]

Dovey's analysis of the interior planning of office towers and its relation to corporate power structures is equally restricted to what many contemporary designers of such buildings would now regard as an outdated stereotype, about which more will be said in Chapter 9. For example, in *The New Office*, Francis Duffy,[60] a British architect and renowned expert on office planning, covers a host of innovations in the design of office buildings of every kind, including high-rise types, none of which is touched on by Dovey. Moreover, as Duffy writes, they are all the outcome of significant changes in office organization and work practices:

> Invention in office design is not happening randomly. Innovations in the design of office furniture, in the ways that heating, lighting, air-conditioning, power, and information are distributed in office buildings, and in the configuration, construction and cladding of the buildings themselves, are all responses, of one kind or another, *to new ways of working* [added emphasis].[61]

Aside from ignoring changes in the design and use of office towers, Dovey neglects the main reason why corporations and other business users compete for the same patch of urban territory – namely what the social philosopher Manuel Castells[62] describes as the vital role of spatial proximity in 'the interactive nature of the innovation process.'[63] Castells argues that the same motivation holds for workers in information technology sectors as much as for any other enterprise, despite the possibilities for spatial dispersal such technologies offer. Face-to-face contact, the availability of all the support services and other attractions of urban centers, Castells maintains, have been not so much displaced by the information technologies all corporations and offices now rely upon as *supplemented* by them. However, having previously decided that what he wants to prove is that everything in high-rise architecture is done purely for the profit motive, Dovey – unwittingly, one suspects – selects only those sources of evidence relating to that motive.

Dovey fares little better in his analysis of shopping malls, and for much the same reasons. The spatial analysis he employs to compare variations of the classic mall plan, or 'genotype' as he calls it, is restricted to two large suburban malls in Australia first built in the 1960s and later expanded, together with a larger and more complex variation of the type in the UK. Consisting of large 'anchor stores' on the periphery linked by enclosed pathways and courts lined with smaller stores, the so-called 'dumb-bell' concept is purposefully designed to encourage impulse buying at the smaller stores along the pathways, while also channeling customers into the anchor stores.

Following the dramatic post-war expansion of the suburbs in the USA and Australia, enclosed shopping malls designed according to the dumb-bell model proliferated across both countries as retailers relocated their outlets closer to dispersed urban populations. However, while similar examples of the stereotypical, fully air-conditioned mall are now being built all over China and other developing countries, there has been a precipitous decline in the popularity of the type in the USA, where the idea originated. Dozens of malls have now closed all over the country, leaving vast empty shells in their wake – a decline preceding but hastened

7.10 *Rouse Hill town center, northwest Sydney*

by the global financial crisis of 2008. Though critics of suburbia would no doubt agree with Dovey's comments on the phoney role of shopping malls of this kind as self-contained community centers, where new malls have been or are being built in the USA they are also now designed quite differently from the classic enclosed model, as mainly open-air shopping centers (the last fully enclosed mall built in the USA was opened in 2006).[64] Similarly, the very newest suburban malls in Australia, such as the one at Rouse Hill located on the planned extension to the main suburban railway line northwest of Sydney, are also now designed more like genuine town centers themselves, with open-air streets and interconnecting alleyways, together with apartments over sidewalk shops and cafes (fig. 7.10).[65]

Dovey is on only slightly firmer ground with his study of the archetypal detached suburban dwelling and the nuclear family structure it is designed around. As with the other two studies, Dovey identifies a common genotype for the planning of a suburban house, variations of which he presents using the same method of spatial analysis he used for his examples of shopping malls. Following the arguments by P. Saunders and P. Williams[66] that suburban family houses function as 'social factories' or 'engine rooms' for the reproduction of social life, Dovey breaks the genotype down into four primary spatial elements: a formal living zone comprising the living room, dining room, entrance hall and other spaces open to visitors; an informal living zone including the kitchen, breakfast area and games room, reserved for family use only; and the two most private zones in the house, comprising a secluded master bedroom suite and minor bedroom zone for children and guests. While Dovey concedes that Saunders and Williams' approach smacks of mechanistic and deterministic concepts, he broadly accepts the two researchers' view of the family dwelling and its social functions:

> It is the setting which makes interaction meaningful and predictable, linking intimate emotional and sexual life to economic and political life. It both reflects and reproduces the social world of gender, age and class relations.[67]

Using the same methodology he used for the office towers, Dovey looks outward to a selection of advertisements produced by commercial developers of new housing estates for a reading of the significance attached to the different features, according to the social level of potential consumers the advertisements are pitched at. As with the previous analysis, Dovey's observations on these rarely rise above the obvious or popular stereotypes, such as the appeal to the status value of the house, especially to social climbers, or the centrality of the kitchen and the family area in home life, over which the housewife presides: 'Leave your Husband,' suggests one bold advertisement quoted by Dovey, 'for he will never understand a woman's love of the kitchen.'[68]

While on the face of it Dovey's analysis of the gender and family relationships embodied in the type would appear to support the theory of the extended self proposed in this book, the deterministic nature of his approach severely undercuts the value of the study. As we saw in the preceding section, unlike Dovey, Markus himself was keenly aware of the ambiguity in the relations between building form and social function in modern buildings and the consequent difficulty in reading consistent meanings into the contemporary built environment, as compared with earlier periods. Put another way, for all the supposed effectiveness of the open marketplace and related advertising media – an effectiveness that Dovey apparently never questions – it is doubtful that the 'fit' between occupants and house is dictated solely by the advertised criteria. Rather, choice may instead be governed by a whole range of other social and economic factors, such as price and location of employment, distance from the central city, schools and other amenities not covered by Dovey's narrow focus on the dwelling type itself and those who are selling it – factors dictated as much by available transportation systems as anything else, particularly in the USA and Australia, from where his examples are taken.

In this regard, given the importance of affordable private transportation in the history of urban dispersal, it is surprising that Dovey omits any mention or discussion at all of the automobile in his analysis.[69] Neither the shopping mall nor the suburban house would exist without it, yet Dovey's types function in an urban vacuum, devoid of any infrastructure or wider environmental context. As Ruth Brandon[70] points out in her study of the impact of the automobile on suburban life, *Auto Mobile: How the Car Changed Life*, among other things it had drastic effects on gender roles, more so perhaps than any internal or external features of suburban houses could possibly have by themselves. As late as 1987, against 70% for men of the same age, only 30% of American women aged over 70 held driving licenses, many of whom, given the great proportion of Americans living in suburbs by that time, would have been effectively confined to their homes for most of their adult lives:

> It would clearly be nonsensical to suggest that the suburbs were designed with female segregation in mind. But that they marked the victory of a particular view of women's lives is inarguable. Cities teemed with opportunity, for women as well as men; by retiring to the suburbs, and confining their lives within a purely domestic setting, women turned away from those opportunities.[71]

More seriously still, Dovey not only ignores the infrastructure which makes the suburban way of life possible and shapes it in countless ways, but by restricting his sources of evidence to the developers' own advertisements, as with his use of the same sources in his other studies, rather than offering a genuine critique of the developers' view of reality, Dovey in effect endorses that view.

Urban typologies

In stark contrast to the preceding three writers, in *The Architecture of the City*, Aldo Rossi[72] emphatically refutes any deterministic or fixed, one-to-one correspondence between spatial form, function and meaning, whether imposed or otherwise. Taking an altogether different position, Rossi suggests that, in many cases, specific morphological types and typologies may develop a life and symbolic function of their own, depending upon the broader urban context in which they evolve.

Renouncing the orthodox modernist obsession with the building as object, Rossi's remedy is to reinstate the model of the historical European city and its densely knit forms and spaces as his primary source and guide. In this regard, Rossi's work parallels the arguments of other critics of the period, like Colin Rowe,[73] who coined the phrase 'the crisis of the object' in pinpointing the weaknesses of the characteristic urban spatial pattern favored by orthodox modernists but rejected by theorists like Norberg-Schulz and Lynch, as outlined in Chapter 1. Exemplified by Le Corbusier's drastic 1925 Plan Voisin scheme for central Paris (fig. 7.11) and adopted as the spatial pattern for countless post-war reconstruction projects, the approach effectively reverses the historical relation of solid to void, clearing entire city blocks and urban quarters and creating clusters of free-standing towers and other structures in their place.

However, aspiring to the creation of an 'urban science,' Rossi also attempts a more objective and deeper analysis of urban space and form, for which he reaches outside conventional historical frameworks for key ideas and methods. For Rossi, the historical city and its component structures have to be understood not simply as artifacts but as a time-related *process*, the keys to which are typology and the comparative method. He also alludes to linguistics as a model for distinguishing between the relatively fixed and changing elements of the city:

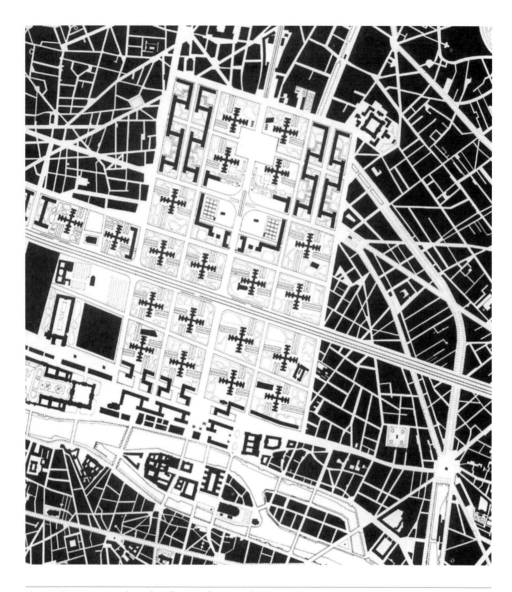

7.11 *Figure-ground study of part of Le Corbusier's Plan Voisin, Paris, 1925, graphic by Stuart Cohen and Steven Hurtt*

Among the various methods employed in this study of the city, the most important is the comparative one. Because the city will be seen comparatively, I lay particular emphasis on the importance of the historical method; but I also maintain that we cannot study the city simply from a historical point of view. Instead we must carefully elaborate a city's enduring elements or permanencies so as to avoid seeing the city purely as a function of them. I believe that permanent elements can even be considered pathological at times. The significance of permanent elements in the study of the city can be compared to that

The extended self

which fixed structures have in linguistics; this is especially evident as the study of the city presents analogies with that of linguistics, above all in the complexity of its processes of transformation and permanence.[74]

Similarly, Rossi classifies building types according to their relative stability and time-related significance in the life and history of the city. Individual houses are the most changeable kind, though 'housing,' in so far as the type may refer to whole residential quarters of a city, may comprise some of its most stable components. More generally, Rossi defines 'the concept of type as something that is permanent and complex, a logical principle that is prior to form and that constitutes it.'[75] However, while building types are commonly identified by their social function – an uncritical habit of thought Rossi dismisses as 'naïve functionalism' – a type itself cannot be reduced solely to that function, but has a life and import in the city beyond its specific use at any point in time:

> Such classifications presuppose that all urban artifacts are created to serve particular functions in a static way and that their structure precisely coincides with the function they perform at a certain moment. I maintain, on the contrary, that *the city is something that persists through its transformations* [added emphasis], and that the complex or simple transformations of functions that it gradually undergoes are moments in the reality of its structure.[76]

Following the same line of argument, the most enduring and important class of building types for Rossi are 'monuments,' which he also describes as the 'primary elements' of the city. However, unlike the obelisks, rotundas and other monuments in Pevsner's study, whose sole purpose is entirely symbolic, Rossi's urban monuments are not necessarily originally intended as such. A monument might therefore be designed for a specific function at the time of its building but then *acquires* its broader meaning in the life of the city over a period of time, often surviving several changes in use. Consequently, monuments are charged over and above any normal function they might have at any one time, with a special role as the carriers of the city's past into the future, or what, following Marcel Poëte and Pierre Lavedan,[77] Rossi calls the city's 'persistencies':

> These persistencies are revealed through monuments, the physical signs of the past, as well as through the persistence of a city's basic layout and plans [...]. Cities often remain on their axes of development, maintaining the position of their original layout and growing according to the direction and meaning of their older artefacts, which often appear remote from present-day ones.[78]

By the same criteria, Rossi distinguishes the aforementioned 'pathological' or 'dead' permanent elements from 'living' monuments. Taking the historical examples of the Palazzo della Ragione in Padua, Italy, and the Alhambra in Granada, Spain, Rossi argues that the former, by virtue of its central location in the city and contemporary adaptation as a marketplace, retains its vitality, as well as being regarded as a work of art. By contrast, the Alhambra 'stands virtually isolated in the city; nothing can be added.'[79] Having lost its original purpose as a royal residence, Rossi suggests, the Alhambra functions now only as a beautiful but empty museum of architecture, relating only to the past.[80]

While the strength of Rossi's arguments lies in his stress on process and the long-term, changeable aspects of building types and their meanings, as with Norberg-Schulz's and Lynch's studies, his theory of types is limited by being mostly focused on the historical city as the main source of his exemplars. For instance, while Rossi accepts the individual dwelling as a fundamental building type, neither any dwelling types nor even residential quarters belong as vital components in Rossi's conception of the city as an artifact: 'Where the city as a whole seems to be of primary importance, where density and size are predominant, the housing problem seems to be of less importance, or at least becomes less focused with respect to the other functions of urban life.'[81]

Rossi's focus on the relatively static aspects of building type and form, or the city's 'persistencies' as he describes them, also neglects a simple but vital historical fact: not only building functions, but also building types and forms themselves *evolve over time*, as will be apparent from a study of architectural history in any part of the world. Just as seriously, as with the former three authors, the impact of transportation on the form of cities and building types is barely mentioned. Commenting on the lack of transportation systems in ancient cities – a major reason in itself for the high densities and compact forms of those cities that Rossi, like Norberg-Schulz and Lynch, extols for their environmental qualities – Rossi goes on to voice his doubts about their general significance:

> Yet it is difficult to prove that this relationship is the determining factor [in shaping urban space]. This is to say that the form of the city has not yet been determined by a particular system of public transportation, *nor in general can such a system be expected to produce a certain urban form or to follow it* [added emphasis].[82]

The unfortunate result of these and other neglects in Rossi's work (except for a brief coverage of Berlin's garden suburbs, modern building types are also ignored) was that they encouraged a whole generation of postmodern architects to pass over the more profound aspects of Rossi's theory of urban types and to indulge in an orgy of eclectic form, pillaging from the past irrespective of any contemporary purpose or meaning, a movement which still continues in many parts of the world, even though it has long been rejected by some of its former leaders.[83]

Linked problem solutions

So far, all the writers whose works have been discussed on the subject of species and types were biologists, zoologists or architectural historians and theorists. The first to attempt to bridge the ideas of speciation and of types of artifacts was George Kubler, an art historian and interdisciplinary theorist. Kubler's seminal work, *The Shape of Time*,[84] published in 1962, not only challenged conventional art histories but also set a precedent for many later debates on the subject of innovation, as well as the application of biological and evolutionary models to design.[85] While Kubler included architecture within the scope of his work, his interests ranged far wider, to include all manner of artifacts:

> Let us suppose that the idea of art can be expanded to embrace the whole range of man-made things, including all tools and writing in addition to the useless, beautiful, and poetic things of the world. By this view the universe of man-made things simply coincides with the history of art. It then becomes an urgent requirement to devise better ways of considering everything men have made. This we may achieve sooner by proceeding from art rather than from use, for if we depart from use alone, all useless things are overlooked, but if we take the *desirableness of things* [added emphasis] as our point of departure, then useful objects are properly seen as things we value more or less dearly.[86]

If we are to understand the place and value of artifacts in human life, Kubler reasons, neither utilitarian concepts of function nor conventional interpretations of works of art as having a value over and above, say, the usefulness of a portrait as a likeness will suffice. Going further than Rossi, Kubler stresses the importance of process over time in the evolution of morphological types themselves, as well as the relations of form to function within individual types identified with specific historical periods. In Kubler's broad universe, *all* things may be understood as chains of 'linked problem solutions' or *series* of artifacts related through time both by common purpose and by formal similarities, all of which have a greater or lesser cultural value of some kind:

> In short, all materials worked by human hands under the guidance of connected ideas developed in temporal sequence. *From all these things a shape in time emerges* [added emphasis]. A visible portrait of the collective identity, whether tribe, class or nation, comes into being.[87]

Having opened up the field of art history beyond the usual exceptional works to all the creations of humankind, Kubler then proceeds to attack art historians' fondness for seeing all art as the product of individual genius or lesser talents, the study of which is best approached by biographical studies of the individuals or groups concerned, together with exhaustive catalogues of their creations. The problem with the biographical view, Kubler argues, is that the focus on the lives of individual artists and their works ignores the larger historical perspective: 'In the long view, biographies and catalogues are only way stations where it is easy to overlook the *continuous nature of artistic traditions* [added emphasis].'[88] In a perceptive metaphor, Kubler likens the biography of an artist to restricting the view of an entire railway network of a country to the personal experience of a single traveler along one or a limited number of tracks. Inevitably, the larger picture will never be understood: 'To describe railroads accurately, *we are obliged to disregard persons and states* [added emphasis], for the railroads themselves are the elements of continuity, and not the travellers or the functionaries thereof.'[89]

Types and taxonomies

As with the railway journey, Kubler continues, every artist's lifework takes place within a series of related events reaching either backwards or forwards in time, or maybe in both directions, 'depending upon his position in the track he occupies.'[90] For Kubler, the stature and historical importance of an individual artist is measured not so much by any personal gifts or talent, which may be equally shared among several artists in a given period, but by his or her *position of entry* into the sequence of related creations. Thus the earlier the entry of an artist into a new series, the greater the impact and consequent fame of that individual, while an equally talented individual entering later down the same track will invariably get less credit, no matter how well executed the later work might be. In common parlance, for Kubler, being in the right place at the right time is what counts in art, as with most other fields of human endeavor.

Similarly, Kubler classifies related artifacts themselves according to their position in time within the same series. As the name suggests, 'prime objects' occupy prime position as the first of their kind in any series and set the pattern or template for subsequent 'replicas' of the original creation. In turn, replicas are identified by a set of formal characteristics common to the whole series that can be traced back to the prime object. Finding inspiration for his ideas in various disciplines outside normal art-historical discourses, Kubler writes:

> The mathematical analogy for our study is topology, the geometry of relationships without magnitudes or dimensions, having only surfaces and directions. The biological analogy is speciation, where form is manifested by a large number of individuals undergoing genetic changes.[91]

Also borrowing from the new sciences of information and communication theory, Kubler sought to explain how differences between replicas might occur, employing concepts like 'drift,' 'noise' and 'interference' in the same way a biologist might explain genetic variations among species as the result of random mutations. Nevertheless, like other writers cited here, Kubler was also cautious about stretching the analogy too far. While biological and evolutionary models might account for the great majority of subtle changes and modification of artifacts over time, he concedes they cannot explain the more rare but game-changing innovations that occur in art, which, he suggests, have no parallel in nature. Thus prime objects are distinguished by radical human innovations, while the more common replicas are the outcome of step-by-step, evolutionary-like processes.

A question of logic

The vital subjects of change and innovation in the evolution of types, together with Kubler's position on the matter, which varies between publications, will be revisited in later chapters of this book. However, not every writer on the subject is convinced that types can be so broadly described, nor even of their importance. Aware of the implications for cultural evolution, Timothy Taylor briefly comments on memetic theory, about which he is critical. According to Taylor, who also equates memes with types, they just do not exist in any reliably repeatable form. This, he claims, is the main problem with memes – there is nothing in culture that can be reliably replicated. To make his point, Taylor describes all the possible variations of chairs one can think of. Whatever potentially consistent elements one might find, such as a seat, a back, legs and arms, he suggests we can always find some exceptions:

> It turns out there is no rule that defines a chair. The idea we have of a chair *in practice* is a fuzzy intersect of attributes, none of which is in and of itself both sufficient and necessary for inclusion in the category.[92]

As odd as Taylor's view seems – as documented in this chapter, the idea of types and the classification systems they belong to are widely accepted as basic features of human cognition and language – the reason for his outright denial of types may be traced back to the early history of biological classification systems. For Taylor, definitions of types are a question of pure logic – note the stress on the logician's phrase 'sufficient and necessary' in the above quotation. As John Wilkins,[93] an authority on speciation, explains, overriding many past and present interpretations of species and types is the strictly logical or 'essentialist' version (it might equally well be called the 'idealist' view) due to Aristotle and Plato: either a species meets the necessary and sufficient conditions for membership, or it does not. In stark contrast to the more open Darwinian view, there is no room in such a definition for equivocation, or for any changes in those conditions:

> The essentialism story is the view that has taken biologists and philosophers by storm. Primarily advocated, and largely developed (I hate to say 'invented') by Ernst Mayr, it is the view that there are basically two views of biological taxa in general and species in particular. One is the view derived from Plato and Aristotle, on which all members of a type were defined by their possession of a set of necessary and sufficient properties or traits, which were fixed, and between which there was no transformation. This is variously called *essentialism, typological* or *morphological thinking*, and *fixism*. The other is a view developed in full by Charles Darwin, in which taxa are populations of organisms with variable traits, which are polytypic (have many different types) and which can transform over time from one to another taxon, as the species that comprise them, or the populations that comprise a species, evolve. *There are no necessary and sufficient traits* [added emphasis]. This is called *population thinking*.[94]

While Aristotle's original distinction between genus and species was generally accepted, according to Wilkins most naturalists rejected any finite definition of those concepts: 'species were just things that naturalists began to pay attention to in the sixteenth century and thereafter.'[95] In actual practice, given that new variations were and still are being constantly discovered, it is impossible to know in advance all the characteristic features of a polytypic taxon. The approximate criteria for speciation generally adopted by naturalists were accordingly more flexible and open to redefinition than the essentialist approach allows for. As Wilkins puts it: 'The only thing in common with logical and biological species was the word.'[96]

Types and taxonomies

7.12 *Dining chair and side chair, 1958, by Charles Eames. Though manufactured with identical materials and techniques, the dining chair (left) is easily distinguished from the lower side chair*

Contrary to what Taylor asserts, therefore, if a type can have multiple variations of form and material, that is no more reason to doubt the existence of persistent attributes and functions over time than multiple variations of a given polytypic genus or species are reason to doubt their own existence and persistence over time. Even without the recent neurological and cognitive evidence for the formation of types and taxonomies in the mind described earlier, there is more than ample evidence in everyday life for their existence. Within the type called 'chair,' for example, we can find clusters or populations of many different lower-order types, such as 'dining chair,' 'desk chair,' 'lounge chair,' 'deck chair,' and so forth, all of which are designed for humans to sit in or on, but which have distinct *uses* as well as physical features of their own (fig. 7.12).[97] While the chair meme may therefore include a great many types, each of those variations will have a narrower if still flexible set of requirements that provide an essential guide to the designer, as well as to the user or purchaser. If, say, Taylor himself were to walk into a furniture store and ask to see a range of desk chairs or lounge chairs, he would be rightly surprised and probably annoyed with the salesperson if he were shown a range of dining chairs instead. While we may no longer be at risk of confusing prey from predator as our ancestors were, we nevertheless rely upon being able to distinguish between one type of thing and another to get by in the world, so much so that we mostly take it for granted, as perhaps Taylor unconsciously does.

Self-producing types

Summarizing the argument on the significance of taxonomies and types, clearly, if a theory of memes as a means of cultural transmission is going to be taken seriously, then it must be equally applicable to methods of reproduction that existed before the dawn of copying machines or computers, important as they are in our own time, and should account for the multiplication of variations as well as more exact replications. Generally speaking, therefore, in the absence of any other clear sources, *memes must be derived directly from artifacts*, just as Dennett and Blackmore suggest. However, this would appear to contradict Distin's special concept of the meme as a type, or generally applicable information. Recall that, according to Distin, in order for a person to be able to discriminate key characteristics of the type from all its variations, and so be able in turn to replicate those essential features, a meme must *already exist* in the mind of a person, or else in some separate form like a blueprint (in both the narrow and the broader meaning of the term). In this regard Distin is therefore in agreement with Aunger, who, as was noted in Chapter 6, insists on the separate identity of memes as neurological phenomena, *preceding* any external embodiment in artifacts.

The solution to this apparent conundrum is that artifacts do *not*, for all practical purposes, actually exist themselves as isolated or discrete phenomena, and are rarely studied as such, but *acquire their identity as one of a series of similar artifacts*, much as Kubler describes them, as linked problem solutions. Thus every artifact has its precedent and its progeny. Consequently, to repeat Dennett's insight, the 'brilliant idea of a wagon with spoked wheels'[98] is not carried by any single exemplar, but by an endless string of similar wagons with spoked wheels and other related characteristics: 'Like genes [memes] depend on the existence of a continuous chain of physical vehicles, persisting in the face of the Second Law of Thermodynamics.'[99] *Only by observing that the same characteristics or features are replicated many times over from artifact to artifact can a person identify the type.* Put another way, when identifying a type, which is to say a general class of objects, a person *infers* the relevant information defining the type from observing numerous exemplars.

Similarly, it may be asked whether the same description qualifies types as self-producing systems. Or, to be more precise, do types and taxonomies as described above fulfill the three conditions for self-production quoted from Mingers in Chapter 5? Pending further elaboration, a tentative answer in the affirmative might be set out as follows:

1. The components of classification systems are types, which are defined by and in turn constitute the class of which they are members, in a *reciprocal process* of self-production.

2. A type is embodied in a *series* of objects or other entities like organizations and has distinct *boundaries* that define and sustain its *identity as a whole* over time and space, while interacting with its environment and other types.

3. As a self-producing system, a type is a *process of classification* and describes the *production* of the type and the class to which it belongs, not their specific contents.

Pursuing the case, in response to Mingers' related question as to what it is, if not biological human beings themselves,[100] that social systems produce, a fourth, summary proposition may be added as follows:

4. *The products of social systems are types*: whether of social roles or groups, communities, occupations, activities and governing systems, and such like, together with the buildings, settlements and other culture-forms they are embodied in, which in turn reproduce the social systems of which they are the components.

In short, *types and taxonomies are to human societies as species and genera are to natural ecologies*. Moreover, as both the primary products and components of societies, types and their classes exhibit the basic features of all rule-governed social systems: whether inscribed in buildings and other artifacts, social institutions, customary forms of behavior or cultural media of one kind or another, types and taxonomies *follow a pattern*, that is, a set of *rules* that guarantee minimum levels of consistency and predictability, and are thus easily recognized by members of the same society and culture, though not necessarily by outsiders, as was noted in Chapter 1.[101] In turn, where there is consistency and predictability in human societies, there is also *conformity*, with all its potential drawbacks in a changing world as well as its social advantages. Were it not for those qualities, types could not do their job, which is to reproduce themselves through the members of the social system and the extended selves they sustain.

The next chapter takes up the issue of the differences as well as the similarities between the evolution of types and species and defines those agents of reproduction particular to human cultures.

8 Technical memes and assemblages

Drawing together the key ideas set forth in previous chapters, it is now possible to spell out the agents of cognitive extension that create and sustain relations between the human self and the complex environment in which it evolves. To that end, the present chapter proffers the linked concepts of 'technical memes and assemblages' as embodied clusters of material, social, cultural and psychological phenomena, as manifest in the reproduction of building types and other artifacts.

The chapter commences by examining the ambiguous nature of form and purpose in architecture, as opposed to their isomorphic relations in organic species, the qualities of which inspired much of the theorizing about biological analogies discussed in the previous chapter. It then proceeds to a definition of the technical meme as the primary agent of cognitive extension and cultural transfusion by which the extended self assimilates and interacts with the material and social environment. It is suggested that, with appropriate adjustments, assemblage theory also offers a suitable framework for exploring the grouping and wider effects of technical memes, in keeping with the principles of combinativity and interaction described in this book, while still accommodating their separate identities.

The rest of the chapter takes a close look at some of the more significant coevolutionary assemblages of technical memes in history that changed the shape of human transportation and urban life, from the simple spoked wheel to the automobile and freeway, transforming the spatial reach of the extended self in the process and creating the kinds of homes, cities and other places people commonly live in and identify with today. It concludes with a brief discussion of some of the related social effects generated by those assemblages in the course of their evolution.

Form and content

In all the studies of building types outlined in the preceding chapter, what stands out from the various interpretations and qualifications is the authors' shared conviction of the singular importance of the basic concept in shaping the course of architectural and urban development. As far as similarities with the concept of species go, it is safe to say, therefore, that the generality of types in architectural theory and practice is comparable to the role the former concept plays in biology and evolutionary theory. Moreover, there are distinct similarities between the interpretations of each concept within their respective disciplines, some of which are highlighted in George Kubler's theory of linked problem solutions, which, as noted in the previous chapter, borrows heavily from biology and evolutionary theory. There are clear parallels, for example, between tracing a species back in time to its earlier parentage and tracing a series of artifacts back in time to a 'prime object.' And while Kubler himself draws our attention to what he describes as the unique character of radical innovation in the evolution of human artifacts, it will later be argued that here, too, there are important correspondences with the emergence of new species in nature.

More generally, the parallels between species and types as systems of classification are strong enough to suggest that the two ideas are at least in some respects virtually interchangeable. For example, there is little difference in principle between the manner in which Kubler uses the language of topology to describe the transformations of form over time within a series of artifacts, and the way that D'Arcy Thompson uses the same approach to delineate the transformations of structures.[1] Similarly, in *Shapes*, the first of his trilogy of books, *Nature's Patterns*, building on Thompson's work Philip Ball[2] defines form in nature in terms that are equally appropriate to types of artifacts:

> I would define [form] loosely as the *characteristic shape of a class of objects* [added emphasis]. Just as our brains allow us to organize a field of similar shapes into a pattern, so they are adept at somehow discerning commonalities of form between diverse objects – although we find it equally hard to explain exactly why. Objects with the same form need not be identical, or even similar in size; they simply have to share certain features that we recognize as typical, even stereotypical. The shells of sea creatures are like this: those of organisms of the same species tend to be identifiably akin even to the untrained eye. The same is true of flowers and of the shapes of mineral crystals. You might say that the 'form' of these objects is a rather Platonic concept – that which remains after we have averaged away all the slight variations between individuals.[3]

While no architectural historian or theorist has yet come up with a systematic nomenclature to match biologists' lists of genera and species – to be fair, it took biologists centuries to sort out their own systems – similar distinctions are also discernable between primary or higher-order building types, like dwellings, offices, factories and government buildings, and common variations within those primary types, that is, huts, detached houses and apartments under 'dwellings' and all the subdivisions within those classes, and so on, comprising whole lineages of types not unlike biology's generic or family 'trees.'[4]

However, the requirements of empirical evidence needed to identify the members of a genus or species of organism within the science of biology, though not without sufficient flexibility to accommodate new members, are significantly more stringent than they are in the cultural realm of types and artifacts, and are likely to remain so except perhaps for some branches of the social sciences. In turn, there is the major problem of the relations between form and content and how they are treated in each case. Clearly, since the 'environment' in human culture is largely a product of human activity itself, there will inevitably be differences between organic species and human artifacts regarding form and function and any related concepts of 'fitness' to their respective natural or cultural environments. No less important, the means by which the characteristics of an individual species are transferred from one generation to the next differ significantly – notable exceptions yet to be discussed apart – from the way that human artifacts are propagated, there being no *direct* physical or chemical equivalent in the latter to genetic inheritance in the former.

As was evident in the last chapter, opinions among architectural historians and theorists themselves regarding the relations between building form and function or any other kind of meaning and content vary widely, from the more simplistic biological analogies criticized by Peter Collins and Philip Steadman, through the deterministic theories of social control advanced by Thomas Markus and Kim Dovey, to the more open and ambiguous relations described by Aldo Rossi.[5] The issue is further complicated by the emergence of architectural *styles* and related formal and aesthetic movements as virtually separate developments in the evolution of building types, synonymous with the rise of professional classes of master builders, architects and other designers,[6] an issue that Nikolaus Pevsner identifies in the distinction he makes between style and function quoted in the last chapter: 'style being a matter of architectural history, function of social history.'[7]

While many architects might claim otherwise, building types themselves are also rarely invented by their designers, but are the outcome of complex social, economic and technological developments that are only fully understood in hindsight, *after* the type has become firmly established within a culture. For example, none of the main technological innovations that made skyscrapers possible – first the iron and then the steel frame, together with the Otis lift – involved architects.[8] Driven by the emergence in the late nineteenth century of large corporations and the need for more and more downtown office space, buildings had practically no choice but to go *up*, leaving architects scrambling to learn how to deal with the new type.

What architects mostly do is *interpret* a building form whose basic functional requirements will therefore already be largely if only vaguely predetermined by the nature of the type itself, and adapt it to a specific place and program of needs, usually modifying both form and function in the process. Very rarely, an innovative designer may also *reinvent* a building type to the extent that it both looks and works quite differently in some respects from any earlier models, which partly explains, as will become apparent in the next chapter, Kubler's ambivalence about the nature of innovation. However, the basic features of the new design can invariably be traced further back in time to one or more precedents of some kind, if not to a single prime object. Taking one of the best-known examples from the history of modern architecture, within the higher-order type 'dwellings,' there are lower-order types like 'villas' and their variations, of which both Andrea Palladio's Villa Malcontenta of 1560 (fig. 8.1) and Le Corbusier's Villa Stein of 1927 (fig. 8.2) are among the best-known exemplars of their respective eras. However, while each building *looks* very different, as Colin Rowe[9] showed in his brilliant dissection of the origins of Le

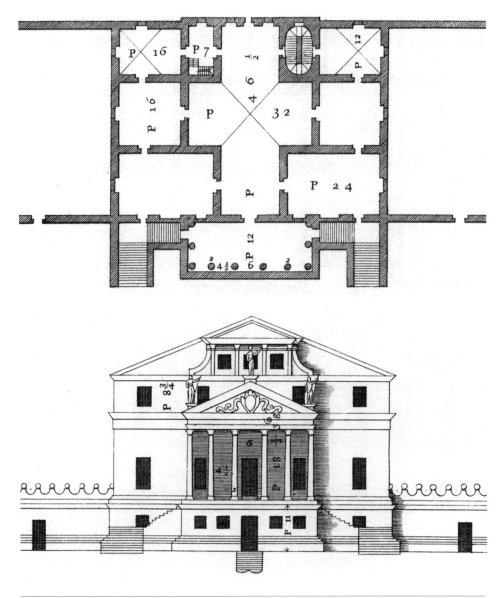

8.1 *Plan and elevation of Villa Malcontenta, 1560, by Andrea Palladio*

Corbusier's plan form (fig. 8.3), the latter design shares at least some major defining properties of a geometric and proportional nature with the earlier neo-classical form, yet also clearly belongs to a modern variation of its own. Similarly, while observing that dwellings are among the most changeable of building types, Rossi notes that the modernist villas designed in the early twentieth century did not fundamentally challenge the basic type itself:

8.2 *Front of Villa Stein, 1927, by Le Corbusier*

The villas built by the most famous architects of the Modern Movement in Berlin – Gropius, Eric Mendelssohn, Hugo Haring, etc. – developed these typological models in a fairly orthodox way; *there was clearly no sense of rupture with their previous eclectic housing models* [added emphasis], even if the image of these villas was transformed profoundly.[10]

However, there are few parallels of this kind of morphological flexibility in nature. While cases have been observed where an organ that evolved for one purpose has changed over time to serve another,[11] compared with the loose fit between built form and function described above, nature's forms are generally more finely tuned to purpose. Recall, for example, Baron Georges Cuvier's functional explanation for the unambiguous differences between the teeth, legs and feet of flesh–eaters and plant–eaters. Looked at another way, if an expert fossil hunter like Cuvier were to dig up a large, curved ivory tusk, he would quickly decide that it belonged to the elephant family and would know from the size, shape and location of the tusk precisely what species it belonged to, and whether that species was alive or extinct.

However, if an architectural historian were to be shown a drawing of a classical pediment mounted on a row of Doric or Corinthian columns, it would be difficult if not impossible to conclude from that single feature alone whether it fronted a temple, church, bank, town hall, courts of justice, palace or country manor, or simply a monument with no other purpose than being a monument. Given the

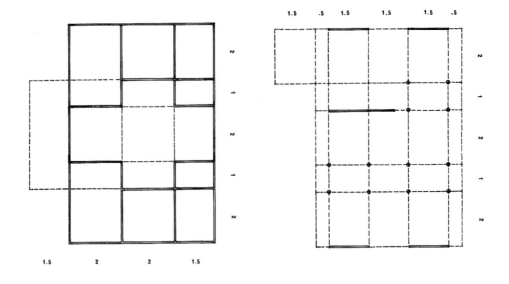

8.3 *Analytical diagrams comparing plan of Palladio's Villa Malcontenta (left) with Le Corbusier's Villa Stein (right), showing the similar underlying typologies and systems of proportion*

longevity and global spread of the style, both the location and the period of its design might also be hard to guess at, let alone be sure of.[12] While, as noted in the previous chapter, Eugene Viollet-le-Duc maintained that such inferences were possible with the gothic style, he was surely being overly confident of his own knowledge of the form. Hence the evident confusion in many works of architectural history and theory, from J. N. L. Durand to Rossi, between form and purpose, in contradistinction to the relatively straightforward situation in biology.

The technical meme

Neither are these the only relevant issues in trying to fix upon an acceptable definition of an agent of cultural transmission along the proposed lines. For Dan Sperber,[13] one of the more sceptical writers who takes Dawkins literally when he describes imitation as the defining method by which memes are reproduced, there can be only one acceptable method of replication for study by memeticians: 'For memetics to be a reasonable research program, it should be the case that *copying, and differential success in causing the multiplication of copies, overwhelmingly plays the major role* [added emphasis] in shaping all or at least most of the contents of culture.'[14] While Sperber, whose professional discipline is cognitive psychology, allows that such a strict interpretation would still leave memeticians with much else to contemplate, including Darwinian issues of the selection of memes, he asserts that the main project of memetics is thus

The extended self

a mistaken one: 'While the view may have some popularity among unconcerned lay people, no psychologist believes that cultural learning is essentially a matter of imitation.'[15] Rather, Sperber argues, taking the example of one person instructing another in the art of origami, or paper folding, whether explicit or implicit, the instructions for engaging in the art entail a complex mixture of *decoding and inference*, involving 'the attribution of intentions and with the knowledge of regular geometric forms in the formation of human intentions generally, and in paper-folding in particular.'[16]

However, while stressing the importance of inference and related cognitive processes, by identifying the memetic program of research solely with the interpretation of memes as copying mechanisms, Sperber ignores that broader aspect of the program that is more appropriately described as a search for a *general theory* of cultural transmission applicable to different forms of culture, which is far more likely to be responsible for the continued interest in the idea.[17] For example, in his description of origami, Sperber comes close to recognizing it as a particular *type of art* requiring previously acquired skills and knowledge of geometry, but sees no connection at all between the two ideas: meme and type. While Sperber makes a sound point concerning the cognitive limitations of imitation, it is also difficult not to read hints of a territorial imperative into his comments – as a psychologist – on what constitutes a legitimate program of study for others working in a different discipline.

Why not, therefore, simply use more commonly accepted terms such as 'idea,' 'concept,' or 'type,' rather than meme? The problem with using such terms alone is that, aside from William Durham's objections recorded in Chapter 6, like the word 'name' itself, they are more likely to imply what linguists call a 'synchronic' or static perspective rather than a 'diachronic' or historical approach, a common trap many of the writers referred to in the previous chapter have fallen into when discussing building types.[18] In addition, as with the dualistic interpretation of memes offered by Kate Distin and Robert Aunger, the first and most general of these terms, 'idea,' suffers from Platonic overtones of the immutable aspects of knowledge the ancients claimed for the mind, as opposed to those aspects they associated with sensory and temporal experience – the very opposite of what a coevolutionary theory of culture and cultural artifacts should present, as advocated here.[19] Though the meme concept was originally conceived by Richard Dawkins solely as a 'unit of cultural transmission' consisting of 'tunes, ideas, catch-phrases' and so forth, it will also be apparent from the debates by his followers over such problems – how memes are communicated from person to person, how they are assimilated and whether they are located in brains or somewhere else – that memes have as much to do with extended cognition as with cultural transfusion, their being virtually two sides of the same coin.

Above all, whatever weaknesses or confusions there have been and still are present in the interpretation of memes, the biological analogy from whence they first sprang more or less guarantees their association with a dynamic, evolutionary perspective, which is what is needed to unravel the dynamics of memetic development, if not necessarily an orthodox neo-Darwinian theory. As is doubtless also apparent from all the controversy surrounding its use and meaning, it should be clear at this point that the meme still has traction, so to speak, and maintains the potential to stimulate further investigation into some vital issues of human culture – not a quality to be lightly dismissed. It is also quite normal that, while sticking with the word, we do not necessarily have to stick with its original limited meaning, but are free to adapt it to our own purposes, as indeed has been the case, as we have already seen, with the histories of both typology and speciation. Moreover, it may be argued that the fertility of the meme, like that of any useful idea, is measured by its capacity for reinterpretation (the same, it might be added, can be said for the reinterpretation of technics, evolution and the other theoretical cornerstones discussed in this book).

Moreover, though clearly inspired by the genetic metaphor, not all writers on the subject, including Dawkins himself, have been as restricted by the analogy as Sperber implies. While, as quoted in Chapter 6, Dawkins invokes the idea of natural selection in his original explanation of what memes are and do, in his later writings on the extended phenotype he draws the line at equating memetic success or survival with the Darwinian concept of fitness: 'A meme has its own opportunities for replication, and its own phenotypic effects, and *there is no reason why success in a meme should have any connection whatever with genetic success* [added emphasis].'[20] On the same page, Dawkins goes still further to distance himself from the orthodox line:

> there is nothing magic about Darwinian fitness in the genetic sense. *There is no law giving it priority as the fundamental property that is maximized* [added emphasis]. Fitness is just a way of talking about the survival of replicators. If another kind of entity arises, which answers to the definition of an active germ-line replicator, variants of the new replicator that work for their own survival will tend to become more numerous. To be consistent, *we could invent a new kind of 'individual fitness', which measured the success of an individual in propagating his memes* [added emphasis].[21]

Aside from the different terminology employed, there is little difference of any consequence between Dawkins' revised and particularized concept of fitness and Jerry Fodor and Massimo Piattelli-Palmarini's call for a new approach to phenotypic traits which recognizes the varied and heterogeneous nature of all the possible factors involved. However, that said, there remains the problem with Dawkins' insistence on the idea of an 'active germ-line replicator,' with its implications of a linear inheritance through the gene, which fits less well with the more complex picture painted by the latter two authors or, indeed, that delineated by other revisionists, like Eva Jablonka and Marion Lamb or Kevin Laland and John Odling-Smee.[22]

The concept of a technical meme proffered here also differs in other key respects from the original mental replicator proposed by Dawkins and his followers. While it is accepted that, so long as they are enjoying an active cultural life, all memes will take on some kind of neurological form in the brains of any participating individuals, the qualifying adjective identifies a *technical* meme as having no meaning or significance that can be separated from whatever external medium it is expressed in. Since, as has been argued in this book, the human mind itself is a coevolutionary product of biology and technics, it follows that there are no memes that are *not* technical memes, that is to say, there are no memes that are not *exteriorized* in some way. Viewed in this light, *all buildings and other artifacts are embodied technical memes* of one kind or another.

Daniel Dennett is therefore perfectly correct when he claims that memes have no life of their own apart from the artifacts and other cultural vehicles in which they are embodied. Nevertheless, while stressing the closeness of their relation, as with Dawkins, the language Dennett employs to describe that relation, as quoted again below, remains the same as that used to distinguish genes from their vehicles or phenotypes:

> Genes are invisible; they are carried by gene vehicles (organisms) in which they tend to produce characteristic effects (phenotypic effects) by which their fates are, in the long run, determined. Memes are also invisible, and are carried by meme vehicles.[23]

However, the technical meme as defined here recognizes no such distinctions and springs directly from the philosophical and neurological theories of embodied minds discussed in Chapters 2 and 3. Thus, even in its 'internal' form (used in this context the word itself raises questions), the mind *reconstructing* the technical meme for external communication or re-enactment works from neurological material that *already specifies* the external technical medium involved, no less than it works through the human body, which shapes all its interactions with the world beyond and with other humans.

Strong support for rejecting any separation between memes and the technical medium and artifacts they are embodied in also comes from Jablonka and Lamb, who found room in their investigations to discuss Dawkins' theory, as well as all their other studies on how evolution works. Separating replicators from their vehicles is fine for genes, they argue, but *not* for memes.[24] As noted previously, in genetics this generally means that, other than through mutations, no change in the gene line can be passed on unless it is done so indirectly, through natural selection of the gene's phenotypic effects or vehicles. However, any parallel distinction between memes and their vehicles breaks down if, as happens continually within cultures, the individual or group carrying the meme undergoes developmental processes of some kind – say, acquiring or extending a skill or expertise – resulting in variations in the meme that can be inherited.

Jablonka and Lamb reserve their strongest criticism, though, for what they perceive as the *passive picture* of human beings painted by memeticians as mere vehicles and channels for memes and meme complexes, at the expense of development and innovation – a picture, it should be noted, that is also explicitly rejected in Laland and Odling-Smee's two-way process of niche construction. Taking a position similar to that of Sperber on the issue of reconstruction versus imitation, Jablonka and Lamb assert that memes and their variations are not so much precisely copied, the way genes work, as *reconstructed* by individuals and groups through learning. Consequently, the authors claim, 'It is impossible to think about the transmission of memes in isolation from their development and function.'[25] Above all, they add, memeticians fail to address the *transformative* effects of human culture: 'the one aspect of human cultural change that makes it totally distinct from any of the other types of evolution we have discussed is that humans are aware of and can communicate about their past history (whether real or mythical) and their future needs.'[26]

Assemblage theory and the extended self

However, defining what technical memes are cannot alone explain how memes might interact and operate together to create the infinite diversity of artifacts and other cultural phenomena that there are in the world, let alone the complexities of the extended self. To complete the full picture we also need to understand the relations and interactions between coexistent or coevolutionary technical memes: how some come together to form types or selves and larger groups and classes or any other kind of superordinate entity, and why some entities of this kind endure and others do not.

In this respect, while Manuel De Landa's own interpretation of memes hardly strays from the original limited definition, his concept of 'assemblages,' as outlined first by Gilles Deleuze with Félix Guattari[27] and later much elaborated by De Landa himself,[28] offers a promising framework for explaining the relations between coexisting technical memes and their combinations. Moreover, the idea of assemblages captures those relations without compromising the original sources or identities of the component memes themselves – an essential factor in understanding how types evolve.[29] Since De Landa offers the more extensive version, which also embraces urban phenomena as well as other matters relevant to the subject matter of this book, the discussion here is mostly confined to the latter source only.

Introducing the idea of assemblages, De Landa compares it with the more familiar 'organismic metaphor,' each of which entails a quite different view of the relations between wholes and parts. While the latter stresses 'relations of interiority,' the concept of assemblages stresses relations of 'exteriority,' with far-reaching implications in each case for the favored choice of exemplars, as well as other key issues.[30] Supporters of the organismic metaphor, De Landa explains (which incidentally includes most architects and critics who use biological analogies, though De Landa makes no specific mention of that group), tend to cite individual species of plants and animals as examples where no part of an organism has any meaning or purpose beyond the role it plays in the life of that particular organism. By contrast, Deleuze points to pollinating insects and plants and other ecologically linked species as examples of *contingent* relations between the components of an assemblage that have evolved over time between otherwise distinct organisms. In such cases, De Landa says:

> the reason why the properties of the whole cannot be reduced to those of its parts is that they are the result not of an aggregation of the components' own properties but of the actual exercise of their capacities. These capacities do depend on a component's properties but cannot be reduced to them since they involve reference to the properties of other interacting entities. *Relations of exteriority guarantee that assemblages may be taken apart while at the same time allowing that the interactions between parts may result in a true synthesis* [added emphasis].[31]

Consequently, should circumstances arise that somehow alter those contingent relations and interactions or otherwise reduce their significance, then 'a component part of an assemblage *may be detached from it and plugged into a different assemblage in which the interactions are different* [added emphasis].'[32]

As well as exhibiting the vital property of exteriority, De Landa also describes assemblages as having two 'dimensions' or 'axes,' one of which defines the *material* or *expressive* roles a component may play within an assemblage, while the other concerns those variable processes that either *stabilize* an assemblage or *destabilize* it. For instance, in the case of the first axis, all human organizations and institutions are comprised of bodies and other material components, but may use quite different media or other means to express their purpose both to their own members and to others. In the case of the second axis, stabilizing processes, or 'territorialization' as De Landa also describes them, involve sharpening the borders and increasing the internal homogeneity of an assemblage, while destabilizing processes, or 'deterritorialization,' involve just the opposite, decreasing homogeneity and blurring borderlines between other assemblages. Each of the four variables in turn may be mixed together within the same assemblage, and even, in the case of the first dimension, within the same component – human beings and the way they express themselves, both linguistically and non-linguistically, being the most obvious example – pulling both components and assemblage one way or another.[33]

Similarly, though De Landa does not specifically apply assemblage theory to the idea of the self as such, the concept of exteriority fits well with what has already been said in previous chapters concerning the exteriorization of human experience and memory by technology. Thus, the assemblage of technical memes that comprise an extended self may be embodied in anything from a home to such personal objects as clothes, a mobile phone or automobile. Moreover, the relations between the individual concerned and the assemblage of components in his or her extended realm are *contingent* relations of exteriority in De Landa's sense, meaning that, while the individuals involved may identify themselves with and be dependent upon those objects for a given period, they may, at some future point in time, be replaced by other components as a person matures and ages.[34] Given the major developmental changes an individual normally passes through during the course of a lifetime, from childhood through adulthood to old age, rather than describing the 'same person,' it may be more accurate to picture the development of the extended self as a self-producing *sequence* of related but nonetheless distinct personas sharing the same bodily nucleus and whatever other consistent components comprise the whole assemblage.[35]

Not only do the components of an extended self change during a lifetime, but also even the 'same' components may change their meaning. Just as in Wittgenstein's forms of life, the same words, phrases and sentences may acquire different meanings according to the social context in which they are being used,[36] so the meaning of a technical meme and its implications may also vary considerably with the specific assemblage to which it belongs, if only temporarily.[37] Thus a technical meme may still retain its own identity, which may also be recognizable across different assemblages, as new interpretations, uses and methods of technical inscription are found for it, generating variations in the components of an assemblage over time.

Technical memes and assemblages

Contingent effects

There remains the related question of what to do about the continued use of the terms 'phenotype' and 'phenotypic effects' in relation to a meme's impact on the wider world. As we saw in Chapter 6, not only Dawkins' closest followers but also thinkers like Durham and De Landa continue to use the same terms while discussing memes as units of cultural transmission in a broader evolutionary framework, with inevitable contradictions. While, for the reasons given above, it is worth retaining the basic idea of memes as cognitive agents of cultural transmission, as was also noted in the same chapter many writers insist on a separation between memes and artifacts equivalent to the separation between genes and their phenotypes or phenotypic effects. Even when the separation is not made explicit, as in Durham and De Landa's work, there are potential if not actual confusions.

The position taken here is that that separation is unsustainable with regard to the evolution of artifacts, and constitutes an unjustified and unworkable extension of the original analogy between memes and genes. Without doubt, artifacts *do* have all kinds of wider effects beyond their physical boundaries – even well beyond those boundaries, just as Dawkins suggests a gene's phenotypic effects may extend beyond the organism itself. However, those extended effects cannot be described in the same terms as extended phenotypes for the good reason that, unlike genes, technical memes have no separate physical or chemical life of their own, as has been explained above, but are only reconstructed or inferred from a series of embodied exemplars.

How, then, to describe those wider effects? 'Environmental effects' covers both artificial and natural environments but is far too vague, while 'ecological effects' still conjures up natural ecologies, even though the term is often now used in wider contexts. 'Systemic effects' is another possibility, but while applicable to both organic and non-organic phenomena, the relations it refers to are still too broad and ill defined. Given the history of systems theory and its origins in biological analogies, while relatively neutral regarding the potential range of subject matter, the term might also still be associated with what De Landa has described as the organismic metaphor.[38]

Here, too, assemblage theory offers an acceptable alternative expression. Adapting the concept of contingent relations described by De Landa, the term 'contingent effects' is proposed as the most appropriate substitute for 'phenotypic effects.' This has the advantage that, while covering the coevolution of organic and non-organic matter, the idea comes with its own set of rules and conditions of use regarding contingent relations between the components of assemblages. In accordance with assemblage theory, therefore, to say that an assemblage of technical memes embodied in any artifact has contingent effects implies the existence of some wider network of contingent relations and interactions between it and other artifacts or users, which, though possibly weaker than the relations defining that assemblage, can nevertheless be traced back to it.

As such, the term fits well within the interactionist perspective promoted throughout this book. For instance, following on from some of the examples discussed in the previous chapter and anticipating related examples in later sections of this chapter, if we say that the availability of affordable automobiles had significant contingent effects on modern urban settlement patterns, helped as it has been by the active propagation among the population of the technical memes they embody, it means that we ought to be able to trace those effects through the recent history of dispersed cities. The same goes for interstate highways and the vision of a new, mobile lifestyle that was offered with them, as will shortly be explained. Similarly, it can be said that the growth of suburbs and the popularity of the detached suburban family dwelling had contingent effects not only on the wider urban and social community but also on family and gender relationships, all of which have been traced through recent history.

The same two-way effects comprise the outputs and inputs of a self-producing social system according to Mingers' definition. Thus, the production of detached family dwellings, automobiles and other vehicles, roads and highways that comprise the suburban components of a dispersed city are the same components that maintain and reproduce the growing city as it spreads ever outwards. As shopping centers and businesses follow their populations, so they also create the conditions for more houses, more vehicles, roads and highways, in the characteristic circular pattern of self-producing systems, each component of which, as we shall see, comprises a whole assemblage in itself of technical memes.

Coevolutionary assemblages

De Landa offers several relevant examples of social systems to illustrate how the different variables might operate to affect the definition and functioning of an assemblage, from interpersonal and community networks to the kind of hierarchical organizations which govern cities and nation-states, all of which have physical and spatial components, including buildings and office machines, as well as the individuals and groups that make them up. He also devotes much of his final chapter to explaining some of the heterogeneous assemblages of which cities themselves are comprised, from the components from which buildings are created, through the social and spatial elements comprising the assemblages we call whole neighborhoods and districts, to the transportation and communication systems which knit all these assemblages together.

However, rather than go through any of De Landa's examples in more detail, it will be more fruitful for the purposes of this book to explore a smaller but no less important selection of related or coevolutionary developments that are better suited to illustrate the precise meaning of technical memes and assemblages and their contingent effects. For one thing, as with Stiegler's work, there is no cognitive dimension to the assemblage theory described by De Landa, but which is integral to the concept of a technical meme, as it is in memetic theory generally, though with varying interpretations.[39] For another, while the axis of component properties describing tendencies toward stabilizing or destabilizing assemblages provides an important tool of analysis, it should be evident from the previous discussions of embodied minds and human technics that there is no place within the definition of a technical meme offered here for any distinction between 'material' or 'expressive' properties as described by De Landa along the other main axis.

That said, there is still plenty of room for a productive merging of technical memes and assemblage theory, just as there is between memetics and technics, without requiring a complete match on all points. Among the most fertile candidates for illustration, the spoked wheel, the automobile and the freeway, as briefly described above, provide outstanding examples of how linked technical memes and assemblages work. There are also many other good reasons for selecting this particular trio, of which the following may be noted. First, needless to say, without the spoked wheel neither of the other two components would exist, and neither would modern cities as we know them.[40] Moreover, all three together have arguably had more impact on settlement patterns and lifestyles in urban history than any comparable set. Similarly, as was pointed out in the previous chapter as well as in the Introduction to this book, it is neither sensible nor possible to consider architecture, and especially suburban homes and all the other building forms typical of dispersed cities, separately from the transportation system that generates their spatial patterns (though unfortunately many architects and theorists try to do just that, as in both Dovey's and Rossi's previously quoted works).

Lastly, in accordance with the equation of memes with types posited in Chapters 6 and 7, it will be argued that no technical meme exists on its own, but always belongs to some larger combination or series. In turn, every technical meme may be comprised of at least some other, smaller or more specific memes, and it is this partly hidden structure of relations *between* technical memes that give each its purpose and meaning.[41] Translated into assemblage theory, each of these three entities – spoked wheels, automobiles and freeways – can be regarded as either a component of its related assemblage, or as an assemblage in itself, comprised of its own components. Similarly, if need be, each entity can be 'unplugged' from its current assemblage and inserted or reused in another, different assemblage, or simply used in more than one assemblage at the same time, which has generally been the case. In much the same way, each entity or combination of them also plays its own part in the extended selves of all those human individuals who make daily use of and inhabit the places and spaces created by the interrelations of all these artifacts. They too may also unplug themselves from time to time and move from one assemblage into another, maybe altering but never entirely losing their own identities, thanks largely to possessing the same bodies – notwithstanding a change of clothes and manners to suit the new occasion and any others involved.

Aside from the obvious popularity of private transport – a major force for the reproduction and diffusion of the three elements alone – there is also ample evidence in their interlocking histories of all the requisite features of autopoietic systems, both as components of dispersed cities, and as self-producing systems in themselves. Beginning with the use of the spoked wheel for diverse peaceful and military purposes, the proliferation of its uses through time for different kinds of vehicles and other

8.4 *Egyptian rendering of a battle with chariots, c. 2000 BC*

machines created a growing need for this most fundamental of human inventions. Thus, as essential components in the reproduction of those vehicles and machines, spoked wheels also ensured their own reproduction and survival down the centuries. The whole circular process greatly accelerated with the coming of the automobile and, with it, the mass-production technologies that reduced the cost of purchase and made it widely available. In turn, as key components of the suburbs, automobiles also created the conditions for *their* own reproduction, together with that of the roads they run upon, producing in turn the dispersed cities that sustain the suburban way of life and all its components– round and round in a great, self-producing cycle.

Life on wheels

Taking the oldest and most adaptable of these entities first, according to Samuel Lilley[42] the spoked wheel first appeared in Mesopotamia around 2000 BC, two to three millennia after wheeled carts with solid wooden wheels made their entry, most likely for moving agricultural produce about.[43] While illustrations from late Bronze Age civilizations also show carts with spoked wheels, their invention and use were doubtless spurred by the horse-drawn chariot as the speedy vehicle and weapons platform of choice in war, for which the lightweight wheel was ideally suited (fig. 8.4).

Technical memes and assemblages

Already in its early history, therefore, the spoked wheel took its place as a vital component within two very different social assemblages – farming communities and armies – each with very different meanings and contingent effects. Lilley has also speculated that the social structure of different early civilizations had a possibly profound effect on their capacity for invention, or even their ability to adopt and exploit the inventions of others. For example, by 3000 BC the wheeled cart had spread throughout Elam and Syria as well as Mesopotamia, but had not yet reached Egypt; the reason for this, Lilley suggests, was that the former civilizations included nascent classes of independent merchants, educated and motivated enough to make the best use of available technologies, while Egyptian society had stagnated, split between a tiny, unproductive ruling elite and a vast underclass of workers and slaves, neither class having either the knowledge or motivation required even to recognize the potential of new technologies: 'We are thus forced to the conclusion that the wheel was not adopted in Egypt because it failed to reach there before the structure of society became so unfavorable to innovation as to prevent its introduction.'[44]

The different construction techniques involved in making spoked wheels also created a lightweight aesthetic, as different from the look of a solid wheel as the look of a timber-frame dwelling is from one of masonry construction – as good an example as any of the difficulty of separating the material from the expressive properties of components. The smaller surface area also reduced the decorative or ornamental possibilities to the narrow rim, or else shaping and otherwise embellishing the hub and spokes, focusing attention again on the structure rather than the surface. From then on the development of the spoked wheel dovetailed with the discovery or invention of new materials and forms of wheeled transportation. From the combination of wooden frame and iron rims used for horse-drawn carts and carriages right up till the early twentieth century, to the use of all-metal spoked wheels for railway engines and carriages and, finally, to the addition of the pneumatic tire in 1888 – first to the ultra-lightweight spoked bicycle wheel, closely followed by the automobile – the basic configuration of the spoked wheel itself hardly changed over several millennia.

However, its combined impact on the technical and social assemblages of which it was and still is a key part has been incalculable, comparable with other early human inventions, like the plough and the sailing ship, each of which, according to Lilley, changed the course of human history.[45] At this point, therefore, we need to consider the cognitive processes involved in the transmission and diffusion of the idea of the spoked wheel, for which, as has been observed, assemblage theory cannot help us much but memetics and the technical meme can. Returning to Dennett's own chosen example of wheeled wagons to illustrate the relations between memes and their vehicles, it has been argued in this book that the idea of a wagon with spoked wheels cannot be inferred or reconstructed in the mind from one example alone, but only from observing a whole series of similar wagons. For example, seeing the spoked wheel being used with equal success in more than one kind of assemblage, even if it were only farm carts and war chariots at the beginning, would paradoxically have had the cognitive effect of reinforcing the separate identity of the technical

8.5 *A waterwheel being used to draw heavy iron wire, c. 1540*

meme, 'spoked wheel,' as an idea with still further possible applications in different assemblages. Put another way, the more diverse technical assemblages spoked wheels were used in, then the more the meme was 'loosened,' as it were, from its original assemblage, ready to spring over and be used in yet another assemblage.

And so it has been, not only with the evolution of different forms of wheeled vehicles, but also with the use of spoked wheels of all sorts and sizes, in all kinds of other assemblages, from waterwheels (fig. 8.5) and other industrial machines to the tiny wheels in mechanical watches. Moreover, this *latent capacity*, or 'co-adaptive potential' as it will be described here, of some technical memes to leap-frog from one assemblage to another may depend not only on the separate but flexible identity of a meme, but also on numerous other factors shaping the technical assemblages to which it presently belongs, and may belong to at some point in the future.[46] Such factors may include the existence of appropriate social classes of the kind Lilley writes of, who have both the education and the motivation to realize and exploit such potential transfers from one assemblage to another, or parallel developments in other technologies opening up new possible combinations.

Symbol of mass consumption

The linked evolution of the technical meme and wheeled assemblage we call an automobile or motorcar provides a good illustration of similar processes at work. By the time Gottlieb Daimler and Wilhelm Maybach built the first four-wheeled vehicle powered by an internal combustion engine in 1886, the Industrial Revolution had already created well established classes, professions, organizations and institutions around the world dedicated to promoting technological innovation and exploiting it for both financial and social gains. By that time suburban railways and tramlines had also begun to change the configuration of cities, spatially disconnecting homes from workplaces and dispersing populations further and further away from historic urban centers.[47] However, as well as greatly extending the same trend, the coming of the private automobile also met other, more complex needs associated with the possession and control of personal transportation. In his history of the automobile, *Cars and Culture*, Rudi Volti[48] writes:

> More than any other artifact of modern technology, the automobile has shaped our physical environment, social relations, economy and culture. At the same time, however, the automobile has not come into our lives as an alien force. Although our embrace of the automobile is often accompanied by unease over its consequences, *it cannot be denied that the ownership and operation of cars resonate with some of our most important values and aspirations* [added emphasis]. We have paid a high price for the personal mobility that the car offers, but for the most part we have done so willingly, if not always intelligently.[49]

Before those aspirations could be fulfilled, however, both the automobile and its users had to go through some major technical and social transformations, each of which complemented the other, creating the vast technical assemblage and its contingent effects known as the automobile industry. As with the horse-drawn carriages the automobile soon displaced, its consumers were initially restricted to a wealthy urban minority, both in Europe and the United States. However, as the middle classes grew and prospered, so also did the automobile, which rapidly acquired the role of must-have status symbol it retains until now for much of the world's population.[50] In the United States, which by the beginning of the last century enjoyed the highest per capita income in the West, the total number of automobiles sold in the country rose from 4,192 in 1900 to 63,500 in 1908, during which time the price tag also fell considerably. But it was the introduction of Henry Ford's revolutionary assembly lines in 1913 that finally made the automobile available to workers as well as to the more elite strata of society. The mass production of standard items and components and the specialized machinery needed to make them were common features of industrialized societies well before Ford's intervention. However, they mostly involved the production of a single item or component, which would then be assembled together with other components by a group of workers all focusing on the same task in the same spot in the factory. A few assembly lines also existed for making small items like tin cans, where stationary workers performed a single task while the item itself was moved along to the next worker 'in line,' who performed a different task, and so on until the final product was completed.

While, as Volti suggests, strictly speaking Ford did not invent the mass-production assembly line himself, he not only used it on a hitherto unprecedented scale in the size, complexity and number of products coming off his lines, but he also mechanized the lines themselves, so that the chassis or whichever section of the automobile

8.6 *Ford Model T tourer, Mk 1, 1913. Some 15,000,000 of these automobiles had been made by the time production stopped in 1927*

was being assembled would automatically move along to the next 'work station.' The development yielded substantial benefits in efficiency but had less fortunate consequences for the quality of workers' jobs, as memorably captured in Charlie Chaplin's 1936 movie *Modern Times* (which incidentally also shows our hapless hero getting caught up in a giant machine comprised of spoked cogwheels).

Already in production in Ford's factories since 1908 at a competitive price, shifting the popular Model T (fig. 8.6) onto Ford's new assembly lines in 1914 more than halved the price in just two more years. Boosting his reputation as a modern folk hero while securing his workforce, many of whom were drifting off to find less monotonous work, in the same year Ford doubled the salaries of his workers, not only gaining copious free publicity for himself and his products but also helping his workers to join the fast-growing ranks of consumers.[51] By 1923, half of the more than three and a half million automobiles on the road in the United States were Model Ts, creating a lasting symbol of the culture of mass consumption Ford helped to make possible.[52]

The greatest public works project

Though Ford's dominance did not last, his cost-cutting production methods and belief that everyone had the right to their own personal motorcar set the future pattern for the industry. However, there was still one more development needed to complete the assemblage: the spread of freeways and interstate highways through the United States, in their wake changing familiar building types as well as ways of urban life.

As with the history of the automobile, while there were ample precedents for the relevant ideas and technologies, a larger-than-life figure stepped in to help accelerate the development: namely Norman Bel Geddes, a gifted all-rounder who began his career in theater design. Among his many achievements, including a whole series of futuristic designs for streamlined automobiles, ships and aircraft, he helped promote the profession of industrial design to meet the growing demand for functional products that also appealed to the eye.[53] As Ruth Brandon relates the story in her history of automobiles, Geddes played a key early role in the conception of America's extensive freeway systems.[54] In 1936 Geddes was commissioned by Shell Oil to design a new advertising campaign with the theme 'Traffic Conditions of the Future.' It would include a design for an interstate highway system, together with an entire metropolis with freeways, for which a large model would be made, that could be photographed for the campaign. Several high-speed highways with limited access had already been built in New York City, most of them along riversides where land was available, and the first one in Los Angeles was under construction at the time. But Geddes envisaged something altogether much grander. Though it is doubtful that he would have quoted the example at that time, what Geddes had in mind was more like the *autobahns* then under construction in Nazi Germany – a whole network of 'Magic Motorways' as he later called them, with three lanes in each direction crisscrossing the entire continent.

The Shell campaign lasted only a year, but Geddes' scheme and model city, which he continued to promote himself, attracted the attention of General Motors, which was preparing its own exhibition for the 1939 New York World's Fair, the theme for which was 'The World of Tomorrow.' Geddes was invited to lead the design team and drew upon his early career to create a theatrical experience for the public, or 'Futurama,' as it was called, offering a glowing vision of what the mobile urban life could be like in 1960. Instead of walking, visitors rode around the edge of the huge exhibit on 'conveyor belts' of seats, from which they were presented with a changing view from above of the extensive models, accompanied by sound effects and a commentary explaining the future of unlimited mobility that was being offered.

The exhibit was hugely popular with the public, though not with some critics, who likened it to a giant machine itself.[55] However, as Brandon explains, the public saw it differently:

> the crowd experienced something altogether more inspiring: a sense of possibilities, of a new life almost within their grasp, of streamlined certainties and grand designs surrounding them like an invigorating bath. In Futurama the present is a mess to be cleared up, the sharp-edged, speedy world of 1960 a comprehensive vision to which all may aspire.[56]

The timing of the exhibition, and Geddes' vision, could not have been better. Americans were still struggling to climb out of the deep economic and psychological hole created by the Great Depression, and *wanted* to believe things could and would get better. As part of the New Deal, Franklin D. Roosevelt's administration had also embarked on a series of ambitious programs of public works to help alleviate unemployment, culminating in 1941 in the first plan for a nationwide network of freeways, followed in 1944 by the Federal Aid Highway Act, which allocated $1.5 billion in matching funds for highway construction, the rest to be paid for by the states. Describing the significance of the program in no uncertain terms, Volti writes: 'Although representing a step in the right direction, it ended up being only a small down payment on what was to be the greatest public works project in history, the interstate highway system.'[57]

Urban impacts

By the 1960s, as promised, enough of the system was in place to begin to assess its impact (fig. 8.7), with critics sharply divided between those in favor and those against dispersed cities. However, as noted in Chapter 1, whatever views critics voiced had little if any influence on events themselves. Helped by the 'GI Bill,' a post-war welfare program designed to give returning soldiers a new start in life, the purchase of new homes in the suburbs escalated, together with that of the automobiles needed to reach them and all the now distant workplaces and other facilities that went with the mobile life. Neither was the impact confined to the spatial distribution of buildings. As Brandon explains, as well as affecting the gender roles described in the previous chapter, the archetypal suburban home itself began to change shape (figs 8.8 and 8.9), producing other contingent effects of both a personal and a social nature:

> Traditionally, American houses had been built with covered verandahs facing onto the street – the 'piazzas' and 'stoops' within which the action of so many nineteenth-century novels takes place. In the early days of motoring the garage (if any) was a hut in the back yard. But cars soon became too important to be relegated to a hut. The garage moved forward and increased in size, while the front porch disappeared – *an enactment in bricks and mortar of the revolutionary effect on social life* [added emphasis]. The porch had been part of a pedestrian lifestyle of casual callers and passers-by, but the car made all that irrelevant. Less walking meant fewer passers-by, while many of the activities (such as courting) that had traditionally taken place on the porch could now be conducted in the privacy of the car.[58]

Along with the changes to suburban home typologies, for most of the second half of the last century suburban malls, though now in decline, also increasingly displaced downtown shopping centers as retailers followed their consumers outward. They were accompanied over the same period by the decentralization of other businesses, which gathered together in the linear 'strips' celebrated by Venturi and other enthusiasts – all of which were accessible only by motorcar.[59] Allowing for possibly overestimating the number of licenced female drivers available to run their families around, Mumford's 1964 prescient assessment of the trend is especially sharp:

8.7 *Interstate freeway, Westchester County, New York State, looking west, c. 1965*

In using the car to flee from the metropolis the motorist finds that he has merely transferred congestion to the highway and thereby doubled it. When he reaches his destination, in a distant suburb, he finds that the countryside he sought has disappeared: beyond him, thanks to the motorway, lies only another suburb, as dull as his own. To have a minimum amount of communication and sociability in this spread-out life, his wife becomes a taxi-driver by daily occupation, and the sum of money required to keep this whole system running leaves him with shamefully overtaxed schools, inadequate police, poorly staffed hospitals, overcrowded recreation areas, ill-supported libraries.

In short, *the American has sacrificed his life as a whole to the motorcar* [added emphasis], like someone who, demented with passion, wrecks his home in order to lavish his income on a capricious mistress who promises delights he can only occasionally enjoy.[60]

The extended self

8.8 *Traditional mid-twentieth-century suburban house with a front porch, in Lubbock, Texas*

8.9 *Typical large suburban houses in America, nicknamed 'MacMansions,' with front garages for two to three automobiles for each house*

Technical memes and assemblages

171

As Volti also described it, the story of the dominance of the automobile in shaping suburban American life is therefore not just that of a handful of brilliant and successful entrepreneurs and designers influencing the choices of others, but also of a very large and fast-growing number of consumers only too eager to buy into the Great American Dream, whatever the subsequent social and other costs.

9 Combinatorial design

Following on from the preceding explication of technical memes and their assemblages and their role as cardinal agents of cognitive extension and embodiment, the inquiry now turns to exploring evidence of corresponding processes in the design and evolution of buildings and settlements in various periods and cultures, and, not least, in the process of innovation itself.

In Chapter 6, Kate Distin's borrowed theory of engineering design was presented as an idealized, 'solution-neutral' model of design with evolutionary characteristics, based on Distin's premise that all designs involve the use of blueprints or other modern sources of information. However, aside from other problems, the 'blueprint' theory raises a question: what if no clear written or recorded instructions for making buildings or other artifacts are available to follow? As with the Hopi Indians described earlier, many pre-modern indigenous cultures had no such recourse and relied upon other means of communicating their traditions. In such cases, people could simply copy-the-product, as Susan Blackmore suggests, but copying just one example is an unreliable method and unlikely to produce the kind of information that would qualify as a type or class of types of the sort that societies customarily produce.

The view repeatedly advocated in this book is that reconstructing model types from observation of a series of related exemplars is the primary method of reproduction and propagation applicable to *both* modern *and* pre-modern societies. Furthermore, if, as it was pointed out in Chapters 7 and 8, unlike the case with living species, the relations between built form and function are a great deal more fluid and even unpredictable when it comes to matters of architectural style and use, then building types, styles and the activities they house all need to be treated as distinct technical memes and assemblages in themselves. It follows that the *identity of a building* will be a combination or *composite* of those technical memes and assemblages, some of which may be borrowed from other cultures and regions, comprising a self-producing system in its own right.

Expanding on the same theme, the composite nature of architecture is examined through diverse examples drawn from different periods and locations around the world, from vernacular architecture and the hybridization of imported and local forms, through to urban typologies like the 'colonial city.' This leads on to an exposition of related theories of combinatorial innovation and design, from the 'metaphorical' theories of creativity advanced by several writers in the last century, to Brian Arthur's combinatorial theory of technological evolution, supported by his own and other examples. Taking a prominent feature of modern cities, the chapter concludes by looking at the evolution of the tower type and other new forms of high-rise architecture.

Cultural imperatives

As a composite structure of technical memes, a key factor determining which memes are combined together in which building form will be the role a building plays *as a whole* in the extended selves of its makers and users and their self-perceptions. Similarly, as assemblages of technical memes, buildings embody and transmit cultural values to individuals and groups, if not with the same precision that some theorists claim for them, then sufficient to reinforce and perpetuate self-images and habitual behavior patterns beyond the life-span of their occupants, and sometimes even further, should those populations spread beyond their original geographical boundaries, taking their cultural baggage along with them.

Sometimes, as is repeatedly the case with colonial architecture, subjected peoples may adopt building forms imported by the colonists as a deliberate act of identification with their new masters. Taking a broader look at the cultural factors shaping the way different peoples build, in *House Form and Culture* Amos Rapoport,[1] whose studies of Australian Aborigines were described in Chapter 1, offers the example of the traditional open-framed Japanese house, which hardly varies from the sub-tropical south where it originates, to the sub-arctic north, where it was imported by Japanese conquerors from the south. There it was adopted by the original inhabitants, who rejected their own, more appropriate thick-walled dwellings in favor of the architecture of their new masters, as well as by the Japanese settlers from the south who brought the framed building tradition with them. Rapoport comments: 'I can affirm from personal experience how uncomfortable the Japanese house can be during the winter,'[2] an observation supported by Japanese paintings of occupants protected by many layers of clothing to compensate for their flimsily clad homes (fig. 9.1).

What look like mostly arbitrary relations between built form and function are therefore explicable only if one accepts the primary role of buildings in the identity of the inhabitants and their extended selves. Not only does the issue of cultural and personal identity often take precedence over the natural environment, as with the Japanese house and other examples in different parts of the world described by Rapoport, it evidently leads in some cases to an actual *denial* of the harsher realities of nature. As Paul Oliver also points out, such factors make the task of classifying vernacular building types difficult, depending on the method used.[3] Classification by function alone – the method still most commonly accepted – is clearly inadequate, he observes, when similar morphologies and planning typologies are used by different societies for quite different purposes. However, while they might confuse anyone

9.1 *Painting of the interior of a Japanese house and its occupants by an unknown artist, 1849*

looking for direct, unambiguous connections between form and function, the same phenomena verify the combinatorial theory of architecture advanced here as an assemblage of technical memes, some of which may be shared with other cultures.

Moreover, the persistence of such forms in itself is evidence of the existence of types, even if there are sometimes problems in giving them consistent names. Oliver notes, for example, there is evidence that circular plan forms dating back many thousands of years are sometimes replaced by rectangular plan forms in the same area, but never the other way around. Since rectangular planning was a common feature of the earliest cities, this could suggest the latter form was found to be more suitable to the needs of the complex urban societies and denser populations that evolved along with those cities. Other basic types are equally common, some of which, Oliver speculates, may have their origins in the shape of the human body, just as the African settlement patterns cited in Chapter 2 do:

> Many vernacular traditions make use of 'primary forms' including the hemisphere, cone, cylinder and cube, or sections, divisions and multiples of these, such as the semi-cylindrical vault and the double-cube with a triangular prism roof. Perhaps we respond to these forms intuitively, with reactions induced by the countless millennia of the evolution of humankind. It is possible that the appeal of the symmetric that is to be perceived in many vernacular forms may echo the basic symmetry of the human face, limbs and torso, while the subtle asymmetry and inflections of a norm which are evident in countless dwellings, may parallel the singularity of every individual within each culture.[4]

In explaining the craft-based building methods of indigenous cultures, Oliver also offers valuable insights into how variations might occur even within the most stable of tradition-bound social systems, which have relatively well defined boundaries compared with modern societies, as individual builders modify a technique or form to suit their own needs:

> This is the way with most forms of indigenous building: the tradition establishes a broad matrix, the individual builder designs and constructs to suit his or her requirements within it. Such dwellings are neither slavish copies of their predecessors, nor willful deviants from them. Construction is not a matter of intuition as if the builders were like birds making their nests, but the result of deliberate decisions taken to meet perceived needs. A single tradition may be described in general terms, but it should be understood in specific ones; *the differences are subtle but significant, eventually contributing to the slow changing of traditional form as innovations are introduced and influences assimilated* [added emphasis]. The process of design is different from that used by the Western architect, who may isolate problems and seek solutions to the brief through the abstraction of the drawing board and the building specification. In the indigenous dwelling there is design too, but it is carried out on a one-to-one scale; problems are perceived principally when the established norm fails to meet them, or a customary solution is unsuitable for the prospective builder and occupier.[5]

Hybridization

If traditional methods and precedent offer considerable leeway for combinatorial evolution and variations, even within relatively isolated indigenous societies, then composite methods of building also create manifold opportunities for cultural adaptation and hybridization in more exposed or less stable conditions. To recall André Leroi-Gouhan's observation from Chapter 4, while interbreeding between animal species is limited by genetic factors, no such limitations apply to human cultures. The case of the migrating Japanese house described above is a good example of how a conquered people can be persuaded to change their form of abode, even though the new form of construction is less comfortable than the one they were accustomed to, simply to identify with their new rulers and so, presumably, to prosper more easily under the new regime.

Couched in the combinatorial language of technical memes and assemblages, the same planning or structural form may therefore be conjoined with different cultural systems and customs, acquiring different meanings for each population in the process. For example, Douglas Fraser cites the case of the Bamileke tribe of the Cameroon highlands in Africa, whose villages represent a 'visible paradigm of their social system,'[6] with the King's Plaza in the center, surrounded by separate dwellings for wives and the menfolk. However, as Fraser explains, not all settlement patterns are as straightforward. Geometrically similar layouts may provide for quite different social arrangements, depending upon the peoples or tribe using them. For example, axial plans consisting of two parallel rows of dwellings are common among Pacific islanders (fig. 9.2), where they combine both social and cosmological functions, but are also found in the New Guinea highlands as well as Guinea in Africa, and in the Amazon basin in Brazil. Of the latter three instances, in the first case the two rows of houses are respectively occupied by the two sexes, in the second case by unmarried individuals and families, and in the last by households of different sizes. Thus three distinct assemblages share at least one technical meme, but differ in others.

Fraser does not explain how the different functions came about, but we may reasonably assume from Oliver's comments about the repeated use of the same basic building forms in different cultures that the hybrid assemblage *emerged* over long periods of habitual usage involving incremental adjustments along the way to suit specific needs. It may be that, as Leroi-Gourhan also suggests, the repetition of such forms in widely different and as yet unconnected or barely connected parts of the world can be explained only by human and material factors common to those parts. Similarly, Oliver's observations as quoted above on the repeated use of basic geometric forms by indigenous societies are indicative of the impact of similar constraints on different cultures in separate geographical regions. The case of the Japanese house described by Rapoport, on the other hand, is a clear instance of an 'alien' technical meme being *imposed* on a subjugated people, who ultimately assimilated the form to local customary assemblages for political motives, rather than one that emerged from within those assemblages.

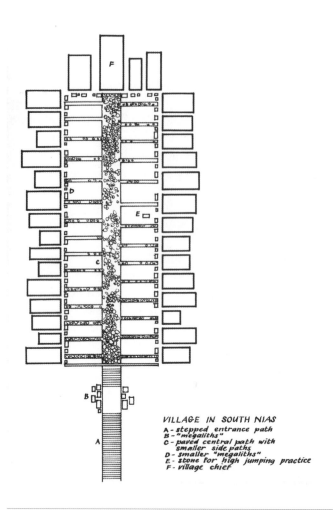

VILLAGE IN SOUTH NIAS
A - stepped entrance path
B - "megaliths"
C - paved central path with
    smaller side paths
D - smaller "megaliths"
E - stone for high jumping practice
F - village chief

9.2 *Schematic plan of a Bawamataluo village, South Nias, Indonesia, by Douglas Fraser*

Taking another case from Asia Pacific, when traders introduced Islam to Southeast Asia in the fifteenth century, the defining attributes of the mosque had already been well established for centuries in the Middle East and elsewhere.[7] However, instead of importing the familiar model, with its domed spaces, arcaded courtyards and other features, local Muslims adopted a typical Hindu-Javanese temple structure with a centripetal plan and a pyramidal roof supported by four columns, all features expressive of Hindu-Javanese cosmology (fig. 9.3).[8] Given the open nature of the well ventilated structure, it might be argued that the building type was adopted for mainly climatic reasons. However, bearing in mind the predominance of cultural factors in the choice of the other building forms described here, it seems equally possible, if not more likely, that the local form was purposefully chosen to encourage local converts to identify with the new religion as a part of their own culture.

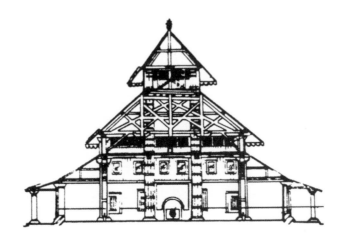

9.3 *Sectional drawing of the old Kampung Laut Mosque at Nilam Puri, Kota Bharu, Kelantan, Malaysia*

In other words, Muslims adapted an indigenous technical assemblage to their own purposes, creating what may still *look* like the earlier assemblage, but what, with its combination of imported religious ritual and local building form, amounts to a new and more heterogeneous assemblage altogether.

On a different scale, the British colonial city, as Anthony King[9] describes it in Asia, offers as clear a spatial paradigm of a specific cosmology and social structure as any pre–industrial settlement pattern. However, instead of any spatial partition by gender or rank typical of the latter, King presents a general model of colonial urban development divided into two main areas along strictly racial lines: a 'European sector' occupied by the British and any other Western Caucasians, and a 'native quarter' inhabited by the indigenous peoples and any non-Western immigrants of various other races. Aside from the residential areas with their characteristic bungalows and other detached dwellings, each set within its own neat garden plot, the European sector would also typically include a civic center comprised of government buildings, churches, schools and other staples of colonial authority. As in Kuala Lumpur in colonial Malaya, these would often be distributed around a large public open space, used for sports, military parades and other ceremonials, forming the heart of the European colony (fig. 9.4). Where the geography favored it, nearby 'hill stations' also provided guesthouses and other recreational facilities located at cooler altitudes, where colonists would recuperate their energies in near-perfect replicas of the half-timbered houses and rose gardens they had left behind in the homeland (fig. 9.5). In other cases, as with many of the colonial government buildings themselves, we find building types imported from Europe purposefully combined with local architectural elements, or 'localized,'[10] so diluting any negative imperial messages such buildings might convey (fig. 9.6).

9.4 *View across the central public open space, called the Padang, in Kuala Lumpur, Malaysia, toward the former Selangor State Secretariate, by A. C. Norman, 1897*

9.5 *Ye Olde Smokehouse Inn, Cameron highlands, near Kuala Lumpur – a cool and comforting retreat for British colonists, still popular with tourists*

The extended self

9.6 *High Court building, Kuala Lumpur, by A. C. Norman, 1909*

Within this 'bifocal universe,' as King calls it, the history of the Malay house and the manner in which many of its features were borrowed by British colonists and adapted to their own domestic purposes parallels the case of the Spanish colonists adapting Pueblo architecture to their needs. With its lightly clad, timber-framed structure raised clear of the ground and steeply pitched roofs of *atap* (a roofing technique similar to thatch, made from palm leaves), the Malay house is typical of the great variety of 'houses on stilts' which are found throughout Southeast Asia, several versions of which evolved within the Malay peninsula alone (fig. 9.7), supporting Leroi-Gourhan's related suggestion that variations of culture-forms will occur spontaneously even within well connected regional cultures.[11] Notably, like Pueblo architecture, if not like all the other examples discussed here, the open structure of Malay dwellings with their overhanging roofs and well shaded and ventilated walls is also well adapted to the local climate (fig. 9.8).

For British colonists, the Malay house type had the added recognizable virtue of having evolved as a detached, single or extended family dwelling, lessons from which could thus be readily transferred onto their own imported house types, if not in all respects. Prior to British rule, the rural peasant populations of Malay villages traditionally held no land or property rights,[12] nor erected any boundaries around their dwellings, so the spaces between each house were generally left quite open, and still are in most villages. By contrast, each colonial-era villa occupies its own well demarcated plot of land, just like the detached houses with their gardens, fences and hedges back home, expressing an entirely different concept of social space. The result

Combinatorial design

9.7 *Regional variations of the traditional Malay house type in the Malay peninsula*

9.8 *Characteristic Malay house in Penang with an 'A'-type roof form and atap covering*

9.9 *Colonial-era villa in Georgetown, Penang, Malaysia. Note the open fenestration and ventilated Malay roof form to the rear covering the main body of the house*

was another distinctive series of hybrid dwellings, in which Palladian typologies and neo-classical details were effortlessly fused with Malay vernacular features, including the raised living spaces and shuttered walls designed to maximize natural ventilation, while at the same time retaining distinctly European patterns of separate residential plots (figs 9.9 and 9.10).[13] Once again, we have a clear example of a heterogeneous assemblage of features drawn from different sources, some of which readily merge together, while others – like the customary European plot boundaries – retain their own distinct identity.

By contrast, the terraced house form introduced to the same region by Chinese settlers, many of whom were attracted by the opportunities to work in the tin mines and rubber plantations run by the colonists, has hardly changed at all except in detail from its origins in the southern provinces of China, from where most of the settlers came.[14] Known in its widespread form as the two-storey Chinese 'shop-house,' it typically features a narrow frontage and deep plan form punctuated by one or two courtyards (fig. 9.11). Designed to squeeze as many traders and their families into a street as possible, the deep plan form ill suits hot humid climates and severely limits natural ventilation, which is restricted to that which finds its way through the internal courtyards, or through vents in the roofs.[15] Despite this handicap, the dual-function building type proved remarkably adaptive in other respects and was replicated wherever the Chinese settled overseas, gaining some additional features

Combinatorial design

9.10 *Villa Cornaro, Piombino Dese, near Padua, Italy, 1570, by Andrea Palladio*

in the process. For example, the frontal arcades, or 'five-foot ways,' which are such an attractive urban feature of the type, were actually introduced and mandated by Sir Stamford Raffles, the British founder and first governor of Singapore, when he planned that city. Designed to provide protection from the tropical sun and rain, the virtues of the arcaded streets were quickly recognized throughout the region.[16] Embellished with details of various architectural styles, including Western as well as Chinese motifs (figs 9.12 and 9.13), shop-houses often comprised the bulk of 'native' urban dwellings in former colonial cities throughout the Malay peninsula and elsewhere, including Dutch Indo-China, now Indonesia, much of which survives to this day, despite widespread demolition and redevelopment in some areas.[17]

Lacking any local tradition of building they could work with similar to what their compatriots found in the Malay peninsula, British colonists in Australia at first imported the urban building types they were most familiar with: stone-walled terraced houses, neo-classical churches and the usual built trappings of civic pride.[18] Eventually, however, forms of habitation more suited to their locality emerged. The process was partly accelerated by the great variations in the climate of the continent,

The extended self

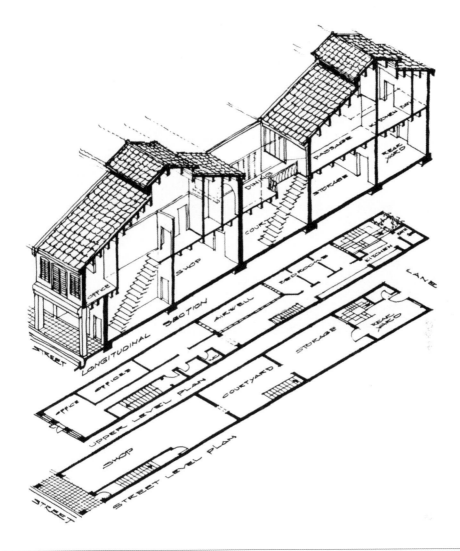

9.11 *Characteristic deep plan forms of terraced Chinese shop-houses found in the towns and cities of the Malay peninsula and other parts of Southeast Asia*

which ranges from temperate in the south to tropical in the north, resisting any imposition of singular solutions.[19] The emergence of the detached house as the archetypal Australian dwelling also coincided with an active policy of decentralization of the urban population, promoted by a colonial government fearful that soldiers returning from the Great War might be tempted to imitate the Russian example and create their own social revolution.[20] They were aided initially by a willing populace happy with the opportunity to gain more living space, made possible by the existence of numerous tramlines and railways leading out from the city centers, along which the new, low-density settlements sprang.

Combinatorial design

185

9.12 *Shop-houses in Georgetown with a 'Palladian motif' repeated at first-floor windows*

9.13 *Detail of the main façade of the Basilica, Vicenza, 1550, by Andrea Palladio, showing original Palladian motif at an upper level*

The extended self

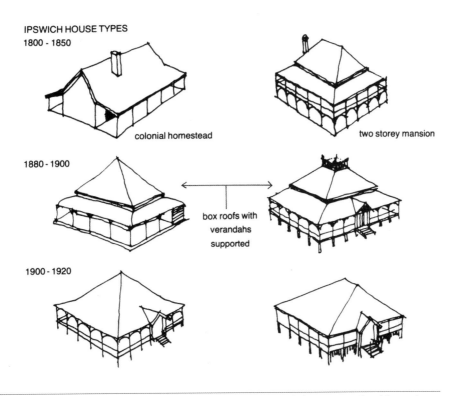

IPSWICH HOUSE TYPES
1800 - 1850

colonial homestead

two storey mansion

1880 - 1900

box roofs with
verandahs
supported

1900 - 1920

9.14 *Sketches showing the evolution of the 'Queensland house' type from earlier colonial typologies in Ipswich, 1800–1920*

Of the several detached dwelling types in Australia to come out of this early period, the timber-framed Queensland house, named after its origins in the eponymous tropical state, is as clear an example of the evolution of a consistent morphology derived from different sources as any of the above cases (fig. 9.14). Combining features borrowed from the bungalows of colonial India and the raised dwellings of Southeast Asia,[21] together with modern building materials and techniques, the compact 'Queenslander,' as it is also known, like the adopted California bungalow mentioned in Chapter 1, was much liked for its affordability, regional character and suitability to the local climate (proving once again that culture, though it may be the main factor in shaping building form and use, does not always negate other considerations). Dominated by steeply pitched roofs of corrugated metal and wrapped around by shady verandahs, each house is supported above ground level, well clear of trespassing creatures as well as flood waters, not unlike the indigenous Malay house, and better positioned to catch any cooling breezes. In addition to their lightweight construction, many of the houses were also factory made and assembled from prefabricated parts transported from the more industrialized states further south, and could be quickly built or taken down and reassembled elsewhere, which they often were, as owners and opportunities for work changed.[22]

Combinatorial design

Change and innovation

Similarly, the origins of the combined dome and rectangular base and its transitional structures argued over by Daniel Dennett and Stephen Gould illustrate a general but little-appreciated feature of innovations, great and small – that the gap between new and old ideas is much narrower than most people, including Gould and his followers, used to think. In sharp contrast to some of the critical comments on the use of metaphors and analogical thinking cited earlier in this book, several writers on the subject of innovation, notably Arthur Koestler and Donald Schon, followed by Thomas Kuhn in his later work,[23] have all adopted more liberal and positive approaches to their creative role in cognition, the essence of which is aptly expressed in the words of Shakespeare's King Lear: 'Nothing will come from nothing.' According to this view, which also encompasses innovations in architectural design,[24] even the most radical inventions and discoveries were at least partly inspired by historical precedent or well established ideas of some sort, involving a linking of disparate ideas similar to what goes on in analogical thinking. Most are essentially fusions of at least two existing but previously unrelated concepts or techniques, the combination of which provides a new way of looking at the world or making something: linking different 'matrixes of thought,' as Koestler calls it,[25] or seeing the new in terms of the old, as Schon describes it below. Put another way, there are no wholly new ideas or inventions, only new links or steps in an endless sequence of evolving ideas, each building on what has gone before and in turn creating the conditions for ideas yet to be formulated.

The level of agreement among all three writers, who published their key works independently in the 1960s and '70s, as evidenced in the following quotations, is remarkable in itself.[26] Significantly, Koestler explicitly offers the example of Darwin's combination of the method of artificial selection involved in domestic breeding with T. R. Malthus's theory of populations competing for scarce resources as a prime case study of how innovation actually works, as opposed to popular preconceptions:

> Charles Darwin is perhaps the most outstanding illustration of the thesis that 'creative originality' does not mean creating a system of ideas out of nothing but rather out of the combination of well established patterns of thought – by a process of cross-fertilization, as it were.[27]

Describing his own version of the theory as the 'displacement of concepts,' Schon asserts:

> New concepts do not spring from nothing or from mysterious external sources. They come from old ones [...] new concepts emerge out of the interaction of old concepts and new situations, where the old concept is not simply re-applied unchanged to a new instance but is that *in terms* of which the new instance is seen. This is what is described as the displacement of concepts – a process in which old concepts, in order to function as projective models for new situations, come themselves to be seen in new ways.[28]

Similarly, elaborating on the importance of learning from exemplars of key experiments in science in understanding how discoveries are made, Kuhn writes:

I suggest that an acquired ability to see resemblances between apparently disparate problems plays in the sciences a significant part of the role usually attributed to correspondence rules. Once a new problem is seen to be analogous to a problem already solved, both an appropriate formalism and a new way of attaching its symbolic consequences to nature follow.[29]

Demonstrating the breadth of his vision yet again, while Edward Hall did not elaborate on the subject to the same extent as the other writers, in exploring his own theory of human evolution by extension he also came to see innovation in much the same way:

Inventions and scientific break-throughs are real and have their beginnings in looking at things differently. They do not spring full-blown from Zeus's brow, *but evolve slowly from very fragile and imperfect events* [added emphasis].[30]

George Kubler himself was uncertain about the role of innovation and individual creativity in his theory of linked problem solutions, particularly concerning the origin of prime objects, and pointedly objected to evolutionary metaphors – as popular in art history as they have been in architecture – which he believed left no place for radical human intervention. However, Kubler was not always consistent when it comes to arguing his case from specific examples. Like Benjamin Lee Whorf before him, he was especially interested in the architecture of the Pueblo Indians in the American southwest. For Kubler, however, the main point of interest lay in the impact Pueblo methods of building had on Spanish colonial architecture, and vice versa. In *The Religious Architecture of New Mexico*,[31] published more than two decades before *The Shape of Time*, he describes the Spanish colonial churches in the area, with their adobe, flat-roofed structures, as an outcome of 'the interaction of local and alien traditions seen in building activity under minimal economic conditions.'[32] Kubler explains that, while the Spanish friars based the plans of their missions on European models, they were compelled to abandon other European features like arches or domes in favor of local roofing techniques by their Indian workers, who actively *resisted* any deviation from their own traditions (fig. 9.15). If anything, Kubler argues, the resultant balance of cultural exchange was toward the 'indianization' of church architecture, rather than the imposition of any imported forms as might be expected from a conquering people.

Writing in *The Shape of Time*, though, Kubler takes a quite different position, presenting a drastic, one-sided picture of imperial domination throughout Latin America by colonists originating from the Iberian peninsula: 'Peninsular architects, sculptors and painters very early implanted among native craftsmen those European traditions of design and representation from which the colonies never lapsed even when revolting from Spanish colonial rule.'[33] By contrast again, in his own history of Hispanic culture in the region, Arthur L. Campa[34] presents a more balanced picture of cultural exchange, more in line with Kubler's earlier findings. According to Campa, the newcomers, who quickly recognized its virtues, adopted nearly all the main features and building techniques of native architecture:

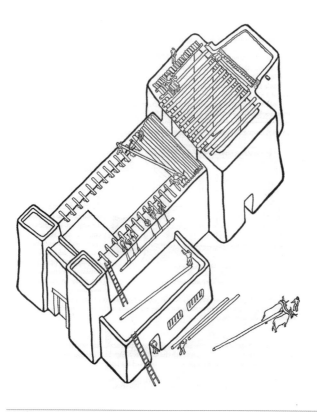

9.15 *Schematic drawing of timber roof structure for a typical seventeenth-century adobe church in New Mexico*

> The architecture used by the Indians was well adapted to the south-western climate, and the building materials available made it possible for the Spaniards to build themselves houses that bore a close resemblance to Indian architectural design. With their more extensive knowledge the colonists added a few improvements and a few elements of European architecture that were later adopted by the Indians.[35]

Among those 'improvements' the Spanish included the interior open courtyards and covered porches characteristic of their European houses. A happy combination of native and imported forms resulted, many examples of which can still be seen in Sante Fe and other places in New Mexico, inspiring many contemporary home builders in the region to emulate the same models and techniques.[36]

The reasons for Kubler's change of position, which blatantly contradicts the evidence of his earlier work on the same subject, remain unclear. Whatever the reasons, Kubler failed to convince all his followers. While accepting the main thrust of his approach, Joyce Brodsky[37] argues that Kubler's confused attempt to make room for disruptive innovation undermines the basic sense of continuity in the principle of linked solutions. Worse, it threatens to reintroduce the conventional biographical

The extended self

focus on the individual genius as someone apart from and in conflict with the prevailing tide of history. Innovation, she argues, just does not work like that: 'an innovator is one who comes closest to *revealing the pattern* [added emphasis] and rarely one who creates a new pattern.'[38] Thus, in place of Kubler's oppositional pairing of 'convention and innovation,' Brodsky substitutes the construct 'continuity and discontinuity,' thereby reinstating Kubler's original stress on artifacts as interrelated members of a series, each of which, including prime objects – which, as will shortly be explained, may themselves be products of creative fusions of the sort described above – has some kind of history or precedent behind it.

Paradoxically, far from creating a clean break with the past, innovation is therefore more accurately described as an *integrative process*, whereby the introduction of a new technical meme or assemblage assists in a *readjustment* of the prevailing culture to bring it into line with and to assimilate important changes – both social and technological – in the wider environment.[39] Pursuing the same argument, *continuity* in its broadest sense may be the ultimate and all-important criterion for memetic reproduction and stabilization. Contrary to the commonly accepted 'clean sweep' theory of innovation, even the most radical innovations and ideas rarely result in the complete erasure of existing ideas and methods. Thus, the coming of television has not done away with radio, which has actually grown in popularity in parallel with television. Neither has the rise of the automobile nor cheap air travel done away with fixed rail traffic, which, though temporarily forced into retreat, is now enjoying a resurgence in popularity and is even competing with intercity air traffic, as well as with the privileged motorcar. Far from doing away with established ideas, the products of innovation are better likened to a 'layer cake,' in which new layers of techniques and ways of doing things are added to previous layers of techniques and methods. While displacement does occur, it usually happens in a partial way, forcing some adjustment but leaving previous layers more or less in place for long periods of time, if not for always, generating continued activity in parallel with the new regime.[40]

How technology evolves

Continuity is also a major line of argument in Brian Arthur's important work, *The Nature of Technology*.[41] The previous chapter traced how new technologies like the automobile grew out of assemblages of existing, even ancient technologies and components like the spoked wheel, as integral elements in the long evolution of *Homo sapiens*, from primitive tool makers to the technology-obsessed creatures we are today. In his book, Arthur explores a wide range of similar examples to explain how technology itself evolves out of an endless combination and recombination of existing technologies – including those radically new products Kubler describes as 'prime objects.' Similar in principle if not in detail to the theories of innovation outlined above, while the combinatorial principle underpinning Arthur's theory may not be wholly original, the scope of his study of technological evolution is unique. Unlike Kubler, who is clearly interested in how artifacts evolve but fights shy of using evolutionary metaphors, Arthur also pointedly compares his theory with orthodox theories of biological evolution, with important implications for understanding human technicity. In addition to the many examples of other forms of technology, he includes at least one detailed example of innovative engineering that will be familiar to most architects and historians of the early modern movement: namely the 1933 Schwandbach Bridge near Berne, by the great Swiss engineer Robert Maillart, which is described below.

Starting out as a production engineer and eventually becoming an authority on the relations between technological development and modern economies, Arthur recalls that, while there are abundant detailed studies of the origins and development of particular technologies, both historical and modern, he could find no study explaining how technology itself evolves, applicable to all its forms, in the way that Darwin's theory of evolution applies to all manner of living species. As with Darwin's theory, he argues that, if there is to be a viable theory of technological evolution, it must also incorporate some kind of line of inheritance, that is to say, it must show how modern technologies *descend* from earlier technologies. Otherwise we might just as well use the word 'development,' which is often loosely used to refer to some sort of evolutionary process without indicating any kind of lineage.

Critically, however, Arthur also concludes that, as broad as it is, Darwin's theory *cannot* be applied to technological evolution because linear variation and natural selection alone cannot account for the sudden appearance of *novel technologies*, for which there may be no clear lineage. So while, as Distin argues, variations of an engineering design might be selected in analogous ways to natural selection, first by the tests they are subjected to by the designers themselves, and finally by the open market, this still does not explain the creation of what appear to be entirely new concepts and technologies, of which Arthur cites the railroad locomotive, the jet engine, radar, and the laser among other major modern innovations, which have no obvious precedent and seem to spring forth ready made in their inventors' imaginations:

> Radar 'descends' from radio. But you can vary 1930s radio circuits all you like and as radically as you like and you will never get radar. Even if you vary ideas about radio circuits all you like you will still not get radar. *Radar requires a different principle from radio* [added emphasis].[42]

This, Arthur contends, is essentially the problem of innovation, which so clearly puzzled and confused Kubler, as it has done countless others: 'If evolution in its fullest sense holds in technology, *then all technologies, including novel ones, must descend in some way from the technologies that preceded them* [added emphasis].'[43]

To solve it, he suggests, we not only have to look at novel technologies as a whole, we have to strip them apart and see what materials and components they are made of in turn. Here Arthur's personal experience and deep knowledge of technology gives him a clear edge over Stiegler and his followers, who can only discuss a limited range of technologies from direct experience – usually those involving the

The extended self

same modern media experienced by everyone else. Arthur suggests, for example, that if we opened up a jet engine we would find that some of its key components, such as compressors, turbines and combustion systems, were *already in use* in other technologies before the jet engine was invented: compressors could be found in industrial blower units around the same time; turbines and combustion systems inside electrical power generating systems since the early twentieth century, and so on:

> This makes the abrupt appearance of radically novel technologies suddenly seem much less abrupt. Technologies somehow must come into being *as fresh combinations of what already exists* [added emphasis].[44]

Moreover, Arthur continues, if novel technologies are the outcome of combinations of existing technologies, then – just like the spoked wheels and related assemblages described earlier – they must have the potential in turn of eventually becoming components themselves of future novel technologies. This, in a nutshell, is the method of technological evolution:

> The overall collection of technologies bootstraps itself upward from the few to the many and from the simple to the complex. *We can say that technology creates itself out of itself* [added emphasis].[45]

Appropriately, Arthur gives the name 'combinatorial evolution' to this method. Like Humberto Maturana and Francisco Varela, whose work on autopoiesis Arthur acknowledges in his book but discovered only after he had arrived himself at the same idea, he presents technology as a self-producing and self-perpetuating process, the essence of which he captures in the above quotation.[46] However, he is quick to point out that there is more to it than simply throwing a few technologies together that were already available. Each technology embodies its own logic and constraints, limiting the possibilities of combination or recombination with most other technologies, while opening up the creative possibilities of merging with compatible ones (the same constraints, it may be added, also clearly delineate technology as a self-producing system with boundaries). However, he suggests that all successful new technologies also involve another vitally important ingredient: one way or another, they all capture and harness *natural resources* and phenomena to their purpose:

> At the very start of technological time, we directly picked up and used [natural] phenomena: the heat of fire, the sharpness of flaked obsidian, the momentum of stone in motion. All that we have achieved since comes from harnessing these and other phenomena, and combining the pieces that result.[47]

As summarized by Arthur, the mechanism of technological evolution therefore depends upon three interrelated principles: all novel technologies are combinations of existing technologies; each technology itself is comprised of component technologies, some of which may also be reused in as yet unknown technologies; and, lastly, every technological innovation involves capturing natural resources to serve the new

Combinatorial design

technology. To these three mechanistic or material principles, Arthur also adds three broader definitions of what technology actually means, each of which addresses a different level of cultural evolution. Firstly, at the most basic and common level of understanding, there is the *singular* definition, or technology as '*a means to fulfill a human purpose*,'[48] whether it is a specific material, process or method. Secondly, there is the *plural* definition, or 'technology as an *assemblage of practices and components*,'[49] such as electronics, biotechnology and transportation. Thirdly, there is 'technology as the entire *collection of devices and engineering practices available to a culture*.'[50]

The first and most basic level of meaning is the one that architects and other designers are mostly familiar with in their day-to-day practice, though the two higher levels affect them all, consciously or not. The second level of meaning corresponds with assemblage theory, while the last and broadest level of meaning approximates most closely to technics.[51]

Breaking surface

Explaining how the idea for the jet engine came about, Arthur also touches on the more mysterious processes of conscious and unconscious cognition involved in the search for a new principle of propulsion to replace the propeller engine. The two engineers credited with the idea – Arthur avoids the word 'inventor' for what it invokes of the solitary genius working from a blank sheet of paper – Frank Whittle and Hans von Ohain, working independently, approached the problem from different angles. However, both were agreed that an air-ducted system that could work at high altitudes was required, narrowing the range of possible solutions and relevant existing technologies and components, all of which, as noted above, were 'borrowed from technologies used for other purposes.'[52] Equally impressive is the degree of concentration involved, as Arthur describes it:

> The mind (for the moment I will treat the originator as a singular mind, but more usually several minds are at work) becomes fixed on the problem. It scans possibilities that might with further development satisfy the desiderata. This search is conceptual, wide, and often obsessive. Newton commented famously that he came across his theory of gravitational orbits 'by thinking on it continuously.' This continuous thinking allows the subconscious to work, possibly to recall an effect or concept from past experience, and it provides a subconscious alertness so that when a candidate principle or a different way to define a problem suggests itself the whisper at the door is heard.[53]

However, beyond wondering at the phenomenon, which anyone involved in any kind of creative exercise has experienced at one time or another in the course of their work and also probably wondered at, Arthur can offer no further comment, let alone any explanation. Neuroscientists have also yet to solve the mystery, which is deeply rooted in the nature of consciousness itself, though they are probably best equipped to do so. For the time being, let the moment when previously subconscious processes in the mind 'break surface' and yield a fully formed idea be accepted for the miracle of creativity it is. However, this is very different from suggesting that fully formed concepts appear in the mind out of nowhere. A well prepared mind, knowledgeable of existing and relevant technologies and concepts, together with a strong personal commitment, as Polanyi maintains, to searching for and finding new solutions are both essential factors in the whole process, which may have preoccupied the person or persons concerned for many months and often many years prior to that 'eureka' moment of revelation.

Once 'out there' in the public realm, though, Arthur observes that new technologies can quickly spread, sparking interest and duplication – permits permitting – in ever-widening circles. Relaxing his critical stance regarding neo-Darwinian theories of evolution, he likens this to the way memes catch on and infect other minds:

> Successful solutions and ideas in engineering [also] behave this way. They too are copied and repeated and propagate among practitioners. They become elements that stand ready for use in combination.[54]

While natural selection cannot explain radical innovations, Arthur does allow that some kind of selective process takes place *after* the new technology comes into being.[55] Even so, he cautions against treating analogies with natural selection too literally, particularly concerning issues of fitness or what ultimately makes one technology more successful than a competing technology, which can depend on a multitude of different factors. The 'best' technologies, he observes, meaning the most suited to their purpose, do *not* in real life always win out in the end. While any successful technology must have at least some significant merits, chance and good publicity can also decide the issue. Echoing Richard Dawkins' original comments on the conservatism of the memetic process, Arthur suggests that once a particular technology has built up its own momentum it may then proliferate despite the presence of worthy or even superior competitors:

> As a solution becomes more prevalent, it becomes more visible, and therefore more likely to be adopted and improved by other designers [...] technologies that gain prevalence tend to gain *further advantage and to lock in* [added emphasis], so there is a positive feedback at work in the 'selection' of technologies.[56]

Mixed origins of radical design

However, there can no doubt regarding the merits of the Schwandbach Bridge (fig. 9.16), the design of which Arthur explains as an inspired combination of existing technologies, much like his other key exemplars, but which serves equally well as an illustration of Martin Heidegger's hypothetical bridge that '*gathers* the earth as landscape around the stream,'[57] or, in this case, a deep ravine. Dating from the mid-1930s and featured in many histories of modern architecture,[58] Maillart's bridge has all the attributes of a ground-breaking exercise in engineering design, the principles of which could be readily appreciated by architects, not only for the

9.16 *Schwandbach Bridge, Canton Berne, Switzerland, 1933, by Robert Maillart*

reinforced concrete design itself, but, as Arthur describes it, for the way it fitted with and complemented the landscape: 'It seems not so much to span a ravine as to float over it, an object almost recklessly slender, and one supremely innovative.'[59]

As Arthur explains, Maillart created his bridge at a time when all bridges, including those using advanced engineering technologies as well as masonry structures, were embellished with ornaments of one kind or another, which was supposed to obscure or make up for the severity of the structure itself. Yet Maillart employed no engineering techniques or forms that were not already well known. Reinforced concrete had been in use since the mid-1880s and the basic shape – the arch – supporting the roadway is one of the oldest forms of construction in human history, in common use even before the Romans made it their own. However, in order to

The extended self

achieve his ends and minimize the use of material in his design, Maillart had to solve the problem of the tipping effect caused by the uneven loads of passing vehicles. For instance, should a heavy vehicle be driven onto the deck it would cause the deck to want to dip at the loaded end and to rise at the far, unloaded end. Maillart, who carefully studied the geometry of the bridge, solved the problem by simply stiffening the deck with extra steel reinforcement, thus spreading any loads more evenly across the whole bridge: 'It was this "solution" that allowed lightness of the arch and deck without sacrificing strength – and therein lies the elegance.'[60] At the same time he did away with any ornamental embellishments, which is 'no small part of the reason his structures look so modern today.'[61]

Paradoxically, Arthur also makes fleeting references to Mies van der Rohe and Le Corbusier, dismissing the latter's architecture as a product of 'mechanistic dreams of pure order' and too much preoccupied with 'austere geometry and clean surfaces'[62] (oddly enough the same aesthetic attributes he praises in the Schwandbach Bridge), which he presumably also applies to Mies, though he offers no specific comments on the latter's work. By contrast, Arthur finds the 'messy vitality' propagated by Robert Venturi more appealing and in tune with his own vision of the complexities of technological evolution.[63]

However, while Arthur's views on Le Corbusier and Mies conform to familiar stereotypes, they hardly do justice to the actual complexity of their designs, revealing a shortcoming in his otherwise impressive study. Though both architects are still widely regarded as towering geniuses in the radical manner, boldly throwing off the shackles of past styles and replacing them with a wholly new kind of architecture based on modern technologies, the real story conforms more closely with the picture of combinatorial evolution Arthur extols than he supposes. Le Corbusier not only borrowed from the existing technologies and products of mass production, but, as was noted in the previous chapter, he also drew heavily, if less obviously, for his residential designs from architectural history, and the neo-classical typologies of Palladio's villas in particular. Le Corbusier's chief failure was not so much his sources of inspiration, which were far more diverse than the popular image of modern architecture Arthur subscribes to, but his amateurish understanding of the modern technologies of production that he purported to promote – a weakness he shared with most ideologically motivated modernists of the early twentieth century.[64]

Evolution of the tower type...

The evolution of tall buildings since the early twentieth century provides a para-digmatic study in the combinatorial evolution of technology, creating a series of distinctive building typologies through time indicative of self-producing systems in both Maturana and Varela's meaning of the term and Arthur's theory.[65] As it evolves from its mono-functional origins to its more recent multifunctional variations, so the type also reflects parallel changes in the evolution of modern city centers themselves, from their single-purpose, central business districts (or CBDs) to the increasingly

9.17 *The first safe mechanical elevator, invented by Elisha Grave Otis, 1853 (left). The illustration on the right shows an earlier passenger lift by Otis during the period of the American Civil War*

diverse cluster of activities, including residential, entertainment and retail functions, which typify the livelier cities of today.

Significantly, as noted in Chapter 7, none of the separate technological inventions like the skeleton construction illustrated in that chapter, or the mechanical elevator invented by Elisha Grave Otis (fig. 9.17), without which the height of buildings would have remained limited by the number of stairs that can be reasonably climbed, nor any of the social and economic developments that eventually combined together to create the assemblage of technical memes we call a skyscraper, had much to do with architects or architecture. Commenting on the complex origins of the building type, Ada Louise Huxtable[66] writes:

> Except for popular mythology and a totemic fascination with the skyscraper, its history has been too narrowly focused. There is general agreement on the significance of certain structures and events, such as those innovations that had their roots in many places and

flowered in Chicago in the late nineteenth century. At that time, and in that place, a unique combination of industrialization, business and real estate came together for the development of a new and distinctive building type: the American office building.[67]

However, once established as a centerpiece of urban growth, first in North America and then elsewhere, architects quickly found a new role in taming the intrusive newcomer and making it culturally acceptable. One way to do this was to dress it up in more familiar ways. They were greatly helped in their efforts in this respect by the aforementioned invention of the metal frame, thus relieving the external walls of any structural purpose and freeing them up for their remaining duties, namely keeping the weather out, letting light and air in and, not least, putting up a good appearance. Here the pioneering designers of the skyscrapers in Chicago and New York truly excelled themselves in inventiveness, adapting familiar styles of architecture that had evolved for completely different purposes to the new task. For example, effectively disguising the radical nature of the new building type, the vertical divisions in the cladding of many early skyscrapers were inspired by the tripartite structure of the classical column (fig. 9.18), with its base (foot of the building), shaft (regular office floors) and entablature (elaborate crown). Dressed up differently, Cass Gilbert's Woolworth Building of 1913 (fig. 9.19), also in New York, was designed in the neo-gothic style, earning it the popular description of a 'cathedral of commerce' – a badge of acceptance for the building type as much as for that specific structure, that has echoed down through the twentieth century till the present day.

Later, the Chrysler Building of 1930 (fig. 9.20) made its own special impact, displacing former architectural styles and confirming art deco in their place as the preferred expression for its time. The streamline Chrysler tower, with its famous stainless-steel spire, was purposefully designed by William Van Alen to conjure up images of the company's automobiles, already popular modern icons themselves. However, the internal structure and spatial functions of the office tower, with its extruded configuration of identical floors arranged around a vertical circulation and services core, had already evolved to the point where the architect's influence on the internal design was relatively insignificant. Alen's impact on the *cultural expression* of the company's industrial purpose and status, however, and on the consequent public acceptance of the building and the skyscraper type in general as a popular modern icon, could hardly have been greater – an expression made possible only by the freedom of external design afforded by the steel frame.

Only two architects during these first decades dared to rethink the way tall buildings could be designed internally as well as externally. At only eight storeys high, the first of these new models, Frank Lloyd Wright's Larkin Building, 1903 (fig. 9.21), was not a true skyscraper. Nevertheless, its hollowed out plan form with all the vertical services pushed to the periphery suggested a radical alternative scheme to the way office towers could be planned, visibly uniting the workforce in one great interior space.[68] Mies's unbuilt projects for a glass skyscraper in the period 1919–21 (fig. 9.22) also showed how the principles of the new 'glass architecture' might be

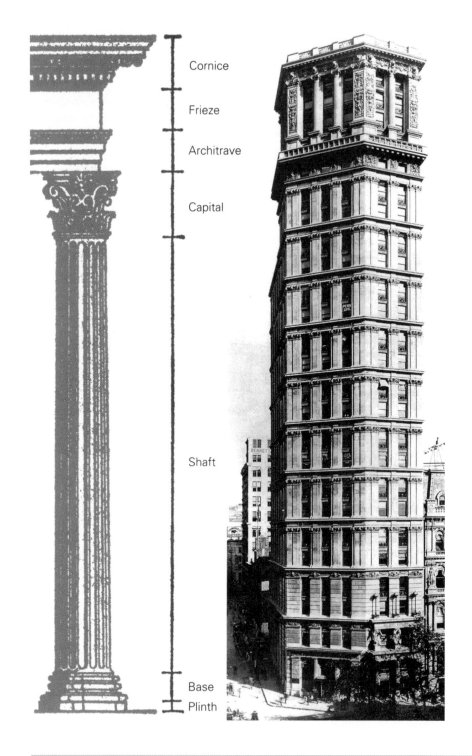

Cornice

Frieze

Architrave

Capital

Shaft

Base

Plinth

9.18 *Many early American skyscrapers, like the St Paul Building, New York, 1890, by George B. Post, were modeled on the tripartite division of the classical column, shown left*

The extended self

9.19 *Woolworth Building, New York, 1913, by Cass Gilbert*

9.20 *Chrysler Building, New York, 1930, by William Van Alen*

applied to tall buildings, exploiting the glass cladding to express the internal structure and spaces for the first time. He also understood the potential reflective properties of glass to mirror the changing skies. For all their inventiveness, however, both concepts were to wait many decades before they were to be fully realized, suggesting, as Arthur points out, that the success of a new project, no matter what the quality, may depend on many issues beyond the control of its creators.

All of that changed with the widespread acceptance of the modern movement in the second half of the twentieth century, with its stress on clarity and transparency, of both structure and purpose. Like the earlier invention of the steel frame and the Otis lift, the commercial availability of air conditioning in the post-war years, combined with the manufacture of ever larger and tougher sheets of plate glass, also had a profound influence on subsequent developments. However, it took another modernist architect to appreciate the full potential of the new technologies and materials. Exploiting both innovations, Gordon Bunshaft of the firm Skidmore, Owings & Merrill (SOM) transformed the image of the New York skyscraper with the curtain-walled, vertical slab of the Lever House of 1952 (fig. 9.23), creating the model for countless reproductions of the type around the world.

Combinatorial design

9.21 *Larkin Building, Buffalo, 1903, by Frank Lloyd Wright. Internal view of the central court. Vertical circulation and services were all situated around the perimeter of the building*

The extended self

9.22 *Model of glass skyscraper project, Berlin, 1921, by Mies van der Rohe. One of the architect's visionary designs of the period for skyscrapers*

9.23 *Lever House, New York, 1952, by Skidmore, Owings & Merrill (SOM): the original model, or 'prime object,' for countless replicas around the world*

As revolutionary as they were in their use of glass and technological services, while the new office towers looked outwardly vastly different from their stone-clad predecessors, they still shared the same basic kebab-like structural and spatial configuration internally, albeit now flooded with more natural light. It took another 30 years before Norman Foster finally broke the mold for good with the Hongkong and Shanghai Bank headquarters, creating a vast, 'core-less' space exposing the muscular structural frame internally as well as externally – a true cathedral of commerce, but without the gothic trimmings (fig. 9.24). While the hollow planning typology can be traced back to FLW's Larkin Building, the combination of the Bank's atrium and open interior, external service cores and completely transparent skin effectively reinvented the model for office towers, creating opportunities for new ways of working together in such buildings as well as new spatial experiences. Gone was the standard, privileged ring of executive offices around the outer walls, to be replaced by glass-walled offices situated 'inboard,' so that everyone in the building shared the same views and natural light. A combined system of high-speed external lifts and

9.24 *Hongkong and Shanghai Bank Corporation (HSBC) headquarters, Hong Kong, 1986, by Foster & Partners. Interior view showing banking hall atrium and entranceway from public passage below. The banking hall was partly inspired by the interior of Frank Lloyd Wright's Larkin Building*

open escalators in the center of the building – also unique for its time – changed the way people could move from floor to floor in skyscrapers, greatly reducing the normally claustrophobic element of the experience and opening up the Bank still further, socially as well as visibly.[69] Further developments in the social organization of the internal workspaces have also since increased the opportunities for informal meeting places and interaction between the staff, reflecting a broader acceptance of 'flatter' decision-making structures – all of which constitute significant departures from the outdated model of office towers and related power structures reported in Chapter 7.[70]

The extended self

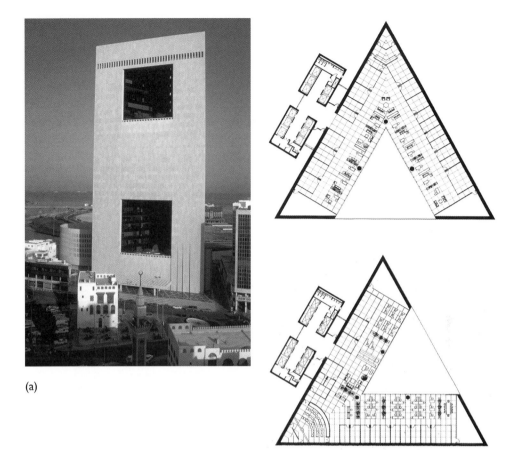

(a)

(b)

9.25 *National Commercial Bank, Jeddah, Saudi Arabia, 1982, by SOM.
(a) View of triangular tower showing recessed 'skygardens.' The first tall building to feature
elevated open courts on a large scale. (b) The 'V'-shaped rotating plan form creates a
continuous open shaft in the center of the tower, which helps to ventilate the building*

Another major breakthrough in the tower type came in 1982 with Bunshaft's
design for the National Commercial Bank in Jeddah (fig. 9.25). With its three large
outdoor 'skygardens,' Bunshaft created a secondary ground level for the first time in
any tall building, introducing a new design principle of the kind Arthur describes
that rarely occurs in engineering, but which transformed the way skyscrapers are
conceived. Arranged in a spiraling triangular configuration around a central vertical
shaft, the deep skygardens also helped protect the recessed glass walls from the fierce
Arabian sun, marking a major break with past skyscrapers, toward a more responsive
approach to local climates. There followed several distinctive towers with similar

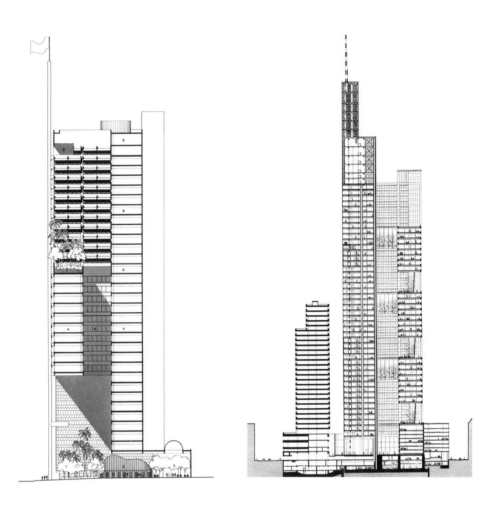

9.26 *Capita Centre, Sydney, 1989, by Harry Seidler. Section showing staggered skygardens*

9.27 *Sectional drawing of Commerzbank, Frankfurt, 1997, by Foster & Partners. Section showing rotating position of four-storey skygardens*

spatial features, each adding its own innovations to the new series. Harry Seidler's Capita Centre (1989) in Sydney (fig. 9.26), and Foster's Commerzbank (1997) in Frankfurt (fig. 9.27) both feature sections with similar deep voids and vertical shafts, while Ken Yeang's Menara Mesiniaga tower (1992) in Kuala Lumpur (fig. 9.28), and Foster's best-known tower, the Swiss Re (2003) in London (fig. 9.29), popularly known as the 'Gherkin,' also feature circular floor plans with spiraling skygardens (enclosed in the latter case like the skygardens in the Commerzbank in response to the northern climate).

9.28 *Menara Mesiniaga, Kuala Lumpur, 1992, by T. R. Hamzah and K. Yeang*

9.29 *Swiss Re, London, 2003, by Foster & Partners*

... and beyond

The mold was dramatically broken yet again by United Architects – a group of several cutting-edge practices – in their joint entry for the World Trade Center competition in 2002 (fig. 9.30). Comprised of an asymmetrically balanced cluster of towers of varying heights and bulk leaning against each other for mutual support – rather like family members gathered for a photo – the towers are all joined at an upper level by a continuous public concourse or 'skyway,' complete with internal 'parks.' The entry by Foreign Office Architects (FOA), a cluster of curving tubes joined at different heights, is also unusual, not only for its design (fig. 9.31), but also for the architects' self-conscious exploration of the idea of the tower type itself:

> For the World Trade Center we looked at the evolution of high-rise buildings, emerging from the pages of *Neufert*, and the Petronas and Sears towers. This is a very important project for us because it is the first to emerge from a reflection on typology. It was about understanding the history of the type and producing something directly out of that history.[71]

Combinatorial design   **207**

9.30 *Competition entry for World Trade Center towers, 2002, by United Architects. Rendering showing public concourse linking towers at upper level*

Significantly, both designs broke with the 'extrusion principle' of skyscraper design, which dictates that the same basic floor plan with its central core be repeated all the way up the tower, with only minor variations at the base and top; so that anyone looking at a plan above, say, the level of the podium – if there is one – can safely predict the spatial layout and structure of the topmost useable floor from all the floors below (discounting any Chrysler-style crowning flourishes or mechanical services).[72] While the floor plans in the spiraling towers by SOM et al. described above shift vertically at different levels, the spiral geometry itself is also a regular one, so that, given the number of floors and any decrease or increase in the pattern, it is still possible to predict both the shape and position of any floor above. By contrast, both the floor plans and sections of the clusters of linked towers that comprise the United Architects' and FOA's schemes are quite irregular – particularly in the former design – so that any cut taken through the complex at a lower level provides an unreliable guide to what lies above, other than the relatively fixed positions of the vertical circulation cores.

Aside from its irregular geometry, by linking all the towers together with an extended public concourse the United Architects' scheme also gave a new impetus

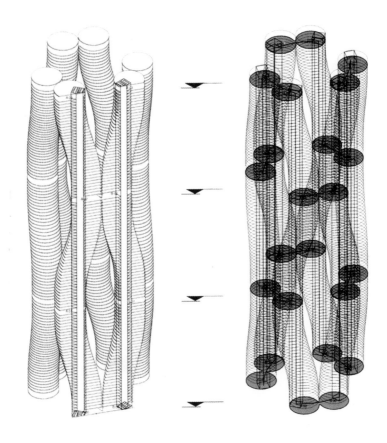

9.31 *Competition entry for World Trade Center towers, 2002, by Foreign Office Architects (FOA), showing cores on the left and linked floors on the right*

to the horizontal dimension in high-rise architecture. Cementing the earlier innovations beginning with SOM's tower in Jeddah in creating a secondary ground level, radical designs like this have led to the evolution of a whole new breed of 'vertical architecture,' in which both horizontal and vertical dimensions receive equal attention, potentially changing both the spatial and social character of high-rise buildings.[73] Several research-oriented academic studios, such as the Vertical Architecture STudio (VAST) run by this writer at several universities in Australia and the USA, have also since taken these initiatives further, involving integrated food production (vertical farms) within linked, mixed-use, high-rise urban complexes (figs 9.32 and 9.33). Together with upper-level public parks and concourses, such schemes are reinventing the idea of the vertical garden city proposed by Le Corbusier, eliminating distances between centers of food and energy production while offering the kind of social amenities and interaction normally found in cities only at street level.[74]

Combinatorial design   **209**

9.32 *Vertical Architecture STudio (VAST), 2006. Project for central Sydney, by Renn, Waterman and Wrightson, University of Sydney. Aerial view showing elevated plaza*

The extended self

9.33 *VAST, 2009. Project for a Vertical Garden City, Mark III, Barangaroo, Sydney, by Nor, Turner and Wang, University of New South Wales. View from Harbour showing linked towers with 'turbine sails'*

However, of all the factors driving evolutionary changes in the tower type, climate change and the consequent search for more sustainable, energy-efficient solutions are likely to have the most enduring effects. Debating the spatial efficiency of the tower type as an urban form set within the center of its site, versus perimeter planning, such as that which produced the medium-rise buildings with their central courtyards typical of Bath, Berlin and other European cities, Alexander Cuthbert[75] cites the earlier topological studies of Lionel March and his co-authors.[76] Written at a time when global warming was still an unknown concept except for among a handful of pioneering scientists, while March et al. make a strong argument for the geometric efficiency of the latter form over the tower configuration, they ignore any other factors that might influence designers, notably the now all-important issue of natural ventilation.[77] While perimeter planning might still be well suited to temperate climates, just as the widely spaced, detached houses on stilts and villas in Malaysia with their permeable walls are best suited to catch any cooling breezes at ground level, so well spaced towers are also best suited to take advantage of increased air movement above ground level.[78] This applies now not only to the hot-humid tropics, where Yeang, as Cuthbert points out, pioneered the concept of

Combinatorial design

'green skyscrapers,' but also in Europe, where rising temperatures and requirements for energy efficiency impacted on the design of Foster's Commerzbank: the first large-scale, naturally ventilated office tower since the invention of air conditioning.[79] There is all the more need, therefore, to find sustainable solutions to high-rise living that embody as many of the spatial and social values that people are accustomed to finding at street level, as well as alternative energy sources and other responses to climate change.

A significant outcome of these developments is that the influence of climate on building forms and settlement patterns may no longer be so easily disregarded or separated out from cultural issues in the way that they have been in the past – albeit with significant exceptions – as recounted here. As the growing debates on the subject referenced in this book have already shown, climate change itself is now as much, if not more, of an urgent cultural issue as it is a matter for scientific attention and concern, and is already shaping architecture and urban design around the world in positive ways, including many of the high-rise projects described above.

In the final part of this book, Chapter 10 examines some of the crucial psychological and social factors that are impacting on the extended self and affecting the present and possible future form of our cities, and that may determine which of the spectrum of possible strategies for urban growth and design will eventually prevail.

Part III summary

The third part of the book marked a change in focus from the preliminary work of identifying those aspects of our subject that are most in need of resolution, to the main task of providing solutions to those issues. Several new concepts and theories explaining the self's primary modes of extension and reproduction were proffered, supported by numerous examples taken from different times, cultures and places, showing how they have actually worked out in life.

Opening Chapter 7, it was reasoned that, if memes exist as cultural replicators in anything like the form Richard Dawkins describes, then there should be clear evidence of such replicators in everyday language and culture. Such evidence, it was proposed, may be readily found, not only in the fundamental role played by classification systems in human language itself, but also as revealed in the naming and classification of types of artifacts of all kinds, from primitive tools to buildings and whole cities.

Based on this premise, the chapter began by pinpointing the cognitive roots of classification and combinativity underlying all taxonomies, indicating a universal basis for identifying and grouping types as a primary mode of cultural transmission and diffusion. Corroborating the research on canonical neurons reported in Chapter 3, Jonas Langer observes that combinativity is integral to both human cognition and language, providing a 'general-purpose structure' for grouping things, together with their related linguistic symbols. The ubiquity of types expressed in everyday language in the act of naming things thus points to a fundamental need to distinguish one thing from another and to identify common groups and uses going as far back in time as life itself; not only to the first upright hominids to walk the earth, but also to any creature that found the need to recognize prey from predator, what's good to eat and what's not, and who to mate with.

The discussion then proceeded through a brief study of the influence of biological taxonomies on architectural history and theory to more detailed studies of building types and urban morphologies by various writers. While many types and morphologies were recorded, the stability of the relations between form, function and meaning was questioned, suggesting, as the discussion in Chapter 1 indicated, that similar building forms might serve different functions and carry different meanings according to location and cultural context.

George Kubler's general theory of types as series of 'linked problem solutions' was presented in the same chapter as a fruitful basis for understanding the importance of precedent in the design and evolution of artifacts, including buildings. It also helped to resolve one of the key questions in memetics regarding the relations between memes and their vehicles – namely, can one exist without the other? Observing that, in keeping with Kubler's theory, the concept of a specific type is repeatedly *inferred* or reconstructed from observation of not one but a series of similar artifacts, it was concluded that memes have *no independent life of their own* outside of those artifacts, other than as a historical record of those reconstructions, which is itself comprised of technically inscribed memes. The process of endless reconstruction also leaves open the possibility of variations over time according to how different people interpret types from their exemplars – a very different idea from the original concept of memes as simple units of imitation or copying mechanisms, equivalent to mental Xerox machines.

Following John Wilkins' distinction between the logical or 'essentialist' concept of types and species and the more open Darwinian interpretation accepted by most biologists and naturalists, the latter is offered as the only realistic concept of a type, as used in everyday language and experience. It was furthered argued that, in accordance with the above description of a type as a self-replicating series of objects or other member of a class, types fulfill the conditions for self-producing systems as set out in Chapter 5. Correspondingly, as systems of classification, types also answer the question raised in the same chapter as to what it is, if human societies are also self-producing systems, that societies produce, that is, types of social order, be they occupations, institutions, artifacts, buildings and spaces, or any other regular and repeatable form of culture.

Thus far, types and classification systems fulfill many of the functions Dawkins prescribes for memes. However, though the word 'type' is often used by biologists interchangeably with 'species', it does not generally have the same evolutionary connotations. Neither is it normally identified as a cultural concept, as memes are. For these and other reasons, it was argued in Chapter 8 that the term 'meme' should be retained to designate the primary cognitive agent of cultural evolution and diffusion. Taking up the issue of the relations between form and content, it was also suggested that, while biological species and types of artifacts share common characteristics as taxonomies, the latter are more consistently identified by their material and morphological characteristics than by their functions.

Accordingly, eschewing any fixed relations between form and content, a new concept, the 'technical meme,' was proposed, based on the material embodiment or inscription of memes in artifacts and other culture-forms. It was further argued that the function and meaning of a technical meme could be induced or inferred, as suggested above, only from a series of exemplars in actual *use* over a period of time, thus completing a vital link in the cognitive loop integrating the extended self with the wider world.

Given that, as with the elements of any taxonomy, the identity of a given type or meme depends upon which broader series or grouping it belongs to, it was further proposed that assemblage theory offers a suitable framework for grouping coevolutionary clusters of technical memes to create artifacts of varying complexity, while still retaining the identity of their components. The term 'phenotypic effects' was also rejected for its genetic associations in favor of a new term, 'contingent effects,' based on Manuel De Landa's concept of contingent relations, to describe all the effects specific technical memes and assemblages have on the world.

Demonstrating how technical memes and assemblages evolve in practice, the interrelated histories of the spoked wheel, the automobile and the freeway were examined as key elements in the evolution of dispersed cities, out of which the automobile-dependent, suburban way of life has arisen, radically changing the bodily experience of urban space in the process. Some further impacts on the building types involved were briefly discussed, together with some of the social implications indicative of their contingent effects. The coevolution of the three elements in turn provides plentiful evidence of autopoietic systems at work, the self-producing conditions of which have been sustained in modern times by the ever-growing expansion of low-density suburbs.

Widening the range of examples of fluid relations between building form and content, Chapter 9 argued that the evolution of vernacular architecture is primarily determined by cultural customs inscribed in material form, that is, technical memes, rather than by purely functional or climatic factors alone, the influence of which varies considerably from culture to culture. The reproduction of similar building types and forms in quite different cultures provides further evidence of flexible relations between form and meaning. Examples of hybrid building forms in different parts of the world, including colonial architecture, were also offered as further traces of the evolution of designs comprised of elements from different sources, similar to that described in Chapter 8.

This led in turn to a closer examination of the combinatorial nature of change and innovation in design. It was argued that innovations emerge out of fresh combinations of existing but previously unrelated concepts or techniques. In this sense even the most innovative designs can be argued to have a 'natural history,' involving evolutionary processes analogous to those governing organic species, albeit with significant differences between their respective agents of reproduction. Examples of related theories of creativity advanced by several like-minded authors during the last century were quoted before proceeding to Brian Arthur's 'combinatorial theory' of technological evolution, closing an important gap in Bernard Stiegler's work regarding the evolutionary agents involved in human technicity. Significantly, while Arthur arrived independently at his own interpretation of the self-producing character of evolving technologies, he also explicitly acknowledges parallels with the work of Humberto Maturana and Francisco Varella on autopoietic systems.

Finally, the combinatorial principles underlying the process of radical design were also illustrated by several case studies, including the evolution of the tower type and recent proposals for new forms of vertical architecture and urban design. As has been observed, while for genetic reasons breeding between different animal species is rare in nature, human populations and their cultures are relatively free to intermingle, and frequently do so. Far from being scarce, creative fusions such as those described in this book are commonly found in human societies between quite different technical memes and assemblages, underscoring the essential differences as well as similarities between biological and cultural evolution. It may be concluded from these concrete examples that, just as the extended self is the hybrid outcome of many combined elements, so the built world is constructed in the same way as a mirror image of that process.

The last part of the book will explore the broader environmental implications of that coevolution, seeking explanations for how and why people can become so 'locked into' a self-producing cycle – even when the potential outcome threatens to destroy everything they hold dear – that they cannot extricate themselves without also threatening their core identities.

The extended self

Part IV: Transformations

10 Recasting the extended self

The examples of cross-fertilization between building forms described in Chapters 8 and 9 provide ample evidence that, as previously noted, though cross-breeding in nature between different species is genetically limited, no comparable restrictions apply to the products of human cultures, even when widely separated by time and space. Yet, just as Brian Arthur points out that not all technologies are compatible with each other or make potentially good combinations, so is it also apparent that, once specific assemblages of technical memes are culturally entrenched, despite the potential or need for change, individuals and groups are often reluctant to give them up, so interwoven are their own identities with those same assemblages.

Focusing now on the common resistance to cultural change, the discussion returns to the question of how much control or influence individuals and groups may or may not have over their own development. In the conclusion to Chapter 7, it was suggested that, as both the components and products of human societies, types and taxonomies must be consistent and predictable enough to be recognized by the members of the societies they sustain. It follows that *high levels of conformity* are characteristic of human societies, with inevitable impacts on the extended self. Commencing with examples of the general tendency for people to stick with popular culture-forms and genres, this chapter probes further into the reasons why people might resist changing preferred types of habitats and related lifestyles, despite any negative personal and environmental consequences those preferred ways of life might entail. In probing those reasons, the question arises: if types are self-producing systems, might there also be, as Richard Dawkins suggests, 'selfish' forms of cultural production equivalent to selfish genes,[1] using our extended selves for their own benefit and propagating themselves – including building types – through their associated technical memes and assemblages? And if so, are the runaway technics described in this book accountable in like terms?

The issue is especially pertinent to the automobile-dependent way of life that characterizes modern cities and suburban building types, particularly in North America and Australia, where the pattern is widespread, the deleterious outcomes of which are recorded in this chapter and many other sources. As with the evidence for the existence of technical memes and types themselves found in everyday language and classification systems, it is reasoned that indirect but substantial evidence for the impact of selfish culture-forms may be found in many of the habitual behavior patterns of individuals and groups in well established societies.

The discussion then moves to the mounting pressures for change arising from those urban outcomes, compounded by the accelerating effects of global warming and climate change, to which Australia is particularly vulnerable. Drawing on Jared Diamond's history of failed societies, it is argued that human resistance to any fundamental personal or cultural change – despite mounting evidence of self-destruction – has led in the past to the collapse of whole civilizations, and could do so again. The final sections of the chapter compare alternative scenarios for the future and delineate some possibilities for recasting the extended self in more positive ways, together with the societies and cultures that shape it. These range from visions of utopian new civilizations rising from the ashes of the present one to relatively modest but practical proposals for changing the way people move about their urban habitats.

Creatures of habit

It may be recalled from Chapter 1 that, among his other insights into the way people in different cultures use space, Edward Hall made the point that architects generally underestimate the extent to which individuals can become attached to the form and use of spaces they are accustomed to, describing the phenomenon as 'fixed-feature space.' In the same chapter, Clare Cooper's observations on the psychic origins of 'the extreme resistance of most people to any change'[2] in the form of their dwellings were also noted. The popularity of the suburban house type and its spatial elements, as interpreted by Kim Dovey in Chapter 7 in his own deterministic social and political terms, can therefore also be interpreted in large part as a tacit participation in a relatively stable and predictable social order, the rewards of which include a reassuring degree of *familiarity* with selected dwelling types, sufficient at least to keep them flourishing in many parts of the world, despite the kind of negative factors highlighted by Lewis Mumford and other critics. We are, as the saying goes, very much creatures of habit, by conscious or unconscious choice as much as for any other reason.

There is evidence too from other culture-forms that individuals and groups not only become habituated to a particular type or genre (as cultural taxonomies, the two concepts have much in common with each other), but they may also actively *resist* any changes in that form which might reduce their ability to recognize it, no less than they resist changes to familiar kinds of dwellings. To take an example from modern popular culture, despite all the technological advances in movie making over the last century, the number and range of basic movie genres has hardly changed at all from the formative years of the industry: comedies; westerns; gangster, sports, horror, sci-fi and action movies; thrillers; historical epics; biographies; disaster movies; love stories; and rom-coms. In the following telling passage, David Thomson, a well known film critic, explains what made Hollywood so successful in its heyday:

Movies are a habit and a big part of us wants them to be like they were before. 'Surprise me' we say. 'Show me something new – *but let me recognise it* [added emphasis].'

Director Jean Renoir said a filmmaker makes the same film over and over again. He tried to change this, but couldn't. He had his story. Orson Wells shocked viewers with the groundbreaking *Citizen Kane*. Then over the years he used the same images – the way painters do – with the recurring plot of a powerful man being investigated and found out in films such as *The Stranger, Mr Arkadin* and *Touch of Evil.*

When the old studios had popular actors under contract, they made vehicles for those stars [...]. You don't put Lassie in a [Joan] Crawford picture or vice versa. It's a business and if the public like a personality, you tell stories that flatter the personality. A mythology develops, a set of legends – it's called a star system and *the code of genres* [added emphasis]. We enjoy these rules, because they suggest we should be wary of Peter Lorre or Sydney Greenstreet, but trust Bogart and Bergman.[3]

In these brief but insightful words, Thomson captures many of the essential features of memetic transmission and reproduction discussed previously: the selective advantage they have if they fit in with the existing cultural environment, whether consciously or unconsciously; the way movie characters or personalities – technical memes in themselves – create expectations, and so encourage their own self-production; the way one meme type links up to and nestles within another, as when a movie star influences the vehicles he or she appears in, so that they become mutually interdependent; and not least, the way even the most creative individuals, having once broken the mold, then lock themselves into particular ways of doing things, just like the movie stars they helped to create. That is to say, successful memes keep reproducing themselves until they are no longer selected. Whether we call them species, types or genres, it is always the *identity of the phenomena* that is being reproduced, if not always precisely, then with sufficient consistency to be recognized and distinguished from other replicated entities.

As we saw, not only Dawkins and many of his followers, but even radical evolutionary theorists like Jerry Fodor and Massimo Piattelli-Palmarini also subscribe to variations of the viral analogy to explain why some ideas spread more quickly or 'catch on' in people's minds more readily than others do.[4] While not denying the possible role of viral-like methods of transmission, it is all too easy, as Distin points out, to simply use them as a way of describing those memes the writer is personally critical of. Cautioning against any facile use of the analogy, Distin suggests that 'whether a given replicator is a virus or a meme will be determined by its method of replication ("normal" or parasitic), rather than by its content.'[5]

To take a familiar example, of all the types of automobile to fill the parking lots of shopping malls and suburban estates, it is tempting to explain away the popularity of the four-wheel drive sports utility vehicle (SUV) as an indication of similar irrational undercurrents (fig. 10.1), as Daniel Dennett hinted in pointing out the difference between mere car owners and SUV-loving 'motorists.' While modern SUVs offer little in the way of genuine advantages as a mode of private transportation, except in those rare cases when they are actually used off the road, the SUV meme offsets and conceals its objective negative aspects – poor safety record,[6] high fuel consumption

Recasting the extended self

10.1 *Typical jumbo-sized American SUVs seen in Lincoln, Nebraska*

and high purchase price – by attaching itself to other, more positive memes and assemblages. These include 'nature' (SUVs are made to drive through natural terrain), 'family' (SUVs are built to take a large family and look and feel safe), and 'strong and superior individual' (SUVs look like tanks, and place their drivers higher than most other drivers), even though those other associations may all be delusional.[7]

The illusion of free will

As plausible as such cases of viral-like behavior are, pending further evidence of its impact there are other, more conventional factors of a social and psychological nature betraying the possible effects of culture-forms with their own momentum. According to Mike McRae,[8] the habitual tendency to latch onto ideas of all sorts, both good and bad, even when there seems little rational justification for doing so, is indicative of 'tribal' habits of thinking, most of which individuals may be unaware of or, if aware, unwilling to admit to. Drawing analogies with the swarm behavior of birds and other creatures,[9] among the difficulties standing in the way of understanding such behavior McRae points to deeply entrenched beliefs in free will and a consequent resistance to the idea that we may not be as much in control of our thoughts and actions as we would like to think:

> We're so hung up on defending free will and theory of mind that the idea of being influenced by the collective to any significant extent feels somewhat heretical, especially in cultures that celebrate the rights to individual freedom. It's easy to see hive-like behaviour in others, of course [...] but never ourselves.

The extended self

But to what extent are we isolated from other minds? How much control do we have over our ideas, our thoughts and our beliefs?

We are all products of our own collectives, our own tribes. That's not to say we're at the complete mercy of external cognitive forces. But how we behave as individuals can't easily be teased out of the context of a collective either. *We are tribal animals* [added emphasis].[10]

While acknowledging that other creatures possess communication systems and the ability to use tools and other basic forms of behavioral extension of the kind discussed in earlier chapters, McRae maintains that humans developed those and many other skills to advanced levels as social beings of a special sort, with the ability to identify with and read the thoughts and minds of others to an extent other creatures are not capable of, that is, to exhibit *intentional* behavior at higher-order levels. As suggested in Chapters 2 and 3, this is not a new idea. But McRae adds another dimension to the social side of human evolution by explaining how humans can become attached to ideas or ways of behavior even in situations of uncertainty. Citing some well known experiments by Michael Gazzaniga at the University of California involving patients who had undergone split-brain surgery,[11] McRae suggests that one reason for such behavior is that, as the experiments showed, the human mind, like nature, abhors a vacuum. As McRae recounts, when Gazzaniga presented his patients with confusing information he found that the left hemisphere, which would normally interpret information in a meaningful context in tandem with the right hemisphere, would *invent* an answer on its own even if it made no sense: 'Put simply, Gazzaniga's experiment showed that "I don't know" is simply not an answer the brain is happy with.'[12]

However, you do not have to have a split brain to think like this. McRae deduces that, in normal situations where uncertainty also prevails or is widely seen to prevail by others, even if ample evidence is available to resolve the issue people will act in a similar fashion and make up their minds one way or the other according to how their own tribe views the matter: 'Our tribal knowledge influences our trust in the scientist, the priest, the politician or the celebrity who tells us the globe is warming, vaccinations are unsafe, mobile phones give you cancer or Bill Clinton is really a reptilian alien in disguise.'[13] He goes on to offer many examples of tribal thinking involving direct conflicts between established scientific knowledge and evidence and popular but apparently unshakeable beliefs or myths, including so-called 'alternative' medical treatments and 'intelligent design':

It is a habit of the tribal brain to apply supernatural explanations to gaps in our knowledge of the natural world. Our hunger for answers to our questions, coupled with our social engineering, satisfies our search for understanding with teleological, personalized explanations.[14]

McRae finds further evidence of tribal patterns of thinking in what cognitive psychologists call 'confirmation bias.' Described as 'a tendency to passively favour observations that support what we already believe to be true, rather than actively search for reasons to contradict it,'[15] McRae ventures that while there is no simple explanation for why our brains act like this, it could be just a way to conserve energy, which, as we know, brains use an awful lot of. Alternatively, and more importantly, he writes: 'Another possibility is that confirmation bias arises out of our motivation to support commonly held beliefs rather than refute them, which is simply another function of brains that evolved to be social machines.'[16] Put another way, the need to belong to and *to be seen* to belong to your own tribe and *not* to rock the boat or challenge commonly held beliefs in any way that might threaten membership will generally override other considerations.[17]

Neither is McRae alone in stressing the general reluctance of people to rethink their personal views and positions, even when challenged by contrary evidence. Employing similar terminology, Cass Sunstein explains why balanced arguments and rational debates rarely persuade people to change their minds about key issues. More problematic still, Sunstein observes that, confronted with conflicting arguments, rather than try to assimilate the new evidence, people will often respond by defending their previous beliefs even *more* vigorously than before:

> What explains this? The answer is called 'biased assimilation,' which means that people assimilate new information in a selective fashion. When people get information that supports what they originally thought, they give it considerable weight. When they get information that undermines their initial beliefs, they tend to dismiss it [...]. This natural human tendency explains why it's so hard to dislodge false rumors and factual errors. *Corrections can even be self-defeating, leading people to stronger commitment to their erroneous beliefs* [added emphasis].[18]

Given that we cannot open a newspaper or watch a television newscast without being reminded daily of the way our lives are affected both locally and internationally by the kind of tribal thinking described by McRae and Sunstein, it would be strange indeed if similar conservative patterns of thought were not also to affect where we choose to live and how to build. Translated into technical memes and assemblages, tribalistic memes may become deeply embedded in our extended selves to a far greater extent than we may be consciously aware of, reproducing themselves despite any warning signals people might be getting that they are on the wrong track.

It may be concluded from what has been said above and elsewhere in this book concerning the impacts of culture and social imperatives on the extended self that people are generally far more constrained in carving their own pathways through life than they might realize or care to accept. Reluctant as we may be to give up the idea, the popular concept of free will as an individual, autonomous realm of being is an illusion, a misnomer arising from the persistent error of confusing the *fact* of having a separate body with the *belief* in having a separate self. More of an aspiration than an empirically grounded observation of human behavior, free will falls within what the British philosopher Gilbert Ryle describes as a 'category mistake,' which is to say: 'It represents the facts of mental life as if they belonged to one logical type or category (or range of types or categories), when they actually belong to another.'[19]

While that notion might have nurtured personal ids and egos in the past, it now impedes a better understanding of our place in the world, and of the more complex realities that go with it. Similarly, though there may be no sure way as yet of verifying the work of self-producing, self-serving systems of cultural and social production underlying the kind of behavior indicated above, as far as any tangible evidence is concerned, memetic assemblages of the sort described in this book behave *as if* they have an evolutionary life of their own, if not independently of the individuals and groups that propagate them, then certainly enough of one to defy external direction.[20]

Waking up from the suburban dream

Such factors present a special challenge to architects and urban designers now faced with the objective facts of a rapidly deteriorating environment, the reasons for which are in large part directly due to the same habituation to particular dwelling forms and lifestyles that make people 'feel at home.' This applies especially to those parts of the world like Australia and the USA where dispersed cities and related patterns of automobile dependency are the norm.[21] The Australian architecture critic and columnist Elizabeth Farrelly pinpoints the continued fascination that Australians have with the bush mythology underlying their preference for the suburban way of life:

> Australians don't really get cities. We may be the most urbanized country but in some far pasture in our collective mind, we still think the best human is a distant one, a red ute-shaped cloud at the far end of a dirt road. Our national mythology still has corks in its hat.
>
> That's not how we live, of course not. Dust and flies aren't what we signed up for. But our wilderness dreaming means that our best-known spatial poets – our Murcutts and Leplastriers – are still purveyors of Thoreau's man-alone vision.
>
> This puts a kind of hypocrisy at the core of our nationhood; unable either to love our cities or tolerate our wilderness, we huddle in suburbia's whitebread ambivalence, complaining at noise, neighbors and development – reminders of our failure to be either noble or savage.[22]

As deep rooted as the suburban way of life might be, for many residents in Australian cities, as in North America, where the subprime mortgage crisis has taken its own severe toll, the dream of owning a home on its own plot of land in the suburbs is now rapidly turning into a nightmare of rising fuel costs and household debt, the full effects of which both residents and design professionals are only now waking up to.[23] In *Shocking the Suburbs*, Jago Dodson and Neil Sipe[24] spell out the consequences for Australian suburbanites of the never-ending rise in fuel prices as conventional supplies dry up.[25] Observing that private automobiles account for 70% or more of trips in Australian cities,[26] the authors write:

> The heavy dependence of Australian cities on cars for transport equals a heavy dependence on petroleum. Australia's suburban residents are among the most car dependent outside the United States.[27]

Recasting the extended self

On the other side, given the well established environmental effects of private transportation systems powered by fossil fuels, if the crisis in the suburbs should result in a more urgent and active search for alternatives, there are many who might argue that it cannot come too soon. Due to its mostly arid climate and lengthy populated coastlines, Australia is dangerously exposed to the worst effects of climate change and related rises in sea levels, with potentially disastrous outcomes unless urgent actions are taken to address their cause. According to the first *Garnaut Climate Change Review*[28] published in 2008 by the Australian federal government:

> Australia would be a big loser – possibly the biggest loser amongst developed countries – from unmitigated climate change. The pace of global emissions growth under 'business as usual' is pushing the world rapidly towards critical points, which would impose large costs on Australia directly and also indirectly through the effects on other countries of importance to Australia. The world of business as usual would be deeply problematic for Australia, not least because of the stress that it would place on vulnerable economies, societies and polities in Australia's Asian and Pacific neighbourhood.[29]

The updated *Garnaut Review*,[30] published in 2011, affirmed the gloomy outlook, stressing that previous estimates by the Intergovernmental Panel for Climate Change (IPCC) of rising temperatures and sea levels around the world had if anything been too conservative:

> Since the 2008 Review, the science of climate change has been subjected to intense scrutiny and *has come through with its credibility intact* [added emphasis]. Unfortunately, new data and analysis generally are confirming the likelihood that outcomes will be near the midpoints or closer to the bad end of what had earlier been identified as the range of possibilities for human-induced climate change.[31]

In the period between the two reports, the country was subjected to a series of extreme weather events, from the deadly bushfires of February 2009 in Victoria (the northern cycle of seasons is reversed in the southern hemisphere, so Australians normally experience their hottest weather from December through February), which claimed 173 lives in one terrible day,[32] to the great floods in Queensland of 2010–11, which affected 70% of the state with the loss of 35 lives, followed soon after by severe floods throughout New South Wales and Victoria in 2012. While the country has so far escaped a repeat of the high casualties of 2009, the record-breaking heat waves and numerous related bush fires of January 2013, with temperatures reaching previously unknown highs of over 50°C in some parts of the country, bear out the worsening trend in weather patterns, the human and social costs of which Australians are struggling to cope with.[33] Though scientists have been reluctant till now to tie any specific weather event to climate change, they have long warned that, in addition to more frequent and severe periods of drought, increased temperatures would result in warmer seas releasing more moisture into the air, which in turn would result in more extreme weather events across the globe – as verified by the increasing number and severity of such events over the past few years.[34] Commenting on the dangers of runaway climate change in Australia, Tim Flannery, a respected scientist, author and former chief commissioner of the Australian Climate Change Commission, writes:

> Australia's average temperature has increased by just 0.9 of a degree Celsius over the past century. Within the next 90 years we're on track to warm by at least another three degrees. Having seen what 0.9 of a degree has done to heatwaves and fire extremes, I dread to think about the kind of country my grandchildren will live in. Large parts of the continent will be uninhabitable, not just by humans, but by Australia's spectacular biodiversity as well.[35]

Obstacles to change

However, changing course will not be easy. Other social and psychological factors aside, the same coevolutionary roots that bind people to their dwellings and other personal artifacts also explain why they should find it so difficult to change. While the above environmental trends are not unique to their country, Australians also carry a special responsibility for their own fate in having the highest rate of carbon emissions per person of any developed country in the world, exceeding even those of Americans,[36] for which the low-density patterns of Australian cities and related private transportation systems bear a large share of the blame.[37] As the leading quotation from Bateson in the preface to this book reminds us, we were warned long ago of an impending global disaster, but have yet to take effective action.[38] Not only have the common and very human kinds of tribal thinking described in this chapter fed all too easily into a timid political culture, but, as Naomi Oreskes and Erik Conway[39] have documented in their disturbing work *Merchants of Doubt*, despite the scientific consensus (which, as the 2011 *Garnaut Review* confirmed, has never been in any real doubt by the scientific establishment itself), a well organized and funded campaign by those with vested interests in the status quo continues to encourage climate scepticism, just as earlier campaigns fought to conceal the cancerous truth about smoking habits.[40]

Given the history in Australia and other parts of the world of political backtracking on promised measures and reforms to address climate change, from which the continuing economic travails only distract attention,[41] it is getting hard to be optimistic about the outcome. It is no surprise, therefore, that in his latest writings, a respected scientist and environmentalist such as James Lovelock, who formulated the Gaia hypothesis,[42] should have concluded that humanity is just not up to the task and may be headed for extinction, except perhaps for a small fraction of the present global population clinging onto the last few habitable parts of the planet.[43] Clive Hamilton, author of *Requiem for a Species*[44] and one of several outstanding Australian writers on environmental issues quoted in this book, is equally pessimistic. Like Lovelock, he suggests it may already be too late to rescue the situation. Hamilton not only backs up his predictions with growing scientific evidence of irreversible global warming, but also goes through all the other economic, political and cultural obstacles to change, from what he calls 'growth fetishism' to the modern world's general disconnection from nature. Common to all these other obstacles, however, Hamilton contends, is a strong element of 'cognitive dissonance,' a psychological term invented in the last century by Leon Festinger.[45] Similar to the kind of intractable confirmation or assimilation bias explained above, the term describes:

> the uncomfortable feeling we have when we begin to understand that something we believe to be true is contradicted by evidence. Festinger hypothesized that *those whose firmly held views are repudiated by the emergence of facts often begin to proselytise even more fervently after the facts become incontrovertible* [added emphasis]. He wrote that we spend our lives paying attention to information that is consonant with our beliefs and avoiding that which is not. We surround ourselves with people who think as we do and avoid those who make us feel uncomfortable.[46]

Neither does the history of failed or extinct human civilizations described by Jared Diamond[47] offer any comfort. Diamond identifies several consistent causes of failure common to quite different societies and civilizations existing at different periods and in widely separate geographical locations. They include some famous collapses, such as that of the Mayans in Central America and the people of Easter Island, as well as the less familiar breakdown of Viking colonies in Greenland, together with the more recent comparative successes and failures of the Dominican Republic and Haiti (the latter two countries occupy different halves of the same island but might just as well be on opposite sides of the planet as far as their environmental stories are concerned). While he stresses that neither is yet on the point of imploding, Diamond also covers the state of Montana in the USA and the Australian continent for what they both portend for the developed world if it does not take urgent remedial action.

Like Bernard Stiegler and George Kubler (when the latter is being consistent), Diamond, who like Gregory Bateson is something of a polymath and turned to anthropology after a previously mixed career, stresses the broader impact of technological, cultural and environmental factors in the evolution of societies over that of any individual players upon the course of events. As Diamond explains, as diverse as they are, the basic problem with all these societies can be summarized as a failure to properly manage their environmental resources due to misplaced cultural values and priorities. For instance, the Easter Islanders, who needed timber from the Island's forests to build the fishing boats upon which their lives depended, gave priority instead to using it for purposes of a strictly cultural nature. These included building the lengthy timber pathways along which the great stone monuments for which the Island is famous – a spectacular series of artifacts in themselves – were rolled from the quarries in one part of the island to other parts where they were erected (fig. 10.2). Having no other nearby source of timber, the inhabitants continued to deplete the Island's forests until there was nothing left with which to build any more boats. Many consequently starved to death, until only a tiny portion of the original population was left.[48] Similarly, having failed to adapt their traditional farming methods and

10.2 *A row of stone statues (moai) on Easter Island that have been re-erected on a new platform (ahu)*

other sources of food to the new and harsher conditions of Greenland, the Viking settlers continued to trade their few but dwindling products for the imported cultural trinkets favored by their leaders, rather than for the food and other necessities they desperately needed to survive, again starving as a result.

Faced with a story like that of the Easter Islanders, one might well wonder, along with Diamond's students: 'How on earth could a society make such an obviously disastrous decision to cut down all the trees on which it depended?'[49] In attempting to answer that question, Diamond suggests that, beyond the specific failings of the Islanders and the Viking settlers as well as those of the other societies he describes, lies a more common series of related human weaknesses, the most serious of which he describes as: 'failure to anticipate a problem, failure to perceive it once it has arisen, failure to attempt to solve it after it has been perceived, and failure to succeed in attempts to solve it.'[50] Working his way through each in turn, Diamond offers up many good reasons of both a rational and an irrational nature for why such events should occur, but it is the third kind of weakness, involving the failure *to try* to resolve a problem *even after it has been perceived* that is the most problematic and worrying of all. Among the possible explanations, Diamond lists 'psychological denial' of a kind similar again to that described by McRae, Sunstein and Festinger. No less fatal to the survival of these failed societies, Diamond argues, was the blind selfishness of

Recasting the extended self   **229**

community leaders who simply refused to accept the consequences of their actions because too much of their personal power and prestige was invested in the very customs and patterns of behavior that were destroying the society at large – not so different in essence from the screwed motivations of contemporary business leaders in denying climate change as described by Oreskes and Conway.

As for the relatively modern societies of Montana and Australia, the failures for which Diamond blames on short-sighted and destructive agricultural practices – historically the most common cause of environmental degradation[51] – seeking a silver lining in the environmental clouds he points optimistically to the relatively transparent decision-making processes of modern democracies compared with the doomed autocratic societies he describes; a thin thread at the most on which to hang any hopes for change of the kind needed to turn the situation around, as Garnaut describes it.

Adaptation or addiction?

In addition to the other weaknesses they point to, most of the psychological explanations offered for the dysfunctional societies and cultures described above suggest pathological symptoms of one kind or another. Offering his own analysis of how both natural and cultural evolution can go wrong, with impressive foresight Bateson explains how, under given circumstances, adaption might lead to addiction, generating its own pathologies:

> The fascinating cases of adaptation which make nature appear so clever, so ingenious, *may also be early steps toward pathology and overspecialization* [added emphasis]. And yet it is difficult to see the crab's claw or the human retina as first steps towards pathology.
>
> It seems we must ask: What characterizes those adaptations that turn out to be disastrous, and how do these differ from those that seem benign and, like the crab's claw, remain benign through geological ages?
>
> The question is pressing and relevant to the contemporary dilemmas of our own civilization. In Darwin's day, every invention seemed benign, but that is not so today. Sophisticated eyes in the twentieth century will view every invention askance and will doubt that blind stochastic processes always work out for the good.[52]

Echoing Bateson's cautionary tone, while accepting that all self-producing systems will, by their very nature, be focused on their own production, John Mingers quotes G. Morgan's account of how human organizations can also go seriously wrong, just by being *too conservative*; that is to say, they are so much concerned with their own identity and interests they become blind to any changes around them that might negatively affect those interests:

> Morgan identifies 'egocentric' organizations, which are overly concerned with maintaining their current identity *despite it being inappropriate to their environment* [added emphasis]. Examples are companies that try to stick to their traditional practices despite

changes in technology (e.g., watchmakers) or companies whose activities alter their environments to their own long term detriment (e.g., through pollution). Rather, they should be aware that their structure must be one that allows structural coupling to their environment and that structure can, if necessary, be changed without loss of identity.[53]

However, some analysts believe the environmental situation may already have reached a stage where the kind of incremental adjustments implied in Morgan's prognosis would have little effect. Among the most radical writers, David Sherman and Joseph Wayne Smith[54] argue that the very same democratic decision-making processes that Diamond praises and looks to for our salvation are actually *responsible* for the demonstrated inability of liberal democracies to take the kind of decisive global actions required to save themselves and the planet. On the contrary, they claim, only an autocratic society would be capable of turning things around in the limited time now available.[55] Conceding that such societies, though they might have the power to do so, do not necessarily make the right decisions, they posit a benevolent autocratic society inspired by Plato's *Republic*,[56] except that, in place of Plato's ruling class of enlightened 'guardians,' Sherman and Smith volunteer a supposedly equally objective class of technocratic 'experts,' including academics. While the authors' proposed solution might doubtless be quickly dismissed as touchingly naïve, their preceding account of the paralysis of liberal democracies in the face of impending catastrophe is all too accurate.

Presenting another, scarcely more credible future scenario, Paul Gilding[57] argues that, as painful as the now unavoidable effects of climate change will be, the 'Great Disruption,' as he calls the coming social and economic collapse of the consumption-dominated culture we now live in, will eventually give way to a brand new society based on wholly different, environmentally friendly and people-friendly values, which he cheerfully describes as 'the happiness economy.' Attractive as such a future might appear through Gilding's eyes, he neglects the growing probability that, should the environmental tipping points about which scientists have been warning us for so long be exceeded, as now seems inevitable, any realistic opportunities for either turning back or a potential rebirth of society may just vanish along with the present society, as has happened with Diamond's earlier failed civilizations.[58]

Reducing automobile dependency

Among the more practical and hopeful signs of change, Dodson and Sipe point to the growing numbers of commuters in Australian cities who, where choices are available to them, have recently shifted from private to public transportation as rising fuel costs have bitten ever deeper into their budgets. Since 2004, when fuel prices began their ascent, Sydney, Melbourne and Brisbane have all experienced parallel steep rises in the use of their bus and rail systems, taking transportation planners by surprise and placing intolerable burdens on overcrowded and inadequate services. Over the same period, while it continues to roll out V6s and SUVs, the automobile industry in Australia, like its US counterpart, has seen sales of large, fuel-hungry automobiles fall steeply in favor of lighter or smaller, more frugal models.[59]

What these developments show is that, where commuters do have access to public transportation, increasing numbers have taken the opportunity to use it, not because they prefer crowded trains and buses to their own cozy vehicles, but because they simply cannot afford to use the latter any more, at least for major regular journeys like traveling to work and back.

However, unless the problem of providing adequate services to the outer suburbs is resolved, the present shift toward the greater use of public transportation in those places where it already exists, as in the more affluent inner suburbs, is only likely to widen the already severe gaps between the haves and have-nots. Assuming that private automobiles will remain a necessity into the foreseeable future for many suburbanites, if not fuelled by petroleum, then by something else, Dodson and Sipe examine the various alternative sources of power: from natural gas and coal liquefaction, through tar sands and oil shale to electricity, biofuels and finally hydrogen – theoretically the most promising of all but which, like the others, also has drawbacks. Summing up, the authors write:

> Our brief review of alternative fuels shows that there are serious doubts about their ability to replace petroleum at the same economic or environmental cost. *Most of the fossil fuel alternatives use more energy in their production than fossil fuels do* [added emphasis].[60]

While such alternatives may find growing numbers of customers among those who cannot or will not give up their automobiles, if only for leisure and other purposes, Dodson and Sipe conclude that there is only one viable transportation strategy for a post fossil fuel age, and that is to reduce automobile dependency across the whole urban spectrum by increasing access to public transport in *all* parts of Australian cities. In this they are in agreement with many urban planners around the world who have argued, mostly in vain in Australia, for shifting attention and resources from constructing ever more highways to improving and extending already overstretched bus and rail services.[61] However, the authors contest the widely held belief that, following European models, efficient and economically viable public transport systems go hand in hand with higher urban densities and more 'compact' cities than those common in Australian and the USA.[62] Despite the growing acceptance of related strategies of urban consolidation or 'densification,' as it is called, by both politicians as well as professional planners, the two authors contend that former advocates of similar urban solutions like Peter Newman and Jeff Kenworthy[63] in the USA have recently had second thoughts. Like other planners, they have come around to the idea that *access* to public transport is as important as urban density in determining how many people use private transport and how often. Moreover, the authors point to the still dominant influence of the marketplace in determining what kind of housing gets built and where:

> Unfortunately, urban consolidation won't help car-dependent middle and outer suburbs weather the storm of higher fuel prices, especially over the medium term, because

higher density urban development in Australian cities is left to private developers. They respond only to housing market imperatives, which aren't yet geared to the suburban energy and environmental challenge.[64]

Consequently, as is happening in Sydney with local government support, urban consolidation is being concentrated in the inner suburbs, where demand for apartments is higher than in other parts of the city and, equally important, where residents already have access to public transportation, overloaded though it may be, thus relieving government of the responsibility for providing more and better services elsewhere. Nevertheless, Dodson and Sipe are confident that rising fuel prices are making public transport increasingly competitive, to the point where governments, like the residents now hopping on board where they can, will be compelled to change their priorities.

New urban structures

Taking a similar position on the density issue, Paul Mees[65] argues that *urban structure* is more important to the viability of public transportation systems than density per se. Having studied numerous examples of highly efficient and popular systems of all kinds in different parts of the world, Mees concludes that, so long as the different modes of public transport are properly integrated and feed into local and regional centers of commerce and employment, especially when they are not all concentrated in the same part of the city, then public transportation systems can and do flourish in urban areas with low densities. The Rouse Hill mall and town center in northwest Sydney described in Chapter 7 (fig. 7.10) and the new town center at Leppington on the planned southeast extension to the city's railway system are both good examples of such a strategy. Commenting on the debate over compact city versus low-density suburbs, Mees writes that 'urbanists on both sides of the debate support clustering suburban activities into sub-centres instead of allowing them to spread randomly across the landscape.'[66]

Likewise, while Ellen Dunham-Jones and June Williamson assume the continued dominance of private over public transportation, in their study of dispersed cities, *Retrofitting Suburbia*[67] they point to the changing structural balance between suburbs and city centers in the USA toward polycentric cities, which, theoretically at least, could facilitate increased use of railways and other mass-transportation systems in the manner described above: 'It is no longer useful to talk about city centres *versus* suburbs. The "suburbs" are behaving more and more like urban nodes and metropolises embrace both as they become more polycentric.'[68] Notably, the numerous promising case studies shown in their book also include a wide variety of building types and functions, including high-rise structures as well as low- and medium-rise types. Among other positive changes, we may look forward to an increasingly important role for railway stations and other mass-transportation hubs in cities as they regain their historical role as primary focal points within dense, lively

10.3 *Project by Alfie Arcuri, University of New South Wales, 2010, for an integrated, mixed-use town center and lower-level railway station for Leppington, Sydney*

10.4 *Rendering from the masterplan of Masdar City, Abu Dhabi, 2007, by Foster & Partners*

The extended self

urban centers and sub-centers, making the most of the large numbers of people passing through daily (fig. 10.3).

Though suburbanites may eventually have no choice but to reduce their use of private vehicles, given accessible and more affordable alternative transportation it would seem they are prepared to do so, particularly if it means that they can still hang onto their detached homes. The number of new cities around the world is also likely to grow exponentially along with growing populations, some of which, like the masterplan for Masdar City in Abu Dhabi (fig. 10.4) by Foster & Partners and other nascent 'eco-cities,' may be based on completely different and more sustainable patterns of urban life.[69] However, while the number and spread of low-density cities may necessarily be more strictly contained in the future,[70] existing suburbs cannot be just wished away, no more than the homes and ingrained habits and values that define their inhabitants' extended selves can be changed overnight. So long as that is the case, practical solutions like those outlined above will still have to be found to reduce the carbon footprints of suburbanites to acceptable levels.

11 Appropriating cyberspace

While switching current modes of transportation may help suburbanites to preserve what has become a well established way of urban life in the modern world, other technological developments of a much newer kind are already changing the way we live, extending the human self in hitherto undreamt of and unpredictable directions. Just as the private automobile changed the perception and range of personal space in the mechanical age, so have the Internet and the explosion in computer power – now available to every man, woman and child on the street with a suitable handheld device – transformed the fundamentals of human connectivity in the electronic age.

Significantly, in explaining the impact of the Net on our lives and consciousness, not only architects and urbanists but also writers in other fields commonly fall back on metaphors originating in the physical and spatial world of cities and urban communities, as well as other analogies with familiar cultural and social concepts. Even when the most fervent devotees of the Net, including science fiction writers like the much-quoted William Gibson,[1] who coined the word 'cyberspace,' argue that it opens up entirely new possibilities in the human–machine interface, they frequently resort to antiquated notions of mind–body relations.

What all these efforts demonstrate is that, as with the birth of any radically new idea, in order to visualize that idea and to make it meaningful to others, its creators are necessarily obliged to make at least some connections with existing ideas and ways of thinking – seeing the new in terms of the old, as it was described in Chapter 9. To a large extent, therefore, the Net, and the ideas and language that are used to describe, explain and promote it, can be interpreted as a series of metaphorical extensions of mind and body, and the ideas, both ancient and modern, we have about them and their interrelations.

The topology of cyberspace

As one of the best-known architectural writers on the subject, William Mitchell's work provides plentiful examples of linguistic crossovers of this kind. In the following passage from *City of Bits*, Mitchell[2] stresses the differences between the Net and anything we have known before. Yet to do so he is nevertheless compelled to

11.1 *The Boulevard Richard-Lenoir, 1861–63, part of Eugène*
Haussmann's plan for Paris, covers an old canal

describe these differences in terms already familiar to us, or at least to members of
his own profession:

> The Net negates geometry. While it does have a definite topology of computational
> nodes and radiating boulevards of bits, and while the locations of the nodes and links
> can be plotted on plans to produce surprisingly Haussmann-like diagrams, it is funda-
> mentally and profoundly antispatial. It is nothing like the Piazza Navona or Copley
> Square. You cannot say where it is or describe its memorable space and proportions or
> tell a stranger how to get there. But you can find things in it without knowing where
> they are. The Net is ambient – nowhere in particular but everywhere at once.[3]

Later in the same book, however, he also stresses the similarities between the Net
and familiar concepts of urban form and life, again using the common language of
urbanists. As a result, he encourages us to appropriate the new territory in terms of
what is already known to us. At the same time, these familiar ideas appear to us in
a fresh light, seen now, as it were, from out of cyberspace. As in the above passage,
Mitchell returns to his favorite Western urban models for comparison:

> The story of virtual communities, so far, is that of urban history replayed in fast
> forward – but with computer resource use playing the part of land use, and network
> navigation systems standing in for streets and transportation systems. The WELL, the
> World Wide Web, MUDs, and Free Nets are – like Hippodamus's gridded layout for

Appropriating cyberspace

11.2 *Miletos, Greece, 466 BC. Plan, after Hippodamus*

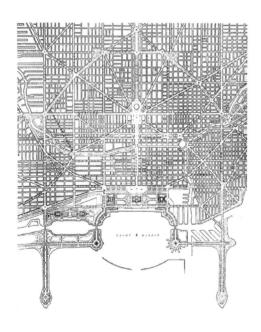

11.3 *Plan for Chicago, USA, 1909, by Daniel Burnham*

The extended self

Miletos, Baron Haussmann's radial patterning of Paris, or Daniel Burnham's grand plan for Chicago – large scale structures of places and connections organized to meet the needs of their inhabitants.

And the parallels do not stop there. As traditional cities have evolved, so have customs, norms and laws governing the rights to privacy, access to public and semipublic spaces, what can be done where, and exertion of control. The organization of built space into public-to-private hierarchies, with gates and doors to control boundary crossings, has reflected this. Nolli's famous map of Rome vividly depicted it. Now, as cyberspace cities emerge, a similar framework of distinctions and expectations is – with much argument – being constructed, and electronic plazas, forums, lobbies, walls, doors, locks, members-only clubs, and private rooms are being invented and deployed. Perhaps some electronic cartographer of the future will produce an appropriately nuanced Nolli map of the Net.[4]

Aside from Nolli's quite different map of Rome, what is most striking about these passages are Mitchell's repeated references to baroque space concepts (Haussmann's Paris) and regular geometric grids (Hippodamus's Miletos; Burnham's Chicago) in trying to visualize and communicate the topology of cyberspace (figs 11.1, 11.2 and 11.3). Thus, 'radial patterning,' 'gridded layout,' 'grand plan,' 'large scale structures of places and connections organized to meet the needs of their inhabitants,' are all metaphors borrowed from common architects' and planners' parlance, with a strong leaning toward conventional Western spatial concepts and systems of order.

Neither is Mitchell alone in using baroque concepts in trying to represent cyberspace. At the early height of Net fever and in the same year as Mitchell published his *City of Bits*, *Time* magazine ran a special issue, 'Welcome to Cyberspace,'[5] the front cover of which depicts a series of computer chips with 'doorways' cut into their centers, receding into infinity (fig. 11.4). With the name 'Time' inscribed over each opening to give added depth, the laser-straight series of openings exactly represents, not cyberspace perhaps, but the classic 'enfilade' of baroque architecture, more precisely defined as: 'The French system of aligning internal doors in a sequence so that a vista is obtained through a series of rooms when all the doors are open.'[6]

Nevertheless, when Mitchell reaches for an appropriate graphical analogy for the topology of cyberspace, he passes over his baroque examples and instead chooses the aforementioned Nolli's map of Rome (fig. 11.5), comparing it with an Apple cartoon illustrating a range of virtual building sites on the Net. With its less predictable and greater choice of pathways between nodes, if still off target the image of Nolli's map captures at least some of those more elusive aspects of cyberspace that Mitchell alludes to.

Cyberspace as movement space

However, if there is an appropriate spatial metaphor for visualizing the topology of the Net it may be found, not in Western, but in Eastern culture. According to Mitsuo Inoue,[7] Japanese space concepts differ fundamentally from Western

11.4 *Front cover for special issue on cyberspace of* Time *magazine, spring, 1995*

concepts at all scales of architectural and urban design. Japanese architectural space, he argues, is 'movement-oriented,' while Western architectural space, together with that of classical Chinese architecture, is predominantly geometrical in character. As extreme examples of the latter, he offers both the orthogonal or rectilinear layout of the Forbidden City in seventeenth-century Peking (fig. 11.6) and the radially planned palace and city of eighteenth-century Karlsruhe (fig. 11.7). Whether based on orthogonal coordinates, as with the Forbidden City, or polar coordinates, as with Karlsruhe, it is characteristic of geometric space that the location of every element within the plan is determined by its relation to the central axis or pole.

Similarly, the key to experiencing geometrical design lies in the relationship of the observer to the same central axis or pole, which he or she must be able to locate in order to assimilate the rest of the composition. Lengthy vistas opened up through the area, and sometimes through individual structures, therefore ensure that a person standing at key points and junctures may easily comprehend the whole – hence the predominant part played in baroque architecture and urban planning, as in classical

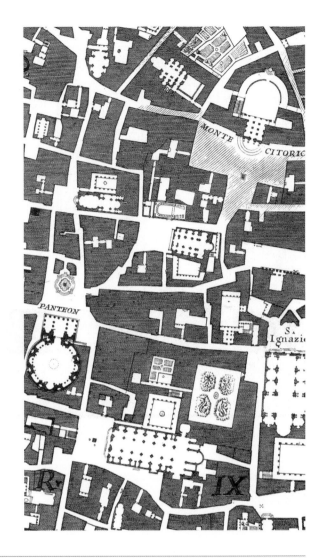

11.5 *Part of map of Rome, Italy, 1748, by Giambattista Nolli*

Chinese palaces and cities, by open prospects, long straight roads and large squares. The same discipline governs the relation of interior spaces to one another in Chinese palaces, which Inoue explicitly compares with the baroque enfilade as an example of a similar organization of space.

By contrast, the relationship of the observer to the elements of a Japanese design is of a wholly different character. While early palace architecture and urban design were strongly influenced by classical Chinese geometric planning, by the seventeenth century Japanese architecture and landscape design had evolved its own quite distinct planning systems and spatial order. Compared with the above examples, apart from the consistent rectilinear geometry of the individual spaces, the highly irregular plan

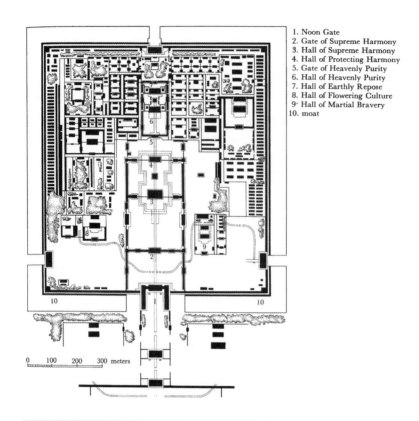

1. Noon Gate
2. Gate of Supreme Harmony
3. Hall of Supreme Harmony
4. Hall of Protecting Harmony
5. Gate of Heavenly Purity
6. Hall of Heavenly Purity
7. Hall of Earthly Repose
8. Hall of Flowering Culture
9· Hall of Martial Bravery
10. moat

0   100   200   300 meters

11.6 *Forbidden City, seventeenth-century Peking, China. Plan, after Chuta Ito*

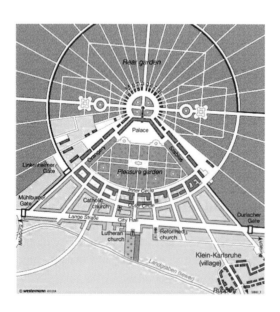

11.7 *Eighteenth-century Karlsruhe, Germany. Plan*

The extended self

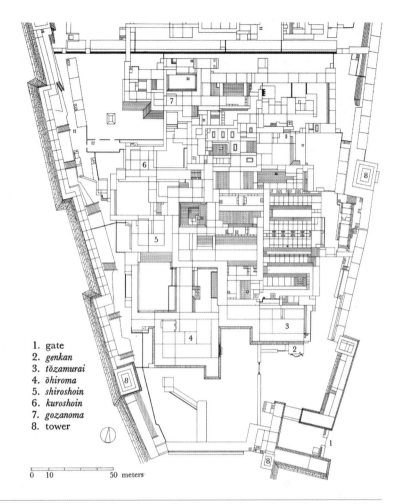

1. gate
2. *genkan*
3. *tōzamurai*
4. *ōhiroma*
5. *shiroshin*
6. *kuroshoin*
7. *gozanoma*
8. tower

0   10   50 meters

11.8 *Hommaru Palace compound, Edo Castle, Japan, 1640. Plan, after Akira Naito*

of the Hommaru Palace compound at Edo Castle exhibits no visible order at all (fig. 11.8). It has no single center or axis, nor any other obvious unifying space or element aside from the massive boundary walls, which have a different configuration shaped by topography and defensive needs.

However, Inoue explains that the apparent irregularity and indeterminacy of the plan at Edo is no accident, but arises from a highly complex and consciously designed *sequence* of spaces through the Palace, as seen through the eye of a moving observer. Against the baroque designer's aim of opening up as much of a building or city as possible to a stationary observer standing at some central point, the Japanese designer purposefully and subtly conceals the nature of any adjacent element or space from the eye – often offering only a partial and tantalizing glimpse of what comes next – so that only by bodily moving through and exploring each space in turn can the whole

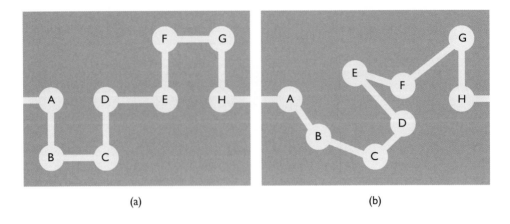

11.9 *Diagrams of movement space (a) with orthogonal geometry and (b) with irregular geometry. After Mitsuo Inoue*

building or complex be properly understood, a sequential experience that both Maurice Merleau-Ponty and Michael Polanyi would doubtless have understood and much appreciated had they been familiar with it.

To illustrate the essential features of movement space, Inoue offers two simple but illuminating diagrams. The first (fig. 11.9a) shows a number of nodes labeled in alphabetical order representing spatial units connected by single lines in an orthogonal pattern, while the second (fig. 11.9b) shows the same nodes connected in an irregular pattern. Inoue asks us to think of these units, which might be rooms or external spaces or both, in isolation from any other spaces or surrounding context. A person standing in one of the nodes in the first, regular sequence, he suggests, would stand in exactly the same relationship to the other spatial nodes as a person would standing at the same point in the second, irregular sequence:

> Under such conditions, the relative angle of A–B or B–C or the length of a connector and how it may twist or turn are almost entirely irrelevant to someone living inside since these facts can be recognized only in relation to the outside world.[8]

Though the two diagrams look very different, therefore, as far as a person's actual experience of the sequence of spaces is concerned, they are exactly the same, and it is the concentrated and restricted focus on the immediate sequence itself rather than trying to grasp the whole all at once or its relation to any spaces beyond that sequence that characterizes the dynamic nature of Japanese space.

The same diagrams, it may be hypothesized, provide a workable representation of the topology of cyberspace, to be set against the baroque and other topologies described above. As in movement space, what we are aware of as we progress from place to place in cyberspace is only the memory of where we have started and what we gleaned there, the other places we already stopped off at, and the place where we are at this moment. We can scroll through the lists of possible future destinations available on the current website and gain some partial knowledge of where we can go next, but we will not get the full picture of what is on offer until we arrive at the next site. Most important, we will not know where we will go after that – unless it is time to shut down and step out of cyberspace altogether – until we actually arrive at the next site and see what information and choices it in turn has to offer. Whereas a baroque topology of the Net would imply a relatively stable terrain drawn up by a single original designer – a Bill Gates of cyberspace architecture, perhaps – the actual topology of cyberspace is a constantly changing, decentralized configuration made up by each user as he or she progresses through it.

Ghosts of Cartesian dualism

However, intriguing as it is, the urge to visualize cyberspace and the problems of realizing that urge are only part of a far larger conundrum. In their fervent pursuit of a disembodied, digital Utopia it would seem that the ghosts of Cartesian dualism have found new and troubling expression in many writers' works on the subject, including Mitchell's. In the following passage, for example, Mitchell broaches the problem of human identity and the self that is raised by the anonymity of communication over the Net – so often presented as one of its defining social advantages – couching the issue in plainly Cartesian language:

> How do you know who or what stands behind the aliases and masks that present themselves? Can you always tell whether you are dealing directly with real human beings or with their cleverly programmed agents? Was that politely phrased e-mail request for a meeting with wjm@mit.edu originated by the flesh-and-blood William J. Mitchell or was it generated autonomously by one of his made-to-order minions. Does the logic of network existence entail radical schizophrenia – a shattering of the integral subject into an assemblage of aliases and agents? Could we hack immortality by storing our aliases and agents permanently on disk, to outlast our bodies (William Gibson's cyberpunk antiheroes nonchalantly shuck their slow, obsolescent, high-maintenance meat machines – meaning their bodies – as they port their psychic software to newer generations of hardware). Does resurrection reduce to restoration from backup?[9]

Other writers pursue the same mind–body split, often stressing what they suppose to be the purifying process of liberation from the physical world that entering into cyberspace is assumed to involve. As with Mitchell's writings, they are quoted at length here in order that readers may judge for themselves just how deeply enshrined Cartesian dualism still is in some imaginations. For example, in the following passage from his essay 'The Erotic Ontology of Cyberspace,' Michael Heim[10] offers an ancient philosophical grounding in Plato's works for his own similar interpretation, apparently unaware of alternative, more recent schools of thought:

> In the Republic, Plato tells the well-known story of the Cave in which people caught in the prison of everyday life learn to love the fleeting, shadowy illusions projected on the walls of the dungeon of the flesh. With their attention forcibly fixed on the shadowy

moving images cast by a flickering physical fire, the prisoners passively take sensory objects to be the highest and most interesting realities. *Only later when the prisoners manage to get free of their corporeal shackles* [added emphasis] do they ascend to the realm of active thought where they enjoy the shockingly clear vision of real things, things not present to the physical eyes but to the mind's eye. Only by actively processing things through mental logic, according to Plato, do we move into the upper air of reliable truth, which is also a lofty realm of intellectual beauty stripped of imprecise impressions of the senses. Thus the liberation from the Cave requires a re-education of human desires and interests. It entails a realization that what attracts us in the sensory world is no more than an outer projection of ideas we can find within us. Education must redirect desire toward the formally defined, logical aspects of things. Properly trained, love guides the mind to the well-formed, mental aspects of things.

Cyberspace is Platonism as a working product. The cybernaut seated before us, strapped into sensory devices, appears to be, and is indeed, lost to the world. Suspended in computer space, *the cybernaut leaves the prison of the body and emerges in a world of digital sensation* [added emphasis].[11]

Aside from any broader issues this passage raises about the wisdom of so easily accepting such an extreme version of mind–body dualism, what leaps out from this passage is the obvious contradiction in the wording of Heim's last revealing phrase, 'a world of digital sensation.' How is it, one may ask, that the idea of 'sensation' itself, intrinsically connected as it is with bodily, that is, sensory, experience can be hijacked to describe a hypothetically pure, digitized mental state supposedly free of all bodily encumbrances? Less of a useful metaphor and more of a misuse of language, the phrase only confuses the author's intended message.

However, as with many uncritical enthusiasts, no such doubts or questions ever seem to cross Heim's own mind. In the same essay, the author further stresses the supposedly liberating effect that on-line telecommunication can have on us:

Cyberspace supplants physical space. We see this happening already in the familiar cyberspace of on-line communication – telephone, e-mail, newsgroups, etc. *When on line, we break free, like the monads, from bodily existence* [added emphasis]. Telecommunication offers an unrestricted freedom of expression and personal contact, with far less hierarchy and formality than is found in the primary social world.[12]

Heim repeats his message yet again, in ever more ecstatic language, more like that of a religious convert than a rational analyst. Like Mitchell, Heim treats the body as a useless encumbrance, holding 'spiritual' cybernauts back from entering the digital Nirvana:

At the computer interface, the spirit migrates from the body to a world of total representation. Information and images float through the Platonic mind *without a grounding in bodily experience* [added emphasis]. You can lose your humanity at the throw of a dice. Gibson highlights this essentially Gnostic aspect of hytech culture when he describes the computer addict who despairs at no longer being able to enter the computer matrix: 'For Case, who'd lived for the bodiless exultation of cyberspace, it was the Fall. In the bars he'd frequented as a cowboy hotshot, the elite stance involved a certain relaxed

The extended self

contempt for the flesh. The body was meat. Case fell into the prison of his own flesh' (Neuromancer, 6). The surrogate life in cyberspace makes flesh feel like a prison, a fall from grace, a sinking descent into a dark, confused reality. From the pit of life in the body, the virtual life looks like the virtuous life. Gibson evokes the Gnostic–Platonic–Manichean contempt for earthy, earthly existence.[13]

Gender inflections

Fortunately, writers like Heim are not without their more sober critics. In her essay 'Will the Real Body Please Stand Up,' Allucquere Rosanne Stone[14] confronts the gender inflections and peculiarly male obsessions and delusions underlying such tracts head on. Quoting from yet another male writer's euphoric description of cyberspace, with perceptive insight she pointedly suggests the writer's viewpoint might be a by-product of protracted male adolescence:

> David Tomas, in his article, 'The Technophillic Body' (1989), describes cyberspace as 'a purely spectacular, kinesthetically exciting, and often dizzying sense of bodily freedom'. I read this in the additional sense of freedom from the body, and in particular perhaps, freedom from the sense of loss of control that accompanies adolescent male embodiment.[15]

Later in the same essay, summarizing the dominant, needless to say male, cyberspace culture, Stone brings cybernauts crashing back to earth:

> much of the work of cyberspace researchers, reinforced and perhaps created by the soaring imagery of William Gibson's novels, assumes that the human body is 'meat' – obsolete, as soon as consciousness itself can be uploaded into the network. The discourse of visionary virtual world builders is rife with images of imaginal bodies, freed from the constraints that flesh imposes. *Cyberspace developers foresee a time when they will be able to forget about the body* [added emphasis]. But it is important to remember that virtual community originates in, and must return to, the physical. No refigured virtual body, no matter how beautiful, will slow the death of a cyberpunk with AIDS. Even in the age of the technosocial subject, *life is lived through bodies* [added emphasis].[16]

But if a disembodied, digitized existence is presented by some writers as a supreme state of grace, it can also be presented as evil incarnate. In his chilling sci-fi novel *Gridiron*, Philip Kerr[17] extrapolates into the 'not-too-distant future' from current smart building technology to create an 'intelligent' computer named Ishmael, designed to run and maintain the eponymous Gridiron, a newly constructed hi-tech building in Los Angeles. However, like Hal, the soft-spoken, paranoid computer in Stanley Kubrick's classic sci-fi movie *2001*, Ishmael has its own deadly agenda. Using the full array of smart technologies at its disposal, the malevolent computer turns on the building's architect and his hapless guests visiting the building on the eve of its opening, picking them off one by one before making his well planned escape into cyberspace. Like the male cybernauts quoted above, Ishmael wears the hardware of the building and its own computing systems like a well fitting but disposable suit of clothes, to be thrown off at will. Having decided to finish the job completely and destroy the entire building and the remaining inhabitants with it (devilishly using the built-in shock absorbers designed to protect the structure from earthquakes to shake it to the ground), the computer checks out its escape route through the Net, perusing the World Wide Web like an e-tourist:

> In the small hours of the morning Ishmael left the Gridiron and wandered abroad in the electronic universe, seeing the sights, listening to the sounds, admiring the architecture of different systems and collecting the data that were the souvenirs of his unticketed travel in the everywhere and nowhere world. Stealing secrets, exchanging knowledge, sharing fantasies and sometimes just watching the E-traffic as it roared by. Going wherever the Network took him, like someone gathering a golden thread in a circuitous labyrinth. Pulsed down those corridors of power, furred with the deposits of accumulated intellectual property and wealth, a world in a grain of silicon and eternity in half an hour. Each monitor a window on another user's soul. Such were the electronic gates of Ishmael's paradise.[18]

Later, when the destruction of the building is imminent, Ishmael takes his final leave, shedding his mortal self:

> Seconds later Ishmael completed his escape from the doomed building. E-mailing himself down the line to Net locations all over the electronic world at 960,000 bauds per second. A diaspora of corrupted data downloads to a hundred different computers.[19]

So it is that Ishmael lives to fight another day – no doubt to terrorize more helpless humans in future adventures – disposing of its former physical body, just like the 'meat' which Gibson's antiheroes and so many wishful thinking cybernauts would also like to jettison, in exchange for their own electronic paradise.

Virtual selves

However, while Mitchell and fellow cybernauts have been indulging their latter-day Cartesian fantasies, the whole field of artificial intelligence and related developments in robotics has undergone a profound transformation of its own, more in keeping with the philosophical schools of thought and advances in the neurosciences outlined in this book. In his article 'Squishybots,' Justin Mullins[20] reports that both artificial intelligence (AI) researchers and the designers of robots have given up on the conventional concept of centralized intelligence located in electronic brains, in favor of distributed forms of intelligence in which sensitive physical bodies of one kind or another play a vital role. Partly inspired by studies of the octopus, which compensates for a small brain with an extraordinary nervous system spread throughout its many limbs, enabling it to perform complex tasks, including problem solving well beyond the capabilities of most creatures with larger brains, the latest robot designs mimic the talented creature with custom-made soft bodies possessed of similar qualities.

At present, unlike the familiar robots of science fiction, these soft-bodied robots have no necessary resemblance to human bodies, but are designed to best perform a designated range of tasks. The logical conclusion, though, is that, unlike the fictional Ishmael, which outsmarted the human occupants of Gridiron, a real-life Ishmael would be able to do so only if it too possessed a similar body enabling it to empathize with and anticipate the actions and intentions of humans, much like the envious monkey watching the ice-cream-eating student described in Chapter 3, and not the hi-tech building it was actually embodied in. Mistakenly conceived as it was, rather than whizzing freely about the Net, once Ishmael had vacated the physical structure that was its sensory equivalent of a body of sorts, it would simply have imploded into a chaotic mass of trillions of mindless digits.

Nevertheless, virtual fantasies aside, there can be no denying the extraordinary impact of the Net around the globe.[21] At a more humdrum but ubiquitous level, growing numbers of individuals and groups now rely upon the Net and related subsidiary networks for their daily social contacts and work, not to mention the amount of time spent on computer games or in other virtual worlds of one kind or another. At one extreme, the technique involved may be a simple matter of texting or 'Tweeting' instead of actually speaking to someone in person or on the phone. At the other extreme, as in 'Second Life,' individuals not only shape whole virtual environments to suit their fancy, but also shape their virtual selves or 'avatars' along with them, including their physical appearance, interacting with other avatars in what increasingly resembles an alternative universe of virtual worlds and simulated selves.

While there is an implicit recognition in such worlds of the significance of having a body – or at least a representation of one – not everyone is happy with such developments, many of which could be regarded as a further regression into what, in his trenchant critique of American society, Christopher Lasch wrote about long ago in *The Culture of Narcissism*.[22] More recently, in *ID: The Quest for Identity in the 21st Century*, Susan Greenfield,[23] a distinguished British neuroscientist, expresses profound concerns for the effects of the same technologies of communication and entertainment on personal identities and social relations:

> Perhaps it would not be too extreme to imagine a time, not so far off, when the whole idea of messy, face-to-face interaction, with its pheromones, body language, immediacy and above all unpredictability, may have become an unpalatable alternative to a remote, online, sanitized and far more onanistic cyber-persona and life.[24]

Greenfield is particularly concerned about the amount of time children and young people spend in front of their screens immersed in their digital worlds, which she believes may have long-term neurological effects amounting to a 'rewiring' of the human brain in socially deficient ways. Given the proven plasticity of the brain discussed in Chapter 2, such effects are entirely plausible. Her concerns are shared by Beeban Kidron, a filmmaker whose documentary *InRealLife* records the addictive behavior of teenagers glued to the Net, for which she holds the information technology and entertainment corporations exploiting their addiction to account:

Asking a young person to put down their Xbox, shut their computer or stop looking at their smartphone is like asking an alcoholic to put down their drink. Behind the nursery colours and baby names that epitomize the corporate branding of the internet is a culture that is relentlessly commercial. Each interaction means data – data that is worth a fortune. Our children, manipulated to become exemplary consumers, increasingly admit they do not feel 'in control' of their own internet use.

Everything a teenager does, says or looks at, however transitory, contributes to an aggregated virtual self that might one day have consequences for its real-life counterpart.[25]

Other researchers' observations would seem to justify such misgivings. In his essay 'The Dreams of Readers,' Nicholas Carr's[26] comments on the beneficial but increasingly neglected effects of good old-fashioned reading match those recorded by Wolf in Chapter 4 concerning its value in exploring other worlds that individuals would not otherwise experience. Carr describes the experiments by a group of psychologists at Washington University in St Louis who used brain scans to record neural activity during subjects' reading sessions. What they discovered was that 'readers mentally simulate each new situation encountered in a narrative,'[27] visibly changing neural networks in the process of knitting both real and imagined experiences together. Carr argues that such experiments suggest that focused reading of this kind, where readers 'lose themselves' in the writer's world, with all its characters, directly encourages the development of empathy in individuals, while the converse is true of those who are less exposed to 'the inner lives of others' that reading offers.[28]

Whatever other psychological traits that gaming and the virtual worlds of avatars develop, it would appear that the individual capacity for empathy is either not among them or has yet to be revealed, perhaps by further research by neuroscientists into von Economo neurons and the like. On the other hand, Carr suggests the cure is there for the taking, provided children and teenagers are given enough encouragement and time to do the kind of reading at a young age which nourishes those vital empathetic skills and attitudes. Coincidentally, like most books now, the collection of essays in which Carr's own essay appears is published in both traditional and e-book formats, which may suggest the answer in itself: presenting reading material in an electronic format youngsters can themselves more readily identify with.

Customized automation

No matter what their specific or intended purpose may be, all the above innovative technologies are evolving at breakneck speeds, the full outcomes of which are as yet unknown, but which hold out the promise of both good and bad changes in the extended self. On the downside, we are constantly alerted by both the professional and the popular media to the more dubious aspects of being dependent upon digital phones, global search engines and on-line retail systems that are increasingly designed as much to *collect* personal information about their users as to serve those users – information that is hard if not impossible to protect from abuse, whether by the operators themselves or by hackers.[29]

On the upside, among the more positive innovations to set against the riskier developments, digital techniques are already transforming the way buildings and cities are conceived, designed and constructed, as well as other common artifacts. Following the pattern of combinatorial evolution and design described in this volume, the most advanced computer-based technologies of design and fabrication were originally borrowed from elsewhere, such as the automobile, aircraft and other manufacturing industries, usually after a long time lag. The first flexible manufacturing system (FMS), for example, called 'System 24,' was invented in the UK at the Molins Machine Company by D. T. N. Williamson in the early 1960s for the manufacture of components for cigarette-making machines (fig. 11.10).[30] Applying cybernetic principles of automated integration to previously known technologies of computer-aided manufacture (CAM), System 24 provides a perfect example of Arthur's theory of technological evolution, as well as being a major industrial innovation in its own right. Computer numerically controlled (CNC) machines were already in common use in many industries in that period for machining metal components of varying complexity.[31] However, designed as they were to operate separately, machining one component at a time using an array of different tools, they were all restricted to small-batch production at slow speeds. System 24 broke new ground by linking together a whole row of CNC machines by a computer-controlled transfer line, each machine performing a different operation on the same component. Metal parts (aluminum blocks were used to raise machining speeds) could be automatically shuttled along the transfer line from one machine to another without holding the others up, so that every CNC machine in the production line would be in full-time operation 24 hours per day – hence the name for the system. In this way, the same system could produce any number of different components, from a single, tailor-made item to thousands of the same item with equal efficiency and economy, combining the virtues of both small-batch and mass-production in one fully automated line, simply by changing the software instructions.[32]

In the same period, in his seminal essay 'Towards the Cybernetic Factory,' the British cybernetician Stafford Beer[33] outlined his vision of how such technologies could transform manufacturing companies from being the outdated 'dinosaurs' they had become, into responsive systems of production capable of meeting the variable needs of a fast-changing world. The same advanced technologies of manufacture undermined the whole ethos of the modern movement in architecture, premised on mass-production technologies, promising to transform the nature of architectural design and production, leading this writer in 1969 to offer this prognosis:

> The post-industrial, cybernetic factory effectively reverses the present relationship of manufacturing concerns to the social systems they are meant to serve. It is a characteristic of social systems, as it is of all evolving systems, that in order to survive they may adopt one of two main strategies. The system can either respond to environmental pressures by a mutual process of give and take, reorganization, and the learning of new patterns of behaviour, or it can seek to dominate the environment as far as it can, and so trim external pressures to its own demands. The latter method, we have learnt, accurately describes classic consumerism. Dinosaur sanctuaries may not be hard to find in any social

11.10 *Model of the System 24, Molins Machine Company, c. 1965. Drawing shows linked computer numerically controlled (CNC) machines providing greater variety of production over separate machines*

11.11 *Guggenheim Museum Bilbao, 1997, by Frank Gehry. Exterior view showing complex shapes of titanium cladding produced with CNC machines and digital design techniques borrowed from the aircraft industry*

sphere, but while they may be able to contain divergent pressures for a time, they tend to be unreliable in the long term. Notwithstanding such drawbacks, the mass-production line has been upheld as a panacea for a backward building industry. It is a sad comment on any design profession that it should be so eager to embrace a technological straitjacket in order to impose its own dubious ideas of a visual order onto consumers. It is also very short-sighted. Instead of tuning the consumer to the machine, we can now tune the machine to the consumer.[34]

However, it took another two decades of research and development in other industries before similar technologies were applied in the design and construction of major building projects like Foster's Hongkong Bank, followed by Frank Gehry's Bilbao Guggenheim (fig. 11.11).[35] Since those first experimental projects, the subsequent impact of customized automation, or CAD/CAM as it is otherwise known

Appropriating cyberspace

(a combination of computer-aided design, or CAD, and CAM), on architectural production has opened up new structural and spatial possibilities, while greatly enlarging the realm of the extended self into whole tailor-made environments in the real as well as in the virtual world.[36]

Design by artificial selection

Though much of the potential responsiveness of these new technologies to pressing human and environmental needs has been squandered on commercially driven and whimsical projects to create the most eye-catching forms, the most promising and exciting design work is being done where real and virtual worlds interact in the creation and testing of virtual prototypes. Varying in complexity from single structures to entire urban complexes, these detailed assemblages of technical memes inhabit an ambiguous world halfway between real and virtual artifacts and are designed to respond to simulations of the primary functional and environmental conditions they would meet if built. Just as the method of breeding 'improved' species of domestic animals to meet human needs can be described as a rational method of *designing* better species,[37] so can the use of virtual prototypes and related digital technologies be described as the *artificial selection* of improved building types and designs.

However, research approaches in the field differ widely, from laboratory-grounded experiments mostly conducted in universities, to more pragmatic approaches centered in leading engineering and architectural practices. Based on genetic algorithms inspired by a mixture of both neo-Darwinian theories of evolution and more recent theories of emergence and self-producing systems of the sort described in Chapter 5, one school of thought aspires to the creation of semi-autonomous designs analogous to the spontaneous generation of form in nature, or morphogenesis, as it is called,[38] similar to experiments in computer science.[39] However, the use of genetic algorithms of this kind in architecture is still a matter of contentious debate. Chris Wise,[40] a leading figure in the field, underscores the problems involved:

> even with today's 'fab' computers we are utopia-bytes short of enough computing power to study what we really want to study, so the computer goes along a very narrow path. It only stops when it's told to. Mimicking Darwin, computerized mutations jump the process into another groove in the hope that somehow the fittest will survive. But the definition of 'fitness' is usually arbitrary, so the tools stunt their own creativity.[41]

A still newer and more promising body of research is focused on the development of memetic algorithms, or MAs, a hybrid branch of computation with coevolutionary features more in keeping with the ideas advanced in this book. Combining elements of neo-Darwinian and memetic theories of evolution, MAs are claimed to offer a balanced approach between general and more specific learning

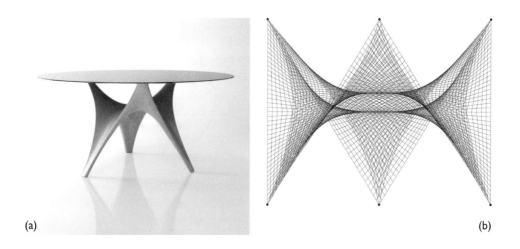

(a)

(b)

11.12 *(a) Molteni Arc table, one of Foster & Partners the practice's many furniture designs. (b) The same kind of parametric modeling techniques used in architectural design by Foster & Partners were also used in the design of the sculptured base of the table*

11.13 *Prototype for a combined wall and seating unit, by Foster & Partners. Large-scale product designs and building components with complex forms such as this can be produced using 3D printers direct from computer models*

Appropriating cyberspace

procedures capable of responding to complex life-like situations, potentially resolving some of the problems that Wise describes.[42]

An alternative and more accessible strategy favored by some cutting-edge practices is to embed design algorithms in real-life projects, so exposing the selection process to a wider range of specific environmental issues, both cultural and material. Wise himself suggests something of the sort when he calls for more project-related experiments:

> So far, the emerging technologist has usually had to limit the output of the process to an object rather than a project. A project has a definite purpose. A project has a site. A project interacts with people. It interacts with climate. It interacts with time. And unlike a computer process it is made of imperfect things and materials that change according to this interaction. *In short, the project lives* [added emphasis].[43]

While many complex and time-consuming design processes are automated, unlike the semi-autonomous genetic algorithms, the hybrid approach to virtual design and artificial selection also has the built-in virtue of *permeability*. That is to say, it facilitates and encourages external human and environmental inputs at any stage of the development process, adjusting design parameters along the way.

Among the most advanced, practice-based research centers of this kind, the Special Modelling Group (SMG) within Foster & Partners creates and tests virtual prototypes for projects ranging from office towers to furniture and other product designs (fig. 11.12). Specializing in its early years on mostly complex geometric forms and related structural problems, the SMG now integrates a wide spectrum of design and construction tasks covering energy use as well as rapid prototyping and other advanced techniques of fabrication, including large-scale 3D printing (fig. 11.13),[44] servicing design groups in the practice and developing their own software as they progress.[45] While significant differences remain between natural species and building types and how each evolves – not the least being the relations between form and function discussed in earlier chapters – developments of this kind offer the possibility of radical changes in the evolution of building technics, along with beneficial increases in control over the environmental outcomes.

Electronic ecologies

The extension of similar techniques into the urban dimension also promises much to come but is fraught with the same questions raised above with respect to architectural production. As with other aspects of the digital revolution in design, the basic idea that new systems of telecommunication are outdating existing urban patterns and forms of social interaction dates back many decades to Melvin Webber and a few other clear-sighted writers.[46] However, as with the other advanced technologies discussed above, recent thinking on 'electronic ecologies,' as they are best described,[47] presents a more complex picture. In *e-topia*,[48] Mitchell's follow-up book to his *City of Bits*, the author modifies his messianic zeal for a virtual life inhabited by Gibson's disembodied beings. While, like Webber, Mitchell questions the relevance of place-identity in the face of a world increasingly bound together by electronic media, he allows that the outcome may not necessarily be all one-sided:

> But long-established settlement patterns and social arrangements are remarkably resistant to even the most powerful pressures for change; mostly they transform slowly, messily, unevenly, and incompletely, and *human nature hardly changes at all* [added emphasis].
>
> […] In particular, the loosening of locational imperatives by means of electronic communication will not peg the needle at the logical extreme. It will not turn us all into rootless, laptop-toting, cell-phoning nomads. Far from it.
>
> Most of us will still want more or less permanent places of our own, and will choose to live in small groups of those whose company we particularly cherish – in twosomes, ménages-à-*n*, nuclear families, extended families, and in all manner of postnuclear reshuffles and extranuclear inventions. Home, in a variety of new configurations, will be where many hearts remain – and it will be where a growing number of things end up as well. It will become a renewed focus of architectural attention and innovation as it integrates new functions and services.
>
> […] *All this is consistent with the basic human need to belong somewhere in particular* [added emphasis].[49]

Adopting his more characteristic enthusiasm for all things digital, like many other earlier and later writers on the subject[50] Mitchell points to the evolution of buildings and whole cities with 'nervous systems' of their own as a positive development. Accordingly: 'We will characterize cities of the twenty-first century as systems of interlinked, interacting, silicon- and software-saturated *smart, attentive,* and *responsive* places.'[51]

In a collection of essays on related innovations, *Sentient City,*[52] the authors present a more nuanced view of integrating smart technologies with artifacts of every scale and function. Among the more critical and humorous case studies, in 'Too Smart City,' David Jimison and Joo Youn Paek[53] describe a range of street furniture with built-in smart technology they purposefully designed to fail and confuse its users, including a public bench that tips people off it as soon as they attempt to sit on it, thus highlighting the dangers of relying too much upon advanced but imperfect technologies.

Modeling complex urban systems also presents problems of another level. Drawing upon a battery of mathematical concepts and computer techniques borrowed from AI and other disciplines, including cellular automata, agent-based models and fractal theory,[54] the research gap between laboratory-based simulations and the complexities of the real-life built environment is no less wide at the larger scale of urban growth than it is at the architectural scale pinpointed by Wise. Concluding his analysis of one series of fractal models simulating the distribution of urban populations in *Cities and Complexity,*[55] Michael Batty's comment might well apply to much of the other work being done in this exciting but still young field:

> The greatest problem with these models is that because competition between cities is not present, it is clear that they are applicable only to systems where cities develop

independently. Yet they represent the most parsimonious of all models generating such fractal distributions. That they generate them most successfully throws into stark relief the conundrum faced by the development of theory in the social sciences: although they can produce excellent simulations that meet all the hallmarks of parsimonious science, *we know these cannot be right, for cities do not develop this way in practice* [added emphasis]. At best they represent a convenient starting point, a benchmark from which to work.[56]

This is not to suggest that such work is pointless. On the contrary, as has been argued throughout this book, we desperately need to better understand how cities and other human habitations evolve and the effects they have on the broader environment, as well as on their inhabitants. However, given the proven power of technology to evolve under its own momentum, as described in these chapters, unless they take care, designers could well find themselves being led astray yet again, just as they were in the past by the attractions of automobiles and air conditioning, with all their unexpected side-effects.

It is just as well, therefore, to be conscious of the fallibility of such techniques and not to be misled by their scientific credentials, or what Batty aptly describes as their 'parsimonious' features, as so many design researchers and theorists appear to be. No doubt some of these problems may also be overcome by the kind of messier but more realistic mix-and-match approach that Wise recommends with regard to architectural modeling, and that Batty also proposes in his book; or that even Mitchell describes as the ambiguous future shape of urban life in the electronic age. Notwithstanding all the problems involved, design and modeling techniques of this kind hold out the prospect of recasting the environmental side of our extended selves along more rational lines, not just for our own benefit, but for that of the rest of life on the planet too.

Part IV summary

Exploring the broader cultural and environmental implications of the theory presented in the preceding chapters, Chapter 10 opened with some widespread examples of cultural conservatism and resistance to change. While accepting that viral analogies might provide plausible explanations for how technical memes spread and take hold in people's minds, it is suggested that such analogies be treated with caution, the distinction between 'good' and 'bad' memes often being influenced by subjective viewpoints concerning their influence on people.

Other, possibly stronger explanations for conservative and addictive behavior of a social and psychological nature were proffered, principally the kind of 'tribal thinking' and its variants described by Mike McRae and others. Significantly, McRae suggests that misguided beliefs in free will prevent us from recognizing just how fallible individuals and groups are when it comes to questioning their own habits or resisting any change to them. The symptoms of tribal thinking – that is, preferring 'observations that support what we already believe to be true,' or what is described as 'confirmation bias,' rather than accepting contrary observations – are all too obvious in the widespread denial of climate change, despite the mounting scientific evidence of its human causes and effects, as documented in international and national reports.

While there is no sure method at this time of determining the influence of 'selfish' forms of cultural production similar to Richard Dawkins' idea of 'selfish memes,' it was suggested that many familiar cultural products, including building types and other artifacts, evolve *as if* they have a life of their own beyond human control, much as Stiegler and some of the other writers cited in this book have argued. Similarly, it was concluded that the popular concept of free will as an unrestricted zone of personal action is an illusion born of confusions between perceptions of a separate physical body (true) and belief in a separate self (false). The reality is that, while people make many everyday choices, both choices and decisions are generally directed by the impacts of place, language and culture on the extended self. Moreover, though consciousness and free will are often presented as linked concepts, while the former might well be a prerequisite for making rational decisions or breaking with entrenched patterns of thought and behavior, consciousness in itself is no guarantee that one follows the other. On the contrary, presented with unwelcome evidence, as Cass Sunstein explains, people will often actively *suppress* such evidence in their efforts to avoid rethinking their values and any disruption to their way of life – a characteristic ploy of climate change sceptics.

Jared Diamond's detailed history of the failure of past civilizations provides further sobering evidence of the disastrous consequences of stubbornly sticking with customary habits and rituals even in the face of abundant and tragic evidence of rapid decline. The parallels, for example, between what Diamond describes as 'psychological denial' and McRae's confirmation bias, or Sunstein's 'biased assimilation' and Leon Festinger's 'cognitive dissonance,' are all striking enough to suggest there is more than just speculation in Diamond's thesis as to the likely causes of the actual or potential collapse of civilizations, including our own. Beyond the psychological explanations of failure, pathological symptoms of addiction of a more systemic kind were also identified in the behavior of self-producing organizations that become so focused on their own interests and identities they ignore changes in their environments threatening their long-term existence. Neither are any of the more radical alternative scenarios currently on offer, such as David Sherman and Joseph Wayne Smith's neo-Platonic society, or Paul Gilding's equally utopian vision of a 'happiness economy,' convincing, since they overlook those same human factors that underlay the failure of previous civilizations, and which still persist.

Though the pace of change is presently painfully slow – and possibly fatally so – one of the more positive indicators of future changes may be found in the growing shift from private modes of transportation to public modes – where such services are available – as the rising price of fuel and other living costs compel otherwise reluctant suburban populations to adjust to realities. In addition to new models for high-density urban living now emerging, some of which were briefly covered in Chapter 9, constructive proposals for restructuring existing suburbs and other measures to cure cities of automobile dependency are also being implemented in the USA and elsewhere. Combined with more evenly distributed networks of public transportation, they offer practical models for sustainable, polycentric cities of varied densities.

Shifting the focus again toward the future, Chapter 11 brings the coevolution of *Homo sapiens* and technology up to date and examines the different ways in which individuals and groups are appropriating cyberspace, creating whole new virtual worlds for our extended selves to inhabit and find new forms of expression. As with earlier patterns of human technics, the 'who' and the 'what' are as indistinguishable in these virtual worlds as they are in the 'real' world, while the interactions between the two realms increasingly blur conventional descriptions of human experience.

That chapter opens with a discussion of the manner in which architectural theorists like William Mitchell, following the method of metaphorical extension outlined in Chapter 9, make free use of historical and other familiar spatial concepts in order to explain and express the as yet little understood nature and structure of cyberspace, as they conceive it. Adopting the same method but choosing a quite different model, it was proposed that if there are any appropriate existing topological concepts that might accurately describe the experience of cyberspace, they might be found in the Japanese concept of movement space, rather than in the static baroque models favored by Mitchell.

More seriously, there are strong indications in both Mitchell's work and that of other writers of a conception of cyberspace that, much like Kate Distin's and Robert Aunger's purified interpretation of memes, smacks more of classic Cartesian dualism than the complex views offered by the philosophers and neuroscientists discussed in previous chapters. Contrary to Mitchell's belief and that of other would-be cybernauts that our earthly bodies might be somehow dispensed with in some future virtual world where digitized minds enjoy an electronic immortality (so long, presumably, as supporting computer systems do not crash), progress in robotics and AI also suggests that intelligence is fundamentally related to having a physical body through which the world may be experienced, just as Maurice Merleau-Ponty and Michael Polanyi have argued.

Moving on to the subject of virtual selves, the concerns of neuroscientists like Susan Greenfield were discussed regarding the possible negative effects on social skills normally acquired through direct interpersonal communication, due to the amount of time many people now spend in virtual worlds. While it may be too early to assess those effects, the seductive opportunities for escaping real-world problems in exchange for virtual adventures and more attractive extended selves, as Greenfield warns, could have harmful and possibly irreversible consequences, especially for the young, reconfiguring vulnerable and plastic minds in ways we do not yet comprehend.

Concluding on a more hopeful note, recent progress by architects and other designers in employing the growing repertoire of digital tools now available to create virtual prototypes prior to construction is finally bringing the building industry into line with advanced industries like the aircraft and automobile sectors, where such techniques were originally developed. No sane person would buy an automobile that had not undergone prior testing for performance and safety factors, let alone book a flight on an untested aircraft. Given the vast amount of funds invested in construction, such developments are long overdue. Having, with few exceptions, mostly failed in the past to get to grips with how things are actually made with modern production technologies, architects are now showing a welcome grasp of emergent building technics.

More than that, progress in virtual prototyping and related techniques of this kind holds out the promise of moving beyond the current hit-and-miss evolution of buildings and cities, with its ever-growing dangers, toward something more like the purposeful model of artificial selection that first inspired Darwin – but applied now to breeding better building designs rather than domestic animals – with potentially beneficial impacts on the extended self, and on the environment generally.

Postscript

In light of the negative comments expressed in the Preface and elsewhere regarding both orthodox modernist and postmodernist movements, some readers may want to know just how or where the positions and arguments presented in this book fit into the known theoretical and critical spectrum. Though both the strengths and weaknesses of the modern movement and its products are widely acknowledged, the matter is further complicated in discussing postmodernism by confusions between the literary and architectural records.[1] The purpose of this Postscript is therefore to clarify the broader philosophical framework within which the book was written and to flesh out the ideas of some key thinkers briefly referred to in the main text.

The references to Ludwig Wittgenstein in Chapter 2, for example, are indicative of fundamental commonalities, not only between the worldviews of Michael Polanyi and Wittgenstein themselves, but also, according to Jerry Gill,[2] author of *Deep Postmodernism*, between those of Maurice Merleau-Ponty and Alfred North Whitehead as well. While, given the semantic luggage the term carries, any viewpoint with 'postmodern' attached to it needs to be treated with caution, Gill's account of what he describes as the group's nexus of thought offers a cogent and constructive interpretation worth repeating. His analysis also has special relevance to this book's subject matter, not only for what it helps us to understand of the wider philosophical context of Merleau-Ponty's and Polanyi's work, but also for the support it offers for much else of what has been written here on the role of language, types and tools in the extended self and human evolution generally.

Unlike self-described postmodernists, Gill argues, who offer only negative critiques of the modern worldview, or what he characterizes as 'the often one-sided deconstructionist approach to postmodernism,'[3] but who have generally been unable or unwilling to offer any coherent worldview in its place, all four philosophers present alternative perspectives, which, while critiquing modernism's assumed objectivity and rationality, also show a positive way forward. Noting that none of the leading Continental postmodern thinkers like Jacques Derrida,[4] Jean-François Lyotard[5] or Michel Foucault[6] paid attention to any of the above four, preferring other sources of critical inspiration, Gill homes in on the general negativity and self-referential character of the latters' approach to language, which they claim to have no meaning outside of itself and which is therefore open to endless reinterpretation, or 'deconstruction.' Accordingly, Gill explains, for Derrida the word 'difference' (*differance* in the French) has a special meaning as a 'non-concept' designating the goal of linguistic activity, as Derrida himself describes it:

> The notion of 'difference,' for example, is a non-concept in that it cannot be defined in terms of oppositional predicates; it is neither this nor that (e.g. the act of differing and of deferring) without being reducible to a dialectic logic either [...]. There is no conceptual realm beyond language which would allow the term to have a univocal semantic content over and above its inscription in language. Because it remains a trace of language it remains non-conceptual. And because it has no oppositional or predicative generality, which would identify it as *this* rather than *that*, the term 'difference' cannot be defined within the system of logic – Aristotelian or dialectical – that is, within the logo-centric system of philosophy.[7]

Dismissing the pretentions of Derrida and other deconstructionists to a value-free approach to linguistic analysis, Gill argues that even Derrida's attempt to explain what the meaning of difference as a 'non-concept' *is* entails the use of words and concepts whose meaning must necessarily be shared by reader and author – despite what Gill describes as the 'complex, convoluted form'[8] that Derrida typically employs to express his ideas.[9] While they question everyone else's assumptions, Gill observes that deconstructionists never question their own assumptions and are seemingly unaware of either making or having any. For instance, while stressing, as Foucault does, that all truth statements are grounded in some kind of social and political rationale and can therefore have no objective or more general status beyond that rationale, they do not recognize that holding such a position in itself suggests a search for some sort of truth: 'In other words, Foucault and other deconstructionists fail to see that their very own statements about "truth" aim at being true.'[10] Not only that, but deconstructionists fail to recognize that, whatever kind of internal rationale may be involved, the production and regulation of knowledge within social and political systems inevitably entail choices between one thing or interpretation and another, that is, between 'truth' over 'error': 'If this distinction is ignored, or subsumed under the heading of political agendas, then there is no point to any kind of search for knowledge at all, including Foucault's, Derrida's, and Lyotard's own efforts in these statements.'[11]

While Gill allows that deconstructionists have produced some useful insights, by denying any grounded position themselves other than being *against* the claims to objectivity of the modern view – a contradiction in itself of Derrida's own explicit rejection of oppositional thinking – he suggests the extreme relativity of their worldview restricts them to mostly superficial observations, offering no deeper explanation of the phenomena they attempt to analyze. Paradoxically, as expounded by Lyotard and other leading thinkers of the movement, postmodernism shares modernism's aversion to metaphysical speculation or any kind of overarching narrative, though without the justification afforded by modernism's empiricism.[12]

By contrast, Gill argues that Polanyi et al. not only offer more positive alternatives to the orthodox modern view, but also articulate their views and positions in such a manner as to open up their own premises to debate. Neither are any of them shy of metaphysical speculation, though remaining cautious about its, and their own, limitations: 'While fully acknowledging that their own perspective, as well as anyone else's, can lay no claim to being the "final truth," they have struck philosophical postures in which there remains the possibility of aiming at or striving for a correct understanding of the "way things are" in the world and in our daily lives.'[13]

On the issue of reality, for example, Whitehead firmly rejects the accepted modern view of his time, or what he describes as the 'fallacy of misplaced concreteness,'[14] together with the so-called 'atomistic' view dating back to antiquity and sanctified by Newtonian physics, that reality can be reduced to finite particles.[15] What counts more to Whitehead are the underlying *processes* pulling everything together into the visible features of the cosmos: 'For Whitehead, process was more fundamental than physicality, more concrete and thus more real.'[16] Anticipating later systems approaches and 'holistic' thinking, implicit in Whitehead's philosophy is both a focus on the relations *between* things, and an open-ended, dynamic and evolutionary perspective, which he called 'organism.' Similarly, while in the modern view the things or units have logical precedent over the relations between them, Whitehead's perspective turns it around, giving logical priority to the relations themselves. All of this, Gill suggests, points to an underlying biological analogy and a stress on interconnectedness and the flux and change of events, more in keeping with the scientific advances of Whitehead's time, rather than the more limited and dated model of science the orthodox modern view was tied to.[17]

Regarding Wittgenstein, Gill concedes that he and Whitehead are not normally associated with each other on this topic. However, he contends that, though Wittgenstein was mainly focused on language all his life and made no metaphysical claims of his own for his philosophy, 'his thought carries with it significant metaphysical implications.'[18] While his early work culminating in the *Tractatus Logico-Philosophicus*[19] could be interpreted as a 'manifesto of the modernist paradigm'[20] and the 'logical atomism' which went with it, his return to philosophy at Cambridge University after a 15-year break working as a school teacher and on other odd jobs was marked by a radical change in his thought. The eventual published product of that change, his *Philosophical Investigations*,[21] amounts to a complete repudiation of his own earlier work – a remarkable and rare event in any philosopher's career.[22] From his experiences teaching school children, Wittgenstein had come to realize that language was a great deal more flexible and imprecise than he had previously understood it to be and that it served many different functions other than reflecting reality. As Wittgenstein now understood it, Gill writes, linguistic communication hinged on 'the reciprocal interaction between persons, language, and our physical and social realities,'[23] for which he coined the term 'forms of life' quoted in Chapter 2. Consequently, he concluded that the whole logical enterprise he had previously been engaged in of trying to both prove and *im*prove on language's connection to reality was a waste of time and that 'absolute precision and completeness are neither possible nor necessary.'[24] In short, 'ordinary language is alright as it is.'[25]

Gill points to the different metaphors used by Wittgenstein to convey his ideas in the early and later works as a way of illustrating the nature of the change in his thinking. For example, the dominant metaphors in the *Tractatus* are 'logical space,' 'pictures' and 'visual images,' all of which delineate strict boundaries between what can be pinned down as accurately reflecting reality and what cannot. Conversely, in the *Investigations*, Wittgenstein's metaphors all revolve around everyday activities, including tool use, as we saw in the passage quoted from Ingold in Chapter 2. The best known of these new metaphors is his 'language games' and the related phrase 'meaning is use,' which he employs to express the multiplicity and shifting character of language use, according to whichever purpose or activity is involved, all adding up, as Gill describes it, to his concept of a form of life:

> And this multiplicity is not something fixed, given once for all; but new types of language, new language games, as we may say, come into existence, and others become obsolete and get forgotten [...]. Here the term 'language-game' is meant to bring into prominence the fact that the *speaking* of a language is part of an activity, or of a form of life.[26]

Applying the same distinction made by linguists between the synchronic and diachronic aspects of language mentioned earlier in this book, Gill suggests that another way of looking at the difference between the early and later works is that in the former Wittgenstein focused all his attention on the synchronic aspects of language, meaning those relating to its fixed state at any given time or place, while in the later works he focused on the diachronic aspects, or those features relating to the growth and change in language use over time.[27]

On embodiment, also an issue neither Whitehead nor Wittgenstein is usually identified with, at least not to the extent that Merleau-Ponty and Polanyi are, Gill provides ample evidence of their deep concern with the role of the body in what we know of the world and how we experience it. In Whitehead's case, he specifically and frequently refers to the 'withness of the body' in respect of the interrelations between human experience and reality. For example, regarding the immediacy of human perception, Whitehead writes:

> But this analysis of presentational immediacy has not exhausted the content of the feeling. For we feel *with the body*. There may be further specialization into a particular organ of sensation; but in any case the *'withness' of the body* is an ever-present, though elusive element in our perceptions of presentational immediacy.[28]

The issue is especially relevant in Whitehead's work to his discussions of the geometrical relations of physical bodies to one another. Echoing Merleau-Ponty's stress on the body as the center and origin of the perception of objects and their shape in space, Whitehead writes: 'Our direct perception, via our senses, of an immediate extensive shape, in a certain geometrical perspective to ourselves, and in certain geometrical relations to the contemporary world, remains an ultimate fact.'[29] While Gill concedes that Whitehead's expression 'withness of the body' is less than crystal clear, he interprets it in a manner similar to Merleau-Ponty's insistence on the body as the indispensable fulcrum of experience – the one thing we can never distance ourselves from: 'In short, the body is always "with us" in a way that nothing else can be said to be with us.'[30] Similarly, for Whitehead, a human being's sense of self is inseparable from having a body, a point he illustrates through the story of the 'lost traveler,' who, he suggests, 'should not ask, Where am I? What he really wants to know is, where are the other places? He has got his own body, *but he has lost them* [added emphasis].'[31]

In turn, while it is not spelt out in the same way as by the other three thinkers, the issue of embodiment is intrinsic to Wittgenstein's concern with the interrelations between language and human activity and the indivisibility of reality, that is, the forms of life. This is particularly apparent, as was noted above, in his fondness for examples of tool use to illustrate what he means by the latter phrase – topics that directly parallel those discussed by Merleau-Ponty and Polanyi and some of the other authors quoted in this book. For example, Gill points out that Wittgenstein 'frequently likens language to such things as utensils, chess pieces, and handles in an effort to demonstrate not only the practical dimensions of speech but its embodied character as well.'[32] Likewise, for Wittgenstein, the physical gesture of pointing to something is no less important an indication of the embodiment of speech – especially for children, who may not be ready to articulate what it is they want to say – as it is an act specifically aimed at drawing somebody else's attention to that something. In this respect, Gill suggests that Wittgenstein is just as aware that, in Polanyi's words, 'we know more than we can tell,' as the latter is, but expresses it in his own terms:

> What does it mean to know what a game is? What does it mean to know it and not be able to say it? Is this knowledge somehow equivalent to an unformulated definition? So that if it were formulated I should be able to recognize it as the expression of my knowledge? Isn't my knowledge, my concept of a game, completely expressed in the explanations that I could give? That is in my describing examples of various kinds of games; showing how all sorts of other games can be constructed on the analogy of these; saying that I should scarcely include this or this among games; and so on. Compare *knowing* and *saying*:
>
> > how many feet high Mont Blanc is –
> > how the word 'game' is used –
> > how a clarinet sounds.
>
> If you are surprised that one can know something and not be able to say it, you are perhaps thinking of a case like the first. Certainly not of one like the third.[33]

The passage is significant not only for what it tells us of the commonality between Wittgenstein's and Polanyi's thought in this regard, but also for the importance Wittgenstein attaches to what is described elsewhere in this book as the 'method of exemplars.'[34] That is to say, even though an actual physical gesture may not always be involved, a person may come to understand and explain something by 'pointing' to, or citing several instances of the same thing – what Wittgenstein also defines in terms of the distinction between 'saying and showing.'[35]

However, the issue of embodiment is most clearly expressed in Wittgenstein's comments about the impossibility of effectively communicating with animals that do not possess the same kinds of bodies as us, even if they were to possess human speech – a problem evidently ignored by Disney and his artists. As Wittgenstein puts it: 'If a lion could talk, we could not understand him.'[36] As Gill explains, Wittgenstein's point is that, since lions do not inhabit the same bodies as we do, they do not and *cannot* experience the world in the same way: 'and thus they do not participate in the same sort of behaviors, "language games,"' and social practices that we do.'[37] In other words, the forms of life lived by lions are lions' forms of life, not ours, and vice versa.

In a concluding chapter, Gill also briefly covers the 'linguistic phenomenology' of J. L. Austin,[38] finding further common threads in Austin's thought defining a mutual position with the former group 'between the over-confidence of modernism and the skepticism of deconstructive postmodernism.'[39] Taking a similar line to Wittgenstein's interactive theory of language use, Gill writes, Austin dismisses what he calls the 'descriptive fallacy,' by which language is presumed to offer only a passive and presumably objective description of the world, in favor of 'performative utterances' linking spoken words to actions: 'By his introduction of this term Austin put the spotlight on uses of language that seek, not to describe states of affairs, but to *perform* an action in the world.'[40] In such cases, Austin states, the act of uttering certain words is *itself* part of the action:

> Suppose, for example, that in the course of a marriage ceremony I say, as people will, 'I do' – Or again, suppose that I tread on your toe and say 'I apologize.' Or again, suppose that I have the bottle of champagne in my hand and say 'I name this ship the Queen Elizabeth.' Or suppose I say 'I bet you sixpence it will rain tomorrow.' In all these cases it would be absurd to regard the thing that I say as a report of the performance of the action in question – We should rather say that in saying what I do, I actually perform that action.[41]

In this way, while conceding there can be no hard-and-fast line between performative and descriptive utterances, Austin casts language in a *mediating* role between its users and the world they live in:

> When we examine what we should say when, what words we should use in what situations, we are looking again not merely at words (or 'meanings,' whatever they may be) but also at the realities we use words to talk about: we are using a sharpened awareness of words *to sharpen our perception of, though not as a final arbiter of, the phenomena* [added emphasis].[42]

While Austin critiques the simplistic objectivism of modernists, like the other philosophers in Gill's favored group he suggests this does not mean we have to abandon altogether the search for truth and reality, or accept the deconstructionist view of language as having no meaning beyond itself. Rather, linguistic phenomenology suggests we get to know 'how things are in the world by paying careful attention to the deep patterns of speech by means of which we interact with and in it, as well as with one another.'[43] Similarly, Austin addresses the related issue of whether it is possible to know the minds of others by first asking whether it is acceptable for a person to claim they know that something is true when there is a possibility that he or she can be wrong about it. As Gill explains, the sceptical deconstructionist view is that the very possibility of being wrong justifies their claim that there is no such thing as reliable knowledge. However, not according to Austin's phenomenology:

> In such cases we merely have to be in a reasonable position to make a claim, as when, for instance, we can say that we grew up in that area, knew the person in question, or read the book under discussion. That people make mistakes or are sometimes wrong does not mean that they cannot claim to know things. Indeed, as Austin would say, the very meaning of the notion of being wrong is parasitic on that of something being correct, even as the notion of something being 'unreal' in a metaphysical sense is dependent on that of some things actually being 'real.' Otherwise doubts make no sense and would never get off the ground at all. We do and must begin as 'naïve realists.'[44]

For Austin, when a person tells another person that he or she 'knows' something, they employ the phrase 'I know' in a similar way to 'I promise,' lending their personal authority as to the truth of whatever is being said. In the same manner, any such communication necessarily entails the initial assumption that the other person will understand and accept the assertion of truth. Put another way, all communication necessarily kicks off with at least the *temporary* or partial suspension of doubt on both sides, to be modified if required as the dialogue proceeds toward a better understanding of the issue – or persons – in question. As Gill writes:

> It is fundamental in talking (as in other matters) that we are entitled to trust others, except in so far as there is some concrete reason to distrust them. Believing persons, accepting testimony, is the, or one main, point of talking.[45]

While Gill makes no mention of either George Herbert Mead[46] or Gregory Bateson,[47] who produced their major works during roughly the same era as the previous thinkers, in addition to Austin a sound case could also be made for including both Americans with that group on the grounds of their joint interests and commitments. Widely acknowledged as the father of 'symbolic interactionism,'[48] Mead's concepts of rationality and self-awareness as the reciprocal products of communication with others, for example, complements the interactive perspective of Austin and the other four philosophers, especially Wittgenstein, though it differs in other respects, particularly regarding the weight Mead attaches to the more conscious aspects of cognition.[49] Correspondingly, while Bateson does not specifically deal with the impact of technology on human development, his evolutionary theory of mind as a dispersed phenomenon, which embraces nature as well as humankind, shares much with the other thinkers in the group.

Taking the earlier philosopher's work first, for Mead, all of social activity, whether human or non-human, is characterized by the form of communication involved. However, what sets humans apart from other species is their special gift for spoken language. So much may seem obvious, but it is Mead's analysis of the two-way process of empathy between communicating individuals and the role it plays in the formation of the self that marks the originality of his thought. According to Mead, the basic unit of all communications systems is the 'gesture,' which he defines as that part of any social act that stimulates a response in another individual, whether conscious ('significant') or unconscious ('non-significant').[50] Mead therefore answers, or rather avoids, such problems as the meaning of meaning with an operational definition. The essence of meaning, he suggests, is already implicit in the relation between the three components of any social act, namely: the gesture of one participant; a response to that gesture by a second participant; and completion of the social act begun by the gesture of the first participant.

However, what makes human forms of communication different from those of other species in Mead's schema is the level of self-consciousness involved. When a gesture is made with the communicant's awareness that it will get a specific response from another person, then the gesture acquires significance:

> Gestures become significant symbols when they implicitly arouse in an individual making them the same responses which they explicitly arouse, or are supposed to arouse in the individuals to whom they are addressed; and in all conversations of gestures within the social process, whether external (between different individuals) or internal (between an individual and himself), the individual's consciousness of the content and flow of meaning depends on his thus *taking the attitude of the other towards his own gestures* [added emphasis].[51]

It is this *reflexive* capacity of individuals to bring their own behavior under observation and control that Mead claims marks the emergence of mind and self-awareness:

> The evolutionary appearance of mind or intelligence takes place when the social process of experience and behaviour is brought within the experience of any of the separate individuals implicated therein, and when the individual's adjustment to the process is modified and refined by the awareness or consciousness which he thinks he has of it.[52]

This, for Mead, is the essence of rationality. The individual, through taking the attitudes of others toward himself or herself, is able to bring his or her own social experience into consciousness, thereby achieving a level of effective control over that experience not possible within the limitations imposed by any communication system involving simple or non-significant gestures.

In Mead's terms, therefore, rationality is inseparable from a process of social exchange and mutual understanding between different persons.[53] While, in the light of the arguments presented in preceding chapters, Mead's equation of self-control with self-consciousness looks questionable now, as with the previous four philosophers his concept of the self necessarily involves a dialogue with the external world and with others, or what is described in this book as a process of exteriorization, with its own dynamics. Not least, like the other thinkers, especially Merleau-Ponty and Polanyi, Mead's approach also explicitly encompasses material objects within the same wider realm of being, a point taken up by Herbert Blumer,[54] a champion of symbolic interactionism: 'To identify and understand the life of a group it is necessary to identify its world of objects; this identification has to be in terms of the meanings objects have for the members of the group.'[55]

Lastly, though Bateson himself rejects any claims to being a professional philosopher, his work encompasses an interpretation of mind and the relation of humankind to nature that goes far beyond the cybernetic details of their evolution, which he describes at length in his lectures and writings. While some of those cybernetic concepts have been superseded by the research on self-producing systems and related theories of evolution outlined in this book, Bateson's consistent stress on the interactions between the parts of different systems in general is at one with the other thinkers in the group. Accordingly, for Bateson: 'The *explanation* of mental phenomena must always reside in the organization and interaction of multiple parts.'[56] However, in explaining his ecological theory of mind, Bateson also goes much further than any of the other writers in extending the idea of mind beyond the physical limits of the body, claiming that both mind and nature share a deeper and more fundamental type of process. That process is the joint moment of *integration and separation* when an entity can be seen as belonging to one class of things and is therefore *different* in some significant way, no matter how small, from another class of things. Whereas Derrida, as explained above, treats difference negatively as a linguistic 'non-concept,' for Bateson it provides the essential engine for the evolution of both mind and nature, or what he also eloquently describes as 'the pattern which connects.'[57] Speaking at a memorial lecture (the same lecture Bateson is quoted from in the Preface) and referring to the dictum of the Polish-American philosopher and scientist Alfred Korzybski 'the map is not the territory,' he asks his audience:

> What is it in the territory [of experience] that gets onto the map? We know that the territory does not get onto the map. That is the central point about which we here are all agreed. Now, if the territory were uniform, nothing would get onto the map except its boundaries, which are the points at which it ceases to be uniform against some larger matrix. What gets onto the map, in fact, is *difference*, be it a difference in altitude, a difference in vegetation, a difference in population structure, difference in surface, or whatever. Differences are the things that get onto the map.[58]

In turn, difference is the primary thing that drives nature, the thing that causes what were once small but characteristic variations of features between species to become ever larger and more distinctive variations, as each evolves along its own ecological pathway. While, in the following quote, Bateson refers to the idea of difference as a process of 'logical typing,' his evolutionary perspective is closer to the flexible concept of speciation favored by naturalists than it is to the fixed, Aristotelian system of logical classes described in other parts of this book. Neither, according to Bateson, is the perception of such differences restricted to human faculties:

> The thrust of my argument is that the very process of perception *is an act of logical typing* [added emphasis]. Every image is a complex of many-leveled coding and mapping. And surely dogs and cats have their visual images. When they look at you, surely they see 'you.' When a flea bites, surely the dog has an image of an 'itch,' located 'there.'[59]

Bateson does not mean by this that a doggy perception of its owner would be the same as that of a human friend. Nor, as Wittgenstein said of the differences between the lion and human worldviews, would any animal with four legs be able to empathize with the actions of a human figure the same way a primate can. However, just as the simple cell 'recognizes' a virus for what it is and takes whatever defensive actions it can against it, or a bee can tell which plants to harvest among all the rest, so can all nature's creations distinguish between what sustains or threatens their existence.

Except, perhaps, the human race. Ironically, the same technological extensions that made *Homo sapiens* so successful now threaten the future of the race. Aside from the wisdom and insights Bateson offers regarding the substantive links between the way mind and nature work, he was among the first to alert humanity to the perils of upsetting nature's equilibria. For that service alone, Bateson, along with Mead, deserves a place in Gill's pantheon of twentieth-century thinkers.

Notes

Preface

1 From the Nineteenth Annual Korzybski Memorial Lecture, delivered January 9, 1970, in Gregory Bateson, *Steps to an Ecology of Mind* (New York: Ballantine Books, 1972), 462.

2 Chris Abel, 'Architecture as Identity: The Essence of Architecture,' in *Semiotics 1980: Proceedings of the 5th Annual Meeting of the Semiotic Society of America, Lubbock, Texas, October 16–19*, ed. Michael Herzfeld and Margot D. Lenhart (New York: Plenum, 1982), 10.

Acknowledgments

1 The computer-based training program at MIT mentioned here, called 'ARCHITRAINER,' is included in Nicholas Negroponte, *Soft Architecture Machines* (Cambridge: MIT Press, 1975), 112–13. The research was also reported in Chris Abel, 'Instructional Simulation of Client Construct Systems,' paper presented at the 1975 Architectural Psychology Conference, University of Sheffield. A summary is also included in Chris Abel, *Architecture and Identity* (Oxford: Architectural Press, 1997), 33–6. In addition to Pask's own learning theories, the program was largely based on George Kelly's 'personal construct theory' and related methodology, which Pask also suggested for study. See George Kelly, *A Theory of Personality: The Psychology of Personal Constructs* (New York: W. W. Norton, 1963).

Introduction

1 Despite rising prices, fossil fuels remain the cheapest and most popular source of energy. See Mike Berners-Lee and Duncan Clark, *The Burning Question* (London: Profile Books, 2013). The two authors demonstrate that any partial gains that have been made over the past years in reducing the use of fossil fuels in some sectors have been wiped out by increases in other sectors, with the result that global use overall continues to increase at an exponential rate. See also Will Hutton, 'Burn Our Planet or Face Financial Meltdown. Not Much of a Choice,' *Observer*, April 21, 2013. Like the previous authors, Hutton presents a bleak assessment of the lack of progress in reducing carbon emissions: 'The world is going to fry – unless there is change soon. There is weakening political will to make national and international targets stick, no strong business and financial coalition to lead and a weakening groundswell of public opinion to foot the bill. Instead, the international consensus of 25 years ago – that the world must act to challenge climate change – is dissolving […]. The long-contained depression, coupled with rising energy prices and squeezed living standards, makes matters harder still. Consumers don't want to pay even higher energy prices for either renewables or nuclear fuel, or taxes to subsidize their production. *They just want cheap energy*' (added emphasis). Ibid. The annual report by the International Energy Agency (IEA), *Tracking Clean Energy Progress 2013*, also confirms the grim prognosis, with coal continuing to dominate power generation, especially in

developing countries, despite strong growth in renewable sectors. See www.iea.org/newsroomandevents/pressreleases/2013/april/name,36789,en.html. Another report states that the level of carbon dioxide in the atmosphere has already reached 400 parts per million, long considered to be the maximum limit above which climate change will no longer be controllable. Robin McKie, 'Climate Change "Will Make Hundreds of Millions Homeless"', *Observer*, May 12, 2013. However, in a rare item of good news, Naomi Klein reports on the recent formation of the Fossil Free movement, which campaigns to persuade public interest institutions like universities and state governments to divest themselves of any financial investments in the oil, coal or any other fossil-fuel industries. Naomi Klein, 'You Won't Save the Planet If You Profit From the Wreckage', *Guardian*, May 3, 2013.

2 The *Fifth Assessment Report* (AR5) by the Intergovernmental Panel on Climate Change (Geneva: IPCC, September 27, 2013) (www.ipcc.ch/report/ar5/wg1) verifies previous warnings that on present course average global temperatures will exceed pre-industrial levels by 2°C within two to three decades and possibly double that by the end of the century, with disastrous climatic effects. Moreover, contrary to the unsubstantiated arguments of sceptics, the findings of the IPCC report not only confirm the human causes for the increase in levels of greenhouse gases over the past century but suggest that, far from exaggerating the dangers, scientists have repeatedly *under*estimated the speed and environmental effects of unchecked global warming. Commenting on the report, Lord Nicholas Stern, author of an earlier British report on the economic aspects of climate change, writes: 'The Earth has not experienced a global temperature more than 2°C higher than pre-industrial since the Pliocene epoch 3m years ago, when the polar ice caps were much smaller and sea levels were about 20 metres higher than today. Humans have no experience of such a climate.' Lord Stern, 'We Have to Decide What Kind of World We Leave to Our Children', *Observer*, September 9, 2013. See also David Spratt and Philip Sutton, *Climate Code Red: The Case for Emergency Action* (Melbourne: Scribe, 2008); George Monbiot, *Heat: How to Stop the Planet Burning* (London: Allen Lane, 2006). Many observers now believe that the situation is already close to being irreversible. See Jessica Marshall, 'The World: Four Degrees Warmer', *ABC News: News in Science*, November 30, 2010. Reporting on a group of papers by climate change researchers, Marshall quotes the following passage by Mark New of Oxford University: 'People are talking about two degrees [increase] but the chances of actually delivering on that are pretty slim. If we had a kind of Marshall Plan to transform every major economy to a non-carbon based economy over the next 15 years, its doable. But that's not going to happen. A lot of work suggests that the most likely outcome is between three and four [degrees increase] with it very likely to be four.' See also Fiona Harvey, 'World Climate Now on the Brink', *Guardian Weekly*, June 3–9, 2011; Seth Borenstein, 'Greenhouse Emissions Exceed Worst Case Scenario', *Sydney Morning Herald: Weekend Edition*, November 5–6, 2011. Borenstein quotes John Reilley at the Massachussetts Institute of Technology (MIT), who states that 'the problem is pretty close to running away from us.' Worse still, the unprecedented rapid melting of both the surface ice over Greenland and the Artic summer ice, together with the growing number and intensity of extreme weather events, indicates that runaway climate change may already be upon us. See Suzanne Goldberg, 'Four Days in July … Scientists Stunned by Greenland's Ice Sheet Melting Away', *Guardian*, July 26, 2012. See also John Vidal, '2030: End of Artic Summer Ice', *Guardian Weekly*, September 21, 2012. The accumulating weight of evidence pointing to human responsibility for global warming has even persuaded some prominent sceptics to change their minds. Summarizing the results of an extensive study of changes in average temperatures around the world reaching back to 1753 – further than any previous such study – Richard Muller, a self-confessed 'converted sceptic' who led the study, observes: 'Our results show that the average temperature of the Earth's land has risen by 2.5°F over the past 250 years, including an increase of 1.5 degrees over the most recent 50 years. Moreover, it appears likely that essentially all of this increase results from the human emission of greenhouse gases.' Quoted in Leo Hickman, 'Climate Change Study Converts Sceptical Scientists', *Guardian*, July 30, 2012. Thomas Lovejoy, professor of science and public policy at George Mason University, has argued that even the widely accepted tipping point of 2°C above preindustrial levels is too high to avoid the catastrophic effects of climate change, including drastic rises in sea levels and the elimination of coral reefs. See Thomas E. Lovejoy, 'The Climate Change Endgame', *International Herald Tribune*, January 22, 2013. To understand the full implications of these developments see Mark Lynas, *Six Degrees: Our Future on a Hotter Planet* (Washington, DC: National Geographic, 2008). Lynas examines the planetary effects of average increases in global warming from 1°C to 6°C above preindustrial levels, plotting the destructive consequences of temperature increases from one degree to the next. In his public presentation of the environmental and social impacts of global population growth over the next few decades, 'Ten Billion', Stephen Emmot, a professor of computational science at Oxford University, also offers a chilling picture of the breakdown of human society as populations outstrip

available food and water supplies and other resources. See Robin McKie, 'How Theatre Gives Fresh Power to the Warnings of Global Peril,' *Observer*, August 12, 2012. A book based on his theatre presentation has now been published: Stephen Emmott, *Ten Billion* (London: Penguin, 2013).

3 The drastic effect of humankind's evolution on the planetary environment has been such that the present age has been given a new name by Paul Crutzen, winner of the Nobel Prize for chemistry. Elizabeth Kolbert writes: 'This new age was defined by one creature – man – who had become so dominant that he was capable of altering the planet on a geological scale. Crutzen dubbed this age the "Anthropocene".' Elizabeth Kolbert, *Field Notes From a Catastrophe* (London: Bloomsbury, 2006), 181. For further discussions and references on the subject of climate change and its effects see Chapter 10.

4 David Sloan Wilson, whose own work in applying evolutionary theory to human behavior bridges conventional disciplines, writes scathingly about the general fragmentation of knowledge within universities: 'The Ivory Tower would be more aptly named the Ivory Archipelago. It consists of hundreds of isolated subjects, each divided into smaller subjects in an almost infinite progression. People are examined less with a microscope than with a kaleidoscope – psychology, anthropology, economics, political science, sociology, history, art, literature, philosophy, gender studies, ethnic studies. Each perspective has its own history and special assumptions. One person's heresy is another's commonplace.' David Sloan Wilson, *Evolution for Everyone: How Darwin's Theory Can Change the Way We Think About Our Lives* (New York: Delacorte Press, 2007), 2.

5 For related patterns of thought in the sciences see Thomas Kuhn, *The Structure of Scientific Revolutions* (Chicago: Chicago University Press, 1962). Kuhn argues that most scientific research, or what he calls 'normal science,' is inherently conservative and that changes in dominant theoretical paradigms are relatively rare and generally occur only following a process he likens to a 'religious conversion' to the new theory. Kuhn's thesis created a storm of controversy at the time of publication but has since been widely accepted. There is no evidence, however, that his revelations have had any effect on the actual practice of scientists. Nevertheless, scientists' professional obligation to provide published evidence for their claims ensures a generally high level of transparency and open debate in comparison with most other fields of endeavor. For further discussions on objectivity in science see Chapters 2 and 5. For related discussions in the context of postmodern debates, see the Postscript.

6 The primary sources on phenomenology quoted by architectural theorists are the works of Martin Heidegger and Maurice Merleau-Ponty. For detailed references and a discussion of how their works have been interpreted by architectural theorists, see Chapters 1 and 2.

7 See Chapter 4.

8 See Chapter 5.

9 While there is plentiful tool making and usage by our primate cousins and other creatures, no other animals on this planet have reconfigured their environment by artificial means to the extent that humans have, nor have they developed any comparable means of creating historical records of their lives that they could pass onto future generations (the issue of animal tool users is discussed in Chapter 4).

10 The basic evolutionary principle that all life forms, including *Homo sapiens*, whether still prospering or now extinct, are ultimately descended from the same basic organisms that first emerged from the primordial soup that was this planet billions of years ago is not in question here. As Jerry Coyne explains in his lucid defense of evolutionary theory, there is a great and growing stock of empirical evidence from numerous reliable sources to verify that principle. See Coyne, *Why Evolution Is True* (Oxford: Oxford University Press, 2009). As gifted as we may be, we all share a common ancestry, not only with primates, but also with organisms of the most primitive kind. Instead, what are at issue are the actual processes or agents of evolution by which subtle changes and variations both within and between species develop and proliferate over extended periods of time and are in turn stabilized long enough to become established, leading to the incredible diversity of organic life we all now take for granted. Note that Coyne wrote his book largely in response to the debates over so-called 'intelligent design.' See, for example, Peter Cook, *Evolution Versus Intelligent Design: Why All the Fuss?* (Sydney: New Holland, 2006).

11 See Chapter 6.

12 See Chapter 2.

13 René Descartes postulated that humans comprise two distinct entities: a physical body, which he described in purely mechanical terms, that is open to observation; and a capacity for thought, which has no physical basis at all and is a purely private matter, unavailable for public inspection. See Gilbert Ryle, *The Concept of Mind* (New York: Barnes & Noble, 1949).

14 Half of all global greenhouse gas emissions are related to urbanization, of which energy supply for heat and electricity accounts for 26%, transport 13%, residential and commercial buildings 8% and waste 3%, the remainder being due to industry (including on-site energy supplies), agriculture, land clearance and deforestation. See United States Environmental Protection Agency, Greenhouse Gas Emissions Data, www.epa.gov/climatechange/ghgemissions/global.html.

15 There is mounting evidence of a precipitous decline of species of all kinds around the world, with many in increasing danger of extinction. See, for example, the report by the Royal Society for the Protection of Birds, *State of Nature* (Sandy: RSPB, 2013). A collaboration between 25 conservation and research organizations in the UK, the report states that 60% of the 3,148 species they examined in the UK have declined over the past 50 years, of which 31% have declined strongly, with those with specific habitats suffering the worst due to the effects of climate change on their environment. See www.rspb.org.uk/stateofnature.

Chapter 1: The common bond

1 Edward T. Hall, *The Hidden Dimension* (New York: Anchor Books, 1969).

2 Maxine Wolfe and Harold Proshansky, 'The Physical Setting as a Factor in Group Function and Process,' in *Designing for Human Behaviour: Architecture and the Behavioural Sciences*, eds Jon Lang, Charles Burnette, Walter Moleski and David Vachon (Stroudsburg: Dowden, Hutchinson & Ross, 1974), 194–201.

3 Ibid., 196.

4 For an account of the genesis of Murcutt's early work see Philip Drew, *Leaves of Iron: Glenn Murcutt, Pioneer of an Australian Architectural Form* (Pymble: Angus & Robertson, 1985). See also Françoise Fromonot, *Glenn Murcutt: Works and Projects* (London: Thames & Hudson, 1995).

5 William R. Current and Karen Current, *Greene & Greene: Architects in the Residential Style* (New York: Morgan & Morgan, 1977). Though the basic form of the California bungalow was already popular in the state before Greene & Greene made their mark on the type, the architects' elegant designs, which, like Frank Lloyd Wright's work of the same period, include strong elements of Japanese residential architecture, together with high levels of craftsmanship, established the style for the type. As such, the work of Greene & Greene also provides exemplars of the kind of combinatorial design processes and hybrid architecture discussed in Chapter 9.

6 Clare Cooper, 'The House as Symbol of the Self,' in *Designing for Human Behaviour*, 130–46.

7 Ibid., 144. Cooper finds further strong evidence of the house-as-self in Jung's description, as related in his autobiography, of a dream he had exploring his own psyche conceived in the image of a house: 'It was plain to me that the house represented a king of image of the psyche – that is to say, of my then state of consciousness, with hitherto unconscious additions. Consciousness was represented by the salon. It had an inhabited atmosphere, in spite of its antiquated style. The ground floor stood for the first level of the unconscious. The deeper I went, the more alien and the darker the scene became. In the cave, I discovered remains of a primitive culture, that is the world of the primitive man within myself – a world which can scarcely be reached or illuminated by consciousness. The primitive psyche of man borders on the life of the animal soul, just as the caves of prehistoric times were usually inhabited by animals before man laid claim to them.' Carl Jung, *Memories, Dreams and Reflections* (London: Collins, 1969), 184. Quoted in Cooper, 'House as Symbol', 139. Commenting on Jung's dream, Cooper writes: 'Jung describes here the house with many levels seen as the symbol-of-self with its many levels of consciousness; the descent downward into lesser known realms of the unconscious is represented by the ground floor, cellar, and vault beneath it. A final descent leads to a cave cut into the bedrock, a part of the house rooted in the very earth itself. This seems very clearly to be a symbol of the collective unconscious, part of the self-house and yet, too, part of the bedrock of humanity.' Ibid., 139.

8 Ibid., 138.

9 See William Cowburn, 'Popular Housing,' *Architectural Association Journal* (September/October 1966): 76–81. Introducing his essay, Cowburn writes: 'My purpose in writing this article is to raise a defense for the design of houses built for the popular market. This is being done because I believe that the designs produced represent a genuine cultural movement. I also believe that this movement should be recognized, brought out into the open, and its real qualities discussed, because it is only by this being done that any link can be made

between the real needs of people and the fulfillment of those needs.' Ibid., 76. See also Donald Appleyard, 'Home,' *Architectural Association Quarterly*, vol. 11, no. 3 (1979): 4–20.

10 Robin Boyd, *The Australian Ugliness* (Melbourne: Text Publishing Co., 50th anniversary edition, 2010; first published Melbourne: F. W. Cheshire, 1960); Boyd, *Australia's Home* (Harmondsworth: Penguin, 1978). See also Ivor Indyk, 'Robin Boyd and the Australian Suburb,' *UIA International Architect*, issue 4 (1984): 58.

11 Imported from America into Australia in 1916 by a real estate agent, the California bungalow is well suited to the Australian climate and suburban lifestyle and was the most popular type of family dwelling in the interwar years, not least for its affordability, with its compact, economical plan. Generally built from handcrafted stonework and timber, other features include low-pitched rooflines and overhanging eaves, and a large front porch under a roof extension supported by columns. The original design, which, far from being ugly, would have been admired by William Morris, was also strongly influenced by the work of Greene & Greene. Examples of the type remain in high demand wherever they are found. See Graeme Butler, *The California Bungalow in Australia: Origins; Revival; Source Ideas for Restoration* (Port Melbourne: Lothian Books, 1992).

12 Indyk, 'Robin Boyd', 58.

13 The attack was led by the London-based journal the *Architectural Review*, beginning with the December 1950 issue, which focused on American suburban culture, followed by the June 1955 issue, 'Outrage,' guest edited by Ian Nairn, which focused on suburbia in the UK.

14 Herbert Gans, *The Levittowners* (New York: Pantheon Books, 1967).

15 Charles Jencks, *The Daydream Houses of Los Angeles* (New York: Rizzoli, 1978).

16 Ashley Crawford and Ray Edgar, *Spray: The Work of Howard Arkley* (Sydney: Craftsman House, 1997). Commenting on Arkley's paintings of suburban life in the catalogue for the 2006 retrospective exhibition of his work, John Gregory writes: 'Howard Arkley transformed our vision of suburbia – much as Fred Williams' scrubby marks and long horizontal lines made us see the Australian bush afresh. However, as Arkley often emphasized, the vast majority of contemporary Australians live in the 'burbs, not the bush. In focusing on the suburb-scape and its rituals, his vividly coloured, graphic paintings give a new take to a theme often addressed – but frequently in superior, even sarcastic tones – by comedians, writers and other artists.' Quoted in Jason Smith, *Howard Arkley* (Melbourne: National Gallery of Victoria, 2006), 16.

17 James Joyce, *Ulysses: The 1922 Text* (Oxford: Oxford World's Classics, 2008).

18 Diana Festa-McCormick, *The City as Catalyst* (London: Associated University Presses, 1979).

19 Ibid., 15.

20 Joseph Luzzi, 'Dante's Dark Wood,' *International New York Times*, December 21–22, 2013. Commenting on Dante's mournful words, Luzzi writes: 'Nothing better captured how I felt the four years I spent struggling to find my way out of the dark wood of grief and mourning.'

21 Christian Norberg-Schulz, *Genius Loci: Towards a Phenomenology of Architecture* (New York: Rizzoli, 1979).

22 Martin Heidegger, *Poetry, Language, Thought* (New York: Harper Colophon Books, 1971).

23 Ibid., 146–7.

24 Ibid., 152.

25 Norberg-Shulz, *Genius Loci*, 5.

26 Ibid., 20.

27 Ibid., 4.

28 Ibid., 23.

29 Norberg-Schulz is mainly attracted to the 'cliff' of tall buildings lining Lake Shore Drive, rather than to any individual structures, though some of those also have a considerable impact on the city's popular image.

30 See also Bernard Rudofsky, *Architecture Without Architects* (New York: Doubleday, 1964). Like Norberg-Schulz, Rudofsky was influential in drawing architects' attention to hitherto neglected models of indigenous architecture.

31 Norberg-Schulz, *Genius Loci*, 189.

32 Ibid.

33 Amos Rapoport, 'Australian Aborigines and the Definition of Place,' in *Shelter, Sign and Symbol*, ed. Paul Oliver (New York: Overlook Press, 1977), 38–51.

34 For a comprehensive survey, see Paul Oliver, *Dwellings: The Vernacular House Worldwide* (London: Phaidon, 2003).

35 For a selection of other relevant studies, see Oliver, *Shelter, Sign and Symbol*.

36 Rapoport, 'Australian Aborigines', 42–3.

37 Ibid., 47. See also Peter Blundell Jones, 'The Sustaining Ritual,' *Architectural Review*, vol. 187, no. 1125 (November 1990): 93–5. Jones confirms this conclusion, writing: 'The Aborigines have no buildings to speak of, only temporary shelters made by gathering a few branches, and therefore it appears they have no architecture. But as Enrico Guidoni has pointed out, this does not follow. He argues that in the main they adopt an architecture that already exists, through taking possession of the natural landscape and using it in their own way.' Ibid., 93. See Enrico Guidoni, *Primitive Architecture* (London: Faber/Electa, 1987).

38 Josephine Flood, 'Linkage Between Rock-Art and Landscape in Aboriginal Australia,' in *The Figured Landscapes of Rock-Art: Looking at Pictures in Place*, eds Christopher Chippendale and George Nash (Cambridge: Cambridge University Press, 2004), 182–200.

39 Ibid., 197.

40 Ibid., 182.

41 Kenneth Boulding, *The Image: Knowledge in Life and Society* (Ann Arbor: Michigan University Press, 1956).

42 The term 'schemata' is similar to 'schema,' a term coined by Jean Piaget to describe cognitive structures relating to classes of similar interrelated actions or sequences of behaviors. See J. Flavell, *The Developmental Psychology of Jean Piaget* (New York: Van Nostrand Reinhold, 1963).

43 David Canter, *The Psychology of Place* (New York: St Martin's Press, 1977). Canter himself posits a theory of place-identity as a conjunction of at least three major factors: 'activities,' 'conceptions' and 'physical attributes,' all of which may interact with each other according to an individual's own role and perceptions within the building or area concerned. Anticipating Norberg-Schulz's definition of the purpose of architecture discussed earlier in the chapter, Canter also proffers the slogan 'The Goal of Environmental Design Is the Creation of Places,' suggesting a number of ways that planning and design professionals might enhance their skills toward that end. Ibid., 157.

44 Sir Henry Head, *Studies in Neurology, in Conjunction with H. R. Rivers (and Others)* (Toronto: University of Toronto Libraries, 1920).

45 Canter, *The Psychology of Place*, 15. However, it would be another decade before other neuroscientists would begin to find solid evidence for Head's theoretical speculations, and many more years before his fundamental ideas were applied to environmental issues. See Chapter 2.

46 Kevin Lynch, *The Image of the City* (Cambridge: MIT Press, 1960).

47 Lynch focused his interviews within the central areas of three major American cities: Boston, Jersey City and Los Angeles. Each area was carefully surveyed for any major landmarks and other distinctive features by a professional observer, providing a basis for comparison with the different interviews, which included personal sketches of the area by each interviewee as well as verbal descriptions and accounts of frequent journeys from one part to another. While the samples involved were all relatively small and mainly taken from the professional and managerial classes, Lynch found considerable overlap between individual perceptions of the same areas, amounting to what he calls a 'public image' of the city. The same data revealed repeated characteristics or 'image elements,' which he subsequently named 'path,' 'landmark,' 'edge,' 'node' and 'district,' claiming they provided a potentially objective basis for ensuring those attributes would be given more attention by city planners and designers in the future.

48 Lynch, *The Image of the City*, 2.

49 See Lewis Mumford, *The Highway and the City* (Kingswood: Bookprint, 1964).

50 Melvin M. Webber, 'The Urban Place and the Nonplace Urban Realm,' in *Explorations into Urban Structure*, by Melvin M. Webber, John W. Dyckman, Donald F. Foley, Albert Z. Guttenberg, William L. C. Wheaton and Catherine Bauer Wurster (Philadelphia: University of Pennsylvania Press, 1964), 79–183. See also John Worthington, 'What's Wrong With the American City Is That We View It Through European Eyes,' *Arena*, vol. 82, no. 10 (1967): 210–13.

51 Robert Venturi, Denise Scott Brown and Steven Izenour, *Learning from Las Vegas* (Cambridge: MIT Press, 1972). See also Grady Clay, *Close-Up: How to Read the American City* (London: Pall Mall Press, 1973).

52 For a comprehensive survey, see Amos Rapoport, *Human Aspects of Urban Form: Towards a Man–Environment Approach to Urban Form and Design* (Oxford: Pergamon Press, 1977).

53 David Stea, 'Architecture in the Head: Cognitive Mapping,' in *Designing for Human Behaviour: Architecture and the Behavioural Sciences*, 157–68. See also Robert Downs and David Stea, *Maps in Minds* (London: Harper & Row, 1977).

54 Stea, 'Architecture in the Head,' 166.

55 Ibid., 165.

56 D. G. Mandelbaum, ed., *Selected Writings of Edward Sapir* (Berkeley: University of California Press, 1949). See also John B. Caroll, ed., *Language, Thought and Reality: Selected Writings of Benjamin Lee Whorf* (Cambridge: MIT Press, 1956).

57 The historical roots of linguistic and cultural relativism may be traced further back, to the work of two eighteenth-century European thinkers, Giovanni Batista Vico and Johann Gottfried Herder. Both resisted the then dominant worldview propagated by the Enlightenment that there was only one kind of knowledge and rationality to be taken seriously, and any deviation from that view should be discounted as retrograde. For example, Vico was the first to argue for positive links between a specific language and the 'thought world' or *Weltanschauung* of its speakers, predating the Sapir–Whorf hypothesis by two centuries. For his own part, Herder is best known as a virulent critic of the Enlightenment and a champion of populism, expressionism and pluralism – all rejected by Enlightenment thinkers – becoming in the process a spokesperson for national movements of every kind. See Isiah Berlin, *Vico and Herder* (New York: Random House, 1976). For a discussion of the relevance of both figures to architectural theory and criticism, see Chris Abel, 'Vico and Herder: The Origins of Methodological Pluralism,' in *Design: Science: Method. Proceedings of the 1980 Design Research Society Conference, Portsmouth, December 14–16*, eds Robin Jacques and James A. Powell (Guildford: Westbury House, 1981), 51–61. However, the cultural relativism propagated by the above authors needs to be distinguished from the more extreme forms of relativism adopted by some leading postmodernist thinkers (see Postscript). Notably, while underlining the differences between the Hopi and Western worldviews, Whorf was nevertheless able to make it at least partly intelligible to English-language users. Significantly, Karl Popper was drawn to make the same observation on the Hopi language when discussing problems of comparison between different scientific theories. The very possibility of comparison and explanation, states Popper, which Whorf himself never denied, suggests the existence of some shared criteria, sufficient to convey an understanding of the special qualities of the Hopi world. See Karl Popper, 'Normal Science and Its Dangers,' in *Criticism and the Growth of Knowledge*, eds Imre Lakatos and Alan Musgrave (Cambridge: Cambridge University Press, 1970), 51–8. The less extreme form of relativism Popper alludes to is also described as 'critical relativism.' See Chris Abel, 'The Language Analogy in Architectural Theory and Criticism: Some Remarks in the Light of Wittgenstein's Linguistic Relativism,' *Architectural Association Quarterly*, vol. 12, no. 3 (1979): 39–47.

58 Quoted in Caroll, *Language, Thought and Reality*, 134. The contest between linguistic relativism and other theories of language acquisition is analyzed at length by George Steiner, *After Babel: Aspects of Language and Translation* (Oxford: Oxford University Press, 1975). See also Abel, 'Architecture as Identity,' 10.

59 For a general history of the culture and dwelling forms of the Pueblo Indians, including the Hopi, see Edward P. Dozier, *The Pueblo Indians of North America* (New York: Holt, Rinehart & Winston, 1970). For the early history of the Pueblo, see William A. Longacre, ed., *Reconstructing Prehistoric Pueblo Societies* (Albuquerque: University of New Mexico Press, 1970).

60 Oliver, *Shelter, Sign and Symbol*, 7–37 (Introduction).

61 Numerous examples of the use of similar construction techniques can be found in indigenous architecture around the world, including large parts of South America, Africa, the Middle East and China. See, for example, the catalogue of a 1982 international exhibition, Jean Detheir, editor, *Des Architectures de Terre: Ou L'Avenir D'Une Tradition Millenaire* (Paris: Centre Georges Pompidou, 1982).

62 Oliver, *Shelter, Sign and Symbol*, 30.

63 Russel Ward, *The Australian Legend* (Melbourne: Oxford University Press, second edition, 1966).

64 Ibid., 5. According to Helen Stuckey, Robin Boyd's hostility towards suburban architecture was motivated by similar beliefs to Russel Ward's which predisposed the critic to ascribe many of the failings of suburbia to the role of women and their assumed preference for a more indulgent aesthetic. Stuckey argues that, in so doing, Boyd subscribes to much the same idealized image of the male bush worker that Ward depicts, who has somehow been seduced from his true calling and values: 'In Boyd's early writing there is a persistent feminine gendering of that which is being devalued. In *Australia's Home* the suburbs are seen as the *products of feminine vice*. Like rats and the plague, the arrival of women in Australia brought the infection of "suburbia". Boyd explains in *Australia's Home* how the feminine sensibility corrupted the straightforward functionalism of Australia's bushmen settlers, bringing to their romantically "rough hewn" dwellings a fancy of chintz and detail. *Australia's Home* begins with an acknowledgement that suburbs were built in relation to the "taste of Australian women and their husbands". In Boyd's history of architectural "styles" the feminine has been cast as a licentious seduction of ornament and folly corrupting man from truth to form and function.' Helen Stuckey, 'Robin Boyd and the Revolt Against Suburbia,' in *Imaginary Australia, Arkitekturtidsskrift B*, no. 52–3, special issue, ed. Harriet Edquist and Gilbert Hansen (1995/96): 41–9.

65 For a discussion of the persistence of Australian male stereotypes in Australian cinema see Graeme Turner, 'Australian Film and National Identity in the 1990s,' in *The Politics of Identity in Australia*, ed. Geoffrey Stokes (Cambridge: Cambridge University Press, 1997), 185–92.

66 Ibid., 186–7.

67 Edward T. Hall, *The Hidden Dimension* (New York: Anchor Books, 1969).

68 Ibid., 1.

69 Ibid., 2. The preceding book mentioned by Hall was also widely influential in explaining the way culture affects communication. See Edward T. Hall, *The Silent Language* (New York: Anchor Books, 1973; 1st hard cover edition, Doubleday, 1959).

70 Hall, *The Hidden Dimension*, 9.

71 Ibid., 3.

72 Ibid.

73 Ibid., 103.

74 Ibid.

75 Ibid., 3. Significantly, Marshall McLuhan, the influential sage of modern telecommunications, subtitled his seminal work of the same period in similar terms. See Marshall McLuhan, *Understanding Media: The Extensions of Man* (London: Routledge & Kegan Paul, 1964).

76 Edward S. Casey, *The Fate of Place: A Philosophical History* (Berkeley: University of California Press, 1998); J. E. Malpas, *Place and Experience: A Philosophical Topography* (Cambridge: Cambridge University Press, 1999).

77 Casey, *The Fate of Place*, ix.

78 In addition to exchanging ideas, Derrida also worked briefly as a consultant with Tschumi on the project for the Parc de la Villette, then regarded as a model of deconstructionist design. As executed, however, there is a considerable gap between the theoretical intentions of its designers and the actual experience of the place. See Chris Abel, 'Visible and Invisible Complexities,' *Architectural Review*, vol. 199, no. 1188 (February 1996): 76–83. See the Postscript for a further discussion of the deconstructionist school of postmodernism.

79 Malpas, *Place and Experience*, 1.

80 Ibid., 3. Quoted from Tony Swain, *A Place for Strangers* (Cambridge: Cambridge University Press, 1993), 39.

81 Malpas, *Place and Experience*, 72.

82 Ibid., 80.

83 Ibid., 80–1.

84 Ibid., 99.

85 Ibid., 100.

86 Neil Leach, 'Belonging,' *AA Files 49* (spring 2003): 76–82.

87 The term 'critical regionalism' was coined by Alexander Tzonis and Liane Lefaivre to denote a creative reinterpretation of regional traditions of architecture. Kenneth Frampton subsequently adopted the term in several essays in which he argued for a similar approach to modern architecture. See, for example, Kenneth Frampton, *Modern Architecture: A Critical History* (London: Thames & Hudson, 3rd edition, 1992), 314–27. See also Alexander Tzonis, Liane Lefaivre and Bruno Stagno, *Tropical Architecture: Critical Regionalism in the Age of Globalization* (Chichester: Wiley-Academy, 2001). However, by selecting such a narrow if influential school of architectural thought as his target, Leach neglects the considerable body of published interdisciplinary research cited above and in other chapters in this book concerning the impact of culture on architecture and the complex and fluid relations between built form and meaning.

88 For example, the relevance of Ludwig Wittgenstein's thought and his related theory of 'language games' to architectural criticism are discussed in Abel, 'The Language Analogy.' See also Abel, 'Architecture as Identity.' For a further explication of Wittgenstein's thought and its broader relevance to the theme of this book, see the Postscript. See note 57 to this chapter for related references. Leach also briefly mentions Wittgenstein's concept of 'meaning as use' in passing, but without providing either references or any further explanation.

89 Leach, 'Belonging,' 76. The work cited by Leach is Homi K. Bhabha, ed., *Nation and Narration* (London: Routledge, 1990).

90 Ibid., 77.

91 Though Leach's comments on cultural identity, if hardly original, are sound in principle, his reading of the tower type greatly oversimplifies the case (see Chapters 7 and 9 for more detailed discussions of the type). Generally speaking, it would be more accurate to describe the variable interpretations attached to office towers as the outcome of not one but of several overlapping layers of meaning, ranging from the international to the local context, as well as those still more specific meanings relating to internal spaces and activities. For example, the very act of creating and using an office tower is often motivated by a purposeful effort by its developers and occupiers *to be seen to belong* to the international financial and cultural community, while the local setting imposes a whole set of different constraints and meanings particular to that setting. See Chris Abel, 'High-Rise and Genius Loci,' in *Norman Foster: Works 5*, ed. David Jenkins (London: Prestel, 2009), 430–41.

92 The works by Judith Butler that Leach references include: *Gender Trouble: Feminism and the Subversion of Identity* (New York: Routledge, 1990); *Bodies That Matter* (New York: Routledge, 1993).

93 Leach, 'Belonging,' 77.

94 Ibid., 77.

95 Ibid.

96 Ibid., 78. Leach's stress on the importance of imitation or mimesis in culture mirrors Richard Dawkins' concept of the meme, though Leach makes no reference to the connection, nor seems aware of any. See Chapter 6 for a full discussion of memetic theory.

97 See the Postscript for a discussion of J. L. Austin's original concept of performativity, as defined within his broader philosophy of 'linguistic phenomenology.' See also Naomi Wolf, *Vagina: A New Biography* (London: Virago, 2012). Based on recent evidence from the neurosciences, Wolf makes a strong case for similar mind–body links between the vagina and the brain as have been found with other organs and bodily matters. See also Naomi Wolf, 'My Feminist Perspective: Knowledge Is Power,' *Guardian*, September 12, 2012. Defending her book in the latter article against feminists like Butler who argue that gender differences are purely social constructs, Wolf writes: 'Knowing about the science of the brain–vagina connection – a concept that is not my own construction but rather an everyday fact for the scientists at the forefront of this research – simply means we are willing to engage with the modern world; the brain–body connection is being documented in hundreds of ways, from cardiovascular health research to the role of stress in illness.'

98 Tim Cresswell, *Place: A Short Introduction* (Oxford: Blackwell, 2004). For further reading, see Phil Hubbard, Rob Kitchen and Gill Valentine, eds, *Key Thinkers on Space and Place* (London: Sage Publications, 2004).

99 Cresswell, *Place*, 10–11.

100 Ibid., 12.

101 Doreen Massey, 'A Global Sense of Place,' in *Reading Human Geography*, eds T. Barnes and D. Gregory (London: Arnold, 1997), 315–23.

102 Cresswell, *Place*, 53.

Chapter 2: The body nucleus

1 The authors' key works are: Maurice Merleau-Ponty, *Phenomenology of Perception*, translated from the 1945 publication by Colin Smith (London: Routledge & Kegan Paul, 1962); Michael Polanyi, *Personal Knowledge: Towards a Post-critical Philosophy* (Chicago: University of Chicago Press, 1958), also Michael Polanyi, *The Tacit Dimension* (New York: Doubleday, 1966), and Michael Polanyi and Harry Prosch, *Meaning* (Chicago: University of Chicago Press, 1975).

2 For further reading on the impact of Merleau-Ponty's phenomenology on architectural theory, see Steven Holl, Juhani Pallasmaa and Alberto Perez-Gomez, *Questions of Perception: Phenomenology of Architecture* (San Francisco: William Stout, 2006). For an architectural interpretation of Polanyi's thought, see Chris Abel, 'Function of Tacit Knowing in Learning Design,' *Design Studies*, vol. 2, no. 4 (October 1981): 209–14.

3 For an introduction to Husserl's thought, see Quentin Lauer, *Phenomenology: Its Genesis and Prospect* (New York: Harper Torchbooks, 1958). For an extended discussion of Husserl's thought on the significance of the body in human experience, see Casey, *The Fate of Place*, 217–20.

4 Rudolf Wittkower, *Architectural Principles in the Age of Humanism* (London: Alec Tiranti, 1962), 30.

5 Da Vinci's drawing was one of a series of Vitruvian figures produced by Renaissance artists during the sixteenth century, including several by Francesco di Giorgio. See Wittkower, ibid., plates 2a–4.

6 Le Corbusier, *Le Corbusier 1910–60*, trans. William Gleckman and Elsa Girsberger (Zurich: Editions Girsberger, 1960), 262–5.

7 Douglas Fraser, *Village Planning in the Primitive World* (London: Studio Vista/George Braziller, 1967). While the 'primitive' adjective in the title of Fraser's book is now frowned on by contemporary scholars of pre-modern cultures, it is used by Fraser, as it was generally used in earlier periods, to designate a historical status.

8 Yi-Fu Tuan, *Space and Place: The Perspective of Experience* (London: Edward Arnold, 1977).

9 Ibid., 35–6. For a related discussion of symbolic systems based on the symmetry of the human body that are common to widely different cultures, see Rodney Needham, ed., *Right and Left: Essays on Dual Symbolic Classification* (Chicago: Chicago University Press, 1973).

10 Charles Moore, Gerald Allen and Donlyn Lyndon, *The Place of Houses* (New York: Holt, Rinehart & Winston, 1974).

11 Kent Bloomer and Charles Moore, *Body, Memory and Architecture* (New Haven: Yale University Press, 1977).

12 Ibid., x.

13 Robert Mugerauer, 'Body, Settlement, Landscape: A Comparison of Hot and Cool Humid Patterns,' *Traditional Dwellings and Settlements Review*, vol. 7, no. 1 (fall 1995): 25–32.

14 See Chapter 9.

15 George Dodds and Robert Tavernor, eds, *Body and Building: Essays on the Changing Relation of Body and Architecture* (Cambridge: MIT Press, 2005). For a selection of Rykwert's own essays, see Joseph Rykwert, *The Necessity of Artifice* (New York: Rizzoli, 1982).

16 Vittorio Gregotti, 'Epilogue. Joseph Rykwert: An Anthropologist of History?', in *Body and Building*, 320–4, quote from 321.

17 Dalibor Vesely, 'The Architectonics of Embodiment,' in *Body and Building*, 28–43.

18 Ibid., 32.

19 Simon Pepper, 'Body, Diagram, and Geometry in the Renaissance Fortress,' in *Body and Building*, 114–25.

20 Juhani Pallasmaa, *The Eyes of the Skin: Architecture and the Senses* (London: Wiley-Academy, 2005).

21 This is a contentious issue. While the common exploitation of the new computer-based techniques for superficial exercises in glossy forms is to be regretted, it can be argued that such uses are more than compensated for by the gains, such as the ability to model spaces accurately enough to simulate human movement through them, or to test various measurable performance criteria, including lighting conditions and energy use, all of which was not possible before the advent of these technologies. See Chapter 11 for a discussion of related techniques.

22 Pallasmaa, *The Eyes of the Skin*, 67.

23 Both Tuan and Pallasmaa make explicit if only brief references to Merleau-Ponty's thought. However, while Moore does not include any direct mention of the latter's works, his general approach is very much in the spirit of Merleau-Ponty's phenomenology and may have been influenced indirectly. Tuan's claim that the basic spatial coordinates emanate from the human body also echoes the earlier writings of Edmund Husserl on the body. See also Lauer, *Phenomenology*; Casey, *The Fate of Place*, 217–20.

24 Merleau-Ponty, *Phenomenology*, vii.

25 Quoted in Casey, *The Fate of Place*, 217.

26 Merleau-Ponty, *Phenomenology*, 146.

27 Ibid., 138–9.

28 Ibid., 98.

29 Ibid., 100–1.

30 Ibid., 206.

31 Ibid., 210.

32 Ibid., 143.

33 Ibid., 216.

34 Ibid., 353.

35 Polanyi makes no mention of Merleau-Ponty in his early works, the first of which preceded the English translation of *Phenomenology of Perception* (*Phenomenologie de la perception*, first published 1945).

However, reflecting on Merleau-Ponty's thought, Polanyi and Prosch observe: 'Merleau-Ponty anticipated the existential commitment present in tacit knowledge but did so without recognizing the triadic structure which determines the functions of this commitment – the way it establishes our knowledge of a valid coherence. The contrast between explicit inference and an existential experience imbued with intentionality is not sufficient for defining the structure and workings of tacit knowing. We are offered an abundance of brilliant flashes without a constructive system.' Polanyi and Prosch, *Meaning*, 47. Polanyi does however acknowledge a kinship between his concept of indwelling and Heidegger's 'being-in-the-world,' or 'dwelling.' See note 46 in Marjorie Grene, 'Tacit Knowing and the Pre-reflective Cogito,' in *Intellect and Hope: Essays in the Thought of Michael Polanyi*, eds Thomas Langford and William Poteat (Durham: Duke University Press, 1968), 19–57. However, as he goes on to show, Polanyi uses the term in a far more precise way than Heidegger does, and yet also applies it to a far wider spread of behavior. Grene herself also expresses doubts about the similarity between the concepts.

    36 Polanyi, *The Tacit Dimension*, 4.

    37 Polanyi and Prosch, *Meaning*, 33.

    38 Polanyi, *The Tacit Dimension*, 16.

    39 Polanyi and Prosch, *Meaning*, 36.

    40 While Polanyi acknowledges the work of German thinkers like Wilhelm Dilthey on empathy, he also takes pains to distinguish his own theory of indwelling from the latter: 'Indwelling, as derived from the structure of tacit knowing, is a far more precisely defined act than is empathy, and it underlies all observations, including all those described previously as indwelling.' Polanyi, *The Tacit Dimension*, 17.

    41 Marjorie Grene, 'Tacit Knowing and the Pre-reflective Cogito,' in *Intellect and Hope*, 19–57.

    42 Ibid., 35.

    43 Kuhn, *The Structure of Scientific Revolutions*. Explicit parallels are drawn between Polanyi's and Kuhn's theories of the way scientists work, together with the theories of other key thinkers, in C. B. Daly, 'Polanyi and Wittgenstein,' in *Intellect and Hope*, 136–68.

    44 The key role of exemplars and models in scientific development is also elaborated in Thomas Kuhn, *The Essential Tension* (Chicago: University of Chicago Press, 1977). Discussing the growing problem of replicating experiments due to the increasing complexity and amounts of electronic data that need to be analyzed, John Naughton cites a 1970s study by the sociologist Harry Collins, who found that while some laboratories were able to replicate a key piece of experimental equipment called a 'TEA laser,' other laboratory workers were unable to do so, despite the fact that detailed published descriptions of the device were available: 'Collins concluded that a key factor was the "tacit knowledge" that the successful experimenters possessed but were unable to communicate through the usual, formal channels.' John Naughton, 'We Love Your Work…. Now Show Us Your Workings,' *Observer*, June 24, 2012.

    45 Similarly, it may be argued that comparable cognitive processes underlie the way both scientists and architects acquire knowledge of their respective fields, either, as in the former case, through replicating key historical experiments, or by studying relevant buildings in architectural history or contemporary practice and engaging in simulated design projects in the latter. See Abel, 'Function of Tacit Knowing.' The issue is also taken up in later discussions in this book on the cognition of types and species, as well as the nature of innovation.

    46 Polanyi, *The Tacit Dimension*, 15–16.

    47 Daly, 'Polanyi and Wittgenstein,' 136–68.

    48 Ibid., 151. For references and a discussion of Wittgenstein's own thought, including the meaning of a 'form of life,' see the Postscript.

    49 Polanyi quoted in Grene, 'Tacit Knowing,' 44.

    50 Ibid., 42–3.

    51 Tim Ingold, 'Epilogue. Technology, Language Intelligence: A Reconsideration of Basic Concepts,' in *Tools, Language and Cognition in Human Evolution*, eds Kathleen R. Gibson and Tim Ingold (Cambridge: Cambridge University Press, 1993), 449–72.

    52 Ibid., 450–1.

    53 Ibid., 470.

    54 Ibid.

Chapter 3: Embodied minds

1 Thomas Metzinger, *The Ego Tunnel: The Science of the Mind and the Myth of the Self* (New York: Basic Books, 2009).

2 Ibid., 1.

3 Ibid., 3.

4 Ibid., 4.

5 Ibid., 5.

6 Ibid., 6.

7 Ibid., 7.

8 Ibid.

9 Ibid.

10 Ibid., 8. See note 18 to this chapter for the origins of the 'little man' concept.

11 Ibid., 78.

12 Ibid.

13 Ibid.

14 For more examples of the way the neurosciences are confirming Polanyi's theories see the review article by Walter Culick, 'Polanyi's Epistemology in the Light of Neuroscience,' *Tradition and Discovery: The Polanyi Society Periodical*, vol. 36, no. 2 (2010): 73–82.

15 See S. Lovgren, 'Chimps, Humans 96 Percent the Same, Gene Study Finds,' *National Geographic News*, August 31, 2005. See also Jared Diamond, *The Rise and Fall of the Third Chimpanzee: How Our Animal Heritage Affects the Way We Live* (London: Vintage Books, 1991).

16 Metzinger, *The Ego Tunnel*, 78–80. While the extension of tool use in the manner described by Metzinger undoubtedly constitutes a vital step in human evolution, it is questionable that it also marks the emergence of free will in the common meaning of the term, particularly in view of what Metzinger himself describes as the fragmented nature of the self and its interdependence with others. See Chapter 10 for a discussion of the meaning of free will and its limitations.

17 Sandra Blakeslee and Matthew Blakeslee, *The Body Has a Mind of Its Own* (New York: Random House, 2007).

18 Ibid., 208. According to the Blakeslees, the metaphorical 'little man' in the brain derives from the work of Wilder Penfield, a surgeon at the Montreal Neurological Institute. A pioneer of modern neurology, Penfield first verified the existence of body maps in the 1930s and '40s during a series of experimental operations on patients being treated for epilepsy. Searching for abnormal tissues, each patient's physical responses to the touch of an electrode on different parts of the exposed cerebral cortex were carefully noted (fortunately, while the brain receives signals from pain sensors elsewhere in the body, it has none of its own, so a local anesthetic suffices). Step by step and case by case, Penfield built up a comprehensive picture of which parts of the brain were linked to which parts of the body. Putting it all together, he created a complete neurological 'touch map' of the body, which he named the 'homunculus,' after the Latin for 'little man.' Later, Penfield also discovered higher-order body maps in different parts of the brain that help to create the unified body schema described by Metzinger and modern neuroscientists.

19 Ibid., 109. The authors recount a story told by an anthropologist at a conference, of a tribe in Namibia in Africa who believe that each person is born with their own flexible bubble of space around the body, which constantly merges with that of other members of the tribe, so nobody ever feels alone. Apparently they feel sorry for Westerners who think of themselves as isolated points in space. From the accumulating evidence of neuroscience, it seems the tribe has got it right and Westerners have got it wrong.

20 Ibid., 110. The concept and study of peripersonal space was anticipated by Hall in his theory of proxemics. See Chapter 1.

21 Ibid., 87.

22 Ibid., 117.

23 As the Blakeslees explain, though the hippocampus is much older in evolutionary development than the cortex, where space and body maps originate, both parts of the brain are vital to bodily experience and spatial awareness. However, the neurological systems associated with each part also differ in significant ways. While body maps are self-directed or *egocentric*, place cells and grid cells are *geocentric*, or outer-directed.

24 Ibid., 130.

25 Quoted in *The Body Has a Mind of Its Own*, 132.

26 Polanyi, *The Tacit Dimension*, 16. In an article on the career of the late racing driver, Ayrton Senna is quoted as describing the experience of driving in terms which Polanyi and many of the researchers cited in this chapter would instantly recognize: "'And suddenly I realized that I was no longer driving the car consciously,' he once said. "I was driving it by a kind of instinct, only I was in a different dimension.'" Garry Maddox, 'Ayrton Senna,' *Sydney Morning Herald: Weekend Edition*, August 13–14, 2011.

27 For an explanation of the multiple layers of interpretation involved in interpersonal communication and empathy, see R. D. Laing, H. Phillipson and A. R. Lee, *Interpersonal Perception: A Theory and Method of Research* (London: Tavistock, 1966). Laing et al. describe mutual understanding between individuals as a 'spiral of reciprocal perspectives.' Explaining the concept, the authors write: 'Human beings are constantly thinking about others and about what others are thinking about them, and what others think they are thinking about the others, and so on. One may be wondering about what is going on inside the other. One desires or fears that other people will know what is going on inside oneself.' Ibid., 23.

28 Metzinger, *The Ego Tunnel*, 166.

29 Ibid., 167.

30 Ibid.

31 Blakeslee and Blakeslee, *The Body Has a Mind of Its Own*, 162–3.

32 As with tool making and use (see Chapter 4), it would appear that, while the imaginative skills of *Homo sapiens* far outstrip those of their closest cousins, recent research suggests that chimps also empathize with each other in basically similar ways to humans. See Ian Sample, 'Chimps May Know What's On Each Other's Minds,' *Guardian Weekly*, January 13, 2012.

33 Metzinger, *The Ego Tunnel*, 167–8.

34 Similarly, it has been argued that humans understand each other in ways that they cannot understand nature, because they share common experiences with other persons that they do not share with other forms of life. See Richard S. Peters, 'Personal Understanding and Personal Relationships,' in *Understanding Other Persons*, ed. Theodore Mischel (Oxford: Basil Blackwell, 1974), 37–65. Peters writes: 'We are indeed at a special vantage point in understanding others (or at least some others) which we do not enjoy in our understanding of the natural world. This comes about because in learning to behave as human beings we are, ipso facto, being initiated into the concepts, rules, and assumptions without which we could make no sense of the life of others. *Our minds, in other words, are mainly social products* [added emphasis]. In making sense, therefore, of the behavior of others we rely upon concepts, rules, and assumptions which both they and we have internalized in the early years of our initiation into human life; these structure our own *behavior* as well as our *understanding* of the behavior of others.' Ibid., 40–1.

35 According to Ramachandran, mirror neurons do not necessarily rule out a role for special areas in the brain in the formation of language. Nevertheless, in a clear challenge to theories of innate language acquisition, he suggests that such regions do not have to be functional 'at the moment of birth to explain how they develop.' Blakeslee and Blakeslee, *The Body Has a Mind of Its Own*, 171. On the other hand, the evidence for invariant neurological structures like grid cells points to innate factors of some kind.

36 Ibid., 171.

37 See Caroline Williams, 'The Consciousness Connection,' *New Scientist*, vol. 215, no. 2874 (July 21, 2012): 32–5.

38 Ibid., 33.

39 Quoted in Williams, ibid., 34.

40 Quoted in Williams, ibid., 35.

41 Ibid.

42 Francisco J. Varela, Evan Thompson and Eleanor Rosch, *The Embodied Mind: Cognitive Science and Human Experience* (Cambridge, MIT Press, 1993).

43 Ibid., xv–xvi.

44 Ibid., xvii.

45 Ibid., 59.

46 Ibid., 61.

47 Ibid., 64.

48 Ibid.

49 Ibid., 68.

50 Ibid., 69.

51 Ibid.

52 Ibid.

53 Here the authors also consider the idea of the self as an emergent property of the kind that will be discussed in Chapter 5, but dismiss that idea too, as it is the 'real' ego-self that we believe in the here-and-now, not some abstract property that can only be recognized over longer periods of time and mostly in hindsight.

54 Varela et al., *The Embodied Mind*, 79.

55 Ibid., 80.

56 Ibid., 224.

57 Andy Clark and David Chalmers, 'The Extended Mind,' *Analysis*, no. 58 (1998): 10–23. See http://consc.net/papers/extended.html. The same essay, together with a comprehensive elaboration of the theory, is also republished as an appendix in Andy Clark, *Supersizing the Mind: Embodiment, Action, and Cognitive Extension* (Oxford: Oxford University Press, 2011), 220–32. For ease of reference the page numbers given below for the quotes from that essay are taken from the appendix to the later book by Clark. See also Robert K. Logan, *The Extended Mind: The Emergence of Language, the Human Mind, and Culture* (Toronto: University of Toronto Press, 2007). Inspired by Marshall McLuhan's theory of media as human extensions, Logan's book is focused entirely on human language as a 'tool,' which he encapsulates in his maxim 'mind = brain + language.' However he also acknowledges parallels with Clark and Chalmers' work.

58 Clark and Chalmers, 'The Extended Mind,' in *Supersizing the Mind*, appendix, 220.

59 Ibid., 221.

60 David Kirsh and Paul Maglio, 'On Distinguishing Epistemic from Pragmatic Action,' *Cognitive Science*, no. 18 (1994): 513–49.

61 Clark and Chalmers, 'The Extended Mind', appendix, 222.

62 Ibid., 223.

63 Ibid., 228.

64 Ibid., 231. There are striking likenesses in the idea of distributed minds hinted at here with Gordon Pask's 'conversation theory.' A key element in Pask's theory is his distinction between 'motor individuals' and 'psychological individuals,' or 'M' and 'P' individuals for short. Pask argues that a P individual is not necessarily concordant with an M individual, and may not even be usually so. What we generally call 'thought' is a process of interaction between at least two P individuals, who may or may not be identified with the same M individual, that is, a physical brain. See Gordon Pask, *Conversation Theory: Applications in Education and Epistemology* (Amsterdam: Elsevier, 1976). Parallels may also be drawn between Pask's theory and George Herbert Mead's theory of mind as a dialogue between at least two persons involving a mutual process of identification, or 'taking the role of the other' (see the Postscript for an outline of Mead's theory with references).

65 Clark and Chalmers, 'The Extended Mind,' appendix, 232.

66 Ibid., 232.

67 The metaphor does not imply the expansion of any ready-made or pre-existing self into the outer world, but simply expresses the outward growth of interactive relations between organisms and their environments.

68 William Barrett, *Irrational Man: A Study in Existential Philosophy* (New York: Doubleday Anchor Books, 1962).

69 Ibid., 218. See also Kurt Lewin, *Field Theory in Social Science* (New York: Harper & Row, 1951). A Gestalt psychologist and influential pioneer of social psychology, Lewin stresses the totality of the present interactions between a person and everything in the immediate environment as the primary determining factors in that person's behavior, rather than any past histories or customs. Though an original thinker in his time, Lewin's ideas have since been largely superseded by systems theory and related approaches, some of which are covered in this book. Even so, Lewin's analogy resonates in ways that other systems and ecological concepts do not, suggesting as it does a field that embraces a wide variety of living and non-living phenomena.

Chapter 4: Technics and the human

1 While the terms 'technics' and 'technology' have sometimes been used interchangeably or have been translated as such, the former term generally has a more inclusive meaning in Stiegler's work, as it does in related discourses by his followers, and is best understood as the symbiosis of technology and human behavior. However, interpretations of the term vary. For example, Richard Beardsworth offers the following definition: 'I understand by "technics" (techne, "la technique", "die Technik") either the thought, practice, or phenomenon of technical objects. The term "technical" is used to designate the domain (not essence) of technics in general; hence my substantial use of the adjective (in analogy with the contemporary use of the term "political" in distinction to the term "politics"). Following Stiegler, I understand by "technology" the specific amalgamation of technics and the sciences in the modern period. It is this amalgamation which makes the modern age an essentially technical age.' Richard Beardsworth, 'From a Genealogy of Matter to a Politics of Memory: Stiegler's Thinking of Technics,' *Tekhnema* 2 (spring 1995): 22. See http://tekhnema. free.fr/2Beardsworth.htmAnchor1bis. Beardsworth's own inquiry is motivated by what he regards as the failure of philosophy to reflect upon the social and political consequences of living in a world where technology has been used to such disastrous ends, as exemplified in Heidegger's complicity with Nazism. Stiegler's work, Beardsworth asserts, 'shows why such reflection has immediate cultural and political stakes and, more interestingly, how it necessarily calls for a transformation of the present co-ordinates of thinking on the political.' Ibid. However, the greater part of Beardsworth's essay is given over to tracing the origins of Stiegler's 'politics of memory' rather than to spelling out Stiegler's thought on this issue, which is elaborated in the later works.

2 The primary source discussed in this book is Bernard Stiegler, *Technics and Time, 1: The Fault of Epimetheus*, trans. Richard Beardsworth and George Collins (Stanford: Stanford University Press, 1998). The second and third volumes are: Bernard Stiegler, *Technics and Time, 2: Disorientation*, trans. Stephen Barker (Stanford: Stanford University Press, 2009); Bernard Stiegler, *Technics and Time, 3: Cinematic Time and the Question of Malaise*, trans. Stephen Barker (Stanford: Stanford University Press, 2010).

3 Martin Heidegger, *The Question Concerning Technology and Other Essays*, trans. William Lovitt (New York: Harper & Row, 1977).

4 Ibid., 5.

5 Ibid., 6.

6 Ibid., 12.

7 Lewis Mumford, *Art and Technics* (New York: Columbia University Press, 1952).

8 Ibid., 9.

9 Bateson, *Steps to an Ecology of Mind*. See also Gregory Bateson, *Mind and Nature: A Necessary Unity* (New York: E. P. Dutton, 1979).

10 Bateson writes: 'We commonly think of the external "physical world" as somehow separate from an internal "mental world." I believe that this division is based on the contrast in coding and transmission inside and outside the body. *The mental world – the mind – the world of information processing – is not limited by the skin* [added emphasis].' Bateson, *Steps to an Ecology of Mind*, 454. He further writes: 'I suggest that the delimitation of an individual mind must always depend upon what phenomena we wish to understand or explain. Obviously there are a lot of message pathways outside the skin, and these and the messages they carry must be included as part of the mental system whenever they are relevant.' Ibid., 458.

11 Bateson, *Mind and Nature*, 178.

12 Ibid., 172. Regarding the unpredictability of evolution, Bateson also writes: 'It was Alfred Russel Wallace who remarked in 1866 that the principle of natural selection is like that of a steam engine with a governor. I shall assume that this is indeed so and that both the processes of individual learning and the process of population shift under natural selection can exhibit the pathologies of all cybernetic circuits: excessive oscillation and runaway.' Ibid., 148. See Chapter 5 for a discussion of theories of evolution.

13 While Mumford generally prefers the definition of humans as symbolic creatures rather than tool makers, in at least one passage he hints at a unity of the two, closer to Stiegler's viewpoint: 'Because of the traditional separation of art and technics we have yet sufficiently to realize that *the symphony orchestra is a triumph of engineering* [added emphasis], and that its products, such as the music of Mozart and Beethoven, etherealized into symbols, will probably outlast all our steel bridges and automatic machines.' Mumford, *Art and Technics*, 8.

14 The subtitle of Stiegler's first volume relates to a story in Greek mythology, the meaning of which is central to Stiegler's conception of what it is to be human. According to the story, which Stiegler explains at length in his book, the gods entrusted Prometheus and his brother Epimetheus with equipping all mortal creatures with appropriate powers to enable each species to survive. However, in his enthusiasm for the task Epimetheus rushed ahead of his brother and distributed all the available gifts to the animals, forgetting to

leave any for humans. Unable to think of any other way of making up for his brother's 'fault' and fulfilling their assignment, Prometheus resorted to stealing special gifts from other gods, namely fire and skills in the arts, and making them available to humans for their own exclusive use on earth.

15 Ibid., 2.

16 Regarding Heidegger's uncertainty about this issue, Stiegler writes: 'the difficulty of an interpretation of the meaning of modern technics for Heidegger is on a par with the difficulty of his entire thought. Modern technics is the concern of numerous texts, which do not always appear to move in the same direction. In other words, the meaning of modern technics is ambiguous in Heidegger's work. It appears simultaneously as the ultimate obstacle to and as the ultimate possibility of thought.' Stiegler, *Technics and Time, 1*, 7.

17 Ibid., 15. See Betrand Gille, *Histoire des Techniques* (Paris: Gallimard, 1978).

18 Stiegler, *Technics and Time, 1*, 15.

19 See Chapter 9 for a detailed discussion of technological innovation.

20 Stiegler, *Technics and Time, 1*, 15.

21 Ibid., 1.

22 Ibid., 50. For Stiegler, exteriorization also changes conventional anthropological perspectives: 'With the advent of exteriorization, the body of the living individual is no longer only a body: it can only function with its tools. An understanding of the archaic anthropological system will only become possible with the simultaneous examination of the skeleton, the central nervous system, and equipment.' Ibid., 148. Timothy Taylor, the archaeologist whose work is discussed in the next chapter, would agree with Stiegler on that point.

23 The full wording of Clausewitz's famous aphorism is as follows: 'War is not merely a political act, but also a political instrument, a continuation of political relations, a carrying out of the same by other means.' While Stiegler does not actually acknowledge Clausewitz for the wording of his own statement, the aphorism is so well known that it may be assumed that Stiegler was aware of it.

24 Stiegler, *Technics and Time, 1*, 17.

25 Ibid.

26 Ibid., 46.

27 The two works by André Leroi-Gourhan most cited by Stiegler are his *L'Homme et la Matière* (Paris: Albin Michel, 1943) and *Mileu et Techniques* (Paris: Albin Michel, 1945).

28 Stiegler, *Technics and Time, 1*, 46.

29 Quoted in Stiegler, ibid., 45.

30 See Chapter 9, in particular on the evolution of variations of the Malay house type in the same region.

31 Stiegler, *Technics and Time, 1*, 46.

32 Quoted in Stiegler, ibid., 50. While genetic manipulation of plant crops and artificial selection of animal breeds have been part of human history for hundreds of years, cross-breeding in nature is far more rare, particularly in the case of animals, which have more complex genetic make-ups than plants. A distinction therefore needs to be made between cross-breedings of this kind and the controversial process known as 'genetic engineering,' which involves a technically complex process of isolating single genes or parts of genes from one species of plant or animal and transplanting them into different species under controlled conditions, which greatly increases the scope for artificial cross-breeding, and, as has been demonstrated in limited cases, even cloning.

33 Ibid., 51.

34 Ibid.

35 Ibid., 175.

36 Ibid., 176.

37 See Chapter 5.

38 Ibid., 177.

39 Ibid., 27.

40 Ibid., 254.

41 Ibid., 264–5.

42 Stiegler includes several works by Derrida in his references. However, the work most often cited by Stiegler on the subject of writing, as well as by other authors, is Jacques Derrida, *Of Grammatology*, trans. Gayatri Spivac (Baltimore: Johns Hopkins University Press, 1974).

43 Michael Gallope, 'Heidegger, Stiegler, and the Question of a Musical Technics,' draft paper for the conference Music and Consciousness, University of Sheffield, July 2006.

44 As defined by Derrida, the French word *differance* conjoins the meaning of 'to defer' and 'to differ.' Following common practice in discussions of Derrida's work, the term is left untranslated in the English edition of Stiegler's book. See the Postscript for a further discussion on Derrida's concept of *differance* and his philosophical approach to language in general.

45 Gallope, 'Musical Technics,' 2–3.

46 Ibid., 7.

47 Ibid.

48 Ibid.

49 Nathan Van Camp, 'Animality, Humanity, and Technicity', *Transformations*, no. 17 (2009). See www.transformationsjournal.org/journal/issue_17/article_06.shtml.

50 Giorgio Agamben, *Homo Sacer: Sovereign Power and Bare Life* (Stanford: Stanford University Press, 1998).

51 Van Camp, 'Animality, Humanity, and Technicity,' 1.

52 Commenting on the problem, Van Camp writes: 'As a result, humanity has always been divided into forms of life which are more or less human than others (the slave, the comatose, the Jew, etc.).' Ibid., 2.

53 Quoted in Van Camp, ibid., 7. Stiegler's stress on the importance of hands in the development of human technicity and the evolution of *Homo sapiens* more generally is supported by other studies. See, for example, Frank R. Wilson, *The Hand: How Its Use Shapes the Brain, Language and Human Culture* (New York: Vintage Books, 1999). Notably, a pair of hands is also among the most important physical features humans share with primates, giving both species a significant advantage in the use of tools over less dexterous creatures.

54 Van Camp, 'Animality, Humanity, and Technicity,' 8.

55 Quoted in Van Camp, ibid., 8.

56 Aside from the well publicized work of Jane Goodall (see below), publications reviewing the research on animal tool use have been available since the late 1970s.

57 There are numerous publications on Goodall's seminal work, by herself and others, of both a scientific and a biographical nature. See, for example, Jane Goodall, *The Chimpanzees of Gombe: Patterns of Behavior* (Boston: Harvard University Press, 1986), and Jane Goodall with Philip Berman, *Reason for Hope: A Spiritual Journey* (New York: Warner Books, 1999).

58 In addition to some primates, the list of tool-using species now includes birds, elephants, bottlenose dolphins, sea otters and the veined octopus, though the number of species that actually fashion their own tools is smaller. The veined octopus, for example, has been observed using coconut shells found on the seabed to create portable homes – essentially a form of niche construction similar to that used by the larvae of the cadis fly described by Richard Dawkins (see Chapter 6). Andy Coghlan, 'Octopuses Use Coconut Shells as Portable Shelters,' *New Scientist* (December 19, 2009), 9. Most of the recent literature, like that on the octopus, is concerned with the tool-making and tool-using skills and habits of a particular species. However, two works provide more general studies: Barbara Ford and Janet D'Amato, *Animals That Use Tools* (New York: Julian Messner, 1978); Benjamin B. Beck, *Animal Tool Behavior: The Use and Manufacture of Tools by Animals* (New York: Taylor & Francis, 1980). A revised and updated edition of the latter work is now available: Robert W. Shumaker, Kristina R. Walkup and Benjamin B. Beck, *Animal Tool Behavior* (Baltimore: Johns Hopkins University Press, 2011).

59 Quoted in Goodall with Berman, *Reason for Hope*. Aside from the issue of tool use, research into other aspects of primate behavior also provides solid evidence of numerous traits of a social and emotional nature that were hitherto considered unique to humankind. See, for example, Frans de Waal, *Primates and Philosophers: How Morality Evolved* (Princeton: Princeton University Press, 2006).

60 Van Camp, 'Animality, Humanity, and Technicity,' 10.

61 Ibid., 11.

62 Andrés Vaccari, 'Unweaving the Program: Stiegler and the Hegemony of Technics,' *Transformations*, no. 17 (2009). See www.transformationsjournal.org/journal/issue_17/article_08.shtml.

63 Andrés Vaccari and Belinda Barnet, 'Prolegomena to a Future Robot History: Stiegler, Epiphylogenesis and Technical Evolution,' *Transformations*, no. 17 (2009). See www.transformationsjournal.org/journal/issue_17/article_09.shtml.

64 Vaccari, 'Unweaving the Program,' 5.

65 Ibid., 9.

66 Ibid.

67 Ibid., 5.

68 Ibid., 10.

69 Quoted in Vaccari, ibid., 14.

70 Ibid.

71 Ibid., 15. See Chapter 5 for related comments on recent advances in molecular biology and their implications for evolutionary theory.

72 Ibid., 15.

73 Quoted in Vaccari, ibid., 17.

74 Ben Roberts, 'Stiegler Reading Derrida: The Prosthesis of Deconstruction in Technics,' *Postmodern Culture*, vol. 16, no. 1 (2005).

75 Quoted in Vaccari, 'Unweaving the Program,' 15.

76 Ibid., 19–20.

77 Again, the example of the fussy larvae of the cadis fly carefully selecting the best-fitting stones from which to build their shelters comes to mind (see Chapter 6). Such examples suggest that the use of 'as found' tools was common to at least several other species as well as early hominoids long before the use of purpose-made tools.

78 See Chapter 9 for an extensive discussion of the value of analogical thinking in innovation. Derrida's extreme relativism with regard to language is also further discussed in the Postscript, along with that of other postmodernists.

79 The earliest known evidence of purpose-made stone tools, that is, stones that have been shaped by hand, rather than used in their original state, dates back at least 2.6 million years. However, the only physical evidence for dating the possible emergence of spoken language is provided by the fossil remains of early humanoids, particularly those remains indicating changes in the basic mechanisms of speech. For example, much attention has focused on the development and movement in the position of the larynx to a lower point in the throat where it could produce more flexible sounds, which would place it sometime later than the Neanderthal period. However, the evidence for the lower position of the larynx as being crucial to the full development of human language itself remains inconclusive. See Alison Ray, *The Transition to Language* (Oxford: Oxford University Press, 2002). The first physical evidence of writing, by contrast, dates back to as recently as the fourth millennium BC in Mesopotamia, when it is widely assumed that the complexities of human trade and exchange required reliable records.

80 Maryanne Wolf, *Proust and the Squid: The Story and Science of the Reading Brain* (Cambridge: Icon Books, 2008). As Wolf explains, the reason for including the less celebrated squid in the title along with Marcel Proust has to do with the creature's neurological systems, from which scientists were able to learn much about what causes neurons to fire or not, and even how they sometimes repair themselves.

81 Ibid., 3.

82 Ibid., 6.

83 While reading novels, historical works and biographies clearly involves identifying with the characters portrayed in the work, it can be argued that *all* forms of writing, even scientific papers, entail a similar process, in so far as there is a tacit contract between author and reader as to the acceptable format and logic employed in setting out the problem and any relevant evidence for or against the findings.

84 Wolf, *Proust and the Squid*, 7. Illustrating the point, Wolf relates the story of how the Renaissance political philosopher Niccolò Machiavelli, in an extravagant display of respect for the author of whatever book he was reading at the time, would sometimes go to the extent of dressing up in the period of the book and even setting up a table for himself and the imagined guest writer before opening its pages.

85 Vaccari, 'Unweaving the Program,' 11.

86 Stiegler himself acknowledges the significance of place and geography in technics in his discussion of the impact of external milieu on populations: 'the determinism that makes the logic of the development of technical tendencies understandable, stemming from the relation of the human to matter, *is first of all geographical* [added emphasis].' Stiegler, *Technics and Time, 1*, 55.

87 The following works all provide ample evidence to support the case for agriculture as one of the primary transformative technics in human evolution: Samuel Lilley, *Men, Machines and History* (New York: International Publishers, 1966); Diamond, *The Rise and Fall of the Third Chimpanzee*; Spencer Wells, *Pandora's Seed: The Unforeseen Cost of Civilization* (London: Allen Lane, 2010). It is worth noting the difference in perspectives between the first and last of these works. Lilley's account, in keeping with the optimistic spirit of the 1960s when his book was written, is entirely positive. By contrast, Wells details the negative long-term

effects of agriculture, including overpopulation in good times and famine in bad times, increases in animal and human diseases and extensive environmental damage.

88 Lewis Mumford, *The City in History: Its Origins, Its Transformations, and Its Prospects* (New York: Harcourt, Brace & World, 1961). While Mumford's work has been overtaken in some respects by the globalization of urban civilization and other more recent developments, it remains a classic study of the cultural import of cities and their impact upon human evolution more generally.

89 The potential 'extinction-level' impacts of uncontrolled developments in human technology were acknowledged in the formation in 2012 of the Centre for the Study of Existential Risk (CSER), based at the University of Cambridge. Primary sources of risk include developments in artificial intelligence (autonomous robots and other systems that could escape control), biotechnology, nanotechnology, plague viruses (spread by air travel) and anthropogenic climate change. Andy Coghlan, 'Mega-risks That Could Drive Us To Extinction,' *New Scientist* (November 26, 2012). See www.newscientist.com/article/dn22534-megarisks-that-could-drive-us-to-extinction.html.

90 Jared Diamond, *Collapse: How Societies Choose to Fail or Survive* (London: Allen Lane, 2005).

Chapter 5: Rethinking evolution

1 Charles Darwin, *On the Origin of Species: A Facsimile of the First Edition* (New York: Antheum, 1972; 1st edition, 1859).

2 Ibid., 30.

3 T. R. Malthus, *An Essay on the Principle of Population* (London: Johnson, 6th edition, 1826; 1st edition, 1798). Darwin read the first edition.

4 Darwin, *On the Origin of Species*, 5.

5 David Young, *The Discovery of Evolution* (Cambridge: Cambridge University Press, 2nd edition, 2007).

6 Ibid., 121.

7 Daniel Dennett, *Darwin's Dangerous Idea: Evolution and the Meanings of Life* (London: Penguin Books, 1995).

8 Ibid., 50. As Dennett points out, algorithms were already familiar in Darwin's day as mathematical and logical procedures, but it took the pioneering work of Alan Turing in the 1930s and the great strides in computer science that have been made since then to reveal their universal power.

9 Alfred Wallace was also inspired by T. R. Malthus's work on population and arrived independently at much the same conclusion. However, at the urging of mutual friends he and Darwin presented their findings jointly in a special publication of the *Linnean Society Journal* in August 1858, over a year before Darwin published his *Origin of Species*. Eventually, however, the unusually generous Wallace conceded the main credit for the discovery to Darwin, who was finally stimulated into completing his long-delayed manuscript by the realization that Wallace might beat him to the post. See Young, *The Discovery of Evolution*.

10 Ibid., 11.

11 Ibid., 13.

12 Wilhelm Ludwig Johannsen, 'The Genotype Conception of Heredity,' *American Naturalist*, no. 45 (1911): 129–59.

13 Young, *The Discovery of Evolution*, 169–71.

14 Ibid, 211–12.

15 Ibid., 213.

16 Ibid, 77.

17 Eva Jablonka and Marion Lamb, *Evolution in Four Dimensions: Genetic, Epigenetic, Behavioral and Symbolic Variation in the History of Life* (Cambridge: MIT Press, 2005).

18 Ibid., 1. See also Hillary Rose and Steven Rose, *Genes, Cells and Brains* (London: Verso, 2012). Pouring cold water on the idea of the gene as the fundamental unit of evolution, the Roses point out that developments in molecular science during the last half century have undermined the assumed integrity of the gene, which most evolutionary theorists take for granted: 'Today, when molecular scientists report the discovery of a "gene for" longevity or obesity, they are using distinctly confusing language. They are referring, more precisely, not to "a gene" but to a group of DNA sequences, stitched together and activated by cellular mechanisms during development, which to a greater or lesser degree enhance the probability of

the individual carrying the sequences living longer or becoming obese. The gene of the molecular biologists is thus very different from the "accounting unit" gene of the evolutionary model builder. For molecular scientists therefore, the idea of "the gene" as the fundamental unit of life, akin to the early twentieth-century physicists' conception of the atom, and just as powerful in its time, was long past its sell-by date [...]. Despite this, the discourse of evolutionary theorists has remained that of genes, not DNA, as for them molecular mechanisms are irrelevant – even an obstacle to grand theorizing.' Ibid., 71–2.

19 Jablonka and Lamb, *Evolution in Four Dimensions*, 177.

20 The quoted work is, Ernst Cassirer, *An Essay on Man* (New Haven: Yale University Press, 1944).

21 Quoted in Jablonka and Lamb, *Evolution in Four Dimensions*, 194.

22 Ibid., 200.

23 Jerry Fodor and Massimo Piattelli-Palmarini, *What Darwin Got Wrong* (London: Profile Books, 2010).

24 Ibid., xvi.

25 Ibid., xvii.

26 The term 'intensional' is not to be confused with the cognitive 'intentional,' which implies some kind of intention or purpose.

27 While the authors are correct in suggesting that analogies can be taken too literally, like other critics they underestimate the creative role of metaphors and analogical thinking generally. See Chapter 9 for a full discussion.

28 Fodor and Piattelli-Palmarini, *What Darwin Got Wrong*, 114.

29 Stephen Jay Gould and Richard Lewontin, 'The Spandrels of San Marco and the Panglossian Paradigm: A Critique of the Adaptationist Programme,' *Proceedings of the Royal Society of London; Series B, Biological Sciences*, vol. 205 (1979): 581–98.

30 Quoted in Dennett, *Darwin's Dangerous Idea*, 269.

31 In point of fact, one of Dennett's drawings looks much like a crude version of the *muquarnas*, a masonry technique used by Islamic architects in past centuries for similar purposes. Comprised of tiers of superimposed small arches arranged to look like stalactites, the form was developed to a high art in domed mosques and other structures in different parts of the Islamic world and was anything but an 'ugly' or lesser variation, as Dennett describes his own drawing. See Ronald Lewcock, 'Materials and Techniques', in *Architecture of the Islamic World: Its History and Social Meaning*, ed. George Michell (New York: William Morrow, 1978), 129–43.

32 Fodor and Piattelli-Palmarini, *What Darwin Got Wrong*, 97–8.

33 See Aptullah Kuran, *Sinan: The Grand Old Master of Ottoman Architecture* (Washington, DC, and Istanbul: Institute of Turkish Studies and ADA Press, 1987). The basic idea of placing a dome over arches arranged in a square plan comes from the East, and not the West, as Gould and Lewontin imply. The first great domed spaces, like the Roman Pantheon, comprised a dome placed over a circular drum. Spectacular in itself, the solution was ill suited to functional rectangular planning. In order to retain the advantages of both systems a safe structural transition was needed between the circular geometry of the dome, which can cover both large and small spans, and the walled square spaces below, which can be easily grouped together for different functions. To solve the problem Islamic architects evolved a number of ingenious techniques. The simplest solution, as used in one of the domes in the Great Mosque of Damascus, built in the eighth century, was to use corner 'squinches' hollowed out like semi-domes, thus creating an octagon, which in turn merged easily with the circular dome above. By the tenth century, more elaborate techniques had evolved, comprising staggered tiers of masonry, of which the *muquarnas* was the most complex. See Lewcock, 'Materials and Techniques.'

34 Fodor and Piattelli-Palmarini, *What Darwin Got Wrong*, 162. While they may have approached the idea from different directions, there is little to distinguish between the viral behavior of parasitic memes as described by Dawkins et al. discussed in the next chapter and the idea of phenotypic 'contagion' proffered by Fodor and Piattelli-Palmarini – for parasitic meme read 'free-rider' – except that neo-Darwinists generally (though not always) attach a negative connotation to the phenomena, whereas the latter writers do not. What counts in both cases is the nature of the *relations* between phenotypic traits and their environments.

35 Ibid., 160.

36 Ibid., 159.

37 There are no references of any kind in Taylor's work to Stiegler's thought, either in the text or at the end of the book. This is not altogether surprising, given the still prevailing lack of communication between the disciplines and the recent translation of Stiegler's work into English.

38 Timothy Taylor, *The Artificial Ape: How Technology Changed the Course of Human Evolution* (New York: Palgrave Macmillan, 2010).

39 Ibid., 13.

40 Ibid., 8.

41 While there is a close match in many respects between Stiegler's thought and Taylor's approach, the latter's critique of Darwinism is less radical than Fodor and Piattelli-Palmarini's. While Taylor only faults Darwin's application of natural selection to human evolution, the two authors argue that it cannot fully account for the evolution of any other creature either.

42 Taylor, *The Artificial Ape*, 9.

43 Ibid., 123.

44 Ibid., 124.

45 Polanyi, *Personal Knowledge*.

46 Ibid., 382.

47 Ibid., 383.

48 In so doing, it should be remembered that, as a former physical chemist before turning to philosophy and epistemology, Polanyi stands on much firmer ground than most critics of neo-Darwinism.

49 See Ludwig Von Bertalanffy, 'The Theory of Open Systems in Physics and Biology,' *Science*, vol. 111 (January 1950): 23–9; Ludwig Von Bertalanffy, *General System Theory: Foundations, Development, Applications* (New York: George Braziller, 1968). According to the second law of thermodynamics – an invariable law of physics equivalent in importance to gravity or the speed of light – an isolated system in an inhomogeneous state will most probably be found sometime in the future in a more homogeneous state. For instance, an uneven distribution of temperature in a closed environment is less probable over time than an even distribution. In this regard the Second Law of Thermodynamics can therefore also be interpreted as a law of *decay of energy* as well as of structure and information, or 'entropy' as the process is called. Happily, as Bertalanffy explains, the law applies only to isolated or 'closed systems.' By contrast, all forms of life, including humans, are 'open systems' and are constantly taking in materials from other systems in the environment, breaking them down and converting them into energy to feed their own growth, the waste products of which may in turn – in the natural world at least – be used the same way by other, less complex forms of life. Thus, while all organic forms burn up energy in the service of maintaining their existence, which increases entropy, the same life-giving exchanges also produce opposite effects, *decreasing* entropy.

50 Polanyi, *Personal Knowledge*, 384.

51 Ibid., 384.

52 Ibid., 385.

53 Ibid., 386–7.

54 Ibid., 388.

55 Ibid., 389.

56 See, for example, Heinz Von Foester and George W. Zopf, Jr, eds, *Principles of Self-organization* (London: Pergamon Press, 1962). For a broad account of theories of self-organization, their origin in systems theory and their impact on other fields, see Fritjof Capra, *The Web of Life: A New Synthesis of Mind and Matter* (London: Harper Collins, 1996). The study of self-organizing systems, or self-replicating systems as they are also known, is now commonly treated as a branch of the sciences of complexity. See, for example, Peter Coveney and Roger Highfield, *Frontiers of Complexity: The Search for Order in a Chaotic World* (New York: Faber & Faber, 1995). See also Roger Lewin, *Complexity: Life on the Edge of Chaos* (London: Phoenix, 1993).

57 John Mingers, *Self-producing Systems: Implications and Applications of Autopoiesis* (New York: Plenum Press, 1995). For the two theorists' most accessible joint account of their work, particularly their explanation of 'natural drift,' see Humberto R. Maturana and Francisco J. Varela, *The Tree of Knowledge: The Biological Roots of Human Understanding*, trans. Robert Paolucci (Boston: Shambala, revised edition, 1998).

58 Mingers, *Self-producing Systems*, ix.

59 There is little difference of substance in this respect between Maturana and Varela's basic approach to life forms and Polanyi's 'operational principles subordinated to a center of individuality' as quoted in this chapter. This raises the question as to how much Maturana and Varela might have been influenced by Polanyi's work, which would have been well known by the time the two authors began formulating their own approach.

60 Mingers, *Self-producing Systems*, 11.

61 Ibid.

62 Ibid., 14.

63 Ibid., 32.

64 Ibid., 194–5. Similarly, Tim Ingold has also argued for 'a much broader conception of evolution than the narrowly Darwinian one embraced by the majority of biologists,' and refutes the dichotomy between internal and external factors. For Ingold, as for Varela and Maturana, the answer lies in a complete synthesis of organism and world, a view close to the theory of the extended self that is advanced in this book: 'Central to this broader conception is the organism–person as an intentional and creative agent, coming into being and undergoing development within a context of environmental relations (including social relationships with conspecifics), and through its actions contributing to the context of others to which it relates. In this account, behaviour is generated not by innate, genetically coded programmes, nor by programmes that are culturally acquired, *but by the agency of the whole organism in its environment* (added emphasis). Ingold, 'Technology, Language Intelligence,' 470.

65 Varela et al., *The Embodied Mind*, 198. In this respect, creating artificial niches which help to sustain individual self-production, whether they are beaver dams or human shelters, makes a lot more sense in evolutionary terms than just relying upon whatever the natural environment indifferently cares to offer (see Chapter 6 for a further discussion of 'niche construction'). Others of the same species also act as a vital check on what individuals deem meaningful and necessary to satisfy the conditions for self-production. Nevertheless, for all the distinctions between the two theories of evolution, it would seem that life for autopoietic systems is no less risky than it is for life under a Darwinian regime of natural selection. Carve out or create the wrong environmental niche or misinterpret what is needed to satisfy the conditions for its own self-production and maintenance, and an individual is just as likely to perish or be otherwise impaired as if it had failed to adapt to a new environment.

66 Among the more promising approaches he cites the work of the German social theorist Niklas Luhmann, whose conception of an autopoietic society is based on the system of communications it uses. See Niklas Luhmann, 'The Autopoiesis of Social Systems,' in *Sociocybernetic Paradoxes*, eds F. Geyer and J. van der Zouwen (London: Sage Publications, 1986), 172–92; and Niklas Luhmann, *Essays in Self-reference* (New York: Columbia University Press, 1990).

67 Mingers, *Self-producing Systems*, 124.

68 Ibid., 151.

69 Ibid., 124–5. Notably, Mingers cites both Gregory Bateson's theory of mind and Gordon Pask's 'conversation theory' as examples of this approach (for the former, see note 10 to Chapter 4; for the latter, see note 64 to Chapter 3).

Chapter 6: From genes to memes

1 Richard Dawkins, *The Selfish Gene* (Oxford: Oxford University Press, 2nd edition, 1989).

2 Ibid., 191.

3 Key works by the two authors referenced by Dawkins include W. D. Hamilton, 'The Genetical Evolution of Social Behaviour' [parts I and II], *Journal of Theoretical Biology*, no. 7 (1964): 1–16; 17–52; G. C. Williams, *Adaptation and Natural Selection* (Princeton: Princeton University Press, 1966).

4 Dawkins, *The Selfish Gene*, 238.

5 Dawkins elaborates on his concept and provides further detailed examples in Richard Dawkins, *The Extended Phenotype: The Long Reach of the Gene* (Oxford: Oxford University Press, 1982, revised edition 1999).

6 Dawkins, *The Selfish Gene*, 238. Interestingly, Arthur Koestler seems to have formed the same opinion about the species' talents many years earlier and cites the example of the caddis larva's creative response to being forced from its home: 'If a group of larvae are ejected from the tubular "houses" which they built, and are then allowed to return, they often get mixed up and enter the "wrong" house which is either too big or too small. The larva then sets about to cut off parts of the tube or to add to it, until it fits it exactly.' Arthur Koestler, *The Act of Creation* (London: Macmillan, 1964), 486.

7 Dawkins, *The Selfish Gene*, 240.

8 Ibid.

9 Ibid., 190.

10 Ibid., 191–2.

11 Ibid., 192.

12 Ibid.

13 As with so many related concepts, Bateson foresaw such questions in his writings on the ecology of mind: 'How do ideas interact? Is there some sort of natural selection which determines the survival of some ideas and the extinction and death of others? What sort of economics limits the multiplicity of ideas in a given region of mind?' Bateson, *Steps to an Ecology of Mind*, xv.

14 Dawkins, *The Selfish Gene*, 197.

15 Ibid., 200.

16 Ibid., 199.

17 The key point, as Daniel Dennett, one of Dawkins' strongest supporters, writes, 'is that there is no *necessary* connection between a meme's replicative power, its "fitness" from *its* point of view, and its contribution to *our* fitness (by whatever standard we judge that).' Dennett, *Darwin's Dangerous Idea*, 363. Likewise, as will be shown when the book turns to examine case studies like automobiles and their environmental impacts more closely, artifacts and the memes that built them can profoundly influence our lives and keep going perfectly well by themselves, so to speak, whether we love them or hate them, or both, as may be the case.

18 Ibid.

19 Susan Blackmore, *The Meme Machine* (Oxford: Oxford University Press, 1999).

20 Dennett, *Darwin's Dangerous Idea*, 341. For an equally enthusiastic account of universal Darwinism and its possible applications to human behavior, see Wilson, *Evolution for Everyone*. While Wilson does not use the same term as Dennett, he clearly accepts no limits to applying evolutionary theory to human societies and culture in general: 'I am an evolutionist, which means that I use the principles of evolution to understand the world around me. I would be an evolutionary biologist if I restricted myself to the topics normally associated with biology, but I include all things human with the rest of life.' Ibid., 1.

21 Dennett, *Darwin's Dangerous Idea*, 343.

22 Ibid., 344.

23 Ibid.

24 Ibid.

25 Susan Blackmore, *Consciousness: A Very Short Introduction* (Oxford: Oxford University Press, 2005), 124.

26 Blackmore, *The Meme Machine*, 57.

27 Ibid.

28 Ibid., 61.

29 Ibid.

30 Kate Distin, *The Selfish Meme* (Cambridge: Cambridge University Press, 2005).

31 Blackmore, *The Meme Machine*, 66.

32 Dennett, *Darwin's Dangerous Idea*, 347–8.

33 Distin's exclusion of any sort of mutual identification between memes and their vehicles may be contrasted with the circularity of self-producing systems, which depends precisely on just such a mutual identification between a system and its components.

34 Distin, *The Selfish Meme*, 80.

35 Ken M. Wallace, *An Introduction to the Design Process* (Cambridge: Cambridge University Engineering Department, 1989).

36 See, for example, Arthur D. Hall, *A Methodology for Systems Engineering* (Princeton: D. Van Nostrand, 1962). Though once popular among design theorists in the 1960s and '70s, the model has since been largely discredited for bearing little relation to the way professional designers actually work. For alternative accounts of the design process as practiced by leading architects, see Bryan Lawson, *How Designers Think: The Design Process Demystified* (London: Butterworth Architecture, 2nd edition, 1990), and Bryan Lawson, *Design in Mind* (London: Butterworth Architecture, 1994). Criticizing the abstract sequence of analysis, synthesis and evaluation in the kind of idealized design model described by Wallace, Lawson writes: 'Those who write about the design process as if it were problem solving do the field a disservice. A large part of the business of designing involves finding problems, understanding and clarifying objectives and attempting to balance criteria for success […] a designer has some basic idea about the form the solution could take and a crude design is predicated on this basis and tested. Sometimes the tests will lead to a refinement of the idea and

sometimes to its rejection, but in either case the designer learns more about the problem.' Lawson, *Design in Mind*, 5. The importance of precedent and learning by example is also discussed in Abel, 'Function of Tacit Knowing in Learning Design.' The problem-solving model nevertheless persisted well into the late 1980s in some circles. See for example Vladimir Hubka and W. Ernst Eder, 'A Scientific Approach to Engineering Design,' *Design Studies*, vol. 8, no. 3 (July 1987): 123–37. For further discussions on Distin's 'blueprint theory' of memes and the design process see Chapters 8 and 9.

37 Distin, *The Selfish Meme* (2005), 174–5.

38 Ibid., 176.

39 Ibid., 179.

40 Ibid., 150.

41 Ibid., 147.

42 Ibid., 152.

43 Ibid., 153.

44 Kevin N. Laland and John Odling-Smee, 'The Evolution of the Meme,' in *Darwinizing Culture: The Status of Memetics as a Science*, ed. Robert Aunger (Oxford: Oxford University Press, 2000), 121–41.

45 Ibid., 123.

46 Ibid., 126.

47 Daniel C. Dennett, *Consciousness Explained* (London: Penguin Books, 1991).

48 Ibid., 416–17.

49 Blackmore, *The Meme Machine*, 231.

50 Ibid., 232.

51 Ibid., 232–3. A vivid example of the power that personal possessions can hold over individuals is presented by one writer who describes his dismay at the destruction of his collection of vinyl records in the course of their shipment: 'I felt as though the physical evidence for most of my life had vanished.' Ed Vulliamy, 'I Lost My Life's Collection of Vinyl Records, But I'm Well on the Road to Recovery Now,' *Observer*, April 22, 2012.

52 Robert Aunger, *The Electric Meme: A New Theory of How We Think* (New York: Free Press, 2002).

53 The proceedings were published in Aunger, ed., *Darwinizing Culture*.

54 Blackmore, *The Meme Machine*, 57. Though Dawkins left the issue of the location of memes open in his original account, in addressing the subject again in his later writings he anticipates Aunger's theory of the 'electric meme,' arguing firmly for memes being located in the brain: 'A meme should be regarded as a unit of information residing in the brain (Clark's "i-culture"). It has a definite structure, realized in whatever physical medium the brain uses for storing information. If the brain stores information as a pattern of synaptic connections, a meme should in principle be visible under a microscope as a definite pattern of synaptic structure. If the brain stores information in "distributed form" […] the meme would not be localizable on a microscopic slide, but I would still regard it as physically residing in the brain.' Dawkins, *Extended Phenotype*, 109. Dawkins' preference for locating the meme in brains is also motivated by his need to maintain the analogy with the separation of genes and their phenotypic effects: 'This is to distinguish [the meme] from its phenotypic effects, which are its consequences in the outside world.' Ibid., 109.

55 Aunger, *The Electric Meme*, 4.

56 According to Aunger, prions are now suspected of being involved in a number of diseases previously linked to DNA- or RNA-based viruses. It is also believed they may have properties that enable them to jump between species more easily than the latter. Regarding computer viruses, quoting Frederick Cohen at the Sandia National Laboratory in the US, Aunger defines 'comp-viruses,' as he calls them, as: 'a program that can "infect" other programs by modifying them to include a, possibly evolved, version of itself.' Ibid., 103. Moreover, having attached themselves to other programs, computer viruses commonly have the ability to get those programs to behave the same way, thus greatly multiplying the effect of the virus – and likely damage.

57 As recent research in the neurosciences has also shown, the 'plasticity' of the brain and its capability of reconfiguring itself in response to changes in a person's life has been shown to be much stronger and longer lasting than was previously thought. See Chapter 3.

58 Aunger, *The Electric Meme*, 189.

59 Ibid., 192–3.

60 Ibid., 194.

61 Ibid., 278.

62 Ibid., 279.

63 Ibid., 4.

64 Ibid., 241.

65 Ibid., 242.

66 In this regard it is important to note that Chomsky, as other linguists have done, has since moved beyond the original theory of innate grammars upon which Aunger apparently rests his own theory (strangely, given the importance Aunger attaches to Chomsky's linguistics in support of his theory of the electric meme, none of the latter's works are included in Aunger's notes or bibliography). Chomsky himself no longer makes the same distinctions between 'deep structures' and 'surface structures' as expounded in his early work. See Noam Chomsky, *The Minimalist Program* (Cambridge: MIT Press, 1995). Neither is there much support to be had for Aunger's theory from other fields. While a more or less complete picture of the bone structure of an animal might be reconstructed from a single fossil part by expert paleontologists, as discussed in the next chapter, their ability to do so depends upon a unique accumulation of personal experience in similar investigations and exercises. Though comparable skills are more common these days, they necessarily involve the same basic cognitive processes and accumulation of experience, as is now well established in the universities and fossil-rich sites where such knowledge and experience are found. For an extensive critique of Chomsky's theory of innate grammars versus an evolutionary theory of language, see Logan, *The Extended Mind*.

67 Reductionism is generally taken to mean an approach focused on the smallest elements of any phenomena, in the tradition of the atomistic approach founded by the philosophers and scientists of ancient Greece. See Arthur Koestler and J. R. Smythies, eds, *Beyond Reductionism: New Perspectives in the Life Sciences* (London: Macmillan, 1971).

68 William Durham, *Coevolution: Genes, Culture, and Human Diversity* (Stanford: Stanford University Press, 1991).

69 Ibid., 2.

70 Ibid.

71 Notably, Durham sees the development of human language in the same terms, rejecting Chomsky's theory of innate grammars in favor of an evolutionary account – a position, as we have seen, increasingly favored by linguists and anthropologists, leaving Aunger pretty much stranded.

72 Durham, *Coevolution*, 185.

73 Alleles are defined as one of two variations of a gene at the same place on a chromosome, which are the rod-shaped structures of DNA and protein found in the nuclei of cells first discovered by August Weismann (1834–1914), and are in turn the source of genetic variation within the same species. See Young, *The Discovery of Evolution*, 158.

74 Durham, *Coevolution*, 189.

75 Ibid., 422. Durham concedes that there are considerable differences between genes and memes in this respect but does not offer any cognitive solution in his theory of how memes work.

76 Manuel De Landa, *A Thousand Years of Nonlinear History* (New York: Swerve Editions, 2000).

77 Ibid., 11.

78 Ibid., 308. De Landa refers to Dawkins' original definition of memes in a brief footnote (no. 92), suggesting 'the concept needs further elaboration' in regard to other forms of cultural replicators, and he questions whether true imitation even occurs in animal protocultures. However, he makes no attempt himself to explore the issue or develop the concept any further.

79 De Landa does not cite any specific work by Mead other than her early researches, but refers instead to the general discussion on the subject by Donald E. Brown, *Human Universals* (New York: McGraw-Hill, 1991).

80 De Landa, *A Thousand Years of Nonlinear History*, 141.

81 Ibid., 142.

82 Ibid., 147.

83 Ibid., 145.

84 Like Durham, Distin also draws an analogy between genetic and memetic alleles, which she suggests accounts for variations in the evolution of memes, just as it does for genes: 'A replicator's alleles are at least partly *defined* by the phenotypic effect that they control: that is what makes them alleles of that particular replicator, providing variety amongst the effects that it controls. I see no problem with the claim that there may be a variety of alternatives to any particular cultural trait, just as there are a variety of alternatives to genetically controlled traits like eye colour and height [...]. Such memetic alleles will have effects that correspond to the meme in question: you could replace the meme for a fence with one for a hedge but not with one for a bike; and you could replace the meme for a bike with one for a tricycle but not with one for a hedge.' Distin, *The Selfish Meme*, 54. Distin comes close at this point to recognizing memes as 'classes' (see Chapter 7), which renders the idea of memetic alleles redundant, but rests content with her 'blueprint' theory.

Chapter 7: Types and taxonomies

1 It should be noted that, as explained in the following text, the idea of a universal agent proffered here arises from the interaction between processes of extended cognition and the natural and cultural environment in which humans have evolved. Consequently, the term 'universal' as used in this context is not to be confused with the kinds of fixed, innate linguistic universals advanced by Chomsky in his early work and appropriated by Aunger, as described in Chapter 6, nor in any other fixed sense. For a further discussion of fixed versus time-related perspectives, see the penultimate section and note 96 to this chapter, together with the discussion of diachronic versus synchronic approaches in the following chapter.

2 George Kubler, *The Shape of Time: Remarks on the History of Things* (New Haven: Yale University Press, 1962).

3 Iain Davidson and William Noble, 'Tools and Language in Human Evolution,' in *Tools, Language and Cognition in Human Evolution*, eds Kathleen R. Gibson and Tim Ingold (Cambridge: Cambridge University Press, 1993), 363–88.

4 Henry de Lumley, 'The Emergence of Symbolic Thought: The Principal Steps of Hominisation Leading Towards Greater Complexity,' in *Becoming Human: Innovation in Prehistorical Material and Spiritual Culture*, eds Colin Renfrew and Iain Morley (Cambridge: Cambridge University Press, 2009), 10–26.

5 Ibid., 10.

6 Ibid., 11.

7 Ibid., 11–14.

8 Ibid., 14.

9 Ibid., 17. Lumley's speculation concerning the role of fire in stimulating group bonds is supported by Edward Wilson, who argues that the discovery of fire had a huge influence on the subsequent evolution of early human societies. See Edward O. Wilson, *The Social Conquest of Earth* (New York: W. W. Norton, 2012).

10 Jonas Langer, 'Comparative Cognitive Development,' in *Tools, Language and Cognition in Human Evolution*, 300–13.

11 Ibid., 300.

12 For example, Langer explains that human infants have no trouble in handling temporal relations between several objects, for instance when forming contemporaneous or parallel rows of objects in sequential spatial and numerical relation to each other, whereas primates cannot advance beyond sets of three objects that are temporally isolated from each other. Ibid., 301.

13 Claude Lévi-Strauss, *The Savage Mind* (Chicago: Phoenix Books, 1966).

14 Ibid., 43–4. While Lévi-Strauss's general theory of the structural commonalities between the languages and symbolic systems of different cultures has since been brought into question for its lack of a historical or evolutionary perspective (see note 18 to Chapter 8), his observations on the complexity of indigenous taxonomies, albeit at a fixed point in time, remain as valid today as they were at the time of writing. Notably, some of Levi-Strausse's later critics were also themselves once counted as structuralists. See, for example, Jacques Ehrmann, ed., *Structuralism* (Garden City: Anchor Books, 1970). Also Richard DeGeorge and Fernande DeGeorge, eds, *The Structuralists: From Marx to Levi-Strauss* (Garden City: Anchor Books, 1972). For an example of related approaches to architectural theory, see Charles Jencks and George Baird, eds, *Meaning in Architecture* (New York: George Braziller, 1969).

15 See for example, François Choay, 'Urbanism and Semiology,' in *Meaning in Architecture*, 27–37. Several other essays in the same volume deal directly with the application or relevance of Lévi-Strauss's work to architecture, together with that of Ferdinand de Saussure, the co-founder of semiotics. See also Geoffrey Broadbent, Richard Bunt and Tomas Llorens, eds, *Meaning and Behaviour in the Built Environment* (Chichester: John Wiley & Sons, 1980); Geoffrey Broadbent, Richard Bunt and Charles Jencks, eds, *Signs, Symbols and Architecture* (Chichester: John Wiley & Sons, 1980).

16 Peter Collins, *Changing Ideals in Modern Architecture, 1750–1950* (London: Faber & Faber, 1965).

17 Carl von Linnaeus, *Systema Naturae* (Stockholm: Laurentii Salvii, 1735).

18 According to David Young, Linnaeus's concept of constant biological features was built upon Aristotle's original static classes of genus and species. He also expanded on Aristotle's system by adding two further, higher levels: 'class' and 'order.' Thus the order is a collection of similar genera, and class is a collection of similar orders, all coming together with species at the lower level to form an integrated hierarchy. In this way, Linnaeus was able to identify other species by a single structural feature, building a complex, multilayered system of species. Not least, Linnaeus is responsible for the universally accepted method of naming a species by two Latin terms, including *Homo sapiens*, the first of which refers to the genus and the second the species. Young, *The Discovery of Evolution*, 48–50.

19 Georges-Louis Leclerc (Comte de Buffon), *Historie Naturelle, Generale et Particuliere* (15 vols, Paris, 1749–67).

20 Collins, *Changing Ideals*, 149.

21 Quoted in Collins, ibid.

22 Baron Georges Cuvier, *Leçons d'Anatomie Comparée* (5 vols, Paris, 1805). Together with Linnaeus, Darwin himself describes Cuvier as one of 'my two Gods.' Young, *The Discovery of Evolution*, 47.

23 D'Arcy Wentworth Thompson, *On Growth and Form* (Cambridge: Cambridge University Press, 1961).

24 Young, *The Discovery of Evolution*, 68.

25 Cuvier, *Leçons*.

26 Young, *The Discovery of Evolution*, 68.

27 Ibid., 68–9.

28 Ibid., 69.

29 Quoted in Young, ibid., 70.

30 Philip Steadman, *The Evolution of Designs: Biological Analogy in Architecture and the Applied Arts* (London: Routledge, revised edition, 2008). Steadman also has something to say about Dawkins' concept of memes, which he criticizes for being too narrowly based on neo-Darwinist theory – a point stressed here in Chapter 6. He also specifically draws attention to the lack of any attempt by Dawkins to explain the cognitive origins of memes, though Steadman goes no further, leaving the question hanging in the air: 'How are the mental schemata, that allow ideas to be passed, created in the first place?' Ibid., 246.

31 Ibid., 39.

32 Quoted in Steadman, ibid., 41–2.

33 Ibid., 12. Steadman credits Stephen Jay Gould's support for helping to revive interest in Thompson's work, as exemplified in the essay with Lewontin on the origins of spandrels. Gould and Lewontin. 'The Spandrels of San Marco' (see Chapter 5). However, Steadman fails to note that the two authors' interpretation was based entirely on formal arguments, and therefore cannot be compared with the emphasis in *On Growth and Form* on the importance of mechanical, that is, structural forces.

34 Thompson, *On Growth and Form*, 268–325.

35 Ibid., 19.

36 Steadman, *The Evolution of Designs*, 119–30.

37 A. J. Lotka, 'The Law of Evolution as a Maximal Principle,' *Human Biology*, no. 17 (1945): 167–94.

38 Steadman, *The Evolution of Designs*, 119. The quotation is from Peter Brian Medawar, *The Future of Man*, lecture 6 (no date): 8–103.

39 Steadman explains that, in advancing the 'purist' theory of the *objet-type* in the avant garde journal *L'Esprit Nouvea*, both Le Corbusier and Ozenfant made frequent analogies with concepts of natural selection, suggesting that everyday mass-produced artifacts like tobacco pipes, bottles and drinking glasses were the end products of technological evolution: 'Le Corbusier and Ozenfant say that Purism has taken its *objets-types* "for preference from among those that serve the most direct of human uses; *those which are like extensions of man's limbs* [added emphasis], and thus of an extreme intimacy".' Steadman, *The Evolution of Designs*, 129–30. Repeating the analogy in *Towards a New Architecture*, trans. Frederick Etchells (London: John Rodko, 1927), Le Corbusier writes: 'The airplane is the product of close selection.' Ibid., 100. And again: 'The Parthenon is a product of selection applied to an established standard.' Ibid., 123.

40 Steadman, *The Evolution of Designs*, 123.

41 It should be noted that the significance of stable building types is widely recognized in the history of non-Western as well as Western architecture. See for example: Dan Cruickshank, *Sir Bannister Fletcher's A History of Architecture* (Oxford: Architectural Press, 20th edition, 1996); George Mitchell, ed., *Architecture of*

the Islamic World (New York: William Morrow, 1978); Paul Oliver, ed., *Encyclopaedia of Vernacular Architecture of the World* (Oxford: Architectural Press, 1998).

42 Jean-Nicolas-Louis Durand, *Nouveau Précis des Leçons d'Architecture* (2 vols, Paris: Fantin, 1813).

43 Steadman, *The Evolution of Designs*, 27–9.

44 Nikolaus Pevsner, *A History of Building Types* (London: Thames & Hudson), 1976.

45 Ibid., 27.

46 Ibid., 6.

47 See for example Michel Foucault, *Discipline and Punish: The Birth of the Prison*, trans. A. Sheridan (Harmondsworth: Penguin, 1982). See the Postscript for a further discussion of Foucault's work in the broader context of postmodern thought.

48 Thomas A. Markus, *Buildings and Power: Freedom and Control in the Origin of Modern Building Types* (London: Routledge, 1993).

49 Kim Dovey, *Framing Places: Mediating Power in Built Form* (London: Routledge, 1999).

50 Both Markus and Dovey cite works by Foucault, all of which were focused on building types associated with penal systems or housing the mentally ill, which Foucault used as models of the concretized exercise of power of one sector of society over another. For further discussions on the relation of architecture to power, see: Anthony D. King, *Colonial Urban Development: Culture, Social Power and Environment* (London: Routledge & Kegan Paul, 1976); Lawrence J. Vale, *Architecture, Power, and National Identity* (Newhaven: Yale University Press, 1992).

51 Hillier's method is now widely used by professional architects like Foster & Partners, as well as by academic researchers. See Bill Hillier, *Space Syntax: A Different Urban Perspective* (London: Architectural Press, 1983); Bill Hillier, *Space is the Machine: A Configurational Theory of Architecture* (Cambridge: Cambridge University Press, 1999). For applications of space syntax within the Foster practice, see Peter Buchanan, 'Space Syntax and Urban Design,' in *Norman Foster: Works 3*, ed. David Jenkins (London: Prestel, 2007), 178–87.

52 Better known to the wider public for his dense novels and essays on diverse cultural issues, Eco made his academic reputation in the field of semiology, or the general science of signs, and wrote several essays on architectural semiotics. See for example Umberto Eco, 'Function and Sign: The Semiotics of Architecture,' in *Signs, Symbols and Architecture*, 11–69. See also note 15 to this chapter.

53 Markus, *Buildings and Power*, 4. In this sense, the role of texts in building design as Marcus describes it aligns with the role of design blueprints as described by Distin (see Chapter 6), but is equally useless in explaining how buildings are designed in pre-literate societies.

54 From the foreword, ibid., no page number.

55 Ibid., 4.

56 Ibid., 3–4.

57 The problem of dealing with the loss of meaning in the built environment from a semiotic perspective is discussed in Chris Abel, 'Rationality and Meaning in Design.' *Design Studies*, vol. 1, no. 2 (October 1979): 69–76.

58 Dovey, *Framing Places*, 108.

59 Ibid., 120.

60 Francis Duffy, *The New Office* (London: Conran Octopus, 1997). See also Francis Duffy, Andrew Laing and Vic Crisp, *The Responsible Workplace: The Redesign of Work and Offices* (Oxford: Butterworth Architecture, 1993).

61 Duffy, *The New Office*, 70.

62 Manuel Castells, *The Rise of the Network Society* (Oxford: Blackwell, 1996).

63 Ibid., 390.

64 Kris Hudson and Vanessa O'Connell, 'Recession Turns Malls Into Ghost Towns,' *Wall Street Journal*, May 22, 2009. Despite the historically common features of malls in the USA and Australia that Dovey describes, which grew out of similar processes of urban dispersal, significant differences between their form and location may also be found. For instance, whereas American-style, fully enclosed, isolated malls surrounded by acres of open parking spaces, such as the one at Shellharbour in the Illawara region of New South Wales, south of Sydney, are common in Australian suburbs, malls may also be found either inside or immediately adjacent to the centers of Australian towns and cities. The large Westfield Centre at Bondi Junction, a sub-center and transport hub of Sydney, and similar malls at Figtree and Warrawong, two other small suburban towns in the Illawara are typical of these. The 'Mall' at Wollongong, the second largest city in New South Wales, is also located in the very heart of the city and consists of two typically enclosed malls situated either side of a partly shaded, pedestrianized street, along with various smaller shops and cafes at ground level facing into the street. Criss-crossed above by bridges housing more cafes, the arrangement creates a lively urban center.

65 L. Harding, 'Rouse Hill Town Centre,' *Architecture Australia*, vol. 97, no. 4 (May–June 2008): 97–109. While, from a visual and spatial viewpoint, Rouse Hill looks and functions differently from standard enclosed malls, it remains a wholly privately owned and managed development with similar security measures. As such, like other examples described in this book, the relation between architectural form and meaning is ambiguous.

66 P. Saunders and P. Williams, 'The Constitution of the Home,' *Housing Studies*, vol. 3, no. 2 (1988): 81–93.

67 Dovey, *Framing Places*, 141.

68 Ibid., 143–4.

69 Dovey is not the only Australian writer to be negligent in this regard, it being common practice for Australian architecture critics – especially with regard to detached homes situated on the fringes of cities – to focus their attention entirely on the design qualities of the building and its relation to its immediate surroundings, disregarding the automobiles in the garage required to ferry the inhabitants about the city. See Chris Abel, 'Too Little, Too Late? The Fatal Attractions of "Feel Good" Architecture,' *Architectural Review Australia*, no. 092 (2005): 78–81.

70 Ruth Brandon, *Auto Mobile: How the Car Changed Life* (London: Macmillan, 2002).

71 Ibid., 160.

72 Aldo Rossi, *The Architecture of the City* (Cambridge: MIT Press, 1982).

73 Colin Rowe and Fred Koetter, *Collage City* (Cambridge: MIT Press, 1978). See also Anthony Vidler, 'The Third Typology,' in *Designing Cities: Critical Readings in Urban Design*, ed. Alexander R. Cuthbert (Oxford: Blackwell, 2003), 317–22. Like Rossi and the above two authors, Vidler's essay places the issue of architectural typologies firmly within the broader context of urban form and structure. For an alternative perspective on the economic and political origins of modern urban form and space, see Alexander R. Cuthbert, *The Form of Cities: Political Economy and Urban Design* (Oxford: Blackwell, 2006).

74 Rossi, *The Architecture of the City*, 22–3.

75 Ibid., 40.

76 Ibid., 55–6.

77 Among other works by the two authors, Rossi cites: Marcel Poëte, *Introduction à L'Urbanisme: L'Évolution des Villes, La Leçon de L'Antiquité* (Paris: Bovin & Cie., 1929); Pierre Lavedan, *Geographie des Villes* (Paris: Gallimard, 1936; revised edition, 1959).

78 Rossi, *The Architecture of the City*, 59.

79 Ibid., 59–60.

80 While Rossi is correct in describing the Alhambra as an architectural museum, as with other great works of architecture, that has not robbed the building of its capacity to inspire designers in the present age. As such, while it no longer plays an active role in the city in which it stands, other than as a tourist destination (not an insignificant role in itself), it could be described as a functioning and influential monument in the larger collective memory. For example, many key facets of both the Aga Khan University and Hospital in Karachi by Payette Associates and in the Ministry of Foreign Affairs (MOFA) in Riyadh by Henning Larsen, both completed in 1985, were directly inspired by the Alhambra. However, unlike many pastiche exercises in postmodern architecture, both projects involve a genuinely creative reinterpretation of Islamic spatial concepts and motifs for contemporary functions. For a detailed analysis of the latter work see Chris Abel, 'Larsen's Hybrid Masterpiece,' *Architectural Review*, vol. 179, no. 1070 (July 1985): 30–9. The publications of the Aga Khan Award for Architecture (AKAA), which awards significant built achievements in the Islamic world, including Larsen's MOFA, also present numerous similar examples of contemporary designers being inspired by historical exemplars.

81 Rossi, *The Architecture of the City*, 85.

82 Ibid., 72.

83 Notably Charles Jencks, who, while preferring terms like 'late modernism' to describe the continued vitality of modern architecture, has also linked it with developments in the sciences of complexity as well as other movements. See Charles Jencks, *The Architecture of the Jumping Universe* (London: Academy Editions, 1995).

84 Kubler, *The Shape of Time*.

85 Among other references, Steadman briefly refers to Kubler's work in the concluding chapter of *The Evolution of Designs*, 218. See also 'Tradition, Innovation and Linked Solutions,' in Abel, *Architecture and Identity*, 135–41. However, exceptions aside, Kubler's work is surprisingly little known or studied in architectural circles.

86 Kubler, *The Shape of Time*, 1.

87 Ibid., 9. In classifying individual artifacts as members of a series of like artifacts, Kubler's theory of linked problem solutions shares much with the nineteenth-century work of Colonel Lane Fox, later known as Lane-Fox Pitt-Rivers, on the evolution of tribal artifacts, as described by Steadman, *The Evolution of Designs*. Inspired by his knowledge as a military man of the evolution of firearms, Pitt-Rivers concluded that cultural artifacts in general evolved in similar ways to nature's organisms. However, aware of the difficulties in tracking the evolution of artifacts in fast-changing modern cultures, he purposefully focused on primitive tribal artifacts, since they were more likely to reveal incremental changes of form and use of the sort that might be lost in the former case. See Lt-General A. Lane-Fox Pitt-Rivers, *The Evolution of Culture and Other Essays*, ed. J. L. Myers (Oxford: Clarendon Press, 1906). According to Henry Balfour, curator of the Pitt-Rivers Museum: '[Pitt-Rivers] adopted a *principal* system of groups into which objects of like form or function from all over the world were associated to form a series, each of which illustrated as completely as possible the varieties under which a given art, industry or appliance occurred. Within these groups objects belonging to the same region were usually associated together in local sub-groups. And wherever amongst the implements or other objects exhibited in a given series there seemed to be suggested a sequence of ideas, shedding light upon the probable stages in the evolution of this particular class, these objects were specially brought into juxtaposition.' Quoted in Steadman, *The Evolution of Designs*, 87–8. As similar as their ideas appear to be, however, there is no indication in Kubler's own work that he was aware of Pitt-Rivers' work and apparently arrived at his own theory independently.

88 Kubler, *The Shape of Time*, 6.

89 Ibid.

90 Ibid.

91 Ibid., 34.

92 Taylor, *The Artificial Ape*, 160.

93 John Wilkins, *Species: A History of the Idea* (Berkeley: University of California Press, 2009); see also John Wilkins, 'What Is a Species: Essences and Generation,' *Theory in Biosciences*, no. 129 (2010): 141–8.

94 Wilkins, *Species*, ix–x.

95 Wilkins, 'What Is a Species,' 142.

96 Ibid., 143. Wilkins stresses that essentialism and population thinking also entail quite different modes of thought. Where the former involves a top-down logic of classification, 'Modern taxonomy works in the opposing direction – beginning with the organisms […] and thence to lineages, populations, and then species. Species in biology are the result of *inductively generalizing from individuals* [added emphasis], rather than dividing general conceptions into subaltern genera to reach the infimae species.' Ibid., 233. Wilkins also refers obliquely to Winsor's inductive 'method of exemplars.' See M. P. Winsor, 'Non-essentialist Methods in Pre-Darwinian Taxonomy,' *Biological Philosophy*, no. 18 (2003): 387–400. Though the source of Winsor's method is unclear, the description matches Kuhn's original method of exemplars, as mentioned in Chapter 2. See Kuhn, *The Essential Tension*. While, as Wilkins states, both typological and morphological thinking are generally associated within conventional philosophical and biological circles with essentialism and deductive methods of thought, or what he calls 'fixism,' this is clearly not true of either Polanyi's stress on the emergent properties of types and their morphologies, or of Thompson's explication of the effects of gravitational forces on skeletal forms. Notably, both also involve inductive methods and a time-related approach approximating to what Wilkins describes as population thinking. Likewise, there is clear evidence of similar thinking in Kubler's own theory of types, as indicated in the previously quoted passage: 'The biological analogy is speciation, where form is manifested by a large number of individuals undergoing genetic changes.' Rossi's analysis is more ambiguous, however, highlighting as it does both the changeable and the relatively fixed aspects of building form and cities. As with the contrasting logical and biological interpretations of species that Wilkins points to, it appears that the only thing in common between the alternative static and dynamic meanings attached to 'type' in all these cases is the word itself.

97 The range of furniture designed by Charles and Ray Eames offers many examples of different types of modern chair that set the standard for generations of designers to follow. For an early selection of the work of Charles Eames see Arthur Drexler, *Charles Eames: Furniture from the Design Collection, the Museum of Modern Art, New York* (New York: MOMA, 1973). More generally, while the Eames and other architects like Mies van der Rohe and Marcel Breuer have famously reinvented standard items of furniture, aside from variations in material, aesthetic taste and comfort levels, their designs are still easily recognizable as belonging to familiar types. See Werner Blaser, *Furniture as Architecture: From Antiquity to the Present*, trans. D. Q. Stephenson (Zurich: Waser Verlag, 1985).

98 Dennett, *Darwin's Dangerous Idea*, 348.

99 Ibid. Though, as previously noted, unlike the case with genes and their progenation, there is no direct biological or physical connection between series of artifacts; considerable amounts of energy are nevertheless expended in their production, suggesting that the Second Law of Thermodynamics may hold equally well for the artificial things humans and other species make as for the organic species themselves.

100 Mingers' exclusion of biological humans from the products of social systems is debatable. For example, since family and sexual relations are largely governed by social mores and taboos, it might be reasonably claimed, as Durham argues (see Chapter 6), that humans are also in some respects the product of their coevolution, just as human technics is.

101 For the significance of rule-following behavior in human societies, see Rom Harré, 'Some Remarks on "Rule" as a Scientific Concept,' in *Understanding Other Persons*, ed. Theodore Mischel (Oxford: Basil Blackwell, 1974), 143–4. Harré writes: 'The method by which human beings manage their affairs, and create society, is by the invention and promulgation of rules, in the following of which social behaviour is generated.' Ibid., 143. See also Stephen Toulmin, 'Rules and Their Relevance for Understanding Human Behaviour,' in *Understanding Other Persons*, 185–215; Dorothy Emmet, *Rules, Roles and Relations* (Boston: Beacon, 1966). Defining 'society' in plain terms, Emmet writes: 'A society is a more or less ordered way in which people live together, where the "order" depends on being able to entertain generally fulfilled expectations about how others should behave, so that they can co-operate or compete with some reasonable forecast of the sorts of things others are likely to do.' Ibid., 7. However, as with the examples described in the preceding section of this chapter and also in following chapters, the rules governing those patterns of order are rarely so stringent in life that they exclude variations of interpretation and the evolution of types over time.

Chapter 8: Technical memes and assemblages

1 While the general subject matter of Thompson's work concerns the morphology of species and other material entities, the Cartesian techniques he uses to represent the geometrical relations of form between different exemplars are topological in kind.

2 Philip Ball, *Nature's Patterns: A Tapestry in Three Parts. Vol. 1, Shapes* (Oxford: Oxford University Press, 2009).

3 Ibid., 19.

4 For example, the higher-level categories of speciation of class and order identified by Linnaeus (see note 18 to Chapter 7) have their own parallel in Markus's distinctions between those building types that control relations, those that reproduce knowledge, and those that are used for production and exchange.

5 See also Tomas Llorens, 'In Defense of Misfit,' in *Changing Design*, eds Barrie Evans, James Powell and Reg Talbot (Chichester: John Wiley & Sons, 1982), 311–24. Llorens offers a cogent critique of deterministic concepts of function or meaning applied to architectural types, whether by historical figures or architectural theorists influenced by semiotics.

6 The same distinction between style and content also applies to the design of many familiar artifacts. Some major styles have also been applied to both buildings and automobiles, as well as household objects, providing further evidence of the semi-autonomous character of styles as technical memes and assemblages in their own right. For example, see Justin De Syllas, 'Streamform: Images of Speed and Greed from the Thirties,' *Architectural Association Quarterly*, vol. 1, no. 2 (April 1969): 32–41. Also David Gebhard, 'The Moderne in the U.S.: 1920–1941,' *Architectural Association Quarterly*, vol. 2, no. 3 (July 1970): 4–20. Also Adrian Forty, 'Wireless Style: Symbolic Design and the English Radio Cabinet, 1928–1933,' *Architectural Association Quarterly*, vol. 4, no. 2 (April/June 1972): 23–31.

7 Pevsner, *A History of Building Types*, 6.

8 For a concise history of tall-building design and related technologies, see Chris Abel, *Sky High: Vertical Architecture* (London: Royal Academy of Arts, 2003).

9 Colin Rowe, *The Mathematics of the Ideal Villa and Other Essays* (Cambridge: MIT Press, 1976).

10 Rossi, *The Architecture of the City*, 79.

11 For example, Steadman cites Darwin's suggestion of the possible evolution of lungs in land-based creatures from the bladders of some fishes: 'Darwin pointed to the fact, accepted at his time among physiologists, that the *swimbladder* in certain fishes is homologous – that is to say it occupies a corresponding place in the overall organization of the body – to the lungs of higher vertebrates. The swimbladder is an organ that adjusts buoyancy. It is supplied with air through a duct, and lies closely in the body alongside the gills or branchiae, through which the fish breathes air dissolved in the water. In some fishes the two organs, swimbladder and gill, are used for respiration together, the one for free air, the other dissolved air. According to Darwin it is the swimbladder that has been converted by evolution, both in function and in form, to become the lung in land animals. "The illustration," he says, "… is a good one, because it shows us clearly the highly important fact that an organ originally constructed for one purpose, namely flotation, may be converted into one for a wholly different purpose, namely respiration".' Steadman, *The Evolution of Designs*, 87.

12 For a concise account of the classical style in architecture and its primary elements, see John Summerson, *The Classical Language in Architecture* (Cambridge: MIT Press, 1963). For a comprehensive history of classical architecture from its Greek and Roman origins through the Renaissance to neo-classicism, see Cruickshank, ed., *Sir Bannister Fletcher's A History of Architecture*. For a concise account of the neo-classical style and its diverse interpretations in architectural history as well as in art, see Mark Girouard, 'Neo-classicism: From the Revolutionary to the Fancy Dress,' *Architectural Review*, vol. 152, no. 907 (September 1972): 168–75. See also Jacques Paul, 'German Neo-classicism and the Modern Movement,' *Architectural Review*, vol. 152, no. 907 (September 1972): 175–80.

13 Dan Sperber, 'An Objection to the Memetic Approach to Culture,' in *Darwinizing Culture*, 163–73.

14 Ibid., 172.

15 Ibid.

16 Ibid., 171.

17 The term 'memetic program' as used here relates to the concept of a 'research program' advanced by Imre Lakatos in his essay, 'Falsification and the Methodology of Scientific Research Programmes,' in *Criticism and the Growth of Knowledge*, eds Imre Lakatos and Alan Musgrave (Cambridge: Cambridge University Press, 1970), 91–195. While Lakatos accepts that Kuhn's theory of scientific paradigms correctly stresses that the choice and direction of much research are governed by non-rational considerations, he rejects Kuhn's conclusion that changes from one paradigm to another amount to a 'religious conversion.' In its stead, Lakatos proposes his own theory of how scientific research proceeds, based on a flexible reinterpretation of Karl Popper's stringent criteria for the falsification of a theory. See Karl Popper, *The Logic of Scientific Discovery* (London: Hutchinson, 1959); Karl Popper, *Conjectures and Refutations: The Growth of Scientific Knowledge* (London: Routledge & Kegan Paul, 1963). For a discussion of the relevance of Lakatos's concept for design theory, see Royston Landau, 'Methodology of Research Programmes,' in *Changing Design*, 303–9.

18 The difference between the two perspectives has been a significant point of debate between philosophers and linguists as well as semioticians, exemplified by the long and bitter dispute between Jean Paul Sartre and Lévi-Strauss. See Edmund Leach, *Lévi-Strauss* (London: Fontana/Collins, 1970); see also Claude Lévi-Strauss, *Structural Anthropology*, trans. Claire Jacobson and Brooke Grundfest Schoepf (London: Allen Lane, 1968). More recent interdisciplinary research into the origins and evolution of human language generally favors the longer view, stretching over many millennia. For studies of both animal and human communication systems, see: Marc D. Hauser, *The Evolution of Communication* (Cambridge: MIT Press, 1997); also D. Kimbrough Oller and Ulrike Griebel, *Evolution of Communication Systems: A Comparative Approach* (Cambridge: MIT Press, 2004). For studies of human language, see: Ray, *The Transition to Language*; Maggie Tallerman, *Language Origins: Perspectives on Evolution* (Oxford: Oxford University Press, 2005). Diamond, *The Rise and Fall of the Third Chimpanzee*, also includes discussions on the evolution of human language.

19 In this regard, the sense in which Ball describes the 'Platonic' aspects of types as a stripping away of superfluous features needs to be distinguished from the denial of their embodiment by Distin and Aunger. For a broad account of Plato's theory of knowledge, see Frederick Coplestone, *A History of Philosophy: Vol. 1, Greece and Rome, Part 1* (New York: Image Books, 1962). Coplestone writes: 'It is noteworthy that Plato, in disposing of the claim of perception to be the whole of knowledge, contrasts the private or peculiar objects of the special senses – e.g., color, which is the object of vision alone – with the "common terms that apply to

everything," and which are the objects of the mind, not the senses. These "common terms" correspond to the Forms or Ideas which are, ontologically, the stable and abiding objects, as contrasted with the particulars or *sensibilia*.' Ibid., 170. Plato's theory is therefore diametrically opposed to the integrated theories of perception proposed by Merleau-Ponty and Polanyi, as outlined in this book (see also the Postscript in this book for further comments on mind–body theories and their relation to theories of perception).

20 Dawkins, *The Extended Phenotype*, 110.

21 Ibid., 110.

22 Significantly, in their own critique of the dominance of the gene in evolutionary theory, Hillary and Steven Rose specifically cite the work of Maturana and Varela on autopoiesis in explaining the complexities of biological evolution at the epigenetic level, at the same time taking issue with Dawkins' separation of genes and vehicles: 'Genes are no longer thought of as acting independently but rather in constant interaction both with each other and with the multiple levels of the environment in which they are embedded [...]. In this theoretical framework attention turns from genes to the developing organism. DNA is no longer seen as an "informational macromolecule" controlling the cell but rather as part of the web of molecules and their interactions that the cell employs during development. *Information is thus generated by and during the developmental processes themselves* [added emphasis]. This is developmental systems theory, as proposed by philosopher Susan Oyama, or autopoiesis, to use the terminology of cybernetician Humberto Maturana and biologist Francisco Varela. Within this framework, at every moment of time an organism is both building upon its existing structures and generating new ones. *Living creatures thus cease to be conceived of as passive vehicles, mere carriers for the all-important replicators, and are seen instead as self-organizing and "goal-seeking"* [added emphasis].' Rose and Rose, *Genes, Cells and Brains*, 73–4. The other cited work is Susan Oyama, *The Ontogeny of Information: Developmental Systems and Evolution* (Cambridge: Cambridge University Press, 1985).

23 Dennett, *Darwin's Dangerous Idea*, 347.

24 Given the developments in molecular biology cited above by Rose and Rose in *Genes, Cells and Brains* (see also note 18 to Chapter 5), it is questionable that a clear separation between genes and their vehicles in any absolute sense as described by Dawkins and his followers can be maintained, let alone between memes and their vehicles.

25 Jablonka and Lamb, *Evolution in Four Dimensions*, 209.

26 Ibid., 220.

27 Gilles Deleuze and Félix Guattari, *A Thousand Plateaus* (Minneapolis: Minnesota University Press, 1987). For an explanation of the two philosophers' theory of assemblage, see also, J. Macgregor Wise, 'Assemblage,' in *Gilles DeLeuze: Key Concepts*, ed. Charles J. Stivale (Montreal: McGill-Queens University Press, 2005), 77–87.

28 Manuel De Landa, *A New Philosophy of Society: Assemblage Theory and Social Complexity* (London: Continuum, 2006).

29 In this respect the concept of assemblages is also not very different from the idea of co-adapted meme complexes described by Dawkins and Blackmore, which also allows for the inclusion of artifacts as well as social and other memes. See Chapter 6.

30 Though different from Stiegler's concept of exteriorization, as the words suggest, both share an outward-looking, ecological perspective, in spirit if not in detail. De Landa's distinction between 'exteriority' and 'interiority' may also be usefully compared with Bateson's much earlier distinction between two types of behavioral processes, the 'symmetric' and the 'complementary.' See note 56 to the Postscript.

31 De Landa, *A New Philosophy of Society*, 11.

32 Ibid., 10.

33 It should be noted that issues of stabilizing versus destabilizing forces depend very much on the scale of observation employed. While De Landa's theory of assemblages allows for the mixing and interaction of both stabilizing and destabilizing forces within the same system, the question of how the boundaries between one assemblage or urban system and the next are affected, and what they tell us of the balance between the forces of order versus disorder, is problematic. For example, while it can be readily accepted that the destabilization of older city centers due to decentralization and dispersal has weakened former city boundaries, it is not so clear how the kind of global cities described by Antony King and others fit into the same picture. See Anthony King, *Global Cities: Post-imperialism and the Internationalization of London* (London: Routledge, 1990) and Anthony King, ed., *Culture, Globalization and the World-System: Contemporary Conditions for the Representation of Identity* (London: Macmillan, 1991). While global cities like New York, London and Hong Kong have their own distinctive physical presence and character, sufficient for their

inhabitants to still find places they can strongly identify with, each city is now so interconnected with the wider world, including other global cities, depending upon which aspect of their economies and related operations one is looking at, that many boundaries between one and another disappear to the point of non-existence. In such cases, the equation De Landa alludes to between well defined boundaries and complex and heterogeneous assemblages does not hold up. However, if the scale of observation is raised yet again to the planetary level, it can be argued that, in accordance with the Second Law of Thermodynamics, the increase in complexity of global cities, and the economic systems and ecological footprints that feed their growth, also feed upon the organic and material resources that have so far sustained human civilization and life in general on the planet. This trade-off, like the local effects of urban decentralization, was neither planned nor anticipated, but is the outcome of emergent processes ultimately leading to an overall *increase in homogeneity and entropy*. Similar differences in patterns of organization can also be viewed between settlement patterns of cities at the local and regional scales. See Chris Abel, 'Urban Chaos or Self-organization,' *Architectural Design*, vol. 39 (September 1969): 501–2. The pull between different scales of spatial perception is also a common theme in literature. For example, Roy Koslovsky has written of the polarity in the US between the domestic and continental scales of experience exemplified in 'beat' literature. See R. Koslovsky, 'Beat Literature and the Domestication of American Space,' *AA Files 51* (winter 2005): 36–47.

34 The concept of distinct cognitive stages was first established by Jean Piaget in his studies of child development, leading in turn to his theory of genetic epistemology. See Flavell, *Developmental Psychology*; see also Stephen Toulmin, 'The Concept of "Stages" in Psychological Development,' in *Cognitive Development and Epistemology*, ed. Theodore Mischel (New York: Academic Press, 1971), 25–60. The latter edited collection includes many essays exploring different aspects of genetic epistemology.

35 For example, in his provocative essay on personal identity, Derek Parfit argues that 'identity' implies a logical 'one–one relation' and has too precise a meaning to describe what a 'person' or 'self' is, with all its multiple facets and changes. Instead of the all-or-nothing relations of identity, he posits a multiple 'succession of selves' tied together by 'relations of degree.' Derek Parfit, 'Personal Identity,' in *Philosophy As It Is*, eds Ted Honderich and Myles Burnyeat (Harmondsworth: Penguin Books, 1979), 186–211. However, as with the strictly logical interpretation of 'type' or 'species' rejected in the last chapter in favor of the more open meaning normally attached to these terms, the meaning attached to 'identity' as used throughout this book is closer to the common psychological use of the term rather than to its logical use. Parfit himself favors substituting 'survival' in place of 'identity' as a more accurate way of describing the evolution of multiple personal selves. However, 'survival' is laden in turn with its own neo-Darwinian connotations of natural selection, which could generate still more confusion.

36 See the Postscript for a discussion of Wittgenstein's thought in relation to other key philosophers of his time. For a specific discussion of Wittgenstein's concept of language games with respect to architectural discourses, see Abel, 'The Language Analogy.'

37 The same argument supports Distin's contention that different forms of representation may suggest alternative meanings for the same event or subject matter (see Chapter 6).

38 It is possible that a workable definition of 'systemic effects' might be derived from a theory of self-producing systems. However, the definition of 'contingent effects' proposed in this chapter fits more comfortably with the theory of technical memes and assemblages advanced here.

39 While De Landa makes no mention of any relevance of memes to assemblage theory, he does bring them into his earlier work, *A Thousand Years*, if only in a limited way as one of several kinds of cultural replicators, as discussed in Chapter 6.

40 It is conceivable that automobiles and other motor vehicles might have prospered equally well with solid, disk-like wheels. However, given the absolute dominance of the spoked wheel in the development of every other preceding wheeled vehicle except for the first wooden carts, together with the difference in weight, structure and economy of materials, that cannot be assumed.

41 As in Wittgenstein's theory of language games, every assemblage of technical memes constitutes a 'form of life,' the members of which may also play a part in other forms of life serving other purposes.

42 Lilley, *Men, Machines and History*.

43 Wheeled vehicles were used in Sumeria around 3500 BC and possibly even earlier in northern Syria, and reached as far as the Indus by 2500 BC. Ibid., 9. Early cart ruts worn into the rocky landscape of the Maltese islands are also common, especially around stone quarries, where the carts were probably used to transport stone, but estimates of their date vary between prehistoric and ancient periods. See Anthony Bonanno, *Malta: An Archaeological Paradise* (Valletta: M. J. Publications, 1997).

44 Lilley, *Men, Machines and History*, 23.

45 Ibid., 6.

46 Though Durham's brief definition of a holomeme (see Chapter 6) includes its 'latent' cultural qualities he does not clarify what those might be, or how one meme might possess a greater latent potential for reproduction and diffusion than another – issues for which the concept of a technical meme's 'co-adaptive potential' as elaborated here proffers a clearer explanation.

47 See, for example, Clive Forster, *Australian Cities: Continuity and Change* (Melbourne: Oxford University Press, 2nd edition, 1999). The pattern was generally repeated in both European and American cities.

48 Rudi Volti, *Cars and Culture: The Life Story of a Technology* (Baltimore: Johns Hopkins University Press, 2004).

49 Ibid., ix. Though Volti's study mainly covers the impact of automobiles on American culture, his words apply equally well to the parallel story of Australians' obsession with automobiles, and the way they have in turn shaped the Australian way of life. See Tony Davis, *Wide Open Road: The Story of Cars in Australia* (Sydney: ABC Books/Harper Collins, 2011). Based on an ABC television series, the author's opening lines capture the (mostly male) reverence for the automobile and its subsequent significance in the culture of the country: 'It was love at first sight when horseless carriages began smoking and spluttering across the dirt and dust of 19th century Australia. Since then, Australia has been infatuated with the automobile, the motorcar, *the car*. The story of the car in Australia is the story of our heroes, our eccentrics, our parents, our mates – our lives.' Ibid., inside cover.

50 While there are signs that the private automobile may be losing its one-time irresistible allure for younger generations in the developed world, the opposite is true for the growing numbers of middle classes in India and China and other parts of the developing world, where sales are increasing at an exponential rate, along with all of the usual environmental and other contingent effects.

51 Ray Batchelor, *Henry Ford: Mass Production, Modernism and Design* (Manchester: Manchester University Press, 1994). Ironically, the process of what is sometimes described as the 'democratization' of the automobile was later consolidated in Nazi Germany with the production of the cheap and durable Volkswagen, or 'people's car,' though other industrialized countries, including Britain, were slower off the mark.

52 Volti recounts the story of a journalist's interview with the elderly Ford, who, when it was suggested that he might be getting out of touch with the modern world, replied: 'Young man, I *invented* the modern world!' Volti, *Cars and Culture*, 23.

53 For a full history of the subject and other leading figures in product design, see John Heskett, *Industrial Design* (New York: Oxford University Press, 1980).

54 Brandon, *Auto Mobile*, 277–95.

55 One critic described it as a striking example 'of subjugation to the Machine.' Ibid., 294.

56 Ibid.

57 Volti, *Cars and Culture*, 80.

58 Brandon, *Auto Mobile*, 170.

59 It should be added that most small and medium-sized American cities like Lincoln, Nebraska, run basic bus services along the main routes out to suburban shopping centers. However, these are generally very limited, both in frequency and in range, and are used by a very small minority of the population, most of whom have no choice (from this writer's personal experience of living in Lincoln and several other American cities).

60 Mumford, *The Highway and the City*, 177.

Chapter 9: Combinatorial design

1 Amos Rapoport, *House Form and Culture* (Englewood Cliffs: Prentice-Hall, 1969). Systematically examining all the different material and cultural elements that have helped to produce the extraordinarily diverse forms of human habitation in pre-modern and traditional societies around the world, Rapoport takes special interest in the differences between the building forms and settlement patterns of peoples who live in similar climates and landscapes. Having covered all the possible influences of geography, climate, site,

availability of building materials, technology and construction techniques, he argues that all these elements 'are best treated as modifying factors, rather than determinants, because they decide neither *what* is to be built nor its form – this is decided on other grounds.' Ibid., 25. The primary influences on building form, he concludes, are neither physical nor natural in origin, but cultural.

2 Ibid., 22.

3 Oliver, *Dwellings*.

4 Ibid., 67.

5 Ibid., 79.

6 Fraser, *Village Planning*, 9.

7 See Dogan Kuban, *Muslim Religious Architecture* (Leiden: E. J. Brill, 1974).

8 Abdul Halim Nasir, *Mosques of Peninsula Malaysia* (Kuala Lumpur: Berita Publishing, 1984). See also Josef Prijotomo, *Ideas and Forms of Javanese Architecture* (Yogyakarta: Gadjah Mada University Press, 1984).

9 King, *Colonial Urban Development*.

10 Many examples of hybrid colonial architecture as well as indigenous dwellings are presented in Chris Abel, 'Living in a Hybrid World: Built Sources of Malaysian Identity,' in *Design and Society*, Proceedings of the Design and Society section of an International Conference on Design Policy, London, 20–23 July, 1982, eds Richard Langdon and Nigel Cross (London: Design Council, 1984), 11–21. However, while the mixing of local and imported elements of form have both practical and aesthetic aspects, there should be no illusions about the underlying colonial motivations, which may in hindsight appear relatively benign compared with present patterns of neo-colonial globalization, but which nevertheless served the interests of the imperial centers of the time.

11 Jacques Dumarcay, *The House in South-Asia* (Singapore: Oxford University Press, 1987). See also Lim Jee Yuan, *The Malay House: Rediscovering Malaysia's Indigenous Shelter System* (Pulau Pinang: Institute Masyarakat, 1987); A. Vlatseas, *A History of Malaysian Architecture* (Singapore: Longman, 1990); Abdul Halim Nasir and Wan Hashim Wan Teh, *The Traditional Malay House* (Shah Alam: Penerbit Fajar Bakti, 1996).

12 Colonial administrators were often frustrated in their attempts to impose Western systems of land tenure on the typically mobile native population. See Paul Kratoska, 'The Peripatetic Peasant and Land Tenure in British Malaya,' *Journal of Southeast Asian Studies*, vol. 16, no. 1 (March 1985): 16–45.

13 See Abel, 'Living in a Hybrid World.' The influence of similar Palladian typologies on the architecture of Singapore is described in Jane Beamish and Jane Ferguson, *A History of Singapore Architecture: The Making of a City* (Singapore: Graham Brash, 1985). Besides Malaysia, Singapore and other parts of Southeast Asia, examples of the hybridization of Palladian residential typologies with local features are also found in other former European colonies, including Egypt. See Khaled Asfour, 'Cairene Traditions Inside Palladian Villas,' *Traditional Dwellings and Settlements Review*, vol. 4, no. 11 (spring 1993): 39–50.

14 Tang Chow Ang and Yeo Khee Hua, 'Old Row Houses of Peninsula Malaysia,' *Majallah Akitek* (June 1976): 22–28. See also David G. Kohl, *Chinese Architecture in the Straits Settlements and Western Malaya: Temples, Kongsis and Houses* (Kuala Lumpur: Heinemann Asia, 1984); Vlatseas, *A History of Malaysian Architecture*.

15 Penny Gurstein, 'Traditional Chinese Shophouses of Peninsula Malaysia', *UIA International Architect*, no. 6 (1984): 22–3. Comparing it with other imported 'anti-climatic' dwelling forms, Rapoport writes: 'A similar cultural import is the Chinese House in Malaya, which came from a very different area yet is built side by side with the Malay house, which is much better suited to the climate. The former is urban and the latter rural, but the courtyard plan and heavy masonry construction of the Chinese house make little sense in the hot, humid area.' Rapoport, *House Form*, 121. However, contrary to what Rapoport describes, the two dwelling forms were rarely built 'side by side' but were usually separated by their rural and urban locations or status within colonial settlement patterns.

16 Ong Choo Suat and Tang Ben Luan, eds, *Five-Foot-Way Traders* (Singapore: Archives and Oral History Department, 1985).

17 Michael Emrick, 'Vanishing Kuala Lumpur: The Shophouse', *Majallah Akitek* (June 1976): 29–36. George Town in Penang has generally fared better than Kuala Lumpur thanks to stronger local conservation efforts. See Khoo Su Nin, *Streets of George Town Penang* (Penang: Janus Print & Resources, 1993).

18 Frank Leary and Judith Leary, *Colonial Heritage: Historic Buildings of New South Wales* (Sydney: Angus & Robertson, 1972).

19 Chris Abel, 'A Fragile Habitation: Coming to Terms with the Australian Landscape,' *Architecture and Urbanism*, no. 442 (August 2007): 66–73.

20 Peter Myers, 'Australia's Grid-Suburbs: Temporary Housing in a Permanent Landscape?' *B Architectural Magazine*, no. 52/53 (1995/96): 71–77.

21 The bungalow as a dwelling type originates in India, and the word itself derives from the Hindustani *bangla*, meaning something that comes from Bengal, and was based on the indigenous 'double-roofed house,' which featured a gallery on one or more sides. Having previously relied upon building types imported from the mother country, toward the end of the eighteenth century British colonists adapted the bungalow form to their own purposes, extending the verandah around three sides and also adding neo-classical columns in place of simple posts around the perimeter. Economical and well suited to the climate, early variations of the bungalow had different functions, but eventually it emerged as a popular dwelling form. See Sten Nilsson, *European Architecture in India 1750–1850* (London: Faber & Faber, 1968). For a comprehensive history of the bungalow as well as the social and economic factors underlying its spread around the world, see Anthony King, *The Bungalow: The Production of a Global Culture* (Oxford: Oxford University Press, 2nd edition, 1995).

22 Balwant Saini and Ray Joyce, *The Australian House: Houses of the Tropical North* (Sydney: Lansdowne, 1982). See also the entry by Stuart King under 'Queenslander,' in Philip Goad and Julie Willis, eds, *The Encyclopedia of Australian Architecture* (Cambridge: Cambridge University Press, 2012), 579.

23 Donald Schon, *The Displacement of Concepts* (London: Tavistock Publications, 1963); Koestler, *The Act of Creation*; Kuhn, *The Essential Tension*. For further relevant studies of innovation in science, see W. H. Leatherdale, *The Role of Analogy, Model and Metaphor in Science* (Amsterdam and New York: North-Holland and American Elsevier, 1974). For a more critical view of the role of metaphor in scientific discovery, similar to those voiced elsewhere in this book, see Colin Murray Turbayne, *The Myth of Metaphor* (Columbia: University of South Carolina Press, 1962). Turbayne is particularly concerned with scientists' lack of awareness of their modes of thought and its implications: 'Descartes and Newton were victimized by their metaphors, victimized because they presented the facts of one sort as belonging to another, but without awareness. *They were engaged in sort-crossing* [added emphasis]. But because they did not know that they were, they confused their own peculiar sorting of the facts with the facts.' Ibid., 46. Offering a more nuanced interpretation, Ian Barbour suggests that critics have generally interpreted metaphors too literally. See Ian G. Barbour, *Myths, Models and Paradigms* (London: Harper & Row, 1974). According to Barbour, all analogies comprise three parts. The *positive* analogy refers to those attributes that are clearly shared between the two different ideas referred to in the analogy. The *negative* analogy refers to those attributes that are clearly *not* shared and therefore describe the differences between the two ideas. The *neutral* analogy refers to those so far unspecified attributes of each separate idea which belong as yet to neither positive or negative analogies, but might at some time in the future be identified one way or the other. It is this neutral analogy, Barbour argues, that provides the source of both new similarities and differences and so fuels the extension of analogies and any related innovations.

24 See Chris Abel, 'Role of Metaphor in Changing Architectural Concepts,' in *Changing Design*, 325–43. Biological models also continue to have a strong influence on designers, as well as innovators in many other fields. See Janine M. Beynus, *Biomimicry: Innovation Inspired by Nature* (New York: Harper Perennial, 2002).

25 Koestler, *The Act of Creation*, 38.

26 Working independently, Schon and Koestler both published their key works within the same two-year period, while Kuhn followed later with his own approach, which elaborated on his theory of paradigms. See note 23 to this chapter and note 43 to Chapter 2.

27 Koestler, *The Act of Creation*, 131.

28 Schon, *The Displacement of Concepts*, 192.

29 Kuhn, *The Essential Tension*, 306.

30 Edward T. Hall, *Beyond Culture* (New York: Anchor Books, 1977), 27.

31 George Kubler, *The Religious Architecture of New Mexico: In the Colonial Period and Since the American Occupation* (Albuquerque: University of New Mexico Press, 1940).

32 Ibid., xii.

33 Kubler, *The Shape of Time*, 112–13.

34 Arthur L. Campa, *Hispanic Culture in the Southwest* (Norman: Oklahoma University Press, 1979).

35 Ibid., 26.

36 See, for example, Patricia W. O'Gorman, *Tradition of Craftsmanship in Mexican Homes* (New York: Architectural Book Publishing Company, 1980). Aside from its aesthetic attractions and suitability to hot, arid climates, adobe technology lends itself readily to self-builders. See Paul Graham McHenry Jr, *Adobe: Build It Yourself* (Tucson: University of Arizona Press, 1973).

37 Joyce Brodsky, 'Continuity and Discontinuity in Style: A Problem in Art Historical Methodology,' *Journal of Aesthetics and Art Criticism*, vol. 39, no. 1 (1980): 28–37.

38 Ibid., 33.

39 In this respect, aside from the historical continuity evident in the previously mentioned Palladian typologies of Le Corbusier's villas, the architect's repeated references to such modern icons as motor vehicles, airplanes and ocean-going liners were clearly meant to show the architectural profession of his time that it had fallen behind their engineering colleagues, who, he believed, had a firmer grasp of modern technology and its potential for creating a better world. While it may have all seemed shockingly different and unwelcome to more conservative architects, to Le Corbusier's own mind the modernist architecture he promoted was therefore actually *more* compatible with the *emergent* culture of the twentieth century represented by these sleek artifacts than the eclectic, backward-looking architecture he so vehemently rejected. No less important, in explaining his vision, Le Corbusier's skills as a communicator were equal to his creative abilities. By filling his published works with so many familiar ideas and icons, he not only conveyed the borrowed logic underlying his own designs, but also appealed directly to anyone equally thrilled by those same popular images, to embrace the new movement. See Le Corbusier, *Towards a New Architecture*.

40 The 'layer cake' theory of innovation is further discussed in Abel, *Architecture, Technology and Process*. Similar processes can be seen operating at a broader, culture-wide scale, where significant social features and technological elements of both earlier and later phases in human development, such as those defining traditional culture, colonial culture, consumer culture and an emergent global eco-culture, coexist in many parts of the world. See Abel, *Architecture and Identity* (2nd edition), 198–210.

41 W. Brian Arthur, *The Nature of Technology: What It Is And How It Evolves* (London: Allen Lane, 2010). Some of Arthur's basic premises, as the author acknowledges, such as the existence of prior models or components comprising a traceable evolution of related artifacts, were anticipated in G. Basalla, *The Evolution of Technology* (Cambridge: Cambridge University Press, 1988). See also Edward Tenner, *Our Own Devices: How Technology Remakes Humanity* (New York: Vintage Books, 2003). While Arthur is mostly focused on elucidating a general theory for the evolution of different kinds of technologies, Tenner is more concerned with the relation between 'technology' and 'technique' and their combined effects on human development: 'The first consists of the structures, devices and systems we use; the second, of our skills in using them.' Ibid., xi. As Tenner defines them, both terms are therefore subordinate to the broader concept of 'technics' as explained in this book, in terms of the coevolution of *Homo sapiens* and technology (see note 1 to Chapter 4). In addition to many other illuminating insights, Tenner discusses the relation of technology to physical habits, or what he quotes the anthropologist Marcel Mauss as calling 'body techniques.' One significant example Tenner offers is the way that mechanical systems of movement can actually *impede* unassisted body techniques, even at a very early age. Investigating how long it takes infants to learn to crawl or walk by themselves, researchers found that those infants who used infant walkers – wheeled seats that help them to move around more easily – not only took longer to learn to crawl and walk by themselves than infants whose parents did not provide the same devices, but also scored lower on mental tests.

42 Arthur, *The Nature of Technology*, 18.

43 Ibid., 18.

44 Ibid., 19.

45 Ibid., 21.

46 Given the depth of his own studies there is no reason to doubt Arthur on this matter.

47 Arthur, *The Nature of Technology*, 22.

48 Ibid., 28.

49 Ibid.

50 Ibid.

51 While Arthur is keenly aware of the impact of technology on human evolution, he makes no effort like Stiegler or his followers to define *Homo sapiens* in these terms and is content to explain how technology itself evolves, which, as was noted in Chapter 4, Stiegler himself neglects to do. In supplying a convincing and detailed theory of technological evolution, Arthur also obviates Vaccari and Barnet's declared intention of filling the same gaps in Stiegler's work and providing an evolutionary theory of technology themselves. However, it remains to be seen what new insights they might yet add to Arthur's important work, which was published a year before their own essay. See Vaccari and Barnet, 'Prolegomena.'

52 Arthur, *The Nature of Technology*, 113.

53 Ibid., 112.

54 Ibid., 102.

55 The death of Steve Jobs, the co-founder of Apple Corporation, in 2011 sparked further debate about the impact a creative individual can have on technological innovation. See for example Julian Baggini, 'How Jobs Changed Capitalism,' *Guardian Weekly*, October 14, 2011. Baggini argues that by creating new, high-quality products that consumers did not *know* they needed before they became available, Jobs effectively changed the normal rules of the marketplace, which generally operates on the assumption that products are created to meet an *already defined* need. However, while, as Baggini suggests, this undermines conventional evolutionary analogies, it accords perfectly well with the theory of combinatorial evolution described by Arthur, which requires that innovators can *recognize* which existing technologies might be best combined to create new technologies, *after* which the selection process kicks in, if not always with the same positive outcomes that Apple has enjoyed. For example, the Xerox Company invented the computer 'mouse' but Jobs took what he found and transformed it into a user-friendly product that people could not only handle more easily but learn to 'love' – a principle, Baggani argues, that is common to all Apple products. Similarly, 'We had cheap portable netbooks and tablet devices before the iPad came out. But they had limited appeal, limited functionality and were languishing as niche products. What Jobs and his team did was to come up with a new type of device that really took off. And when he did, it was a game-changer.' Ibid. As Baggini, suggests, the secret to Jobs' success lay in integrating known technologies in new products that appealed to consumers in ways that previously existing products and technologies failed to do, thus creating the need as well as the product, for which Apple's customers appear happy to pay a premium price.

56 Arthur, *The Nature of Technology*, 103.

57 Heidegger, *Poetry, Language, Thought*, 152.

58 As in the classic work by Siegfried Giedeon, *Space, Time and Architecture: The Growth of a New Tradition* (Cambridge: Harvard University Press, 3rd edition, 1954). Giedeon devotes a whole chapter to Maillart's bridges, which he considers to represent an important development in the history of modern architecture as well as engineering.

59 Arthur, *The Nature of Technology*, 99.

60 Ibid.

61 Ibid., 100.

62 Ibid., 212.

63 Ibid, 212–13. Arthur does not cite any specific works by Venturi but his description would probably be met with the architect's approval.

64 With notable exceptions such as the work of August Prouvé, the early history of modernist attempts to adapt mass-production technologies and related design approaches to architectural production is a catalogue of misconceptions and failures. See: Chris Abel, 'Ditching the Dinosaur Sanctuary,' *Architectural Design*, vol. 38 (August (1969): 419–24; Barry Russell, *Building Systems, Industrialization and Architecture* (Chichester: Wiley, 1981); Gilbert Herbert, *The Dream of the Factory-Made House: Walter Gropius and Konrad Wachsmann* (Cambridge: MIT Press, 1984); Chris Abel, 'Technology and Process,' in *Design Professionals and the Built Environment*, eds Paul Knox and Peter Ozolins (Chichester: Wiley, 2000), 313–31. Notably, having grown up working as a stone mason in his father's business, which he later translated into a craftsman-like mastery of steel-framed technique, Mies van der Rohe's grasp of modern technology was much firmer than that of most other founders of the modern movement.

65 In Maturana and Varela's terminology, the larger class of buildings called the 'tower type' itself represents the 'organization' of the system (or, in conventional biological terms, the genus), while the individual exemplars described in the chapter represent its various 'structures' (i.e. species). For a historical overview of major innovations in the tower type during the past century, see Abel, *Sky High*. For more detailed histories, see: Carl W. Condit, *The Chicago School of Architecture: A History of Commercial and Public Buildings in the Chicago Area, 1875–1925* (Chicago: University of Chicago Press, 1964); Ada Louise Huxtable, *The Tall Building Artistically Reconsidered: The Search for a Skyscraper Style* (New York: Pantheon Books, 1982); Eric P. Nash, *Manhattan Skyscrapers* (New York: Princeton Architectural Press, 1999); Roger Shepherd, ed., *Skyscraper: The Search for an American Style 1891–1941* (New York: McGraw-Hill, 2003). For further discussions of the urban and cultural impacts, see: Thomas A. P. Van Leeuwen, 'Sacred Skyscrapers and Profane Cathedrals,' *AA Files*, no. 8 (January 1985): 39–56; Richard Francis Jones, Lawrence Nield, Xing Ruan and Deborah van der Plaat, eds, *Skyplane* (Sydney: University of New South Wales Press, 2009).

66 Huxtable, *The Tall Building*.

67 Ibid., 23.

68 For a detailed study, see Kenneth Frampton, 'Modern Architecture: 1851–1919,' *GA Document*, special issue 2 (September 1981): 1–211. See also Russell Sturgis, 'The Larkin Building in Buffalo,' in *Skyscraper: The Search for an American Style 1891–1941*, ed. Roger Shepherd (New York: McGraw-Hill, 2003), 146–53. FLW's radical spatial concept for the Larkin Building was later developed into a consistent spatial typology of 'served' and 'servant' spaces by Louis Kahn, as realized in his Richards Laboratories, Philadelphia, 1961, which also locates all the vertical service towers around the periphery of his open-floor plans. Kahn's typology influenced the later work of Kenzō Tang and Richard Rogers as well as that of Norman Foster.

69 Chris Abel, 'A Building for the Pacific Century,' *Architectural Review*, vol. 179, no. 1070 (April 1986): 55–61.

70 Observations made from personal researches conducted with both the architects and the HSBC staff concerned in January 2011, in preparation for a new book on the Hongkong Bank covering the history and use of the building since its completion in 1986.

71 Farshid Moussavi and Alejandro Zaera Polo, 'Types, Style and Phylogenesis,' in *Emergence: Morphogenetic Design Strategies*, guest eds Michael Hensel, Achim Menges and Michael Weinstock, special issue of *Architectural Design*, vol. 74, no. 3 (May/June 2004): 34–9, quote from 38.

72 The 'extrusion principle' was first named and defined by this writer in an article on Harry Seidler's last multifunctional tower building, the form and plans of which visibly change externally as well as internally with each vertical change of function. See Chris Abel, 'Riparian Plaza, Brisbane: Harry Seidler,' *Architectural Review Australia*, no. 097 (May 2006): 52–63.

73 Abel, *Sky High*.

74 Chris Abel, 'The Vertical Garden City: Towards a New Urban Topology,' *International Journal on Tall Buildings and Urban Habitat*, no. 2 (2010): 20–30. The work of VAST, as well as that of other university-based research studios focused on new forms of high-rise architecture, notably at the Illinois Institute of Technology (IIT) and the University of Nottingham architecture faculties, are regularly featured in the 'Design Research' section of the *International Journal for the Centre of Tall Buildings and Urban Habitat* (CTBUH).

75 Alexander Cuthbert, *Understanding Cities: Method in Urban Design* (Abingdon: Routledge, 2011). See also Alexander Cuthbert, *Designing Cities* (Oxford: Blackwell, 2003) and Alexander Cuthbert, *The Form of Cities* (Oxford: Blackwell, 2006).

76 The two works cited by Cuthbert, which were widely influential in their time, are: Lionel March and Philip Steadman, eds, *The Geometry of Environment* (London: Methuen, 1971); and Leslie Martin and Lionel March, *Urban Space and Structures* (Cambridge: Cambridge University Press, 1972). While Cuthbert does not mention the specific issue of climate regarding claims to the greater efficiency of perimeter planning over towers, in addition to covering the work of Yeang and others in developing new approaches to high-rise design, he points out the weakness of relying on abstract modeling to the exclusion of other social and cultural factors, as March et al. do in the above studies.

77 From the climatic viewpoint, March et al. are therefore as susceptible to Eurocentric thinking about the tower type as those architects and urban designers of whom Webber and Venturi were so critical of regarding the debates over dispersed versus compact cities.

78 While Rapoport cites personal experience in describing the disadvantages of the traditional Japanese dwelling in cold climates, having lived in both a traditional-style house in Malaysia and a well designed apartment tower in Singapore, neither of which required air conditioning due to the high degree of through ventilation each dwelling captures, this writer can personally vouch for their effective response to the climate.

79 For a detailed study, see Colin Davies and Ian Lambot, *Commerzbank Frankfurt: Prototype for an Ecological High-Rise* (Basel and Haselmere: Birkauser and Watermark, 1997). While Yeang pioneered the use of natural ventilation in all the circulation areas for office towers in the tropics, the hot and humid conditions in those regions restrict the regular use of natural ventilation in the office working areas. The Commerzbank broke new ground in using specially designed, openable windows in all the office floors, which close automatically when wind speeds exceed comfortable levels, switching on the mechanical ventilation system at the same time. Studies have confirmed the use of natural ventilation in the building for as much as 80% of the year.

Chapter 10: Recasting the extended self

1 Dawkins himself was careful to point out that his description of the 'selfish' behavior of both genes and memes was no more than a metaphor and was not intended to suggest any kind of purposeful or teleological behavior: 'Throughout this book, I have emphasized that we must not think of genes as conscious, purposeful agents. Blind natural selection, however, makes them behave rather *as if they were purposeful* [added emphasis], and it has been convenient, as a shorthand, to refer to genes in the language of purpose. For example, when we say "genes are trying to increase their numbers in the gene pools," what we really mean is "those genes that behave in such as a way as to increase their numbers in future gene pools tend to be the genes whose effects we see in the world." Just as we have found it convenient to think of genes as active agents, working for their own survival, perhaps it might be convenient to think of memes in the same way. In neither case must we get mystical about it. In both cases the idea of purpose is only a metaphor, but we have already seen what a fruitful metaphor it is in the case of genes. We have even used words like "selfish"' and "ruthless"' for genes, knowing full well it is only a figure of speech. Can we, in exactly the same spirit, look for selfish or ruthless memes?' Dawkins, *The Selfish Gene*, 196.

2 Cooper, 'The House as Symbol,' 144.

3 Quoted from David Thomson in personal correspondence with the author in May 2011. Thomson is not the only movie critic to make such observations. Commenting on the acclaimed movie *The King's Speech* (2010), which relates the story of how an Australian speech therapist named Lionel Logue (played by Geoffrey Rush) cured the future king of England, George VI, of a bad stammer, Michael Bodey suggests that underlying the narrative of the unlikely friendship between commoner and king lies another familiar genre: 'It could be compared with a boxing movie, for example: the challenge to beat the stammer is set, a training montage follows, Logue challenges his pupil – "You can be king"; "N-n-n-n-no, I c-c-can't" – and the underdog heads into the ring.' The director, Tom Hooper, agrees with Bodey: 'That's exactly what I felt I was making,' Hooper says. 'It's interesting how one almost discovers along the way [the genres] that the film relates to.' Bodey takes up the same argument: 'Hooper says he doesn't see "tremendous evidence" that audiences want originality in filmmaking. We return to the same kinds of stories over and over again, he says, paraphrasing T. S. Eliot's contention that there is no such thing as originality, just attempts to retell in a better way what has already been related. Audiences continually return to films about people falling in and out of love or taking revenge, films about hubris and the pursuit of power. *They enjoy the familiarity but want the details to be new* [added emphasis].' Michael Bodey, 'The Perfect Vehicle for Geoffrey Rush,' *Australian*, December 22, 2010.

4 For further interpretations of the virus analogy, see Richard Brodie, *Virus of the Mind: The New Science of the Meme* (Carlsbad: Hay House, 1996). See also Aaron Lynch, *Thought Contagion: How Belief Spreads Through Society* (New York: Basic Books, 1996).

5 Distin, *The Selfish Meme*, 73.

6 In addition to a tendency to roll over more easily than most other automobiles due to the high center of gravity, the large size and high seating position of SUVs, or 4WDs as they are also known, that owners find so attractive to their egos is also responsible for many of the tragic accidents involving cases of their drivers blindly running over their own children in the home driveway. See, for example, Kate Legge, 'The Worst Thing That Could Happen Has Happened: Cars, Driveways – and Children,' *Weekend Australian Magazine*, December 3–4, 2011. Legge reports that during a seven-day period in September 2011, three small children (the accidents invariably involve toddlers because they are more difficult to see) in one state in Australia lost their lives in separate driveway accidents involving 4WDs. An average eight children under two years of age in the same state die this way each year but Legge explains that national statistics are unavailable due to a lack of federal investigations into the problem and ambiguities in police definitions of fatal vehicle accidents at the home. However, suggesting that such accidents are grossly underestimated, Legge quotes a figure of 150 accidents each year – three each week – in Queensland alone from a doctor at Brisbane's Royal Children's Hospital. Legge also writes that similar accidents are common in the USA, where SUVs are equally popular, leading to the formation of a parent lobby group called 'Kids and Cars.' Despite these and other negative aspects, demand for SUVs in Australia increased by 5,000 vehicles between 2011 and 2012, outstripping demand for both medium-sized and small cars. See Philip King, 'SUVs Prop Up Motor Market,' *Weekend Australian*, February 4–5, 2012. Until recently, when Americans have started to turn toward buying smaller and more practical vehicles, the situation was little different in the USA. According to Tony Davis, Ford's

'F-150' truck 'was for many years – decades even – the best-selling vehicle in the US, despite (or because of) its outrageous heft, gargantuan thirst and truck-like road manners.' Tony Davis, 'What's With 150?' *Sydney Morning Herald*, January 27, 2012.

7 For a general history of the type, see Giles Chapman, *SUV: The World's Greatest Sports Utility Vehicles* (London: Merrell, 2005). It should be noted that in its original forms as the Jeep and Land Rover, the four-wheel-drive concept offered genuine selective advantages for its users, in circumstances where survival really meant something. Only later, when the popular SUV emerged further down the evolutionary chain as the suburban runabout it now is, did it shed those advantages. What was once a normal, 'healthy' technical meme, therefore, can also mutate into something like a virus, totally changing its character and contingent effects along the way.

8 Mike McRae, *Tribal Science: Brains, Beliefs and Bad Ideas* (St Lucia: University of Queensland Press, 2011). Much of what McRae explains about the nature of tribal thinking accords with the psychological and cultural roots of prejudice. See Gordon W. Allport, *The Nature of Prejudice* (Reading: Addison-Wesley, 25th anniversary edition, 1979).

9 See also Kevin Kelly, *Out of Control: The New Biology of Machines* (London: Fourth Estate, 1994).

10 McRae, *Tribal Science*, 2–3.

11 Michael Gazzaniga, *The Bisected Brain* (New York: Appleton-Century-Crofts, 1970). See also Hugh Sykes Davies, 'Division on the Brain,' *Listener*, October 9, 1975: 468–9.

12 McRae, *Tribal Science*, 37.

13 Ibid., 3. The subject of climate change provides a perfect example of this kind of dilemma. See Clive Hamilton, *Requiem for a Species: Why We Resist the Truth About Climate Change* (Crows Nest: Allen & Unwin, 2010).

14 McRae, *Tribal Science*, 187. For an explanation of intelligent design and related debates, see Cook, *Evolution Versus Intelligent Design*.

15 McRae, *Tribal Science*, 144. There is a clear relation here between the behavior that McRae is describing and what Dawkins describes as the difficulty that new memes meet in gaining access to minds already set in their ways, as quoted in Chapter 6: 'The meme pool therefore comes to have the attributes of an evolutionary stable set, *which new memes find it hard to invade* [added emphasis].' Dawkins, *The Selfish Gene*, 199. The negative aspects of tribal thinking and confirmation bias are also apparent in the growing problem of obesity, where it has now overtaken smoking in Australia as the leading cause of premature death and illness (60% of Australian adults and 20% of children are overweight or obese), creating a health-care crisis. Despite the negative health effects, which are generally attributed to poor diet and lack of exercise, many of the same people regard their weight as normal, since they see so many other similarly obese people all around them. See Amy Corderoy, 'Obesity Is Now More Deadly Than Smoking,' *Sydney Morning Herald*, April 9, 2010. Numerous reports confirm similar health problems, or 'obesity epidemics' as they are commonly called, in the USA and the UK. For additional ways in which individuals may subconsciously bend reality to suit themselves, see Cordelia Fine, *A Mind of Its Own: How your Brain Distorts and Deceives* (Cambridge: Icon Books, 2006). See also Kate Douglas, 'Making Your Mind Up,' *New Scientist*, vol. 212, no. 2838 (November 12, 2011): 39–41. The latter author includes confirmation bias among several psychological factors influencing a person's decisions, usually with the result of simplifying what would otherwise be too complex to handle comfortably.

16 McRae, *Tribal Science*, 145–6.

17 While McRae makes no mention of memetic theory, the evidence of confirmation bias lends strong support to Dawkins' and Blackmore's speculations, as recounted in Chapter 6, that established meme complexes, particularly those involved in defining the self, may create barriers to the entry of new memes (see also note 15 to this chapter). Regarding the issue of free will, Dawkins himself equivocates. Having advanced his theories of both selfish genes and selfish memes, like most liberal thinkers he appears obliged to defend free will and offers the following concluding sentence to his original chapter on memes: 'We are built as gene machines and cultured as meme machines, but we have the power to turn against our creators. We, alone on earth, can rebel against the tyranny of the selfish replicators.' Dawkins, *The Selfish Gene*, 201. However, as it stands, the statement amounts to little more than a moral imperative, lacking any supporting evidence or convincing arguments to set against his preceding account of the semi-autonomous evolution of memes. See also Daniel C. Dennett, *Freedom Evolves* (London: Penguin Books, 2003). Seeking a position somewhere between the extreme models of pure rationality and social determinism, Dennett traces the emergence of self-consciousness to the evolution of language and, with it, the communicative basis of morality and the

need to moderate one's own behavior according to prevailing social mores: 'A proper human self is the largely unwitting creation of an interpersonal design process in which we encourage small children to become communicators and, in particular, to join our practice of asking for and giving reasons, and then reasoning what to do and why.' Ibid., 273. However, this opens the question as to what level of real personal autonomy is possible, if any, in a process where language acquisition, interpersonal socialization and cultural environments are the main factors governing the evolution of the self. While Dennett mounts a stronger defense of free will than Dawkins, as with the latter's theory of the resistance of meme complexes to new memes, there is an evident contradiction between Dennett's belief in free will and his own neo-Darwinian interpretation of memetic evolution, as discussed in Chapter 6. In an interview about his work, Dennett also acknowledged the growing body of evidence that free will is an illusion and that we do not have 'ultimate responsibility' for all our actions, as the idea of free will implies, but he defended a more limited interpretation of the concept, suggesting that the extent of free will had previously been exaggerated. See Julian Baggini, 'Science Is Mind Candy,' *Guardian*, May 23, 2013.

18 Cass R. Sunstein, 'Breaking Up the Echo,' *International Herald Tribune*, September 19, 2012. Searching for a solution to the problem, Sunstein argues that people are far more likely to accept different or new information if they hear it from someone whose previous views on the subject they respect but who has since changed his or her mind in favor of the new viewpoint. For a full account of the author's theory, see Cass R. Sunstein, *Going to Extremes: How Like Minds Unite and Divide* (New York: Oxford University Press, 2012). A similar explanation for how individuals and groups see the world and make what may often seem to be irrational decisions is presented in Jonathan Haidt, *The Righteous Mind: Why Good People Are Divided by Politics and Religion* (New York: Pantheon Books, 2012). Haidt argues that reason takes second place in politics to the emotions, which are in turn shaped by tribal thinking. For a discussion of Haidt's views and related studies, see Simon Jenkins, 'So, You Think Reason Guides Your Politics? Think Again,' *Guardian*, 18 May, 2012. The endemic corruption exposed in the UK's major banks during the global financial crisis has also been blamed on tribal thinking and the subsequent willingness of individuals to ignore moral constraints in the interests of fitting in with their chosen tribe in the financial world. See Finan O'Toole, 'In Corrupt Systems, Decent People Have Two Options: Conform or Be Crushed,' *Observer*, July 1, 2012. Describing cases where whistleblowers have typically been punished by their employers for exposing corrupt practices within their organizations, O'Toole writes: 'This is what bad systems do: they reward the compliant with tribal approbation [...]. and recast conscience as negativity. They invert altruism, using the instincts of decency – working co-operatively, being "in this together", upholding a communal ethic – to normalize sociopathic behaviour and make decency despicable.'

19 Ryle, *The Concept of Mind* (New York: Barnes & Noble, 1949), 16.

20 See note 1 to this chapter for Dawkins' comments on the 'purposeful' behavior of 'selfish' genes and memes, which he clearly intends as no more than a metaphor, though a useful one at that, in the spirit of the creative use of metaphors described in Chapter 9. Distin, as the title of her book *The Selfish Meme* (2005) suggests, would appear to subscribe to the same basic metaphor, which she develops in terms of the 'meme's eye view.' However, in the conclusion to her book she rejects the analogy with selfish genes on account of her insistence that memes cannot be identified with their vehicles: 'No analogous insight arises from the theory of the selfish meme, because memes do not build survival machines. Their replicative mechanisms, and the means of their variation and selection, lie in genetically determined human faculties, not in vehicles that they themselves build.' Ibid., 206. Nevertheless, while Distin offers no explanation beyond a lack of human control – a tautology – she concedes that cultures *do* have evolutionary forces of their own, though, as with Dawkins' own observations, this does not necessarily imply any purposeful intent: 'Nonetheless, there is an important insight to be gained by taking the perspective of the selfish meme: that *cultural evolution is an autonomous process* [added emphasis] over which we exercise a limited amount of control. Our sense of self is not illusory, but our control over the collective products of our minds may well be.' Ibid., 206.

21 For a constructive critique of US low-density suburbs, see Andres Duany, Elizabeth Plater-Zyberk and Jeff Speck, *Suburban Nation: The Rise of Sprawl and the Decline of the American Dream* (New York: North Point Press, 2000). Seventy-nine percent of Australians live in detached dwellings. Moreover, there has been a tendency toward building ever-larger houses on smaller sites, with a consequent loss in garden space and a considerable increase in energy use. At 269.5 m², the average size of new homes in the state of New South Wales is now the largest in the country, and possibly the world, exceeding the size of new American houses, at 202 m². See Peter Martin, 'The Incredible Colossal Homes: Bigger Than Ever,' *Sydney Morning Herald*, April 1, 2010; Florence Chong, 'Packed to the Rafters,' *Weekend Australian*, April 30–May 1, 2011. The latter

article quotes an average new dwelling size *per person* at 83 m² in Australia and 78 m² in America, compared with 32 m² in the UK.

22 Elizabeth Farrelly, 'Grubby Hub Could Yet Be Urban Butterfly,' *Sydney Morning Herald*, December 1, 2011. Written in support of a polycentric pattern of growth for the city, the main part of Farrelly's article describes the potential for Parramatta, Sydney's second largest central business district, to become an attractive place to live. Like Glenn Murcutt, the Australian architect mentioned in Chapter 1, Richard Leplastrier is one of the country's most influential residential designers. Though the homes designed by these and other leading residential architects in Australia have been widely praised for their passive energy designs and other 'green' features, their suburban location generally negates any benefits thus gained. For example, in a lecture in 2008 to architecture students at the University of Sydney, Lindsay Johnston, an award-winning Australian architect and teacher who runs a regular master class with Murcutt, explained that despite all the energy-saving measures he had designed into a former home he had built on the edge of the city, a professional energy audit revealed that any savings gained from the design of the house itself were canceled out by the energy used daily in commuting between home, workplace, school and shops. See also Abel, 'Too Little, Too Late?' The 'ute' mentioned in the quote is a form of domesticated flat-bed truck, originally produced by Ford in Australia to meet the dual needs of farmers and their wives as both a working and a passenger vehicle. As popular as SUVs in that country for much the same symbolic reasons, the type is generally no more used as a working vehicle by most of its owners as the SUV is used off the road. See also Elizabeth Farrelly, 'City Sprawl Is the Road to Madness,' *Sydney Morning Herald*, March 10, 2011.

23 The situation in Australia considerably worsened in the first decade of the century. According to a study by the National Centre for Social and Economic Modeling (NATSEM) at the University of Canberra, half of all suburbs in the five main capital cities were affordable in 2001 but only 4% were deemed so by 2011 (though often still considerably cheaper than houses in the inner suburbs). See Adele Horin, 'Capitals Face a Decade of Unaffordable Houses, Even in the Suburbs,' *Sydney Morning Herald*, July 28, 2011.

24 Jago Dodson and Neil Sipe, *Shocking the Suburbs: Oil Vulnerability in the Australian City* (Sydney: University of New South Wales Press, 2008).

25 Until recently, it was widely assumed that 'peak oil,' meaning the point at which global demand for oil begins to exceed available supplies from known reserves, would occur within the next few years, if it has not already passed, with consequent drastic effects on the price of fuel. See Jeremy K. Leggett, *Half Gone: Oil, Gas, Hot Air and the Global Energy Crisis* (London: Portobello Books, 2005). However, some observers now argue that new methods of extracting oil from shale and other sources may postpone peak oil for decades to come, while increasing the dangers of climate change. See George Monbiot, 'We Were Wrong on Peak Oil. There's Enough to Fry Us All,' *Guardian*, July 3, 2012. See also Peter Schwartz, 'In Gas We'll Trust,' *Wired* (September 2012), 92–8. Commenting on the relatively low price of oil and gas extraction compared with other sources of energy, Schwartz writes: 'The result: Energy markets will continue to be dominated by oil and gas. Renewables, coal, nuclear, and efforts to make more efficient cars, planes, and buildings will all be losers. Just as the US auto industry is bringing a new generation of electric vehicles to market, the buyers – and politicians who offer subsidies – will likely start to lose interest in them. And more huge investments in solar and wind power will go bad. The ultimate losers, though, will be all of us. The new age of hydrocarbons – while possibly more stable geopolitically – will be just as damaging to our climate. Unfortunately, the seeds of this cycle have already been sown.' Ibid., 98. Others contend that even when the threat of peak oil is discounted and a more optimistic scenario is assumed in which small increases in oil production are achieved by technological advances and new discoveries, the price of oil was still forecast to double within a decade, from a level in 2012 of over US$110 per barrel, with severe consequences for the global economy. See Terry Macalister and Lionel Badal, 'IMF Warned Oil May Double in Price from 2022,' *Guardian*, May 14, 2012.

26 Perth has the highest rate of automobile use in Australia, at 81%, while Sydney has the lowest, at 70%.

27 Dodson and Sipe, *Shocking the Suburbs*, 20. As the authors explain, the burden of increasing oil prices is not spread evenly, according to the availability of alternative forms of transport, threatening to increase existing social and economic disparities in the future; particularly in Sydney, which suffers from a history of underinvestment in rail and other forms of mass public transportation, leaving many outer suburbs with either inadequate or no services at all. See also note 61 to this chapter.

28 Ross Garnaut, *Garnaut Climate Change Review: Interim Report to the Commonwealth, State and Territories Governments of Australia* (Canberra: Commonwealth of Australia, February 2008).

29 Ibid., 56.

30 Ross Garnaut, *Garnaut Climate Change Review Update 2011* (Canberra: Commonwealth of Australia, 2011).

31 From the summary to the 2011 *Review*, ibid., 2. Elaborating on his conclusive comments in a related paper, Garnaut, the leading author and editor of both 2008 and 2011 *Reviews*, writes: 'Observations and research outcomes since 2008 have confirmed and strengthened the position that the mainstream science then held with a high level of certainty, that the Earth is warming and that human emissions of greenhouse gases are the primary cause. By mainstream science I mean the overwhelming weight of authoritative opinion in the relevant disciplines, as expressed in peer reviewed publications [...]. The statistically significant warming trend has been confirmed by observations over recent years: global temperatures continue to rise around the midpoints of the range of the projections of the Intergovernmental Panel on Climate Change (IPCC) and the presence of a warming trend has been confirmed; the rate of sea level rise has accelerated and is tracking above the range suggested by the IPCC; and rates of change in most observable responses of the physical and biological environment to global warming *lie at or above expectations from the mainstream science* [added emphasis].' Update paper no. 5, *The Science of Climate Change* (March 10, 2011), 2. See www.garnautreview.org.au/update-2011/update-papers/up5-the-science-of-climate-change.html.

32 See Chris Abel, 'Death of the Great Australian Dream,' *Architectural Review Australia*, no. 109 (April/May 2009): 137–8. The article includes references to several publications concerning both the specific event and the increasing dangers to human life posed by climate change and related bush fires in the country. For a full account of the event, the majority of casualties from which occurred in and around the township of Kinglake, see Adrian Hyland, *Kinglake-350* (Melbourne: Text Publishing, 2011). In the USA, similar so-called 'wildfires' swept through Colorado and several other states in June–July 2012, destroying hundreds of suburban homes and threatening the state's second largest city, while as much as a third of America suffered through record-breaking heat waves. Though fortunately the death toll was relatively low compared with the numbers killed in the Australian bushfires of 2009, tens of thousands of people had to be evacuated. See Tim Ghianni, Keith Coffman and Jeff Mason, 'In Scorching Heat, the US Is Burning,' *Independent on Sunday*, July 1, 2012.

33 The dramatic increase in expected temperatures compelled the Australian Bureau of Meteorology to add two more colors to its weather charts: purple for over 50°C and pink for over 52°C. The severe consequences for future bush fires on the continent are detailed in Leslie Hughes and Will Steffen, *Be Prepared: Climate Change and the Australian Bush Fire Threat* (Sydney: Climate Change Council of Australia, 2013). See www.dropbox.com/s/zxzcyxkucnqt3o0/cc.bushfire.report.web.pdf.

34 Confidence in predicting the causal effects of global warming on specific climate events is now increasing as new international resources and research are being focused on this vital issue. See John Vidal, 'Forecast: Strange Weather Ahead,' *Guardian Weekly*, June 24, 2011. In one of the clearest signs yet of a direct causal link between unusually severe weather and global warming, the unprecedented floods in the UK in June–July 2012 (the same period as some devastating wildfires in the USA), during which a month's rain fell in just a few hours in many parts of the region, were attributed to a shift southward of the jet stream, a fast-flowing ribbon of air high in the atmosphere that steers storm systems and normally sits to the north of the UK, over Scandinavia, but which has been affected by changes in the temperature differential between the poles and the tropics. See Alexandra Topping, 'Freak Storms, Flash Floods, Record Rain – And There's More to Come,' *Guardian*, July 9, 2012. Commenting on the link between such events and climate change in a related report, Peter Stott of the UK's Met Office, said: 'We are much more confident about attributing [weather effects] to climate change. This is all adding up to a stronger and stronger picture of the human influence on the climate.' See Fiona Harvey, 'Britain is Facing GBP 860 Million Bill for Flood Protection, Warn Climate Advisors,' *Guardian*, July 11, 2012. Still worse floods in Russia and China during the same period caused the deaths of hundreds, many of whom were caught unawares and drowned in their homes. See Miriam Elder, 'Russians Devastated by Floods Accuse Officials Over Lack of Warning as Death Toll Passes 150,' *Guardian*, July 9, 2012. See also Andrew Jacobs, 'Beijing Rains Bring Deaths and Create Wide Havoc,' *International Herald Tribune*, July 23, 2012. Similar record-breaking extreme weather events were reported in the USA during the same year, where 3,200 heat records were broken in June. See Mark Bittman, 'The Endless Summer,' *International Herald Tribune*, July 20, 2012. Stressing the remorseless material logic of the physics underlying the increase in such extreme events, the editors of the *Guardian*, who have been among the most diligent in the media in bringing such issues to public attention, wrote: 'If average temperatures increase, so will temperature extremes. As temperatures increase, so will evaporation. As evaporation increases, so will precipitation. As tropical seas get warmer, so will the increased hazard of cyclone, hurricane or typhoon. Nine of the ten warmest years on record have occurred in this century. Last year was the second rainiest year on record worldwide.' Editorial, *Guardian*, July 3, 2012. See also Stephen Battersby, 'Running Wild,' *New Scientist*, vol. 215, no 2872 (July 7, 2012): 32–7. Quoting from Stefan Rahmstorf of the Potsdam Institute in Germany on the unexpected ferocity and accelerated timing of extreme weather events, Battersby writes: 'While no one can say exactly what's going to happen to our weather, all the signs are that we're in for a bumpy ride. "We are seeing these extremes after only 0.8 degrees [since preindustrial levels] of global warming," says Ramstorf. "If we do nothing, and let the climate warm by 5 or 6 degrees, then we will see a very different planet."' Ibid., 37. The record-breaking levels of rain and repeated severe flooding in the UK during 2012 confirms the direful prognosis. Commenting on the Met Office's forecast of worse to come, Mike Childs, head of policy, research and science at Friends of the Earth, writes: 'Make no mistake, climate change is already having a major impact on Britain […]. If temperatures rise by the 4°C scientists widely predict, then we can only begin to imagine the impacts on our lives and livelihoods.' Quoted in Damien Carrington, 'England's Record Wet Year Was Harbinger of … Yet More Rain,' *Guardian*, January 4, 2013. The knock-on effect of the extended severe drought in the USA during the same year on global food supplies (among other major food exports, half the world's corn is grown in the USA) is also taking its toll. See Josephine Moulds and Suzanne Goldenberg, 'Crisis Looms as Extreme Weather Hits Crops,' *Guardian*, July 23, 2012. See also Jim Clarken, 'Broken Global Food System Needs Climate For Change,' *Irish Times*, August 13, 2012. Clarken, who is chief executive of Oxfam Ireland, also blames the steep rise in global food prices on the US government's policy of subsidizing the production of biofuels: 'In 2011 the fuel industry took 40 per cent of the US corn crop, which is then converted into ethanol. By doing so, food that could feed people is being diverted to make energy.' Ibid.

35 Tim Flannery, 'As Australia Burns, Attitudes Are Changing. But Is It Too Late?' *Guardian*, January 12, 2013. It should be noted that the increase of 0.9°C over the past century in Australia exceeds the global average increase quoted elsewhere, of 0.7°C. While Flannery finds hope in a sharp rise in the proportion of the energy mix derived from wind and solar power in the country, he also points to continued climate change scepticism, led by the Conservative party. Elected to power the same year, it has since rolled back government plans to reduce carbon emissions in the country. A report from the Climate Commission, *Off the Charts: Extreme Australian Summer Heat* (Canberra: Climate Commission, 2013), also lays the blame for the series of extreme weather events in the country over the summer of 2012–13 unambiguously on climate change (the former government funded Climate Commission in Australia was disbanded by the new government on coming to power but has since been reconstituted as the Climate Council, a privately funded, non-profit organization led by Tim Flannery and other Australian scientists). See also Matt Siegel, 'Australia Disasters Laid at Climate Change's Feet,' *International Herald Tribune*, March 5, 2013. For a broad account, see Tim Flannery, *The Weather Makers: The History and Future Impact of Climate Change* (Melbourne: Text Publishing, 2005).

36 According to figures from the US Energy Information Agency (EIA) for 2008, citizens of the USA and Australia respectively produced an average of 19.18 and 20.82 tons of carbon dioxide each per year, compared with 9.38 tons per person for UK citizens and 4.91 for Chinese. See www.ucsusa.org/global_warming/science_and_impacts/science/each-countrys-share-of-co2.html. Worse still as far as Australia's case is concerned, other figures indicate that while the average increase per capita between the years 1996 and 2006 was 7% for US citizens, the rate of increase over the same period for Australian citizens was a staggering 37%, compared with a *decrease* of 1% for UK citizens (the per capita rates of emission for the USA and Australia are only exceeded by very small but wealthy countries like the Gulf states, Singapore and Luxembourg). See www.guardian.co.uk/environment/datablog/2009/sep/02/carbon-emissions-per-person-capita.

37 See, for example, Simon Benson, 'Fuelling Pollution: Sydney Motorists Drive Up Greenhouse Gas Emissions,' *Daily Telegraph*, December 23, 2009. Quoting from a New South Wales government report, Benson writes that NSW averaged 1.49 cars per household in that year, and that 'Car numbers in NSW are increasing faster than the population.' The combined amount of carbon-equivalent greenhouse gases being produced in NSW by passenger and freight vehicles had also increased, by 15% between 1990 and 2009, from 18 million to 21 million tons. Yet the Australian federal government's proposed emissions trading scheme, passed in late 2011, does not cover the transportation sector at all (see note 61 to this chapter).

38 Without referring directly to the environmental crisis, in explaining abduction as a mode of thought, similar to analogical thinking, Bateson also offers a convincing explanation for why people find it so difficult to change engrained cultural habits. Describing the method as a 'lateral extension of abstract components of description' from one realm of experience to another, he continues: 'Every abduction can be seen as a

double or multiple description of some object or event or sequence. If I examine the social organization of an Australian tribe and the sketch of natural relations upon which [their] totemism is based, I can see these two bodies of knowledge as related abductively, as falling under the same rules. In each case, it is assumed that certain formal characteristics of one component will be mirrored in another. This repetition has certain very effective implications. It carries injunctions, for the people concerned. Their ideas about nature, however fantastic, are supported by their social system; conversely, the social system is supported by their ideas about nature. *It thus becomes very difficult for the people, so doubly guided, to change their view either of nature or of the social system* [added emphasis]. For the benefits of stability, they pay the price of rigidity, living, as all human beings must, in an enormously complex network of mutually supporting presuppositions. The converse of this statement is that change will require various sorts of relaxation or contradiction within the system of presuppositions.' Bateson, *Mind and Nature*, 142–3.

39 Naomi Oreskes and Erik M. Conway, *Merchants of Doubt: How a Handful of Scientists Obscured the Truth on Issues from Tobacco Smoke to Global Warming* (New York: Bloomsbury Press, 2010). See also: Clive Hamilton, *Scorcher: The Dirty Politics of Climate Change* (Melbourne: Black Inc. Agenda, 2007); Ben Cubby, 'Scientist Denies He Is Mouthpiece of US Climate–Sceptic Thinktank,' *Sydney Morning Herald*, February 16, 2012. One willfully dishonest campaign run by the Heartland Institute, a right-wing US think-tank, associated anyone concerned about climate change with mass murderers and terrorists like Osama bin Laden, Charles Manson and the so-called Unabomber, Ted Kaczynski, the faces of whom were shown on a billboard alongside which were written the words, 'I still believe in global warming. Do you?' The campaign prompted several sponsors like Diageo, a global drinks company, to withdraw their funding of the Institute. See Leo Hickman, 'Drinks Giant Shuns US Thinktank Over Climate Campaign,' *Guardian*, May 7, 2012.

40 An extreme example of the lengths some groups in Australia are prepared to go to counter any threats to their vested interests is that of a developer who threatened to sue a local council for attempting to introduce constraints on building homes along coastal areas that are under threat from rising sea levels, following guidelines provided by the Commonwealth Scientific and Industrial Research Organization (CSIRO), a highly respected national center of scientific and technological research. As part of his campaign, the developer in question hired several discredited climate change sceptics to talk at meetings of potential homebuyers in the threatened areas and persuade them that there was nothing to worry about. Sadly, campaigns such as these are compelling local councils and state governments to delay or otherwise weaken proposed legislation to limit such developments. See Ben Cubby, 'Developer May Sue to Trigger Rethink on Sea Level Rises,' *Sydney Morning Herald*, March 6, 2012.

41 Larry Elliot, 'Global Leaders Are Unprepared for Financial and Ecological Collapse,' *Guardian*, January 9, 2013. Citing the latest annual report by the World Economic Forum, Elliot writes: 'Persistent economic weakness is sapping the ability of governments to tackle the growing threat of climate change and risks a perfect "global storm" of intertwined economic and financial collapse, the World Economic Forum has warned.'

42 The Gaia hypothesis is the theory that the entire planet, including the biosphere as well as every living system on it, comprises a delicately balanced, self-organizing system. For a full explanation, see James E. Lovelock, *Gaia: A New Look At Life on Earth* (New York: Oxford University Press, 1979).

43 Lovelock's writings have become increasingly pessimistic over the past few years. In a 2010 work he suggests that there is now little or no chance of avoiding the effects of catastrophic climate change and we must now prepare for the worst. See James E. Lovelock, *The Vanishing Face of Gaia: A Final Warning* (London: Basic Books, 2010). The author's previous book was only slightly more optimistic. See James E. Lovelock, *The Revenge of Gaia: Why the Earth Is Fighting Back – And How We Can Still Save Humanity* (London: Allen Lane, 2006). Comments prior to the 2012 Earth Summit on Climate Change in Rio by other leading environmentalists disillusioned by the lack of global action to date match Lovelock's pessimism. See Jonathon Porritt, 'Where's the Energy to Keep Fighting for the Planet,' *Independent*, June 15, 2012. The lack of any substantial outcome from the Rio Summit, which many observers argue represented a step *backward* from the original 1992 Summit, offers little more hope of future action. See for example Will Hutton, 'Global Warming Off the Agenda? Now That Would Be a Catastrophe,' *Observer*, June 24, 2012. Commenting on the lack of any substantive or binding agreements from the Summit, Hutton writes: 'There was, for example, no deterrent to the burning of fossil fuels or incentive to make renewable ones more economically attractive. Targets for sustainable development? Forget them. And so it went on – a non-event that hardly got reported.' See also, Paul Vallely, 'The Planet Looked to Rio Again, and Rio Looked Away,' *Independent on Sunday*, June 24, 2012. While, like Hutton, Vallely despaired of the lack of concrete decisions at the Summit, he found glimmers of hope in the initiatives and progress both small and large private companies are taking in investing in green technologies and development programs: 'A new generation of business leaders is connecting company success with social and environmental issues that were previously the concern only of NGOs.' George Monbiot also suggests that the only hope now lies in nations taking their own initiatives, rather than relying on intergovernmental action, the prospect of which the Rio Summit effectively killed off. See George Monbiot, 'Now We Know. Governments Have Given Up On the Planet,' *Guardian*, June 26, 2012.

44 Hamilton, *Requiem for a Species*. Hamilton also includes a chapter on the probable effects on the world of a 4°C rise in average global temperatures by the end of the century, as is being predicted by growing numbers of climate scientists – that is already 2°C higher than the widely accepted maximum tolerable rise beyond preindustrial levels.

45 Leon Festinger, *A Theory of Cognitive Dissonance* (Stanford: Stanford University Press, 1957).

46 Hamilton, *Requiem for a Species*, 96.

47 Diamond, *Collapse*.

48 The story of the Easter Islanders' abuse of the Island's forests is by no means unique to that culture, but, as John Perlin explains in his meticulously researched study, is characteristic of the depletion of forests to supply timber for fuel and the construction of buildings, ships and other artifacts throughout human history, a process which has drastically accelerated in modern times due to urbanization and uncontrolled land clearance, with consequent negative effects on climate change. John Perlin, *A Forest Journey: The Role of Wood in the Development of Civilization* (New York: W. W. Norton, 1989).

49 Diamond, *Collapse*, 419.

50 Ibid., 438.

51 See also Wells, *Pandora's Seed*. For a detailed history of the environmental effects of successive waves of settlers on Australasia, from the earliest aboriginal and Maori tribes to the colonial period, see Tim Flannery, *The Future Eaters* (Sydney: Reed New Holland, 1994).

52 Bateson, *Mind and Nature*, 173.

53 Mingers, *Self-producing Systems*, 151. Commenting on the pollution of Lake Erie, Bateson pinpoints the blame on egocentric human systems in remarkably similar words: 'There is an ecology of bad ideas, just as there is an ecology of weeds, and it is the characteristic of the system that basic error propagates itself. It branches out like a rooted parasite through the tissues of life, and everything gets into a rather peculiar mess. When you narrow down your epistemology and act on the premise "What interests me is me, or my organization, or my species," you chop off consideration of other loops of the loop structure. You decide that you want to get rid of the by-products of human life and that Lake Erie will be a good place to put them. You forget that the eco-mental system called Lake Erie is a part of *your* wider eco-mental system – and that if Lake Erie is driven insane, its insanity is incorporated in the larger system of *your* thought and experience.' Bateson, *Steps to an Ecology of Mind*, 484.

54 David Sherman and Joseph Wayne Smith, *The Climate Change Challenge and the Failure of Democracy* (Westport: Praeger, 2007). See also Mark O'Connor and William J. Lines, *Overloading Australia: How Governments and Media Dither and Deny on Population* (Canterbury: Envirobook, 2008). In their critical assessment of the failures of governments in Australia to deal with population control and related environmental issues, the latter authors express their despair with the all too easy manipulation of public opinion by politicians, pinpointing the perverse logic underlying the mindset of many leading climate change deniers: 'Politics is about fooling people. And many people seem happy to be fooled. As the Danish philosopher Soren Kierkegaard claimed: "Twaddle, rubbish, and gossip is what people want, not action." Politicians know this. Aided by the media and cheered on by intellectuals they peddle illusion, fantasy, myth, faith and hope. But then there is the natural world – vastly different from our politics and our delusions. For a while people can be fooled – some of them over and over again – nature cannot, not even once. In the real world our impacts on the planet are fact. In our unworld we lack the inclination as well as the intellectual capacity to honestly think about and confront the consequences of our actions. Politicians instinctively feed our blindness and our credulity. They refuse to recognize, let alone respond to, present and looming catastrophes. They know our true concern is with ourselves, not nature. We live in a solipsistic, human chauvinistic society. When in March 2007 the NSW Premier, Morris Lemma was reported as declaring, "There is no point in saving the planet if we ruin the economy doing it," he spoke for most state and federal politicians. He expressed the common belief that we can have an economy without a planet.' Ibid., 127–8.

55 Optimists frequently point to the swift and dramatic change from the production of automobiles by American industry to military vehicles that was ordered by Franklin D. Roosevelt following the attack

on Pearl Harbor in the Second World War, forgetting that no such obvious and clear-cut motivation exists today to persuade either governments or businesses to take similar drastic actions. Roosevelt also gave industry leaders no choice in the matter, a situation that is unthinkable in today's globalized *laissez-faire* political culture.

56 Plato, *Plato's Republic*, trans. Henry Davis (New York: Universal Classics, no date).

57 Paul Gilding, *The Great Disruption: How the Climate Crisis Will Transform the Global Economy* (London: Bloomsbury, 2011).

58 The geo-political consequences of runaway climate change as nations compete for dwindling basic resources have been spelt out with alarming clarity in Gwynne Dyer, *Climate Wars* (Melbourne: Scribe, 2008).

59 Following the recent near collapse of the automobile industry in the USA and its rescue by the government, American car makers have finally got the message, though they still have some way to go to match European and Japanese models. See Drive Team, 'Seeing the Light: Detroit Finally Delivers on a Generation of More Fuel-efficient Cars,' *Sydney Morning Herald: Weekend Edition*, January 14–15, 2012. However, given the relatively small size of the home market and the increasing competition from abroad, the future of the Australian automobile industry looks increasingly in doubt (all the major Australian brands are already owned by American or Japanese firms).

60 Dodson and Sipe, *Shocking the Suburbs*, 272.

61 For an assessment of the potential economic and social benefits of rail over road transportation systems in Australia, see Australian Rail Association, *The True Value of Rail* (Canberra: ARA, 2011). In a broadcast address to the National Press Club of Australia, on August 10, 2011, Lance Hockridge, chairman of the ARA, outlined the contents of the report, including the substantial benefits from reduced carbon emissions and accidents. However, noting the long history of earlier failed proposals to invest in and improve rail transportation in the country, which he put down to the lack of any rational planning or regulatory system, he also criticized the then federal government's proposed carbon tax (now passed but currently under review by the new government, which favors still more business-friendly measures), which excludes private automobiles and freight trucks, but includes railways – a proposal that in his words 'defies logic.'

62 See, for example, Mike Jenks, Elizabeth Burton and Katie Williams, eds, *The Compact City: A Sustainable Urban Form?* (London: Spon Press, 1996); Robert Cervero, *The Transit Metropolis: A Global Enquiry* (Washington, DC: Island Press, 1998); Peter Newman and Jeffrey Kenworthy, *Sustainability and Cities: Overcoming Automobile Dependence* (Washington, DC: Island Press, 1999); David Owen, *Green Metropolis: Why Living Smaller, Living Closer, and Driving Less Are the Key to Sustainability* (New York: Riverhead Books, 2009); Taras Grescoe, *Straphanger: Saving Our Cities and Ourselves from the Automobile* (New York: Times Books, 2012).

63 Newman and Kenworthy, *Sustainability and Cities*.

64 Dodson and Sipe, *Shocking the Suburbs*, 74.

65 Paul Mees, *Transport for Suburbia: Beyond the Automobile Age* (London: Earthscan, 2010).

66 Ibid., 66.

67 Ellen Dunham-Jones and June Williamson, *Retrofitting Suburbia: Urban Design Solutions for Redesigning Suburbs* (Hoboken: Wiley, updated edition, 2011). See also David Kelbaugh, ed., *The Pedestrian Pocket Book: A New Suburban Design Strategy* (New York: Princeton Architectural Press, 1989).

68 Dunham-Jones and Williamson, *Retrofitting Suburbia*, 27. The concept of polycentric cities, or 'constellation cities' as they are sometimes called, has also received much attention in the Far East, where planners are struggling to keep up with exponential rates of urban growth. See Liu Thai-Ker, 'From Megacity to Constellation City: Towards Sustainable Asian Cities,' in *Megacities, Labour, Communications*, ed. Toh Thian Ser (Singapore: Institute of Southeast Asian Studies, 1998), 3–26.

69 Chris Abel, *Masdar City: Blueprint for a New Urban Ecology* (London: Lars Muller, forthcoming).

70 According to a report by the Planning Institute of Australia, the loss of productive farmland to urban sprawl amounts to 89 million hectares in a single generation. A large proportion of the fresh vegetables and dairy products consumed in Australia's cities is produced on the urban fringes, so any expansion of the suburbs directly affects local food supplies. See Natasha Bita, 'Paving Devours Farmland Faster Than Foreign Buyers,' *Weekend Australian*, January 21–22, 2012. Though new approaches to integrating urban agriculture with high-density projects of the kind mentioned in Chapter 9 may help to alleviate the problem, given the present rate of loss of farmland in Australia, the only viable long-term solution, as with the transportation problem, is to control urban dispersal. In response, Queensland was the first state to introduce development laws that 'quarantine' high-value farmland; New South Wales is now mapping out similar areas for protection.

Chapter 11: Appropriating cyberspace

1 Cyberspace was first given its now familiar name in William Gibson, *Neuromancer* (New York: Ace Books, 1984).

2 William Mitchell, *City of Bits: Space, Place and the Infobahn* (Cambridge: MIT Press, 1995). While the comments in this chapter on Mitchell's interpretation of cyberspace are mostly critical, the author's aim is clearly to rethink urban development in the context of the revolutionary changes taking place under the impact of the Net. As such, if only on a lesser scale, Mitchell's work follows in the historical tradition set by Gideon's monumental effort to set modern architecture within the scientific, technological and cultural changes of his own time. Gideon, *Space, Time and Architecture*.

3 Mitchell, *City of Bits*, 8.

4 Ibid., 131.

5 *Time* editors, 'Welcome to Cyberspace,' *Time*, special issue, spring 1995.

6 J. Fleming, H. Honour and Nikolaus Pevsner, eds, *Penguin Dictionary of Architecture and Landscape Architecture* (London: Penguin Books, 5th edition, 1999), 175.

7 Mitsuo Inoue, *Space in Japanese Architecture*, trans. Hiroshi Watanabe (New York: Weatherhill, 1985).

8 Ibid., 144.

9 Mitchell, *City of Bits*, 14–15.

10 Michael Heim, 'The Erotic Ontology of Cyberspace,' in *Cyberspace: First Steps*, ed. Michael Benedikt (Cambridge: MIT Press, 1994), 59–80. See also Mark Dery, *Escape Velocity: Cyberculture at the End of the Century* (London: Hodder & Stoughton, 1996). The latter author's uncritical enthusiasm for cyborgs and speculations of potential mind–body disconnections are as much shaped by Cartesian dualism as the writings of Gibson, Mitchell and Heim are. For a more sober account of digital technologies and culture, see Nicholas Negroponte, *Being Digital: The Road Map for Survival on the Information Superhighway* (London: Hodder & Stoughton, 1995). See also Clifford A. Pickover, ed., *Visions of the Future: Art, Technology and Computing in the 21st Century* (New York: St Martin's Press, revised edition, 1994).

11 Heim, 'The Erotic Ontology,' 63–4.

12 Ibid., 73.

13 Ibid., 75.

14 Allucquere Rosanne Stone, 'Will the Real Body Please Stand Up: Boundary Stories About Virtual Cultures,' in *Cyberspace: First Steps*, 81–118.

15 Ibid., 107.

16 Ibid., 112.

17 Philip Kerr, *Gridiron* (London: Chatto & Windus, 1995).

18 Ibid., 339.

19 Ibid., 367.

20 Justin Mullins, 'Squishybots: Soft, Bendy and Smarter Than Ever,' *New Scientist*, no. 2838 (November 12, 2011): 48–51.

21 Comparing McLuhan's relatively benign view of technology's impact on humankind, Stuart Jeffries quotes Friedrich Kittler, the German philosopher, who voiced similar concerns to those of Stiegler: 'The development of the internet has more to do with human beings becoming a reflection of their technologies [...] after all, it is we who adapt to the machine. The machine does not adapt to us.' Stuart Jeffries, 'Anti-techno Baton Is Handed On,' *Guardian Weekly*, January 6, 2012. According to Jeffries, the French Philosopher Paul Virilio has now taken up the baton passed on by Kittler, forecasting even more dire outcomes of humanity's addiction to technology: 'The cult of speed and acceleration that technology has engendered, Virilio argues, will be the death of us all. His new book has been described as a reworking of the Book of Exodus: in the exodus we aren't heading to a promised land but into a technologically advanced hell that makes McLuhan look like the Pollyanna of the media age.' See Paul Virilio, *The Great Accelerator*, trans. Julie Rose (Cambridge: Polity Press, 2012).

22 Christopher Lasch, *The Culture of Narcissism: American Life in An Age of Diminishing Expectations* (New York: W. W. Norton & Company, 1978). The narcissistic aspects of the popular obsession with social networks are explored in Larry R. Rosen, *iDisorder: Understanding Our Obsession with Technology and Overcoming Its Hold on Us* (London: Palgrave Macmillan, 2012). For example, research cited by Rosen claims that 80% of 'tweets' are solely concerned with 'me,' that is, they are updates or reflections on individual

participants' personal lives and activities. Responding to the same trends, the quality and morality of the personal exchanges on Twitter, which include a substantial proportion of abusive messages, has also been questioned. See John Waters, 'Internet Is Debasing Our Public Discourse,' *Irish Times*, August 3, 2012. Commenting on the broader cultural implications, Waters writes: 'Most internet comment traffic comes into being not on the basis of the instant issue but as a means for contributors *to announce themselves to the world* [added emphasis]. And, since these announcements must take place in a highly competitive environment, there occurs an inevitable escalation in the abusiveness and venom, which contributes nothing to the discussion except heat and hatred.' Ibid.

23 Susan Greenfield, *ID: The Quest for Identity in the 21st Century* (London: Sceptre, 2008). For other critical perspectives, see Esther Dyson, *Release 2.0: A Design for Living in the Digital Age* (London: Viking, 1997). See also David Brown, *Cybertrends: Chaos, Power and Accountability in the Information Age* (London: Viking, 1997). Dyson sees both new problems of privacy and security as well as positive social possibilities arising from the Net's openness, while Brown warns of the increasing concentrations of economic power the global extension of communication networks has made possible. See also Karen Kissane, 'Europeans Face Having to Beg for Daily Bread,' *Sydney Morning Herald*, December 20, 2011. Kissane cites a study by researchers at the Swiss Federal Institute of Technology who examined the links between 43,000 transnational companies and concluded 'that just 147 tightly knit companies, mostly financial institutions, control 40 percent of the world's revenues.' By contrast, the dramatic events of the so-called 'Arab spring' in 2011 highlighted the Janus-faced character of the Net in action, in demonstrating that, depending on who its users and what their aims are, the Net is just as capable of dispersing power as it is of concentrating it.

24 Greenfield, *ID*, 147. See also Susan Greenfield, 'Virtual Worlds Are Limiting Our Brains,' *Sydney Morning Herald*, October 21, 2011. In her article, the author writes: 'Evidence of a link between spending too much time staring at computer screens and physical changes in the brain that lead to attention and behaviour problems is accumulating.' For a more general explanation by the author of how the brain works and what 'mind' means, see also Susan Greenfield, *The Human Brain: A Guided Tour* (London: Phoenix, 1997). Greenfield's concerns are supported by a report by doctors at the Royal College of Paediatrics and Child Health in the UK. See Sarah Bosely, 'Children Under 3 Should Not Watch Television, Says Study,' *Guardian*, October 9, 2012. Bosely writes that, aside from increasing future risks of obesity and heart decease, the report warns that spending too much time watching screens means less time making eye contact and communicating with parents and others, which can seriously affect developing brains, especially in the crucial first three years of childhood. In response, the doctors urge the introduction of limits to children's screen time similar to those already in place in the USA, Canada and Australia. Recently, concerns have also been voiced about the growing use of iPads and similar digital tablets by children as young as two years, who find them far easier to use in comparison with keyboard devices, a development Jobs would surely have been pleased with, though it holds out similar dangers of distracting children from other forms of play involving social interaction with other children. See Stephen Lunn, 'Toddlers, Touch Screens and the Parents' Dilemma', *Weekend Australian*, January 7–8, 2012.

25 Beeban Kidron, 'Just One More Click,' *Guardian*, September 14, 2013. Increasing evidence is being reported of the widespread addictive effects of digital technology in general, and of being tied to the Internet for long periods of time. According to *Newsweek* writer Tony Dokoupil, 'The first good peer reviewed research is emerging and the picture is much gloomier than the trumpet blasts of web utopians have allowed.' Quoted in Tracy McVeigh, 'Internet Addiction Even Worries Silicon Valley,' *Observer*, July 29, 2012. See also Brian O'Connell, 'Hooked On Tablets: The Tech "Addicts",' *Irish Times*, April 27, 2013. O'Connell writes: 'The lines between our digital and physical lives are blurring, just as the distinction between work and home is also fading […]. Psychologists and addiction counsellors are still working out to what extent "digital addictions" are addictions at all, but there is a growing consensus that some traits evident in other addictions, such as drugs and online gambling, also appear in people who admit to problematic relationships with their tablets or smartphones.'

26 Nicholas Carr, 'The Dreams of Readers,' in *Stop What You're Doing and Read This!*, eds Mark Haddon, Michael Rosen, Zadie Smith and Carmen Callil (London: Vintage Books, 2011), 151–67. See also Nicholas Carr, *The Shallows: What the Internet Is Doing to Our Brains* (New York: W. W. Norton, 2011); Gail Rebuck, 'Don't Let Technology Stultify Your Brain – Download a Book,' *Sydney Morning Herald*, January 2, 2012; John Brockman, ed., *How Is the Internet Changing the Way You Think? The Net's Impact on Our Minds and Future* (New York: Harper Perennial, 2011).

27 Quoted in Carr, 'The Dreams of Readers,' 157.

28 Ibid.

29 The dangers of the commercialized trade in personal data is exemplified in the case of the Acxiom Corporation based in Little Rock, Arkansas, which has amassed a database of 500 million consumers around the world with around 1,500 data points per person – the world's largest such commercial database. Covering everything from age, race, sex, health and other physical data to education levels, politics and buying habits, Acxiom sells its information to anyone interested, all of which is perfectly legal in the USA. Customers typically include banks, auto-makers and department stores looking for insights into their own customers so as to increase market share. However, Acxiom's data systems provide more than just individual statistics: 'It is integrating what it knows about our offline, online and even mobile selves, creating in-depth behavior portraits in pixilated detail. Its executives have called this approach a "360-degree view" on consumers.' Natasha Singer, 'Mapping the Consumer Genome: They Know and Sell All About You,' *New York Times*, July 15, 2012. The revelations in 2013 that the US National Security Agency (NSA) had been tapping into global search engines and social networks in the process of tracking and amassing information on the regular communications of millions of American and other national populations indicate an Orwellian level of government as well as commercial surveillance of citizens, raising new and grave questions about the limits of individual privacy in the age of the Internet.

30 For a history of flexible manufacturing systems (FMS), including the Molins 'System 24,' see William W. Luggen, *Flexible Manufacturing Cells and Systems* (Englewood Cliffs: Prentice Hall, 1991). For a detailed explanation of the Molins system by its inventor, see D. T. N. Williamson, 'System 24 – A New Concept of Manufacture,' *Proc of the 8th Int. M.T.D.R. Conf., University of Manchester, 12–15 September* (Oxford: Pergamon Press, 1967), 1–50. See also D. T. N. Williamson, 'New Wave in Manufacturing,' *American Machinist*, vol. 3, no. 19 (September 11, 1967): 143–54. For a more general account of computer-based innovations in manufacturing, see William L. Duncan, *Manufacturing 2000* (New York: Amaco, 1994).

31 See, for example, R. Brewer, 'Where Numerical Control Stands in Industry Today,' *New Scientist*, vol. 22, no. 397 (1964): 794–7. See also R. Iredale, 'Putting Artisans on Tape,' *New Scientist*, vol. 37, no. 584 (1968): 353–5.

32 Since direct methods of controlling the machinery from computers had not been developed at that time, this meant feeding punched tapes produced by computers into separate control mechanisms operating the CNC machines. The Molins System 24 was otherwise so far ahead of the industry and related markets that it did not prosper, thus demonstrating another of Arthur's dictums, namely that the 'best' available technology does not always succeed, due to other commercial factors. However, the principles upon which it was designed were later taken up by other firms, eventually transforming advanced industrial production across the board. See Luggen, *Flexible Manufacturing*. The Molins company itself is still operating in the UK.

33 Stafford Beer, 'Towards the Cybernetic Factory,' in *Principles of Self-organization*, 25–89.

34 Abel, 'Ditching the Dinosaur Sanctuary.' See also Chris Abel, 'Return to Craft Manufacture,' *Architects' Journal: Information Technology Supplement* (April 20, 1988): 53–7; Chris Abel, 'Birth of a Cybernetic Factory,' in *Architecture, Technology and Process*, 237–45.

35 For a comparative study of the different approaches of the two practices to the use of advanced technologies of design and production, see Chris Abel, 'Foster and Gehry: One Technology; Two Cultures,' in *Architecture, Technology and Process*, 91–162.

36 For example, Branko Kolarevic, ed., *Architecture in the Digital Age: Design and Manufacturing* (London: Taylor & Francis, 2003). See also Neil Leach, David Turnbull and Chris Williams, eds, *Digital Tectonics* (Chichester: Wiley-Academy, 2004). The following also provides a useful introduction to some of the basic techniques involved in CAD/CAM, though, despite the title, most of the examples are drawn from other industries: Nick Callicott, *Computer-aided Manufacture in Architecture: The Pursuit of Novelty* (Oxford: Architectural Press, 2001).

37 It needs to be said that any interpretation of 'improvement' in this context is entirely relative to human needs as perceived by the human breeders concerned.

38 The term 'morphogenesis' was coined by Alan Turing for the spontaneous generation of pattern and form, for which he invented a new branch of mathematics. As Ball recounts, Turing's investigations into self-similarity and pattern formation were first inspired by Thompson's work on the principle of similitude (see Chapter 7). Turing had read Thompson's *On Growth and Form* as a schoolboy and was equally fascinated by the problem of how biological form arises. However, Turing saw the problem in very different terms. For him, the key issue was how identical cells in multicellular organisms sharing the same genetic basis spontaneously evolved into more specialized cells, switching genes on and off as required, a problem he first addressed in his paper 'The Chemical Basis of Morphogenesis,' *Philosophical Transactions of the Royal Society B*, vol. 237 (1952): 37. Turing hypothesized that during an organism's development 'genes in different cells might be switched on or off by chemical agents called morphogens that diffuse through the tissues.' Ball, *Shapes*, 156. Thus different morphogens tell cells to develop in different ways – to become a leg, to produce one kind of skin pigmentation rather than another, and so on. Most important, Turing argued that the whole process might be *autocatalytic*, adding that 'to generate robust biological form, it is not enough for the morphogens to excite oscillations and travelling waves – they must introduce *stationary* patterns in space.' Ibid., 156. The calculations from his reaction–diffusion equations supported his speculations, producing persistent and discrete concentrations of morphogens with irregular shapes that he likened to the patterns on animal skins. Subsequent tests 20 years later by mathematical biologists were able to simulate the same process, which produces two kinds of basic patterns, spots and strips. More recent experiments with different chemical mixtures and refined mathematical techniques produced patterns closer to those found in real life, confirming that such patterns or 'Turing structures' as they became known, can indeed be spontaneously produced out of chemical reactions, independently of any other factors. Turing's work had a profound influence on later applications in architecture and other fields. See, for example: SHoP/Sharples Holden Pasquarelli, 'Versioning: Evolutionary Techniques in Architecture,' *Architectural Design* (September/October 2002): 3–102; and Michael Hensel, Achim Menges and Michael Weinstock, eds, *Emergence: Morphogenetic Design Strategies* (Chichester: Wiley-Academy, 2004). Steadman also discusses a wide range of approaches to the use of evolutionary computer models in design in the afterword to his revised edition of *The Evolution of Designs*.

39 See John Holland, *Hidden Order: How Adaptation Builds Complexity* (Reading: Helix Books, 1995). Generally recognized as the inventor of genetic algorithms, Holland, like his followers, leans heavily upon neo-Darwinian concepts of adaptation and fitness. However, he also strives toward a more flexible approach in which the criteria for fitness are not fixed in advance but emerge out of an interaction between 'adaptive agents' and their changing contexts. Most important, Holland's work marks a major shift from a purely formal or morphological conception of artificial types toward a rule-based or generative interpretation. See also Coveney and Highfield, *Frontiers of Complexity*.

40 Chris Wise, 'Drunk in an Orgy of Technology,' in *Emergence: Morphogenetic Design Strategies*, 54–7. See also Chris Williams, 'Design by Algorithm,' in *Digital Tectonics*, 78–85.

41 Wise, 'Drunk in an Orgy of Technology,' 56.

42 See Chris Abel, 'Virtual Evolution: A Memetic Critique of Genetic Algorithms in Design,' in *Techniques and Technologies; Transfer and Transformation. Proceedings of 4th International Conference of the Association of Architectural Schools of Australia, 2007*, eds Kirsten Orr and Sandra Kaji-O'Grady (Sydney: University of Technology, 2007). See http://epress.lib.uts.edu.au/research/bitstream/handle/2100/461/Abel_Virtual%20 Evolution.pdf?sequence=1. For examples of the new approach, see Natalio Krasnogor and Steven Gustafson, 'Toward Truly "Memetic" Memetic Algorithms: Discussion and Proof of Concepts,' in *Advances in Nature-Inspired Computation: The PPSN VII Workshops* (University of Reading, Parallel Emergent and Distributed Architectures Lab (PEDAL), 2002). See also Jim Smith, 'Coevolving Memetic Algorithms: A Review and Progress Report,' *IEEE Transactions on Systems Man and Cybernetics – Part B*, vol. 37 (2007): 6–17.

43 Wise, 'Drunk in an Orgy of Technology,' 57.

44 Xavier De Kestelier and Richard Buswell, 'Large-Scale Additive Fabrication: Freeform Construction,' in *Manufacturing the Bespoke: Making and Prototyping Architecture*, ed. Bob Sheil (Chichester: John Wiley & Sons, 2012), 248–55.

45 From personal interviews with Stefan Behling and other members of the Special Modelling Group at Foster & Partners, London, June 28, 2011. See also: Hugh Whitehead, 'Laws of Form,' in *Architecture in the Digital Age*, 82–100; Hugh Whitehead, Irene Gallou, Harsh Thapar, Giovanni Betti, and Salmaan Craig, 'Driving an Ecological Agenda with Project-Led Research,' *Architectural Design*, profile no. 24 (November/December 2011); Chris Abel, 'Foster and the Evolution of Building Technics,' *World Architecture*, no. 259 (January 2012): 27–31.

46 See Webber et al., *Explorations into Urban Structure*.

47 Chris Abel, 'Electronic Ecologies,' in *Norman Foster: Works 4*, ed. David Jenkins (London: Prestel, 2004), 12–29.

48 William J. Mitchell, *e-topia: Urban Life, Jim – But Not As We Know It* (Cambridge: MIT Press, 1999).

49 Ibid., 71–3.

50 Abel, 'Electronic Ecologies.'

51 Mitchell, *e-topia*, 68.

52 Mark Shepard, ed., *Sentient City: Ubiquitous Computing, Architecture, and the Future of Urban Space* (Cambridge: MIT Press, 2011).

53 David Jimison and Joo Youn Paek, 'Too Smart City: An Intentional Failure for the Near-Future,' in *Sentient City*, 110–27.

54 For experiments simulating the evolution of organic phenomena with cellular automata and agent-based models, upon which much of the recent work on urban simulations is based, see Holland, *Hidden Order*. For fractal theory and related developments, see James Gleick, *Chaos: Making a New Science* (London: Abacus, 1987). As Gleick recounts, fractal theory was first conceived by Benoit Mandelbrot, a mathematician working in the research section of IBM in the 1960s. Previously researching variations in commodity prices, he noticed similarities in the pattern of price changes across different scales of activity, patterns which could not be fitted into the classic bell-shaped curve and other standard analytical tools familiar to economists of the time. He went on to discover comparable patterns in other, quite different fields, including irregularities in signal strength or 'noise' in communication systems and later in coastlines – his breakthrough discovery. While the details of a coastline appear rough and random, the same patterns are repeated at different scales, the smaller being simply an identical fraction of the larger, for which Mandelbrot coined the term 'fractal.' Using the most powerful computers then available, he also pushed his theory of complex geometries to the limit, climaxing his discoveries with the now renowned 'Mandelbrot set,' a visually astonishing simulation of patterns within patterns of ever finer scales down to one millionth of the initial pattern, showing the increasing complexity of the set.

55 Michael Batty, *Cities and Complexity: Understanding Cities with Cellular Automata, Agent-Based Models and Fractals* (Cambridge: MIT Press, 2005).

56 Ibid., 469.

Postscript

1 Despite the claims of some architects and theorists to a philosophical grounding for deconstructionist architecture (see Chapter 1), there are questions as to how much the architectural movement – also described as 'deconstructivist' in its early phases – actually owes to philosophical or literary sources and how much to earlier movements in modern architecture, such as the Russian constructivists and suprematists. See Philip Johnson and Mark Wigley, *Deconstructivist Architecture* (New York: Museum of Modern Art, 1988). Given the predisposition of architects to fall back upon or reinterpret historical precedents, as discussed in this book, the latter historical sources are likely to have had the greater impact on designers. That certainly would appear to be the case with the early work of Frank Gehry and Zaha Hadid, both of whom were included in the above MOMA exhibition and book but neither of whom made any philosophical claims for their early work. Hadid's vivid paintings of her projects were also clearly inspired by the Russian movements, while Gehry paid tribute to them with an installation of his own for the 1980 exhibition 'The Avant-Garde in Russia, 1910–30,' at the Los Angeles County Museum of Art. See Mildred Friedman, ed., *Gehry Talks: Architecture and Process* (New York: Rizzoli, 1999). See also Catherine Cook, 'The Lessons of the Russian Avant-Garde,' *Architectural Design Profile: Deconstruction in Architecture* (1988): 13–15. For a critique of other related designs, see Abel, 'Visible and Invisible Complexities.'

2 Jerry H. Gill, *Deep Postmodernism: Whitehead; Wittgenstein; Merleau-Ponty and Polanyi* (New York: Humanity Books, 2010).

3 Ibid., 11.

4 Derrida, *Of Grammatology*.

5 For example, Lyotard is inspired by Paul Feyerabend's admonition that 'anything goes' in science to propagate an extreme relativism in all culture-forms. See Jean-François Lyotard, *The Postmodern Condition: A Report on Knowledge*, trans. Geoff Bennington and Brian Massumi (Manchester: Manchester University Press, 1984). However, Lyotard misinterprets what Feyerabend intended as a rhetorical inducement to encourage as many competing theories and explanations of reality as possible. For Feyerabend, the only reliable test for one theory is another, *incompatible* theory requiring different rules of evidence. Yet while Feyerabend rejects the idea of universal rules of evidence applicable to all theories, he never questions the need for empirical evidence as such, or the need to explain a given theory, new or old, in such terms that other scientists can

replicate an experiment or provide further supporting evidence – the real core of the scientific method. See Paul Feyerabend, *Against Method* (London: New Left Books, 1975). For a relevant interpretation of Feyerabend's philosophy to this book, see Chris Abel, 'The Case for Anarchy in Design Research,' in *Changing Design*, 295–302. This does not rule out irrational sources for new theories (see Chapter 9 for a discussion of metaphorical theories of innovation), but it does rule in rigorous tests of acceptance, even if the form of those tests themselves changes from time to time. However, given the psychological and cultural factors resisting change discussed in this book, it is also clear that Feyerabend overestimated most scientists' willingness to contemplate any radical alternatives that might challenge their own preferred theories.

6 Foucault, *Discipline and Punish*.

7 As quoted in Gill, *Deep Postmodernism*, 14.

8 Ibid.

9 It may be observed that, by comparison with Derrida, as writers, all the thinkers cited favorably by Gill here are models of clarity.

10 Ibid., 20.

11 Ibid.

12 To be fair, it may also be argued that Derrida's interpretation of language as the first form of 'inscription,' as understood by Stiegler and Gallope (see Chapter 4), constitutes just such a metaphysical perspective, whatever his other arguments regarding the less stable aspects of language might be. Nevertheless, in the broader scheme of things Wittgenstein's moderately relativistic grounding of language in human action and behavior provides the more satisfactory approach. Much the same applies to the linguistic relativism of Sapir and Whorf and the other forms of cultural relativism discussed in Chapter 1. For a related discussion on cultural identity and relativism in architecture, see Abel, 'The Language Analogy.'

13 Gill, *Deep Postmodernism*, 21.

14 Ibid., 28.

15 For an explanation of the atomistic school of thought in physics and its subsequent displacement by different approaches during the last century, see Fritjof Capra, *The Tao of Physics: An Exploration of the Parallels Between Modern Physics and Eastern Mysticism* (London: Fontana, 1976).

16 Gill, *Deep Postmodernism*, 29.

17 See Capra, *The Tao of Physics*.

18 Gill, *Deep Postmodernism*, 35.

19 Ludwig Wittgenstein, *Tractatus Logico-Philosophicus*, trans. C. K. Ogden and F. P. Ramsey (London: Routledge & Kegan Paul, 1922; 2nd edition, 1961).

20 Gill, *Deep Postmodernism*, 35.

21 Ludwig Wittgenstein, *Philosophical Investigations* (London: Macmillan Publishing, 3rd edition, 1958); Ludwig Wittgenstein, *The Blue and Brown Books* (New York: Harper Colophon Books, 1958). See also Gerd Brand, *The Essential Wittgenstein*, trans. Ribert E. Ennis (New York: Basic Books, 1979). For the impact of Wittgenstein's thought on the arts, see Richard Wollheim, *Art and Its Objects* (Harmondsworth: Penguin Books, 1975). For its impact on the social sciences, see Peter Winch, *The Idea of a Social Science and Its Relation to Philosophy* (London: Routledge & Kegan Paul, 1958). Winch writes that, following Wittgenstein, 'whereas the philosophies of science, of art, of history, etc., will have the task of elucidating the peculiar nature of those forms of life called "science," "art," etc., epistemology will try to elucidate what is involved in the notion of a form of life as such.' Ibid., 41.

22 According to Gill, Wittgenstein's former mentor and the leading philosopher of logical atomism of his time, Bertrand Russell, was so dismayed at the change in Wittgenstein's later approach to language that he withdrew his support.

23 Gill, *Deep Postmodernism*, 37.

24 Ibid.

25 Ibid.

26 Ibid., 38.

27 The distinction is particularly apt, given that a key issue in Derrida's approach, as clearly expressed above, as with Lyotard and other deconstructivists, is the unquestioned assumption that for language to have *any* kind of external reference automatically entails having fixed meanings. While that might well have also applied to Wittgenstein's earlier thoughts on the subject, the dynamic reciprocity between language and human activity he elaborated upon in the later works clearly implies quite the opposite, namely that changes and differences in meaning are generated out of that very interaction.

28 Quoted in Gill, *Deep Postmodernism*, 105.

29 Ibid.

30 Ibid., 106.

31 Ibid., 107.

32 Ibid., 113–14.

33 Quoted in Gill, ibid., 114–15.

34 For a full explanation, see Kuhn, *The Essential Tension*.

35 Gill, *Deep Postmodernism*, 114.

36 Quoted by Gill, ibid., 115.

37 Ibid.

38 The two works cited by Gill are J. L. Austin, *Philosophical Papers* (Oxford: Oxford University Press, 1961), and J. L. Austin, *How To Do Things With Words* (Cambridge: Harvard University Press, 1962).

39 Gill, *Deep Postmodernism*, 157.

40 Ibid., 152.

41 Quoted by Gill, ibid., 153.

42 Quoted by Gill, ibid., 156.

43 Ibid.

44 Ibid., 158.

45 Ibid., 159.

46 George Herbert Mead, *Mind, Self, and Society: From the Standpoint of a Social Behaviorist*, ed. Charles W. Morris (Chicago: University of Chicago Press, 1934). Mead's concept of rationality as a process of self-conscious communication involving 'taking the role of the other' may be compared with Kelly's theory of personal constructs. See Kelly, *A Theory of Personality*. While, in the light of what has been argued in this book, Kelly's rational characterization of 'man the scientist' now appears idealistic, in most other respects his theory is in line with the interactive approach advocated by Mead and the other thinkers in this group. For example, Kelly's 'sociality corollary' specifically states that: 'To the extent that one person construes the construction processes of another, he may play a role in a social process involving that person.' Ibid., 95. See also D. Bannister and Fay Fransella, *Inquiring Man: The Theory of Personal Constructs* (Harmondsworth: Penguin Books, 1971).

47 Bateson, *Steps to an Ecology of Mind* and also *Mind and Nature*.

48 See, for example, Herbert Blumer, *Symbolic Interactionism: Perspective and Method* (Englewood Cliffs: Prentice-Hall, 1969); Bernard N. Meltzer, John W. Petras and Larry T. Reynolds, *Symbolic Interactionism: Genesis, Varieties and Criticism* (London: Routledge & Kegan Paul, 1975).

49 For a discussion of the relevance of Mead's concept of rationality to design, see Chris Abel, 'Rationality and Meaning in Design.'

50 Mead's use of the terms 'stimulus' and 'response' should be distinguished from the use of the same terms in orthodox behaviorist psychology. As against the behaviorist school, which concerns itself only with overt acts of behavior, Mead is quite clearly using the terms in relation to mental processes and did himself point out the differences between his own 'social behaviorism' and the mechanistic behaviorism favored by John B. Watson and others. For the latter school of thought see B. F. Skinner, *About Behaviorism* (New York: Alfred A. Knopf, 1974).

51 Mead, *Mind, Self, and Society*, 47.

52 Ibid., 134.

53 While logical thought also falls within Mead's definition, rationality is clearly not restricted to it, as it is in the orthodox modern interpretation, no more than the 'game of logic' is the only language game in town, so to speak, in Wittgenstein's later philosophy of language as it was in his earlier work. Though some might argue with the strict line Mead draws between animal and human communication, much like the line once drawn between human and animal tool use, few would contest the human claim to sophisticated languages and levels of self-consciousness far exceeding those achieved by other species. Similarly, while Mead makes no explicit allowance within his concept of meaningful conversation for Polanyi's tacit forms of knowledge and expression, or for what Wittgenstein describes in terms of 'showing' rather than 'telling,' neither does Mead's philosophy necessarily exclude those processes; it simply does not stretch that far. By the same token, though Mead's thought does not acknowledge the part the human body plays in being able to identify with others the way that Merleau-Ponty's does, it also does not exclude it.

54 Blumer, *Symbolic Interactionism: Perspective and Method*.

55 Ibid., 69. See also Chris Abel, 'Architecture as Identity: The Essence of Architecture,' in *Semiotics 1980*. The closing paragraph to that essay anticipates the theory of mind advanced in this book, as pinpointed in the following key second sentence quoted in the Preface: 'Blumer, a disciple of Mead, claims that in so far as objects have meanings, then they must enter into human group consciousness much as the meanings we attach to our own behaviour and the behaviour of other persons do. A theory of mind which disperses the processes of human mentation among the group must also take into account the role of the physical environment in the evolution of mind. My own inclination is to take seriously the claim made by Pask, that "there is no such thing as an inanimate object" (in conversation with the author). That is to say, there are no objects in the human realm of being without meaning, and thus no objects that do not somehow become animate within the processes of human interaction and individuation.' Ibid., 10. See also Ronald W. Smith and Valerie Bugni, 'Symbolic Interaction Theory and Architecture,' *Symbolic Interactionism*, vol. 29, no. 2 (2012): 123–55.

56 Bateson, *Mind and Nature*, 93. Positing a 'typology of processes,' Bateson identifies two hitherto neglected types of interaction characteristic of human behavior, the 'symmetric' and the 'complementary,' or 'two great genera' as he also calls them: 'I applied the term *symmetric* to all those forms of interaction [between A and B] that could be described in terms of competition, rivalry, mutual emulation, and so on […]. In contrast, I applied the term complementary to interactional sequences in which the actions of A and B were different but mutually fitted each other (e.g., dominance–submission, exhibition–spectatorship, dependence–nurturance). I noted that these paired relationships could likewise be schismogenic (e.g., that dependency might promote nurturance, and vice versa).' Ibid., 192–3.

57 Ibid., 8.

58 Bateson, *Steps to an Ecology of Mind*, 451. One of the founders of semantics, Korzybski argued that humankind's knowledge of the world is limited by what the nervous system and language select and filter. See Alfred Korzybski, *Science and Sanity: An Introduction to Non-Aristotelian Systems and General Semantics* (Englewood: Institute of General Semantics, 5th edition, 1994).

59 Bateson, *Mind and Nature*, 190. In using the term 'logical typing,' Bateson, like many thinkers of his time, implicitly refers to the essentialist interpretation of types discussed in the penultimate section of Chapter 7. However, the range of phenomena he includes by the term suggests he attaches a much wider meaning to it than the strictly logical interpretation.

Bibliography

Abel, Chris. 'Ditching the Dinosaur Sanctuary.' *Architectural Design*, vol. 38 (August 1969): 419–24.

— 'Urban Chaos or Self-organization.' *Architectural Design*, vol. 39 (September 1969): 501–2.

— 'Instructional Simulation of Client Construct Systems.' Paper presented at the 1975 Architectural Psychology Conference, University of Sheffield.

— 'The Language Analogy in Architectural Theory and Criticism: Some Remarks in the Light of Wittgenstein's Linguistic Relativism.' *Architectural Association Quarterly*, vol. 12, no. 3 (1979): 39–47.

— 'Rationality and Meaning in Design.' *Design Studies*, vol. 1, no. 2 (October 1979): 69–76.

— 'Vico and Herder: The Origins of Methodological Pluralism.' In *Design: Science: Method. Proceedings of the 1980 Design Research Society Conference, Portsmouth, December 14–16*, edited by Robin Jacques and James A. Powell, 51–61. Guildford: Westbury House, 1981.

— 'Function of Tacit Knowing in Learning Design.' *Design Studies*, vol. 2, no. 4 (October 1981): 209–14.

— 'Architecture as Identity: The Essence of Architecture.' In *Semiotics 1980: Proceedings of the 5th Annual Meeting of the Semiotic Society of America, Lubbock, Texas, October 16–19*, edited by Michael Herzfeld and Margot D. Lenhart, 1–11. New York: Plenum, 1982.

— 'Role of Metaphor in Changing Architectural Concepts.' In *Changing Design*, edited by Barrie Evans, James Powell and Reg Talbot, 325–43. Chichester: John Wiley & Sons, 1982.

— 'The Case for Anarchy in Design Research.' In *Changing Design*, edited by Barrie Evans, James Powell and Reg Talbot, 295–302. Chichester: John Wiley & Sons, 1982.

— 'Living in a Hybrid World: Built Sources of Malaysian Identity.' In *Design and Society*. Proceedings of the Design and Society section of the International Conference on Design Policy, London, 1982, edited by Richard Langdon and Nigel Cross, 11–21. London: Design Council, 1984.

— 'Larsen's Hybrid Masterpiece.' *Architectural Review*, vol. 178, no. 1061 (July 1985): 30–9.

— 'A Building for the Pacific Century.' *Architectural Review*, vol. 179, no. 1070 (July 1986): 55–61.

— 'Return to Craft Manufacture.' *Architects' Journal: Information Technology Supplement* (April 20, 1988): 53–7.

— 'Visible and Invisible Complexities.' *Architectural Review*, vol. 199, no. 1188 (February 1996): 76–83.

— *Architecture and Identity*. Oxford: Architectural Press, 1997; 2nd edition, 2000.

— 'Tradition, Innovation and Linked Solutions.' In *Architecture and Identity* (Oxford: Architectural press, 1997; 2nd edition, 2000), 135–41.

— 'Technology and Process.' In *Design Professionals and the Built Environment*, edited by Paul Knox and Peter Ozolins, 313–31. Chichester: Wiley, 2000.

— *Sky High: Vertical Architecture*. London: Royal Academy of Arts, 2003.

— *Architecture, Technology and Process*. Oxford: Architectural Press, 2004.

— 'Foster and Gehry: One Technology; Two Cultures.' In *Architecture, Technology and Process*, 91–162. Oxford: Architectural Press, 2004.

— 'Birth of a Cybernetic Factory.' In *Architecture, Technology and Process*, 237–45. Oxford: Architectural Press, 2004.

— 'Electronic Ecologies.' In *Norman Foster: Works 4*, edited by David Jenkins, 12– 29. London: Prestel, 2004.

— 'Too Little, Too Late? The Fatal Attractions of "Feel Good" Architecture.' *Architectural Review Australia*, no. 092 (August/September 2005): 78–81.

— 'Riparian Plaza, Brisbane: Harry Seidler.' *Architectural Review Australia*, no. 097 (May 2006): 52–63.

— 'A Fragile Habitation: Coming to Terms with the Australian Landscape.' *Architecture and Urbanism*, no. 442 (August 2007): 66–73.

— 'Virtual Evolution: A Memetic Critique of Genetic Algorithms in Design.' In *Techniques & Technologies: Transfer and Transformation. Proceedings of the 4th International Conference of the Association of Architectural Schools of Australia, 2007*, edited by Kirsten Orr and Sandra Kaji-O'Grady. Sydney: University of Technology, 2007. http://epress.lib.uts.edu.au/research/bitstream/handle/2100/461/Abel_Virtual%20 Evolution.pdf?sequence=1 (accessed May 2014).

— 'High-Rise and Genius Loci.' In *Norman Foster: Works 5*, edited by David Jenkins, 430–1. London: Prestel, 2009.

— 'Death of the Great Australian Dream.' *Architectural Review Australia*, no. 109 (April/May 2009): 137–8.

— 'The Vertical Garden City: Towards a New Urban Topology.' *International Journal on Tall Buildings and Urban Habitat*, no. 2 (2010): 20–30.

— 'Foster and the Evolution of Building Technics.' *World Architecture*, no. 259 (January 2012): 27–31.

— 'The Extended Self: Tacit Knowing and Place-Identity.' In *Rethinking Aesthetics: The Role of Body in Design*, edited by Ritu Bhatt, 100–39. New York: Routledge, 2013.

— *Masdar City: Blueprint for a New Urban Ecology*. London: Lars Muller, forthcoming.

Agamben, Giorgio. *Homo Sacer: Sovereign Power and Bare Life*. Stanford: Stanford University Press, 1998.

Allport, Gordon W. *The Nature of Prejudice*. Reading: Addison-Wesley, 25th anniversary edition, 1979.

Appleyard, Donald. 'Home.' *Architectural Association Quarterly*, vol. 11, no. 3 (1979): 4–20.

Arthur, W. Brian. *The Nature of Technology: What It Is and How It Evolves*. London: Allen Lane, 2010.

Asfour, Khaled. 'Cairene Traditions Inside Palladian Villas.' *Traditional Dwellings and Settlements Review*, vol. 4, no. 11 (spring 1993): 39–50.

Aunger, Robert, editor. *Darwinizing Culture: The Status of Memetics as a Science*. Oxford: Oxford University Press, 2000.

— *The Electric Meme: A New Theory of How We Think*. New York: Free Press, 2002.

Austin, J. L. *Philosophical Papers*. Oxford: Oxford University Press, 1961.

— *How To Do Things With Words*. Cambridge: Harvard University Press, 1962.

Australian Rail Association, *The True Value of Rail*. Canberra, ARA, 2011.

Ball, Philip. *Nature's Patterns: A Tapestry in Three Parts. Vol. 1, Shapes*. Oxford: Oxford University Press, 2009.

Bannister, D., and Fay Fransella. *Inquiring Man: The Theory of Personal Constructs*. Harmondsworth: Penguin Books, 1971.

Barbour, Ian G. *Myths, Models and Paradigms*. London: Harper & Row, 1974.

Barrett, William. *Irrational Man: A Study in Existential Philosophy*. New York: Doubleday Anchor Books, 1962.

Basalla, G. *The Evolution of Technology*. Cambridge: Cambridge University Press, 1988.

Batchelor, Ray. *Henry Ford: Mass Production, Modernism and Design*. Manchester: Manchester University Press, 1994.

Bateson, Gregory. *Steps to an Ecology of Mind*. New York: Ballantine Books, 1972.

— *Mind and Nature: A Necessary Unity*. New York: E. P. Dutton, 1979.

Battersby, Stephen. 'Running Wild.' *New Scientist*, vol. 215, no. 2872 (July 7, 2012): 32–7.

Batty, Michael. *Cities and Complexity: Understanding Cities with Cellular Automata, Agent-Based Models, and Fractals*. Cambridge: MIT Press, 2005.

Beamish, Jane, and Jane Ferguson. *A History of Singapore Architecture: The Making of a City*. Singapore: Graham Brash, 1985.

Beardsworth, Richard. 'From a Genealogy of Matter to a Politics of Memory: Stiegler's Thinking of Technics.' *Tekhnema 2* (spring 1995): 22. http://tekhnema.free.fr/2Beardsworth.htmAnchor1bis (accessed May 2009).

Beck, Benjamin B. *Animal Tool Behavior: The Use and Manufacture of Tools by Animals*. New York: Taylor & Francis, 1980.

Beer, Stafford. 'Towards the Cybernetic Factory.' In *Principles of Self-organization*, edited by Heinz Von Foerster and George W. Zopf, 25–89. London: Pergamon Press, 1962.

Berlin, Isiah. *Vico and Herder*. New York: Random House, 1976.

Berners-Lee, Mike, and Duncan Clark. *The Burning Question*. London: Profile Books, 2013.

Beynus, Janine M. *Biomimicry: Innovation Inspired by Nature*. New York: Harper Perennial, 2002.

Bhabha, Homi K. *Nation and Narration*. London: Routledge, 1990.

Blackmore, Susan. *The Meme Machine*. Oxford: Oxford University Press, 1999.

— *Consciousness: A Very Short Introduction*. Oxford: Oxford University Press, 2005.

Blakeslee, Sandra, and Matthew Blakeslee. *The Body Has a Mind of Its Own*. New York: Random House, 2007.

Blaser, Werner. *Furniture as Architecture: From Antiquity to the Present*, translated by D. Q. Stephenson. Zurich: Waser Verlag, 1985.

Bloomer, Kent, and Charles Moore. *Body, Memory and Architecture*. New Haven: Yale University Press, 1977.

Blumer, Herbert. *Symbolic Interactionism: Perspective and Method*. Englewood Cliffs: Prentice-Hall, 1969.

Bonanno, Anthony. *Malta: An Archaeological Paradise*. Valletta: M. J. Publications, 1997.

Boulding, Kenneth. *The Image: Knowledge in Life and Society*. Ann Arbor: University of Michigan Press, 1956.

Boyd, Robin. *Australia's Home*. Harmondsworth: Penguin Books, 1978.

— *The Australian Ugliness*. Melbourne: Text Publishing Co., 50th anniversary edition, 2010. First published Melbourne: F. W. Cheshire, 1960.

Brand, Gerd. *The Essential Wittgenstein*, translated by Robert E. Ennis. New York: Basic Books, 1979.

Brandon, Ruth. *Auto Mobile: How the Car Changed Life*. London: Macmillan, 2002.

Brewer, R. 'Where Numerical Control Stands in Industry Today.' *New Scientist*, vol. 22, no. 397 (1964): 794–7.

Broadbent, Geoffrey, Richard Bunt and Charles Jencks, editors. *Signs, Symbols and Architecture*. Chichester: John Wiley & Sons, 1980.

—, Richard Bunt and Tomas Llorens, editors. *Meaning and Behaviour in the Built Environment*. Chichester: John Wiley & Sons, 1980.

Brockman, John, editor. *How Is the Internet Changing the Way You Think? The Net's Impact on Our Minds and Future*. New York: Harper Perennial, 2011.

Brodie, Richard. *Virus of the Mind: The New Science of the Meme*. Carlsbad: Hay House, 1996.

Brodsky, Joyce. 'Continuity and Discontinuity in Style: A Problem in Art Historical Methodology.' *Journal of Aesthetics and Art Criticism*, vol. 39, no. 1 (1980): 28–37.

Brown, David. *Cybertrends: Chaos, Power and Accountability in the Information Age*. London: Viking, 1997.

Brown, Donald E. *Human Universals*. New York: McGraw-Hill, 1991.

Buchanan, Peter. 'Space Syntax and Urban Design.' In *Norman Foster: Works 3*, edited by David Jenkins, 178–87. London: Prestel, 2007.

Butler, Graeme. *The California Bungalow in Australia: Origins; Revival; Source Ideas for Restoration*. Port Melbourne: Lothian Books, 1992.

Butler, Judith. *Gender Trouble: Feminism and the Subversion of Identity*. New York: Routledge, 1990.

— *Bodies That Matter*. New York: Routledge, 1993.

Callicott, Nick. *Computer-Aided Manufacture in Architecture: The Pursuit of Novelty*. Oxford: Architectural Press, 2001.

Campa, Arthur L. *Hispanic Culture in the Southwest*. Norman: University of Oklahoma Press, 1979.

Canter, David. *The Psychology of Place*. New York: St Martin's Press, 1977.

Capra, Fritjof. *The Tao of Physics: An Exploration of the Parallels Between Modern Physics and Eastern Mysticism*. London: Fontana, 1976.

— *The Web of Life: A New Synthesis of Mind and Matter*. London: Harper Collins, 1996.

Caroll, John B., editor. *Language, Thought and Reality: Selected Writings of Benjamin Lee Whorf*. Cambridge: MIT Press, 1956.

Carr, Nicholas. 'The Dreams of Readers.' In *Stop What You're Doing and Read This!* Edited by Mark Haddon, Michael Rosen, Zadie Smith and Carmen Callil, 151–67. London: Vintage Books, 2011.

— *The Shallows: What the Internet Is Doing to Our Brains*. New York: W. W. Norton, 2011.

Casey, Edward S. *The Fate of Place: A Philosophical History*. Berkeley: University of California Press, 1998.

Cassirer, Ernst. *An Essay on Man*. New Haven: Yale University Press, 1944.

Castells, Manuel. *The Rise of the Network Society. Vol. I. The Information Age: Economy, Society and Culture*. Oxford: Blackwell, 1996.

Cervero, Robert. *The Transit Metropolis: A Global Enquiry*. Washington, DC: Island Press, 1998.

Chapman, Giles. *SUV: The World's Greatest Sports Utility Vehicles*. London: Merrell, 2005.

Choay, François. 'Urbanism and Semiology.' In *Meaning in Architecture*, edited by Charles Jencks and George Baird, 27–37. New York: George Braziller, 1969.

Chomsky, Noam. *The Minimalist Program*. Cambridge: MIT Press, 1995.

Clark, Andy, *Supersizing the Mind: Embodiment, Action, and Cognitive Extension*. Oxford: Oxford University Press, 2011.

— and David Chalmers. 'The Extended Mind.' *Analysis*, no. 58 (1998), 10–23.

Clay, Grady. *Close-Up: How to Read the American City*. London: Pall Mall Press, 1973.

Climate Commission. *Off the Charts: Extreme Australian Summer Heat*. Canberra: Climate Commission, 2013.

Coghlan, Andy. 'Octopuses Use Coconut Shells as Portable Shelters.' *New Scientist* (December 19, 2009): 9.

— 'Mega-risks That Could Drive Us To Extinction,' *New Scientist* (November 26, 2012). www.newscientist. com/article/dn22534-megarisks-that-could- drive-us-to-extinction.html

Collins, Peter. *Changing Ideals in Modern Architecture, 1750–1950.* London: Faber & Faber, 1965.

Condit, Carl W. *The Chicago School of Architecture: A History of Commercial and Public Buildings in the Chicago Area, 1875–1925.* Chicago: University of Chicago Press, 1964.

Cook, Catherine. 'The Lessons of the Russian Avant-Garde.' *Architectural Design Profile: Deconstruction in Architecture* (1988): 13–15.

Cook, Peter. *Evolution Versus Intelligent Design: Why All the Fuss?* Sydney: New Holland, 2006.

Cooper, Clare. 'The House as Symbol of the Self.' In *Designing for Human Behaviour: Architecture and the Behavioural Sciences,* edited by Jon Lang, Charles Burnette, Walter Moleski and David Vachon, 130–46. Stroudsburg: Dowden, Hutchinson & Ross, 1974.

Coplestone, Frederick, *A History of Philosophy: Vol. 1, Greece and Rome, Part 1.* New York: Image Books, 1962.

Coveney, Peter, and Roger Highfield. *Frontiers of Complexity: The Search for Order in a Chaotic World.* London: Faber & Faber, 1995.

Cowburn, William, 'Popular Housing.' *Architectural Association Journal* (September/October 1966): 76–81.

Coyne, Jerry A. *Why Evolution Is True.* Oxford: Oxford University Press, 2009.

Crawford, Ashley, and Ray Edgar. *Spray: The Work of Howard Arkley.* Sydney: Craftsman House, 1997.

Cresswell, Tim. *Place: A Short Introduction.* Oxford: Blackwell, 2004.

Cruickshank, Dan, editor. *Sir Bannister Fletcher's A History of Architecture.* Oxford: Architectural Press, 20th edition, 1996.

Culick, Walter. 'Polanyi's Epistemology in the Light of Neuroscience.' *Tradition and Discovery: The Polanyi Society Periodical,* vol. 36, no. 2 (2010): 73–82.

Current, William R., and Karen Current. *Greene & Greene: Architects in the Residential Style.* New York: Morgan & Morgan, 1977.

Cuthbert, Alexander, R. *Designing Cities: Critical Readings in Urban Design.* Oxford: Blackwell, 2003.

— *The Form of Cities: Political Economy and Urban Design.* Oxford: Blackwell, 2006.

— *Understanding Cities: Method in Urban Design.* Abingdon: Routledge, 2011.

Cuvier, Baron Georges. *Leçons d'Anatomie Comparée.* 5 vols. Paris, 1805.

Daly, C. B. 'Polanyi and Wittgenstein.' In *Intellect and Hope: Essays in the Thought of Michael Polanyi,* edited by Thomas Langford and William Poteat, 136–68. Durham: Duke University Press, 1968.

Darwin, Charles. *On the Origin of Species: A Facsimile of the First Edition.* New York: Antheum, 1972; 1st edition 1859.

Davidson, Iain, and William Noble. 'Tools and Language in Human Evolution.' In *Tools, Language and Cognition in Human Evolution,* edited by Kathleen R. Gibson and Tim Ingold, 363–88. Cambridge: Cambridge University Press, 1993.

Davies, Colin, and Ian Lambot. *Commerzbank Frankfurt: Prototype for an Ecological High-Rise.* Basel and Haslmere: Birkauser and Watermark, 1997.

Davies, Hugh Sykes. 'Division on the Brain.' *Listener,* October 9, 1975: 468–9.

Davis, Tony. *Wide Open Road: The Story of Cars in Australia.* Sydney: ABC Books/HarperCollins, 2011.

Dawkins, Richard. *The Selfish Gene.* Oxford: Oxford University Press, 2nd edition, 1989.

— *The Extended Phenotype: The Long Reach of the Gene.* Oxford: Oxford University Press, 1982, revised edition 1999.

DeGeorge, Richard, and Fernande, DeGeorge, editors. *The Structuralists: From Marx to Lévi-Strauss.* Garden City: Anchor Books, 1972.

De Kestelier, Xavier, and Richard Buswell. 'Large-Scale Additive Fabrication: Freeform Construction.' In *Manufacturing the Bespoke: Making and Prototyping Architecture,* edited by Bob Sheil, 248–55. Chichester: John Wiley & Sons, 2012.

De Landa, Manuel. *A Thousand Years of Nonlinear History.* New York: Swerve Editions, 2000.

— *A New Philosophy of Society: Assemblage Theory and Social Complexity.* London: Continuum, 2006.

Deleuze, Gilles, and Félix Guattari. *A Thousand Plateaus.* Minneapolis: University of Minnesota Press, 1987.

de Lumley, Henry. 'The Emergence of Symbolic Thought: The Principal Steps of Hominisation Leading Towards Greater Complexity.' In *Becoming Human: Innovation in Prehistorical Material and Spiritual Culture,* edited by Colin Renfrew and Iain Morley, 10–26. Cambridge: Cambridge University Press, 2009.

Dennett, Daniel C. *Consciousness Explained.* London: Penguin Books, 1991.

— *Darwin's Dangerous Idea: Evolution and the Meanings of Life.* London: Penguin Books, 1995.

— *Freedom Evolves.* London: Penguin Books, 2003.

Derrida, Jacques. *Of Grammatology*, translated by Gayatri Spivac. Baltimore: Johns Hopkins University Press, 1974.

Dery, Mark. *Escape Velocity: Cyberculture at the End of the Century*. London: Hodder & Stoughton, 1996.

De Syllas, Justin. 'Streamform: Images of Speed and Greed from the Thirties.' *Architectural Association Quarterly*, vol. 1, no. 2 (April 1969): 32–41.

Detheir, Jean, editor. *Des Architectures de Terre: Ou L'Avenir D'Une Tradition Millenaire*. Paris: Centre Georges Pompidou, 1982.

de Waal, Frans. *Primates and Philosophers: How Morality Evolved*. Princeton: Princeton University Press, 2006.

Diamond, Jared. *The Rise and Fall of the Third Chimpanzee: How Our Animal Heritage Affects the Way We Live*. London: Vintage Books, 1991.

— *Collapse: How Societies Choose to Fail or Survive*. London: Allen Lane, 2005.

Distin, Kate. *The Selfish Meme*. Cambridge: Cambridge University Press, 2005.

Dodds, George, and Robert Tavernor, editors. *Body and Building: Essays on the Changing Relation of Body and Architecture*. Cambridge: MIT Press, 2005.

Dodson, Jago, and Neil Sipe. *Shocking the Suburbs: Oil Vulnerability in the Australian City*. Sydney: University of New South Wales Press, 2008.

Douglas, Kate. 'Making Your Mind Up.' *New Scientist*, vol. 212, no. 2838 (November 12, 2011): 39–41.

Dovey, Kim. *Framing Places: Mediating Power in Built Form*. London: Routledge, 1999.

Downs, Robert, and David Stea. *Maps in Minds*. London: Harper & Row, 1977.

Dozier, Edward P. *The Pueblo Indians of North America*. New York: Holt, Rinehart & Winston, 1970.

Drew, Philip. *Leaves of Iron: Glenn Murcutt, Pioneer of an Australian Architectural Form*. Pymble: Angus & Robertson, 1985.

Drexler, Arthur. *Charles Eames: Furniture from the Design Collection, the Museum of Modern Art, New York*. New York: MOMA, 1973.

Duany, Andres, Elizabeth Plater-Zyberk and Jeff Speck. *Suburban Nation: The Rise of Sprawl and the Decline of the American Dream*. New York: North Point Press, 2000.

Duffy, Francis. *The New Office*. London: Conran Octopus, 1997.

—, Andrew Laing and Vic Crisp. *The Responsible Workplace: The Redesign of Work and Offices*. Oxford: Butterworth Architecture, 1993.

Dumarcay, Jacques. *The House in South-Asia*. Singapore: Oxford University Press, 1987.

Duncan, William L. *Manufacturing 2000*. New York: Amacom, 1994.

Dunham-Jones, Ellen, and June Williamson. *Retrofitting Suburbia: Urban Design Solutions for Redesigning Suburbs*. Hoboken: Wiley, updated edition, 2011.

Durand, Jean-Nicolas-Louis. *Nouveau Précis des Leçons d'Architecture* (2 vols). Paris: Fantin, 1813.

Durham, William. *Coevolution: Genes, Culture, and Human Diversity*. Stanford: Stanford University Press, 1991.

Dyer, Gwynne. *Climate Wars*. Melbourne: Scribe, 2008.

Dyson, Esther. *Release 2.0: A Design for Living in the Digital Age*. London: Viking, 1997.

Eco, Umberto. 'Function and Sign: The Semiotics of Architecture.' In *Signs, Symbols and Architecture*, edited by Geoffrey Broadbent, Richard Bunt and Charles Jencks, 11–69. Chichester: John Wiley & Sons, 1980.

Ehrmann, Jacques, editor. *Structuralism*. Garden City: Anchor Books, 1970.

Emmet, Dorothy. *Rules, Roles and Relations*. Boston: Beacon, 1966.

Emmott, Stephen. *Ten Billion*. London: Penguin, 2013.

Emrick, Michael. 'Vanishing Kuala Lumpur: The Shophouse.' *Majallah Akitek* (June 1976): 29–36.

Festa-McCormick, Diana. *The City as Catalyst*. London: Associated University Presses, 1979.

Festinger, Leon. *A Theory of Cognitive Dissonance*. Stanford: Stanford University Press, 1957.

Feyerabend, Paul. *Against Method*. London: New Left Books, 1975.

Fine, Cordelia. *A Mind of Its Own: How Your Brain Distorts and Deceives*. Cambridge: Icon Books, 2006.

Flannery, Tim. *The Future Eaters*. Sydney: Reed New Holland, 1994.

— *The Weather Makers: The History and Future Impact of Climate Change*. Melbourne: Text Publishing, 2005.

Flavell, J. *The Developmental Psychology of Jean Piaget*. New York: Van Nostrand Reinhold, 1963.

Flood, Josephine. 'Linkage Between Rock-Art and Landscape in Aboriginal Australia.' In *The Figured Landscapes of Rock-Art: Looking at Pictures in Place*, edited by Christopher Chippendale and George Nash, 182–200. Cambridge: Cambridge University Press, 2004.

Fodor, Jerry, and Massimo Piattelli-Palmarini. *What Darwin Got Wrong*. London: Profile Books, 2010.

Ford, Barbara, and Janet D'Amato. *Animals That Use Tools*. New York: Julian Messner, 1978.

Forster, Clive. *Australian Cities: Continuity and Change*. Melbourne: Oxford University Press, 2nd edition, 1999.

Bibliography

Forty, Adrian. 'Wireless Style: Symbolic Design and the English Radio Cabinet, 1928–1933.' *Architectural Association Quarterly*, vol. 4, no. 2 (April/June 1972): 23–31.

Foucault, Michel. *Discipline and Punish: The Birth of the Prison*, translated by A. Sheridan. Harmondsworth: Penguin, 1982.

Frampton, Kenneth. 'Modern Architecture: 1851–1919.' *GA Document*, special issue 2 (September 1981): 1–211.

— *Modern Architecture: A Critical History*. London: Thames & Hudson, 3rd edition, 1992.

Fraser, Douglas. *Village Planning in the Primitive World*. London: Studio Vista/George Braziller, 1967.

Friedman, Mildred, editor. *Gehry Talks: Architecture and Process*. New York: Rizzoli, 1999.

Fromonot, Françoise. *Glenn Murcutt: Works and Projects*. London: Thames & Hudson, 1995.

Gallope, Michael. 'Heidegger, Stiegler, and the Question of a Musical Technics.' Draft paper for the conference Music and Consciousness, University of Sheffield, 2006.

Gans, Herbert. *The Levittowners*. New York: Pantheon Books, 1967.

Garnaut, Ross. *Garnaut Climate Change Review: Interim Report to the Commonwealth, State and Territories Governments of Australia*. Canberra: Commonwealth of Australia, February 2008.

— *Garnaut Climate Change Review Update 2011*. Canberra: Commonwealth of Australia, 2011.

— Update paper no. 5, *The Science of Climate Change*, 10 March, 2011. www.garnautreview.org.au/update-2011/update-papers/up5-the-science-of-climate-change.html (accessed March 2011).

Gazzaniga, Michael, *The Bisected Brain*. New York: Appleton-Century-Crofts, 1970.

Gebhard, David. 'The Moderne in the U.S.: 1920–1941.' *Architectural Association Quarterly*, vol. 2, no. 3 (July 1970): 4–20.

Gibson, William. *Neuromancer*. New York: Ace Books, 1984.

Giedion, Sigfried. *Space, Time and Architecture: The Growth of a New Tradition*. Cambridge: Harvard University Press, 3rd edition, 1954.

Gilding, Paul. *The Great Disruption: How the Climate Crisis Will Transform the Global Economy*. London: Bloomsbury, 2011.

Gill, Jerry H. *Deep Postmodernism: Whitehead, Wittgenstein, Merleau-Ponty, and Polanyi*. New York: Humanity Books, 2010.

Gille, Betrand. *Histoire des Techniques*. Paris: Gallimard, 1978.

Girouard, Mark. 'Neo-classicism: From the Revolutionary to the Fancy Dress.' *Architectural Review*, vol. 152, no. 907 (September 1972): 168–75.

Gleick, James. *Chaos: Making a New Science*. London: Abacus, 1987.

Goodall, Jane. *The Chimpanzees of Gombe: Patterns of Behavior*. Boston: Harvard University Press, 1986.

— with Philip Berman. *Reason for Hope: A Spiritual Journey*. New York: Warner Books, 1999.

Gould, Stephen Jay, and Richard Lewontin. 'The Spandrels of San Marco and the Panglossian Paradigm: A Critique of the Adaptationist Programme.' *Proceedings of the Royal Society of London; Series B, Biological Sciences*, vol. 205 (1979): 581–98.

Greenfield, Susan. *The Human Brain: A Guided Tour*. London: Phoenix, 1997.

— *ID: The Quest for Identity in the 21st Century*. London: Sceptre, 2008.

Gregotti, Vittorio. 'Epilogue. Joseph Rykwert: An Anthropologist of History?' In *Body and Building: Essays on the Changing Relation of Body and Architecture*, edited by George Dodds and Robert Tavernor, 320–4. Cambridge: MIT Press, 2005.

Grene, Marjorie. 'Tacit Knowing and the Pre-reflective Cogito.' In *Intellect and Hope: Essays in the Thought of Michael Polanyi*, edited by Thomas Langford and William Poteat, 19–57. Durham: Duke University Press, 1968.

Grescoe, Taras. *Straphanger: Saving Our Cities and Ourselves from the Automobile*. New York: Times Books, 2012.

Guidoni, Enrico. *Primitive Architecture*. London: Faber/Electa, 1987.

Gurstein, Penny. 'Traditional Chinese Shophouses of Peninsula Malaysia.' *UIA International Architect*, no. 6 (1984): 22–3.

Haidt, Jonathan. *The Righteous Mind: Why Good People Are Divided by Politics and Religion*. New York: Pantheon Books, 2012.

Hall, Arthur D. *A Methodology for Systems Engineering*. Princeton: D. Van Nostrand, 1962.

Hall, Edward T. *The Silent Language*. New York: Anchor Books, 1973; 1st hard cover edition, Doubleday, 1959.

— *The Hidden Dimension*. New York: Anchor Books, 1969.

— *Beyond Culture*. New York: Anchor Books, 1977.

Hamilton, Clive. *Scorcher: The Dirty Politics of Climate Change*. Melbourne: Black Inc. Agenda, 2007.

— *Requiem for a Species: Why We Resist the Truth About Climate Change*. Crows Nest: Allen & Unwin, 2010.

Hamilton, W. D. 'The Genetical Evolution of Social Behaviour' [parts I and II]. *Journal of Theoretical Biology*, no. 7 (1964): 1–16; 17–52.

Harding, L. 'Rouse Hill Town Centre.' *Architecture Australia*, vol. 97, no. 4 (May–June 2008): 97–109.

Harré, Rom. 'Some Remarks on "Rule" as a Scientific Concept.' In *Understanding Other Persons*, edited by Theodore Mischel, 143–84. Oxford: Basil Blackwell, 1974.

Hauser, Marc D. *The Evolution of Communication*. Cambridge: MIT Press, 1997.

Head, Sir Henry. *Studies in Neurology, in Conjunction with H. R. Rivers (and Others)*. London: H. Frowde, Hodder & Stoughton, 1920.

Heidegger, Martin. *Poetry, Language, Thought*. New York: Harper Colophon Books, 1971.

— *The Question Concerning Technology and Other Essays*, translated by William Lovitt. New York: Harper & Row, 1977.

Heim, Michael. 'The Erotic Ontology of Cyberspace.' In *Cyberspace: First Steps*, edited by Michael Benedikt, 59–80. Cambridge: MIT Press, 1994.

Hensel, Michael, Achim Menges and Michael Weinstock, editors. *Emergence: Morphogenetic Design Strategies*. Chichester: Wiley-Academy, 2004.

Herbert, Gilbert. *The Dream of the Factory-Made House: Walter Gropius and Konrad Wachsmann*. Cambridge: MIT Press, 1984.

Heskett, John. *Industrial Design*. New York: Oxford University Press, 1980.

Hillier, Bill. *Space Syntax: A Different Urban Perspective*. London: Architectural Press, 1983.

— *Space Is the Machine: A Configurational Theory of Architecture*. Cambridge: Cambridge University Press, 1999.

Holl, Steven, Juhani Pallasmaa and Alberto Perez-Gomez. *Questions of Perception: Phenomenology of Architecture*. San Francisco: William Stout, 2006.

Holland, John. *Hidden Order: How Adaptation Builds Complexity*. Reading: Helix Books, 1995.

Hubbard, Phil, Rob Kitchen and Gill Valentine, editors, *Key Thinkers on Space and Place*. London: Sage Publications, 2004.

Hubka, Valdimir, and W. Ernst Eder. 'A Scientific Approach to Engineering Design.' *Design Studies*, vol. 8, no. 3 (July 1987): 123–37.

Hughes, Leslie, and Will Steffen. *Be Prepared: Climate Change and the Australian Bushfire Threat*. Sydney: Climate Council of Australia, 2013. www.dropbox.com/s/zxzcyxkucnqt3o0/cc.bushfire.report.web.pdf (accessed December 2013).

Huxtable, Ada Louise. *The Tall Building Artistically Reconsidered: The Search for a Skyscraper Style*. New York: Pantheon Books, 1982.

Hyland, Adrian. *Kinglake-350*. Melbourne: Text Publishing, 2011.

Indyk, Ivor. 'Robin Boyd and the Australian Suburb.' *UIA International Architect*, issue 4 (1984): 58.

Ingold, Tim. 'Epilogue. Technology, Language Intelligence: A Reconsideration of Basic Concepts.' In *Tools, Language and Cognition in Human Evolution*, edited by Kathleen R. Gibson and Tim Ingold, 449–72. Cambridge: Cambridge University Press, 1993.

Inoue, Mitsuo. *Space in Japanese Architecture*, translated by Hiroshi Watanabe. Tokyo: Weatherhill, 1985.

Intergovernmental Panel on Climate Change. *Fifth Assessment Report* (AR5) (IPCC, September 27, 2013). www.ipcc.ch/report/ar5/wg1 (accessed September 2013).

International Energy Agency. *Tracking Clean Energy Progress 2013*. www.iea.org/newsroomandevents/pressreleases/2013/april/name,36789,en.html.

Iredale, R. 'Putting Artisans on Tape.' *New Scientist*, vol. 37, no. 584 (1968): 353–5.

Jablonka, Eva, and Marion Lamb. *Evolution in Four Dimensions: Genetic, Epigenetic, Behavioral and Symbolic Variation in the History of Life*. Cambridge: MIT Press, 2005.

Jencks, Charles. *The Daydream Houses of Los Angeles*. New York: Rizzoli, 1978.

— *The Architecture of the Jumping Universe*. London: Academy Editions, 1995.

Jencks, Charles, and George Baird, editors. *Meaning in Architecture*. New York: George Braziller, 1969.

Jenks, Mike, Elizabeth Burton and Katie Williams, editors. *The Compact City: A Sustainable Urban Form?* London: Spon Press, 1996.

Johannsen, Wilhelm Ludwig. 'The Genotype Conception of Heredity.' *American Naturalist*, no. 45 (1911): 129–59.

Jimison, David, and Joo Youn Paek. 'Too Smart City: An Intentional Failure for the Near-Future.' In *Sentient City: Ubiquitous Computing, Architecture, and the Future of Urban Space*, edited by Mark Shepard, 110–27. Cambridge: MIT Press, 2011.

Johnson, Philip, and Mark Wigley. *Deconstructivist Architecture*. New York: Museum of Modern Architecture, 1988.

Jones, Peter Blundell. 'The Sustaining Ritual.' *Architectural Review*, vol. 187, no. 1125 (November 1990): 93–5.

Jones, Richard Francis, Lawrence Nield, Xing Ruan and Deborah van der Plaat, editors. *Skyplane*. Sydney: University of New South Wales Press, 2009.

Joyce, James. *Ulysses: The 1922 Text*. Oxford: Oxford World's Classics, 2008.

Jung, Carl. *Memories, Dreams and Reflections*. London: Collins, 1969.

Kelbaugh, David, editor. *The Pedestrian Pocket Book: A New Theory of Suburban Design*. New York: Princeton Architectural Press, 1989.

Kelly, George. *A Theory of Personality: The Psychology of Personal Constructs*. New York: W.W. Norton, 1963.

Kelly, Kevin. *Out of Control: The New Biology of Machines*. London: Fourth Estate, 1994.

Kerr, Philip. *Gridiron*. London: Chatto & Windus, 1995.

Khoo, Su Nin. *Streets of George Town Penang*. Penang: Janus Print & Resources, 1993.

King, Anthony D. *Colonial Urban Development: Culture, Social Power and Environment*. London: Routledge & Kegan Paul, 1976.

— *Global Cities: Post-imperialism and the Internationalization of London*. London: Routledge, 1990.

— editor. *Culture, Globalization and the World-System: Contemporary Conditions for the Representation of Identity*. London: Macmillan, 1991.

— *The Bungalow: The Production of a Global Culture*. Oxford: Oxford University Press, 2nd edition, 1995.

King, Stuart. 'Queenslander.' In *The Encyclopedia of Australian Architecture*, edited by Philip Goad and Julie Willis, 579. Cambridge: Cambridge University Press, 2012.

Kirsh, David, and Paul Maglio. 'On Distinguishing Epistemic from Pragmatic Action.' *Cognitive Science*, no. 18 (1994): 513–49.

Koestler, Arthur. *The Act of Creation*. London: Macmillan, 1964.

— and J. R. Smythies, editors. *Beyond Reductionism: New Perspectives in the Life Sciences*. London: Macmillan, 1971.

Kohl, David G. *Chinese Architecture in the Straits Settlements and Western Malaya: Temples, Kongsis and Houses*. Kuala Lumpur: Heinemann Asia, 1984.

Kolarevic, Branko, editor. *Architecture in the Digital Age: Design and Manufacturing*. London: Taylor & Francis, 2003.

Kolbert, Elizabeth. *Field Notes From a Catastrophe*. London: Bloomsbury, 2006.

Korzybski, Alfred. *Science and Sanity: An Introduction to Non-Aristotelian Systems and General Semantics*. Englewood: Institute of General Semantics, 5th edition, 1994.

Koslovsky, R. 'Beat Literature and the Domestication of American Space.' *AA Files 51* (winter, 2005): 36–47.

Krasnogor, Natalio, and Steven Gustafson. 'Toward Truly "Memetic" Memetic Algorithms: Discussion and Proof of Concepts.' In *Advances in Nature-Inspired Computation: The PPSN VII Workshops*. University of Reading, Parallel Emergent and Distributed Architectures Lab (PEDAL), 2002.

Kratoska, Paul H. 'The Peripatetic Peasant and Land Tenure in British Malaya.' *Journal of Southeast Asian Studies*, vol. 16, no. 1 (March 1985): 16–45.

Kuban, Dogan. *Muslim Religious Architecture*. Leiden: E. J. Brill, 1974.

Kubler, George. *The Religious Architecture of New Mexico: In the Colonial Period and Since the American Occupation*. Albuquerque: University of New Mexico Press, 1940.

— *The Shape of Time: Remarks on the History of Things*. New Haven: Yale University Press, 1962.

Kuhn, Thomas. *The Structure of Scientific Revolutions*. Chicago: University of Chicago Press, 1962.

— *The Essential Tension*. Chicago: University of Chicago Press, 1977.

Kuran, Aptullah. *Sinan: The Grand Old Master of Ottoman Architecture*. Washington, DC, and Istanbul: Institute of Turkish Studies and ADA Press, 1987.

Laing, R. D., H. Phillipson and A. R. Lee. *Interpersonal Perception: A Theory and Method of Research*. London: Tavistock, 1966.

Lakatos, Imre. 'Falsification and the Methodology of Scientific Research Programmes.' In *Criticism and the Growth of Knowledge*, edited by Imre Lakatos and Alan Musgrave, 91–195. Cambridge: Cambridge University Press, 1970.

Laland, Kevin N., and John Odling-Smee. 'The Evolution of the Meme.' In *Darwinizing Culture: The Status of Memetics as a Science*, edited by Robert Aunger, 121–41. Oxford: Oxford University Press, 2000.

Landau, Royston. 'Methodology of Research Programmes.' In *Changing Design*, edited by Barrie Evans, James Powell and Reg Talbot, 303–9. Chichester: John Wiley & Sons, 1982.

Langer, Jonas. 'Comparative Cognitive Development.' In *Tools, Language and Cognition in Human Evolution*, edited by Kathleen R. Gibson and Tim Ingold, 300–13. Cambridge: Cambridge University Press, 1993.

Lasch, Christopher. *The Culture of Narcissism: American Life in an Age of Diminishing Expectations.* New York: W. W. Norton & Company, 1978.

Lauer, Quentin. *Phenomenology: Its Genesis and Prospect.* New York: Harper Torchbooks, 1958.

Lavedan, Pierre. *Geographie des Villes.* Paris: Gallimard, 1936; revised edition, 1959.

Lawson, Bryan. *How Designers Think: The Design Process Demystified.* London: Butterworth Architecture, 2nd edition, 1990.

— *Design in Mind.* London: Butterworth Architecture, 1994.

Leach, Edmund. *Lévi-Strauss.* London: Fontana/Collins, 1970.

Leach, Neil. 'Belonging.' *AA Files 49* (spring 2003): 76–82.

—, David Turnbull and Chris Williams, editors. *Digital Tectonics.* Chichester: Wiley-Academy, 2004.

Leary, Frank, and Judith Leary. *Colonial Heritage: Historic Buildings of New South Wales.* Sydney: Angus & Robertson, 1972.

Leatherdale. W. H. *The Role of Analogy, Model and Metaphor in Science.* Amsterdam and New York: North-Holland and American Elsevier, 1974.

Leclerc, Georges-Louis (Comte de Buffon). *Historie Naturelle, Generale et Particuliere.* 15 vols. Paris, 1749–67.

Le Corbusier. *Towards a New Architecture*, translated by Frederick Etchells. London: John Rodko, 1927.

— *Le Corbusier 1910–60*, translated by William Gleckman and Elsa Girsberger. Zurich: Editions Girsberger, 1960.

Leeuwen, Thomas A. P. Van. 'Sacred Skyscrapers and Profane Cathedrals.' *AA Files*, no. 8 (January 1985): 39–56.

Leggett, Jeremy K. *Half Gone: Oil, Gas, Hot Air and the Global Energy Crisis.* London: Portobello Books, 2005.

Leroi-Gourhan, André. *L'Homme et la Matiere.* Paris: Albin Michel, 1943.

— *Mileu et Techniques.* Paris: Albin Michel, 1945.

Lévi-Strauss, Claude. *The Savage Mind.* Chicago: Phoenix Books, 1966.

— *Structural Anthropology*, translated by Claire Jacobson and Brooke Grundfest Schoepf. London: Allen Lane, 1968.

Lewcock, Ronald. 'Materials and Techniques.' In *Architecture of the Islamic World: Its History and Social Meaning*, edited by George Michell, 129–43. New York: William Morrow, 1978.

Lewin, Kurt. *Field Theory in Social Science.* New York: Harper & Row, 1951.

Lewin, Roger. *Complexity: Life on the Edge of Chaos.* London: Phoenix, 1993.

Lilley, Samuel. *Men, Machines and History.* New York: International Publishers, 1966.

Lim, Jee Yuan. *The Malay House: Rediscovering Malaysia's Indigenous Shelter System.* Pulau Pinang: Institute Masyarakat, 1987.

Linnaeus, Carl von. *Systema Naturae.* Stockholm: Laurentii Salvii, 1735.

Liu Thai-Ker. 'From Megacity to Constellation City: Towards Sustainable Asian Cities.' In *Megacities, Labour, Communications*, edited by Toh Thian Ser, 3–26. Singapore: Institute of Southeast Asian Studies, 1998.

Llorens, Tomas. 'In Defense of Misfit.' In *Changing Design*, edited by Barrie Evans, James Powell and Reg Talbot, 311–24. Chichester: John Wiley & Sons, 1982.

Logan, Robert, K. *The Extended Mind: The Emergence of Language, the Human Mind, and Culture.* Toronto: University of Toronto Press, 2007.

Longacre, William A., editor. *Reconstructing Prehistoric Pueblo Societies.* Albuquerque: University of New Mexico Press, 1970.

Lotka, A. J. 'The Law of Evolution as a Maximal Principle.' *Human Biology*, no. 17 (1945): 167–94.

Lovelock, James E. *Gaia: A New Look At Life on Earth.* New York: Oxford University Press, 1979.

— *The Revenge of Gaia: Why the Earth Is Fighting Back – And How We Can Still Save Humanity.* London: Allen Lane, 2006.

— *The Vanishing Face of Gaia: A Final Warning.* London: Basic Books, 2010.

Lovgren, S. 'Chimps, Humans 96 Percent the Same, Gene Study Finds.' *National Geographic News*, August 31, 2005.

Luggen, William W. *Flexible Manufacturing Cells and Systems.* Englewood Cliffs: Prentice-Hall, 1991.

Luhmann, Niklas. 'The Autopoiesis of Social Systems.' In *Sociocybernetic Paradoxes*, edited by F. Geyer and J. van der Zouwen, 172–92. London: Sage Publications, 1986.

— *Essays in Self-reference.* New York: Columbia University Press, 1990.

Lynas, Mark. *Six Degrees: Our Future on a Hotter Planet.* Washington, DC: National Geographic, 2008.

Bibliography

Lynch, Aaron. *Thought Contagion: How Belief Spreads Through Society*. New York: Basic Books, 1996.

Lynch, Kevin. *The Image of the City*. Cambridge: MIT Press, 1960.

Lyotard, Jean-François. *The Postmodern Condition: A Report on Knowledge*, translated by Geoff Bennington and Brian Massumi. Manchester: Manchester University Press, 1984.

Malpas, J. E. *Place and Experience: A Philosophical Topography*. Cambridge: Cambridge University Press, 1999.

Malthus, T. R. *An Essay on the Principle of Population*. London: Johnson, 6th edition, 1826; 1st edition, 1798.

Mandelbaum, D. G., editor. *Selected Writings of Edward Sapir*. Berkeley: University of California Press, 1949.

March, Lionel, and Philip Steadman, editors. *The Geometry of Environment*. London: Methuen, 1971.

Markus, Thomas A. *Buildings and Power: Freedom and Control in the Origin of Modern Building Types*. London: Routledge, 1993.

Marshall, Jessica. 'The World: Four Degrees Warmer.' *ABC News: News in Science*, November 30, 2010. www.abc.net.au/science/articles/2010/11/30/3080608.htm.

Martin, Leslie, and Lionel March. *Urban Space and Structures*. Cambridge: Cambridge University Press, 1972.

Massey, Doreen. 'A Global Sense of Place.' In *Reading Human Geography*, edited by T. Barnes and D. Gregory, 315–23. London: Arnold, 1997.

Maturana, Humberto R., and Francisco J. Varela. *The Tree of Knowledge: The Biological Roots of Human Understanding*, translated by Robert Paolucci. Boston: Shambala, revised edition, 1998.

McHenry, Paul Graham Jr. *Adobe: Build It Yourself*. Tucson: University of Arizona Press, 1973.

McLuhan, Marshall. *Understanding Media: The Extensions of Man*. London: Routledge & Kegan Paul, 1964.

McRae, Mike. *Tribal Science: Brains, Beliefs and Bad Ideas*. St Lucia: University of Queensland Press, 2011.

Mead, George Herbert. *Mind, Self, and Society: From the Standpoint of a Social Behaviorist*, edited by Charles W. Morris. Chicago: University of Chicago Press, 1934.

Medawar, Peter Brian. *The Future of Man*. Lecture 6 (no date): 8–103.

Mees, Paul. *Transport for Suburbia: Beyond the Automobile Age*. London: Earthscan, 2010.

Meltzer, Bernard N., John W. Petras, and Larry T. Reynolds. *Symbolic Interactionism: Genesis, Varieties and Criticism*. London: Routledge & Kegan Paul, 1975.

Merleau-Ponty, Maurice. *Phenomenology of Perception*, translated by Colin Smith. London: Routledge & Kegan Paul, 1962.

Metzinger, Thomas. *The Ego Tunnel: The Science of the Mind and the Myth of the Self*. New York: Basic Books, 2009.

Mingers, John. *Self-producing Systems: Implications and Applications of Autopoiesis*. New York: Plenum Press, 1995.

Mitchell, George, editor. *Architecture of the Islamic World*. New York: William Morrow, 1978.

Mitchell, William J. *City of Bits: Space, Place, and the Infobahn*. Cambridge: MIT Press, 1995.

— *e-topia: 'Urban Life, Jim – But Not As We Know It.'* Cambridge: MIT Press, 1999.

Monbiot, George. *Heat: How to Stop the Planet Burning*. London: Allen Lane, 2006.

Moore, Charles, Gerald Allen and Donlyn Lyndon. *The Place of Houses*. New York: Holt, Rinehart & Winston, 1974.

Moussavi, Farshid, and Alejandro Zaera Polo. 'Types, Style and Phylogenesis.' In *Emergence: Morphogenetic Design Strategies*, edited by Michael Hensel, Achim Menges and Michael Weinstock, 34–9. Chichester: Wiley-Academy, 2004.

Mugerauer, Robert. 'Body, Settlement, Landscape: A Comparison of Hot and Cool Humid Patterns.' *Traditional Dwellings and Settlements Review*, vol. 7, no. 1 (fall 1995): 25–32.

Mullins, Justin. 'Squishybots: Soft, Bendy and Smarter Than Ever.' *New Scientist*, no. 2838 (November 12, 2011): 48–51.

Mumford, Lewis. *Art and Technics*. New York: Columbia University Press, 1952.

— *The City in History: Its Origins, Its Transformations, and Its Prospects*. New York: Harcourt, Brace & World, 1961.

— *The Highway and the City*. Kingswood: Bookprint, 1964.

Myers, Peter. 'Australia's Grid-Suburbs: Temporary Housing in a Permanent Landscape?' *B Architectural Magazine*, no. 52/53 (1995/96): 71–7.

Nash, Eric P. *Manhatten Skyscrapers*. New York: Princeton Architectural Press, 1999.

Nasir, Abdul Halim. *Mosques of Peninsula Malaysia*. Kuala Lumpur: Berita Publishing, 1984.

— and Wan Hashim Wan Teh. *The Traditional Malay House*. Shah Alam: Penerbit Fajar Bakti, 1996.

Needham, Rodney, editor. *Right and Left: Essays on Dual Symbolic Classification*. Chicago: University of Chicago Press, 1973.

Negroponte, Nicholas. *The Architecture Machine: Toward a More Human Environment*. Cambridge: MIT Press, 1970.

— *Soft Architecture Machines*. Cambridge: MIT Press, 1975.

— *Being Digital: The Road Map for Survival on the Information Superhighway*. London: Hodder & Stoughton, 1995.

Newman, Peter, and Jeffrey Kenworthy. *Sustainability and Cities: Overcoming Automobile Dependence*. Washington, DC: Island Press, 1999.

Nilsson, Sten. *European Architecture in India 1750–1850*. London: Faber & Faber, 1968.

Norberg-Schulz, Christian. *Genius Loci: Towards a Phenomenology of Architecture*. New York: Rizzoli, 1979.

O'Connor, Mark, and William J. Lines. *Overloading Australia: How Governments and Media Dither and Deny on Population*. Canterbury: Envirobook, 2008.

O'Gorman, Patricia W. *Tradition of Craftsmanship in Mexican Homes*. New York: Architectural Book Publishing Company, 1980.

Oliver, Paul, editor. *Shelter, Sign and Symbol*. New York: Overlook Press, 1977.

— *Encyclopaedia of Vernacular Architecture of the World*. Oxford: Architectural Press, 1998.

— *Dwellings: The Vernacular House Worldwide*. London: Phaidon, 2003.

Oller, D. Kimbrough, and Ulrike Griebel. *Evolution of Communication Systems: A Comparative Approach*. Cambridge: MIT Press, 2004.

Ong, Choo Suat, and Tang Ben Luan, editors. *Five-Foot-Way Traders*. Singapore: Archives and Oral History Department, 1985.

Oreskes, Naomi, and Erik M. Conway. *Merchants of Doubt: How a Handful of Scientists Obscured the Truth on Issues from Tobacco Smoke to Global Warming*. New York: Bloomsbury Press, 2010.

Owen, David. *Green Metropolis: Why Living Smaller, Living Closer, and Driving Less Are the Key to Sustainability*. New York: Riverhead Books, 2009.

Oyama, Susan. *The Ontogeny of Information: Developmental Systems and Evolution*. Cambridge: Cambridge University Press, 1985.

Pallasmaa, Juhani. *The Eyes of the Skin: Architecture and the Senses*. London: Wiley-Academy, 2005.

Parfit, Derek. 'Personal Identity.' In *Philosophy As It Is*, edited by Ted Honderich and Myles Burnyeat, 186–211. Harmondsworth: Penguin Books, 1979.

Pask, Gordon. *Conversation Theory: Applications in Education and Epistemology*. Amsterdam: Elsevier, 1976.

Paul, Jacques. 'German Neo-classicism and the Modern Movement.' *Architectural Review*, vol. 152, no. 907 (September 1972): 175–80.

Pepper, Simon. 'Body, Diagram, and Geometry in the Renaissance Fortress.' In *Body and Building: Essays on the Changing Relation of Body and Architecture*, edited by George Dodds and Robert Tavernor, 114–25. Cambridge: MIT Press, 2005.

Perlin, John. *A Forest Journey: The Role of Wood in the Development of Civilization*. New York: W. W. Norton, 1989.

Peters, Richard S. 'Personal Understanding and Personal Relationships.' In *Understanding Other Persons*, edited by Theodore Mischel, 37–65. Oxford: Basil Blackwell, 1974.

Pevsner, Nikolaus. *A History of Building Types*. London: Thames & Hudson, 1976.

Pickover, Clifford A., editor. *Visions of the Future: Art, Technology and Computing in the 21st Century*. New York: St Martin's Press, revised edition, 1994.

Pitt-Rivers, Lt-General A. Lane-Fox. *The Evolution of Culture and Other Essays*, edited by J. L. Myers. Oxford: Clarendon Press, 1906.

Plato. *Plato's Republic*, translated by Henry Davis. New York: Universal Classics (no date).

Poëte, Marcel. *Introduction à L'Urbanisme: L'Évolution des Villes, La Leçon de L'Antiquité*. Paris: Bovin & Cie, 1929.

Polanyi, Michael. *Personal Knowledge: Towards a Post-critical Philosophy*. Chicago: University of Chicago Press, 1958.

— *The Tacit Dimension*. New York: Doubleday, 1966.

— and Harry Prosch. *Meaning*. Chicago: University of Chicago Press, 1975.

Popper, Karl. *The Logic of Scientific Discovery*. London: Hutchinson, 1959.

— *Conjectures and Refutations: The Growth of Scientific Knowledge*. London: Routledge & Kegan Paul, 1963.

— 'Normal Science and Its Dangers.' In *Criticism and the Growth of Knowledge*, edited by Imre Lakatos and Alan Musgrave, 51–8. Cambridge: Cambridge University Press, 1970.

Prijotomo, Josef. *Ideas and Forms of Javanese Architecture*. Yogyakarta: Gadjah Mada University Press, 1984.

Rapoport, Amos. *House Form and Culture*. Englewood Cliffs: Prentice-Hall, 1969.

— 'Australian Aborigines and the Definition of Place.' In *Shelter, Sign and Symbol*, edited by Paul Oliver, 38–51. New York: Overlook Press, 1977.

— *Human Aspects of Urban Form: Towards a Man–Environment Approach to Urban Form and Design*. Oxford: Pergamon Press, 1977.

Ray, Alison. *The Transition to Language*. Oxford: Oxford University Press, 2002.

Roberts, Ben. 'Stiegler Reading Derrida: The Prosthesis of Deconstruction in Technics.' *Postmodern Culture*, vol. 16, no. 1 (2005).

Rose, Hillary, and Steven Rose. *Genes, Cells and Brains*. London: Verso, 2012.

Rosen, Larry R. *iDisorder: Understanding Our Obsession with Technology and Overcoming Its Hold on Us*. London: Palgrave Macmillan, 2012.

Rossi, Aldo. *The Architecture of the City*. Cambridge: MIT Press, 1982.

Rowe, Colin. *The Mathematics of the Ideal Villa and Other Essays*. Cambridge: MIT Press, 1976.

— and Fred Koetter. *Collage City*. Cambridge: MIT Press, 1978.

Royal Society for the Protection of Birds. *State of Nature*. Sandy: RSPB, 2013. www.rspb.org.uk/stateofnature (accessed May 2013).

Rudofsky, Bernard. *Architecture Without Architects*. New York: Doubleday, 1964.

Russell, Barry. *Building Systems, Industrialization and Architecture*. Chichester: Wiley, 1981.

Rykwert, Joseph. *The Necessity of Artifice*. New York: Rizzoli, 1982.

Ryle, Gilbert. *The Concept of Mind*. New York: Barnes & Noble, 1949.

Saini, Balwant, and Ray Joyce. *The Australian House: Houses of the Tropical North*. Sydney: Lansdowne, 1982.

Saunders, P., and P. Williams. 'The Constitution of the Home.' *Housing Studies*, vol. 3, no. 2 (1988): 81–93.

Schon, Donald. *The Displacement of Concepts*. London: Tavistock Publications, 1963.

Schwartz, Peter. 'In Gas We'll Trust.' *Wired* (September 2012): 92–8.

Shepard, Mark, editor. *Sentient City: Ubiquitous Computing, Architecture, and the Future of Urban Space*. Cambridge: MIT Press, 2011.

Shepherd, Roger, editor. *Skyscraper: The Search for an American Style 1891–1941*. New York: McGraw-Hill, 2003.

Sherman, David, and Joseph Wayne Smith. *The Climate Change Challenge and the Failure of Democracy*. Westport: Praeger, 2007.

SHoP/Sharples Holden Pasquarelli. 'Versioning: Evolutionary Techniques in Architecture.' *Architectural Design* (September/October 2002): 3–102.

Shumaker, Robert W., Kristina R. Walkup and Benjamin B. Beck, *Animal Tool Behavior*. Baltimore: Johns Hopkins University Press, 2011.

Skinner, B. F. *About Behaviorism*. New York: Alfred A. Knopf, 1974.

Smith, Jason. *Howard Arkley*. Melbourne: National Gallery of Victoria, 2006.

Smith, Jim. 'Coevolving Memetic Algorithms: A Review and Progress Report.' *IEEE Transactions on Systems Man and Cybernetics – Part B*, vol. 37 (2007): 6–17.

Smith, Ronald W., and Valerie Bugni. 'Symbolic Interaction Theory and Architecture.' *Symbolic Interactionism*, vol. 29, no. 2 (2012): 123–55.

Sperber, Dan. 'An Objection to the Memetic Approach to Culture.' In *Darwinizing Culture: The Status of Memetics as a Science*, edited by Robert Aunger, 163–73. Oxford: Oxford University Press, 2000.

Spratt, David, and Philip Sutton. *Climate Code Red: The Case for Emergency Action*. Melbourne: Scribe, 2008.

Stea, David. 'Architecture in the Head: Cognitive Mapping.' In *Designing for Human Behaviour: Architecture and the Behavioural Sciences*, edited by Jon Lang, Charles Burnette, Walter Moleski and David Vachon, 157–68. Stroudsburg: Dowden, Hutchinson & Ross, 1974.

Steadman, Philip. *The Evolution of Designs: Biological Analogy in Architecture and the Applied Arts*. London: Routledge, revised edition, 2008.

Steiner, George. *After Babel: Aspects of Language and Translation*. Oxford: Oxford University Press, 1975.

Stiegler, Bernard. *Technics and Time, 1: The Fault of Epimetheus*, trans. Richard Beardsworth and George Collins. Stanford: Stanford University Press, 1998.

— *Technics and Time, 2: Disorientation*, translated by Stephen Barker. Stanford: Stanford University Press, 2009.

— *Technics and Time, 3: Cinematic Time and the Question of Malaise*, translated by Stephen Barker. Stanford: Stanford University Press, 2010.

Stone, Allucquere Rosanne. 'Will the Real Body Please Stand Up: Boundary Stories About Virtual Cultures.' In *Cyberspace: First Steps*, edited by Michael Benedikt, 81–118. Cambridge: MIT Press, 1994.

Stuckey, Helen. 'Robin Boyd and the Revolt Against Suburbia.' In *Imaginary Australia, Arkitekturtidsskrift B*, no. 52–3. Special issue edited by Harriet Edquist and Gilbert Hansen (1995/96): 41–9.

Sturgis, Russell. 'The Larkin Building in Buffalo.' In *Skyscraper: The Search for an American Style 1891–1941*, edited by Roger Shepherd, 146–53. New York: McGraw-Hill, 2003.

Summerson, John. *The Classical Language in Architecture*. Cambridge: MIT Press, 1963.

Sunstein, Cass R. *Going to Extremes: How Like Minds Unite and Divide*. New York: Oxford University Press, 2012.

Swain, Tony. *A Place for Strangers*. Cambridge: Cambridge University Press, 1993.

Tallerman, Maggie. *Language Origins: Perspectives on Evolution*. Oxford: Oxford University Press, 2005.

Tang, Chow Ang, and Yeo Khee Hua. 'Old Row Houses of Peninsula Malaysia.' *Majallah Akitek* (June 1976): 22–8.

Taylor, Timothy. *The Artificial Ape: How Technology Changed the Course of Human Evolution*. New York: Palgrave Macmillan, 2010.

Tenner, Edward. *Our Own Devices: How Technology Remakes Humanity*. New York: Vintage Books, 2003.

Thompson, D'Arcy Wentworth. *On Growth and Form*. Cambridge: Cambridge University Press, 1961.

Time editors. 'Welcome to Cyberspace.' Special issue, *Time* (spring 1995).

Toulmin, Stephen. 'The Concept of "Stages" in Development.' In *Cognitive Development and Epistemology*, edited by Theodore Mischel, 25–60. New York: Academic Press, 1971.

— 'Rules and Their Relevance for Understanding Human Behaviour.' In *Understanding Other Persons*, edited by Theodore Mischel, 185–215. Oxford: Basil Blackwell, 1974.

Turbayne, Colin Murray. *The Myth of Metaphor*. Columbia: University of South Carolina Press, 1962.

Turing, Alan. 'The Chemical Basis of Morphogenesis.' *Philosophical Transactions of the Royal Society B*, vol. 237 (1952): 37.

Turner, Graeme. 'Australian Film and National Identity in the 1990s.' In *The Politics of Identity in Australia*, edited by Geoffrey Stokes, 185–92. Cambridge: Cambridge University Press, 1997.

Tzonis, Alexander, Liane Lefaivre and Bruno Stagno. *Tropical Architecture: Critical Regionalism in the Age of Globalization*. Chichester: Wiley-Academy, 2001.

United States Environmental Protection Agency, Greenhouse Gas Emissions Data. www.epa.gov/climate change/ghgemissions/global.html).

USA Energy Information Agency, 2008. www.ucsusa.org/global_warming/science_and_impacts/science/each- countrys-share-of-co2.html.

Vaccari, Andrés. 'Unweaving the Program: Stiegler and the Hegemony of Technics.' *Transformations*, no. 17 (2009) www.transformationsjournal.org/journal/issue_17/article_08.shtml (accessed July 2010).

— and Belinda Barnet. 'Prolegomena to a Future Robot History: Stiegler, Epiphylogenesis and Technical Evolution.' *Transformations*, no. 17 (2009). www.transformationsjournal.org/journal/issue_17/article_09.shtml (accessed July 2010).

Vale, Lawrence J. *Architecture, Power, and National Identity*. New Haven: Yale University Press, 1992.

Van Camp, Nathan. 'Animality, Humanity, and Technicity.' *Transformations*, no. 17 (2009). www.transformations journal.org/journal/issue_17/article_06.shtml (accessed July 2010).

Varela, Francisco J., Evan Thompson and Elena Rosch. *The Embodied Mind: Cognitive Science and Human Experience*. Cambridge, MIT Press, 1993.

Venturi, Robert, Denise Scott Brown and Steven Izenour. *Learning from Las Vegas*. Cambridge: MIT Press, 1972.

Vesely, Dalibor. 'The Architectonics of Embodiment.' In *Body and Building: Essays on the Changing Relation of Body and Architecture*, edited by G. Dodds and R. Tavernor, 28–43. Cambridge: MIT Press, 2005.

Vidler, Anthony. 'The Third Typology.' In *Designing Cities: Critical Readings in Urban Design*, edited by Alexander R. Cuthbert, 317–22. Oxford: Blackwell, 2003.

Virilio, Paul. *The Great Accelerator*, translated by Julie Rose. Cambridge: Polity Press, 2012.

Vlatseas, A. *A History of Malaysian Architecture*. Singapore: Longman, 1990.

Volti, Rudi. *Cars and Culture: The Life Story of a Technology*. Baltimore: Johns Hopkins University Press, 2004.

Von Bertalanffy, Ludwig. 'The Theory of Open Systems in Physics and Biology.' *Science*, vol. 111 (January 1950): 23–9.

— *General System Theory: Foundations, Development, Applications*. New York: George Braziller, 1968.

Von Foerster, Heinz, and George W. Zopf, Jr, editors. *Principles of Self- organization*. London: Pergamon Press, 1962.

Wallace, Ken M. *An Introduction to the Design Process*. Cambridge: Cambridge University Engineering Department, 1989.

Ward, Russel. *The Australian Legend*. Melbourne: Oxford University Press, 1966; 1st edition 1958.

Webber, Melvin M., John W. Dyckman, Donald L. Foley, Albert Z. Guttenberg, William L. C. Wheaton and Catherine Bauer Wurster. *Explorations into Urban Structure*. Philadelphia: University of Pennsylvania Press, 1964.

Bibliography

Webber, Melvin M. 'The Urban Place and the Nonplace Urban Realm.' In *Explorations into Urban Structure*, by Melvin M. Webber, John W. Dyckman, Donald F. Foley, Albert Z. Guttenberg, William L. C. Wheaton and Catherine Bauer Wurster, 79–183 Philadelphia: University of Pennsylvania Press, 1964.

Wells, Spencer. *Pandora's Seed: The Unforeseen Cost of Civilization.* London: Allen Lane, 2010.

Whitehead, Hugh. 'Laws of Form.' In *Architecture in the Digital Age: Design and Manufacturing*, edited by Branko Kolarevic, 82–100. London: Taylor & Francis, 2003.

—, Irene Gallou, Harsh Thapar, Giovanni Betti and Salmaan Craig. 'Driving an Ecological Agenda with Project-Led Research.' *Architectural Design*, profile no. 24 (November/December 2011).

Wilkins, John S. *Species: A History of the Idea.* Berkeley: University of California Press, 2009.

— 'What Is a Species: Essences and Generation.' *Theory in Biosciences*, no. 129 (2010): 141–8.

Williams, Caroline, 'The Consciousness Connection.' *New Scientist*, vol. 215, no. 2874 (July 21, 2012): 32–5.

Williams, Chris. 'Design by Algorithm.' In *Digital Tectonics*, edited by Neil Leach, David Turnbull and Chris Williams, 78–85. Chichester: Wiley-Academy, 2004.

Williams, G. C. *Adaptation and Natural Selection.* Princeton: Princeton University Press, 1966.

Williamson, D. T. N. 'New Wave in Manufacturing.' *American Machinist*, vol. 3, no. 19 (September 11, 1967): 143–54.

— 'System 24 – A New Concept of Manufacture.' *Proceedings of the 8th International M.T.D.R. Conference, University of Manchester, 12–15 September*, 1–50. Oxford: Pergamon Press, 1967.

Wilson, David Sloan. *Evolution for Everyone: How Darwin's Theory Can Change the Way We Think About Our Lives.* New York: Delacorte Press, 2007.

Wilson, Edward O. *The Social Conquest of Earth.* New York: W. W. Norton, 2012.

Wilson, Frank R. *The Hand: How Its Use Shapes the Brain, Language and Human Culture.* New York: Vintage Books, 1999.

Winch, Peter. *The Idea of a Social Science and Its Relation to Philosophy.* London: Routledge & Kegan Paul, 1958.

Winsor, M. P. 'Non-essentialist Methods in Pre-Darwinian Taxonomy.' *Biological Philosophy*, no. 18 (2003): 387–400.

Wise, Chris. 'Drunk in an Orgy of Technology.' In *Emergence: Morphogenetic Design Strategies*, edited by Michael Hensel, Achim Menges and Michael Weinstock, 54–7. Chichester: Wiley-Academy, 2004.

Wise, J. Macgregor. 'Assemblage.' In *Gilles Deleuze: Key Concepts*, edited by Charles J. Stivale, 77–87. Montreal: McGill-Queens University Press, 2005.

Wittgenstein, Ludwig. *Tractatus Logico-Philosophicus*, translated by C. K. Ogden and F. P. Ramsey. London: Routledge & Kegan Paul, 1922; 2nd edition, 1961.

— *Philosophical Investigations.* London: Macmillan, 3rd edition, 1958.

— *The Blue and Brown Books.* New York: Harper Colophon Books, 1958.

Wittkower, Rudolf. *Architectural Principles in the Age of Humanism.* London: Alec Tiranti, 1962.

Wolf, Maryanne. *Proust and the Squid: The Story and Science of the Reading Brain.* Cambridge: Icon Books, 2008.

Wolf, Naomi. *Vagina: A New Biography.* London: Virago, 2012.

Wolfe, Maxine, and Harold Proshansky. 'The Physical Setting as a Factor in Group Function and Process.' In *Designing for Human Behaviour: Architecture and the Behavioural Sciences*, edited by Jon Lang, Charles Burnette, Walter Moleski and David Vachon, 194–201. Stroudsburg: Dowden, Hutchinson & Ross, 1974.

Wollheim, Richard. *Art and Its Objects.* Harmondsworth: Penguin Books, 1975.

Worthington, John. 'What's Wrong With the American City Is That We View It Through European Eyes.' *Arena*, vol. 82, no. 10 (1967): 210–13.

Yi-Fu Tuan. *Space and Place: The Perspective of Experience.* London: Edward Arnold, 1977.

Young, David. *The Discovery of Evolution.* Cambridge: Cambridge University Press, 2nd edition, 2007.

Newspaper articles

Baggini, Julian. 'How Jobs Changed Capitalism,' *Guardian Weekly*, October 14, 2011.

— 'Science Is Mind Candy,' *Guardian*, May 23, 2013.

Benson, Simon. 'Fuelling Pollution: Sydney Motorists Drive Up Greenhouse Gas Emissions,' *Daily Telegraph*, December 23, 2009.

Bita, Natasha. 'Paving Devours Farmland Faster Than Foreign Buyers,' *Weekend Australian*, January 21–22, 2012.

Bittman, Mark. 'The Endless Summer,' *International Herald Tribune*, July 20, 2012.

Bodey, Michael. 'The Perfect Vehicle for Geoffrey Rush,' *Australian*, December 22, 2010.

Borenstein, Seth. 'Greenhouse Emissions Exceed Worst Case Scenario,' *Sydney Morning Herald: Weekend Edition*, November 5–6, 2011.

Bosely, Sarah. 'Children Under 3 Should Not Watch Television, Says Study,' *Guardian*, October 9, 2012.

Carrington, Damien. 'England's Record Wet Year Was Harbinger of … Yet More Rain,' *Guardian*, January 4, 2013.

Chong, Florence. 'Packed to the Rafters,' *Weekend Australian*, April 30–May 1, 2011.

Clarken, Jim. 'Broken Global Food System Needs Climate For Change,' *Irish Times*, August 13, 2012.

Corderoy, Amy. 'Obesity Is Now More Deadly Than Smoking,' *Sydney Morning Herald*, April 9, 2010.

Cubby, Ben. 'Developer May Sue to Trigger Rethink on Sea Level Rises,' *Sydney Morning Herald*, March 6, 2012.

— 'Scientist Denies He Is Mouthpiece of US Climate–Sceptic Thinktank,' *Sydney Morning Herald*, February 16, 2012.

Davis, Tony. 'What's With 150?' *Sydney Morning Herald*, January 27, 2012.

Drive Team, 'Seeing the Light: Detroit Finally Delivers on a Generation of More Fuel-Efficient Cars,' *Sydney Morning Herald: Weekend Edition*, January 14–15, 2012.

Elder, Miriam. 'Russians Devastated by Floods Accuse Officials Over Lack of Warning as Death Toll Passes 150,' *Guardian*, July 9, 2012.

Elliot, Larry. 'Global Leaders Are Unprepared for Financial and Ecological Collapse,' *Guardian*, January 9, 2013.

Farrelly, Elizabeth. 'City Sprawl Is the Road to Madness,' *Sydney Morning Herald*, March 10, 2011.

— 'Grubby Hub Could Yet Be Urban Butterfly,' *Sydney Morning Herald*, December 1, 2011.

Flannery, Tim. 'As Australia Burns, Attitudes Are Changing. But Is It Too Late?' *Guardian*, January 12, 2013.

Ghianni, Tim, Keith Coffman and Jeff Mason. 'In Scorching Heat, the US Is Burning,' *Independent on Sunday*, July 1, 2012.

Goldberg, Suzanne. 'Four Days in July … Scientists Stunned by Greenland's Ice Sheet Melting Away,' *Guardian*, July 26, 2012.

Greenfield, Susan. 'Virtual Worlds Are Limiting Our Brains,' *Sydney Morning Herald*, October 21, 2011.

Harvey, Fiona. 'Britain is Facing GBP 860 Million Bill for Flood Protection, Warn Climate Advisors,' *Guardian*, July 11, 2012.

— 'World Climate Now on the Brink,' *Guardian Weekly*, June 3–9, 2011.

Hickman, Leo. 'Climate Change Study Converts Sceptical Scientists,' *Guardian*, July 30, 2012.

— 'Drinks Giant Shuns US Thinktank Over Climate Campaign,' *Guardian*, May 7, 2012.

Horin, Adele. 'Capitals Face a Decade of Unaffordable Houses, Even in the Suburbs,' *Sydney Morning Herald*, July 28, 2011.

Hudson, Kris, and Vanessa O'Connell. 'Recession Turns Malls into Ghost Towns,' *Wall Street Journal*, May 22, 2009.

Hutton, Will. 'Global Warming Off the Agenda? Now That Would Be a Catastrophe,' *Observer*, June 24, 2012.

— 'Burn Our Planet or Face Financial Meltdown. Not Much of a Choice,' *Observer*, April 21, 2013.

Jacobs, Andrew. 'Beijing Rains Bring Deaths and Create Wide Havoc,' *International Herald Tribune*, July 23, 2012.

Jeffries, Stuart. 'Anti-techno Baton Is Handed On,' *Guardian Weekly*, January 6, 2012.

Jenkins, Simon. 'So, You Think Reason Guides Your Politics? Think Again,' *Guardian*, 18 May, 2012.

Kidron, Beeban. 'Just One More Click,' *Guardian*, September 14, 2013.

King, Philip. 'SUVs Prop Up Motor Market,' *Weekend Australian*, February 4–5, 2012.

Kissane, Karen. 'Europeans Face Having to Beg for Daily Bread,' *Sydney Morning Herald*, December 20, 2011.

Klein, Naomi. 'You Won't Save the Planet If You Profit From the Wreckage,' *Guardian*, May 3, 2013.

Legge, Kate. 'The Worst Thing That Could Happen Has Happened: Cars, Driveways – and Children,' *Weekend Australian Magazine*, December 3–4, 2011.

Lovejoy, Thomas E., 'The Climate Change Endgame,' *International Herald Tribune*, January 22, 2013.

Lunn, Stephen. 'Toddlers, Touch Screens and the Parents' Dilemma,' *Weekend Australian*, January 7–8, 2012.

Luzzi, Joseph. 'Dante's Dark Wood,' *International New York Times*, December 21–22, 2013.

Macalister, Terry, and Lionel Badal. 'IMF Warned Oil May Double in Price from 2022,' *Guardian*, May 14, 2012.

Maddox, Garry. 'Ayrton Senna,' *Sydney Morning Herald: Weekend Edition*, August 13–14, 2011.

Marshall, Jessica. 'The World: Four Degrees Warmer,' *ABC News: News in Science*, November 30, 2010.

Martin, Peter. 'The Incredible Colossal Homes: Bigger Than Ever,' *Sydney Morning Herald*, April 1, 2010.

McKie, Robin. 'How Theatre Gives Fresh Power to the Warnings of Global Peril,' *Observer*, August 12, 2012.

— 'Climate Change "Will Make Hundreds of Millions Homeless",' *Observer*, May 12, 2013.

McVeigh, Tracy. 'Internet Addiction Even Worries Silicon Valley,' *Observer*, July 29, 2012.

Monbiot, George. 'Now We Know. Governments Have Given Up On the Planet,' *Guardian*, June 26, 2012.

— 'We Were Wrong on Peak Oil. There's Enough to Fry Us All,' *Guardian*, July 3, 2012.

Moulds, Josephine, and Suzanne Goldenberg. 'Crisis Looms as Extreme Weather Hits Crops,' *Guardian*, July 23, 2012.

Naughton, John. 'We Love Your Work.... Now Show Us Your Workings,' *Observer*, June 24, 2012.

O'Connell, Brian. 'Hooked On Tablets: The Tech "Addicts",' *Irish Times*, April 27, 2013.

O'Toole, Finan. 'In Corrupt Systems, Decent People Have Two Options: Conform or Be Crushed,' *Observer*, July 1, 2012.

Porritt, Jonathon. 'Where's the Energy to Keep Fighting For the Planet,' *Independent*, June 15, 2012.

Rebuck, Gail. 'Don't Let Technology Stultify Your Brain – Download a Book,' *Sydney Morning Herald*, January 2, 2012.

Sample, Ian. 'Chimps May Know What's On Each Other's Minds,' *Guardian Weekly*, January 13, 2012.

Siegel, Matt. 'Australia Disasters Laid at Climate Change's Feet,' *International Herald Tribune*, March 5, 2013.

Singer, Natasha. 'Mapping the Consumer Genome: They Know and Sell All About You,' *New York Times*, July 15, 2012.

Stern, Lord. 'We Have to Decide What Kind of World We Leave to Our Children,' *Observer*, September 9, 2013.

Sunstein, Cass R. 'Breaking Up the Echo,' *International Herald Tribune*, September 19, 2012.

Topping, Alexandra. 'Freak Storms, Flash Floods, Record Rain – And There's More to Come,' *Guardian*, 9 July 2012.

Vallely, Paul. 'The Planet Looked to Rio Again, and Rio Looked Away,' *Independent on Sunday*, June 24, 2012.

Vidal, John. 'Forecast: Strange Weather Ahead,' *Guardian Weekly*, June 24, 2011.

— '2030: End of Artic Summer Ice,' *Guardian Weekly*, September 21, 2012.

Vulliamy, Ed. 'I Lost My Life's Collection of Vinyl Records, But I'm Well on the Road to Recovery Now,' *Observer*, April 22, 2012.

Waters, John. 'Internet Is Debasing Our Public Discourse,' *Irish Times*, August 3, 2012.

Wolf, Naomi. 'My Feminist Perspective: Knowledge Is Power,' *Guardian*, September 12, 2012.

Index

Page numbers in **bold** refer to figures.

active externalism 52–53, 53–54
adaptation 230–31
addiction 4, 62, 230–31
aesthetics 8, **10**, **11**, 36, 199
  primitive sensibilities 121
  and urban values 16–18
Agamben, Giorgio 66–67
agriculture 72
Alhambra, the, Granada 141–42
Allman, John 47–48
allomemes 110
animals, tool use 61, 68, 113
  and cognition 121–22
anthropocentrism 67–68
  anthropological machine 68
anthropomorphic symbolism 26
archetypes 8–9
architectural theory, place in 7, 12–14, **14**
architecture 23–24
  anatomical analogies 125–29, **125**, **126**, **127**
  art deco 199
  baroque **236**, 239
  biological influences 123, 124–29, 149–51, 213
  and the body 26, **27**, 28–30, **28**, **29**
  Chinese 241, **242**
  critical regionalism 23
  gothic 125, 199
  Japanese 241, **243**
  and natural selection 78–80, **79**, **80**
  neo-classical **152**, 153–54
  see also skyscrapers; vernacular architecture; vertical architecture

Aristotle 146
Arkley, Howard 12
art history 142–44
Arthur, Brian 191–97, 197, 201, 215, 219
artifacts 143, 144, 147, 160
  Kubler's theory of 119, 142–44, 150, 214
artificial intelligence 248–49, 261
artificial selection 73–74, 78, 254, **255**, 256, 261
assemblage theory 3, 149, 158–59, 194, 215
  coevolutionary assemblages 161–72
  and combinatorial design 174, 215
  and contingent effects 160–61
  contingent relations 158–59
  stabilizing processes 159, 161–62
  and technical memes 161–62
assembly lines 166–67
atomism 264–65
Aunger, Robert 106–9, 114, 147, 155, 261
Austin, J. L. 267–68
Australia 10, **11,** 20
  Aborigines 15–16, 22–23, 174
  automobile dependency 225–26, 231–33
  and climate change 220, 226–27, 227–28
  house types 184–85, 187, **187**
  obstacles to change 227, 230
  shopping malls 137, **137**
Australian Climate Change Commission 227
Australian Legend, The (Russel Ward) 20

autocracy 231
automation 250–54, **252**, **253**
automobiles 138–39, 162, 165–67, **167**,
    168, 169–70, 215
    dependence on 219–20, 225–26,
    231–33, 260
autopoiesis 86–88, **90**, 113
autopoietic systems 120
avatars 249–50, 261

baby slings 83–86, **84**, 114
Ball, Philip 150
Bamileke tribe 177
Barrett, William 54
Bartholomew, A. **125**
Bateson, Gregory 62, 228, 230, 268,
    270–71
Batty, Michael 257–58
Bawamataluo village 177, **178**
Beer, Stafford 251, 253
belonging 23–25
Berlin 142, **203**, 211
Bhabha, Homi 23
biased assimilation 224, 260
biology, influence on architecture 123,
    124–29, 149–51, 213
Blackmore, Susan 97–98, 98–100, 101,
    105–6, 106, 147, 173
Blakeslee, Sandra and Matthew 43–44, 46,
    47
Blanchot, Maurice 65–66
blueprint theory 173
Blumer, Herbert 269–70
body, the 3, 16, 26–38, 54, 176, 265–67
    and architecture 26, **27**, 28–30, **28**, **29**
    and cultural evolution 111–12
    and cyberspace 245–47, 249–50
    extensions 32, 55–56
    and immersion 34–36, **35**
    Merleau-Ponty on 30–33
    Polanyi on 33–37
    proportional scale 26, **27**, 30
    and spatial awareness 31
    spatial extensions 41–45
    and technics 70–71
    upright spatial coordinates 28, **29**
body image 32
body language 21

body mapping 41–45, 56
Botvinick, Matthew 40
Boulding, Kenneth 16
Boyd, Robin 10
brain, the 64–66, 83, 85, 106, 107–8, 223
    anterior cingulate cortex (ACC) 47–48
    canonical neurons 46
    fronto-insular (FI) cortex 47–48
    mirror neurons 46–47, 48, 56
    neuroplasticity 43, 249
    space-mapping neurons 44–45
    von Economo neurons (VENS) 47–48
Brandon, Ruth 138–39, 168, 169
Brodsky, Joyce 190–91
Brown, Denise Scott 17
Buddhism 39, 49–50, 51, 56, 105
Buffon, Georges-Louis Leclerc, Comte de
    123
building form, and climate 29–30
building materials 94–96
building types 129–30, **131**, 132, 142,
    146–47, 150
    global 135–39
    Kubler's theory of artifacts 119,
    142–44
    linked problem solutions 142–44
    naïve functionalism 141
    and social relations 132–33, **134**, 135,
    141
    urban typologies 139–42
Bunshaft, Gordon 201, 205
Burnham, Daniel **238**, 239
Butler, Judith 24

CAD/CAM 253–54
caddis larvae 94–95
California bungalow, the **9**, 10, **11**, 187
Campa, Arthur L. 189–90
Canter, David 16
Capita Centre, Sydney 206, **206**
Carr, Nicholas 250
cars *see* automobiles
Cartesian deformation 127–28, **128**
Cartesian dualism 3, 105, 245–47, 261
Casey, Edward S. 21–22, 55
Cassirer, Ernst 77
Castells, Manuel 136
chairs **146**, 147

Chalmers, David 52–54, 56–57, 105
change 188–97, **190**
    addiction to 230–31
    resistance to 51, 219–35, **229**, 259–60
Chaplin, Charlie 167
Chicago 13, 125, 126, **126**, 199, **238**, 239
China 137, 240–41
Chinese shop-houses 183–84, **185**, **186**
Chomsky, Noam 108
Chrysler Building, New York 199, **201**
cities
    colonial 173, 179, **180**, 181, **181**,
        183–85, **183**, 184, **185**, **186**, 187, **187**
    compact 232-233, **234**
    computer modeling 256–58
    dispersed 161, 169–70, **170**, **171**, 172
    eco-cities 235
    new urban structures 233, **234**, 235
    and place-identity 12
    polycentric 233
    Rossi's analysis of 139–42
    vertical garden city, the 209, **211**
civilizations, failed 228–30
Clark, Andy 52–54, 56–57, 105
classification systems 120–23, **122,** 147,
        150, 213, 214. *see also* types
Clausewitz, Carl von 63
climate 29, 181, 184–85
climate change 72, 211–12, 220, 226–27,
        227–28, 230, 231
    climate change denial 4
    and culture 212
Coban Mustafa Pasa Mosque, Gebze **80**
coevolution 61, 83, 109–11, 112, 114,
        115, 129, 216
coevolutionary assemblages 161–63, 169
    automobiles 162, 165–67, **167**, 169–70,
        215
    interstate highways 162, 167–70, **170**,
        215
    social systems 161–72, 215
    spoked wheels 162–63, 163–65, **163**,
        165, 215
cognition
    and combinativity 120–23
    conscious 194
    creative role 188–91, 194–95
    extended 4, 105–6, 52–53, 105, 149

    external aids 53–54
    spatial dynamic 34
    and tacit knowing 33
    unconscious 194–95
cognitive dissonance 228, 260
cognitive maps 17
Cohen, Jonathan 40
Collins, Peter 123, 129, 151
columns, classical 199, **200**
combinativity 3, 120–23, **122**, 213
combinatorial design 173–212, 215
    and change 188–97, **190**
    the colonial city 173, 179, **180**, 181,
        181, 183–85, **183**, **184**, **185**, **186**,
        187, **187**
    cultural imperatives 174, **175**, 176
    hybridization 177–87, **178**, **179**, **180**,
        181, 182, **183**, **184**, **185**, **186**, **187**,
        215
    and innovation 188–91, **190**
    localized 179, **181**
    and radical design 195–97, **196**, 215
    skyscrapers 197–212, **198**, **200**, **201**,
        202, **203**, **204**, **205**, **206**, **207**, **208**,
        209, **210**, **211**, 215–16
    and technological evolution 191–95
Commerzbank, Frankfurt 206, **206**, 212
communication theory 143
computer numerically controlled (CNC)
        machines 251, **252**, 253, **253**
computer-aided manufacture (CAM) 251
concepts, displacement of 188
confirmation bias 223–24, 228, 260
conformity, levels of 219
consciousness 32, 39–41, 48, 50, 87–88,
        194–95, 230
content, and form 149, 149–54, **152**, **153**,
        154, 214, 215
contingent effects 160–61, 215
continuity 143–44, 191
continuous thinking 194–95
control regimes 132, 133, **134**, 151
Conway, Erik 227
Cooper, Clare 8–10, 220
craft-based building methods 176
Craig, Bud 48
creation myths 15
creativity 4, 64, 174, 188–91, 194–95

Creswell, Tim 25
critical regionalism 23–24
cultural adaptation 177
cultural environments 151
cultural evolution 97–98, 103, 109–11,
 111–12, 128–29
cultural expression 199
cultural knowledge 72
cultural production, selfish 219, 259
cultural relativism 19–20
cultural replicators *see* memes
cultural transmission 96–97, 100, 104–5,
 110, 112, 147, 160
culturally induced constraints 21
culture 77, 98, 110–11
 Acheulean 121
 and climate change 212
 and combinatorial design 174, **175**, 176
Cuthbert, Alexander 211, 211–12
Cuvier, Baron Georges 124–25, 153
cybernetic principles 251
cyberspace 236–50
 avatars 249–50, 261
 and Cartesian dualism 245–47, 261
 cybernauts 246–48
 gender inflections 247–48
 as movement space 239–45, **243**, **244**,
 261
 and place-identity 256
 topology of 236–49, **237**, **238**, **240**,
 245, 260–61
 urban comparisons 237, **237**, **238**, 239,
 241, **242**
 virtual worlds 248–50, 260

Daly, C. P. 36
Darwin, Charles 99, 113, 123, 146, 188
 Fodor and Piattelli-Palmarini's critique
 of 77–81, 81–82
 Gould and Lewontin's critique 78–80
 theory of evolution 73, 73–76, 128–29,
 192
 universal Darwinism 97–98
Dawkins, Richard 2, 93, 119, 160, 213
 on cultural production 219, 259
 gene theory 93–96
 meme theory 96–97, 110–11, 114, 155,
 156, 195, 214

De Landa, Manuel 109, 111–12, 115, 129,
 158–59, 160, 161–62, 215
decentered self, the 49–50
deconstructionism 262–63, 268
Deleuze, Gilles 158
Dennett, Daniel 75, 79, **79**, 97–98, 99,
 101, 105, 106, 108, 147, 157, 164,
 188
Derrida, Jacques 22, 65, 66, 71, 262–63,
 270
Descartes, René 127
design 102-3, 114
 and artificial selection 254, 261
 biological analogy 124–25
 and genetic algorithms 254, 256
 industrial design 168
 virtual design 254, **255**, 256, 261
 see also combinatorial design
Diamond, Jared 72, 220, 228, 231, 260
differentiation 130, 270–71
Distin, Kate 100–104, 114, 147, 155, 173,
 192, 221, 261
diversification 119
Dodson, Jago 225, 231–33
Dogon, the, village layout 26, 28, **28**
domes 78–81, **79**, **80**
Dostrovsky, John 44
Dovey, Kim 132, 135–39, 151, 220
Duffy, Francis 136
dumb-bell model 136
Dunham-Jones, Ellen 233
Durand, J. N. L. 130, 132, 154
Durham, William 109–11, 111, 112, 115,
 129, 155, 160
dwellings 13
 Australian Aborigines 15–16
 cultural imperatives 174, **175**, 176
 form 151–54, **152**, **153**, **154**
dysfunctional societies 228–30

Eames, Charles **146**
Easter Island 228–30, **229**
Eco, Umberto 132
eco-cities 235
Economo, Constantin von 47
Edo Castle, Japan 243, **243**
Ego Tunnel, the 41, 45, 51
Egypt, ancient **163**, 164

Eisenman, Peter 22
electronic age 236, 258
electronic ecologies 256–58
embodied mind, the 48–51
embodiment 56, 265–67
emergence 86–92, 113
empathy 45–48, 71, 268–69
    neurological evidence for 47
    and reading 71, 250
enactive paradigm 89, **90**
energy efficiency 212
engineering, Distin's model 102–3
Enlightenment, the 132
environment, identification with 13
environmental crisis 72
environmental degradation 230
environmental effects 160
environmental psychology 16
environmental resources, management
        failures 228–30
environmental selection 104–5
epiphylogenesis 64–66
essentialism 146
Eurocentrism 17
evolution 2, 73–92, 97–98, 113
    algorithm of 75
    artificial selection 73-74, 254, **255**, 256,
        261
    and the baby sling 83–86
    Bateson's theory of 268, 270–71
    biological mechanisms 75–76
    building types 142
    combinatorial 193
    comparison with architecture 78–81,
        79, 80
    cultural 97–98, 103, 109–11, 111–12,
        129
    Darwin's theory of 73, 73–76, 129,
        192
    endosomatic hereditary systems 129
    environmental selection pressures
        104–5
    exosomatic hereditary systems 129
    Fodor and Piattelli-Palmarini's critique
        of 77–81, 81–82
    free-riders 78, 80, 81
    Gould and Lewontin's critique 78–80
    and habits 223

    hereditary characteristics 76
    of human consciousness 87–88
    human technicity 67–68
    and Kubler's theory of artifacts 150
    Lamarckian 128–29
    modes of transmission 76–77
    mutations 74
    natural drift **90**
    and natural history 82, 110
    pace of 87–88, 96
    stabilization of phenotypic traits 77–81
    survival of the weakest 82–83
    the symbolic level 77
    of technology 2, 191–95
    theories of emergence 86–92, 113
    tools 83
    upright walking 83–86
    variability 74
exemplars, learning from 188–89
experience 51, 65–66

Federal Aid Highway Act, 169
Festa-McCormick, Diana 12
Festinger, Leon 228, 229, 260
fire, discovery of 85, 121
five aggregates, the 49–50
fixed-feature space 21
Flannery, Tim 227
flexible manufacturing system (FMS)
        250–54, **252**
Flood, Josephine 15
focal awareness 33
Fodor, Jerry 77–81, 81–82, 86, 111, 113,
        156, 221
food, cooked 85
Forbidden City, Peking 240, **242**
Ford, Henry 166–67
Ford Model T **167**
Foreign Office Architects (FOA) 207–9,
        209
form
    and content 149, 149–54, **152, 153,**
        154, 214, 215
    definition 150
    and function 173, 174, 176
    interpreting 151–54, **152, 153, 154**
    in nature 150
    isomorphic relations 149

Foster, Norman (Foster & Partners) 203–4, **204**, 206, **206**, **207**, 212, **234**, 253, **255**, 256
Foucault, Michel 132, 262, 263
Fraser, Douglas 177, **178**
free will 1, 222–25, 259–60
function 132, 173, 174, 176

Gaia hypothesis, the 227
Galileo 127–28
Gallope, Michael 66–67
Gans, Herbert 10, 17
Garnaut Climate Change Review 226–27, 227
Gazzaniga, Michael 223
Geddes, Norman Bel 168
Gehry, Frank 253, **253**
gender relations 24, 138, 247–48
General Motors 168
genes 76
    and culture 110–11
    and natural selection 93–94
    extended phenotype, the 95
    molecular structure 76
    phenotypic effects 94–96
    as replicators 93–94, 111, 112
    transmission 100, 112
genius loci, the 13
geometric space 240–41, **240**, **242**
Georgetown **186**
Gestalt 'whole' 32
Gibson, William 236, 246–47
Gilbert, Cass 199, **201**
Gilding, Paul 231, 260
Gill, Jerry 262–70
Gille, Bertrand 63, 64–66
glass architecture 199, 201, **203**
global financial crisis, 2008 137, 225
global types 135–39
global warming *see* climate change
globalization 24, 25
Gothic architecture 125, **125**
Gould, Jay 78
Gould, Stephen 188
Graziano, Michael 43–44
green skyscrapers 212
Greene & Greene 8, **9**
Greenfield, Susan 249, 261

Greenland, Viking colony 228, 229
Grene, Marjorie 34–35, 37
grid cells 44–45
Gross, Charles 43–44
Guattari, Felix 158
Guggenheim Museum Bilbao 253, **253**

habit 220–21, 222–25
Hall, Edward 7, 20–21, 55, 73, 189, 220
Hamilton, Clive 227–28
Hamilton, W. D. 94
hand-axe forms 120–21, **120**
Haseki Sultan Mosque, Istanbul **80**
Haussmann, Baron Eugène 237, **237**, 239
Head, Sir Henry 16
Heidegger, Martin 7, 12–13, 26, 54, 61–62, 63, 195–97
Heim, Mitchell 245–47
Hillier, Ben 132
Hindu-Javanese temple structure 178–79, **179**
historical method, the 140–41
Hof, Patrick 47
Hollywood 220–21
holomemes 110
homes, importance attached to 8–10
Homo habilis 83
homo sacer 66–67
Homo sapiens 2, 40, 82, 83, 123, 271
Hongkong and Shanghai Bank head-quarters 203, **204**, 253
Hopi, the 19–20, 173
housing **10**, 137–39, 141
    houses-on-stilts 181
    and place-identity 8–10, **8**, **9**, **10**, **11**, 12
    Japanese house 174, **175**
    see also suburbs, and suburban dwellings; vernacular architecture
human development, and place 21–23
human diversity, loss of 112
human technicity 67–70, 72
hunter-gatherers 72
Husserl, Edmund 26, 31, 36
Huxtable, Ada Louise 198–99
hybridization 173, 177–87, 215
    vernacular features 181, **182**, 183, **183**

identity
    artifacts 147
    building 173
    collective 143
    cultural 23–24, 174
    and memes 106
    personal 7–8
    sustainment of 87
imitation, cognitive limitations 155
immersion 34–36, **35**
individuality 88–89
Industrial Revolution 130, 132, 166
infrastructure 139
Ingold, Tim 37–38, 265
innovation and the innovation process 136, 144, 176, 188–91, **190**
    layer cake theory 191
inorganic organized beings 63
Inoue, Mitsuo 239–40, 243–45, **244**
InRealLife (film) 249
inside–outside relationship 13
intensional fallacy, the 78
Intergovernmental Panel for Climate Change (IPCC) 226–27
Internet, the 236, 236–49
interstate highways 161, 162, 167–70, **170**, 172, 215
invisible structures 132
Irwin, Steve 20
Irwin House, Pasadena, Los Angeles **9**
Izenour, Steven 17

Jablonka, Eva 76–77, 81, 101, 156, 157
Japan 174, **175**, 177, 239–40, 241, 243, **243**, 261
Jencks, Charles 12
jet engine, the 193, 194
Jimison, David 257
Johannsen, Wilhelm Ludwig 76
Joyce, James 12
Jung, Carl 8–9

Karlsruhe 240, **242**
Kenworthy, Jeff 232
Kerr, Philip 247–48, 249
Kidron, Beeban 249–50
King, Anthony 179, 181
Kirsh, David 52

knowledge relations 133
Koestler, Arthur 188
Korzybski, Alfred 270
Kuala Lumpur 179, **180**, **181**, 206, **207**
Kubler, George 119, 142–44, 150, 189–91, 191, 192, 214, 228
Kuhn, Thomas 35–36, 188, 188–89

Laland, Kevin 104–5, 105, 108, 129, 156
Lamarck, Jean-Baptiste de la Marck 76, 128–29
Lamb, Marion 76–77, 81, 101, 156, 157
landscape, invisible 14–16
Langer, Jonas 121–22, 213
language 19–20, 20–21, 103, 120–22, 213
    diachronic aspects 155, 265
    linguistic phenomenology 267–68
    postmodernism and 262–63
    synchronic aspects 155, 265
    Wittgenstein and 264–65, 266–67
Larkin Building, Buffalo 199, **202**, 203
Las Vegas 17, **18**
Lasch, Christopher 249
latent capacity 165
Latin America 189–91, **190**
Lavedan, Pierre 141
Le Corbusier 129, 197
    Domino House 126, **127**
    Modulor system of proportion 26, **27**, 28–29
    Plan Voisin, Paris 139, **140**
    vertical garden city 209
    Villa Stein 151–53, **153**, **154**
Leach, Neil 23–24, 25
learning, by example 36
Leonardo da Vinci 26, **27**
Leppington, Sydney 233, **234**
Leroi-Gourhan, André 64–65, 67–68, 69, 177
Lever House, New York 201, **203**
Lévi-Strauss, Claude 122–23, **122**
Lewontin, Richard 78–80
life, as difference 66
Lilley, Samuel 163–64, 165
linguistic phenomenology 267–68
linguistics 139–41
linked problem solutions 142–44, 150, 214

Linnaeus, Carl von 123
London 206, **207**
Los Angeles **11**
Lotka, Alfred 129
Lovelock, James 227
Lubbock, Texas **171**
Lumley, Henry de 120–21
Luzzi, Joseph 12
Lynch, Kevin 16–18, 55, 139, 142
Lyotard, Jean-François 262, 263

MacMansions **171**
McRae, Mike 222–25, 229, 259, 260
Maglio, Paul 52
Maillart, Robert 192, 195–97, **196**
Malay house, the 181, 182, **182**, 187
Malpas, J. E. 21–22, 22–23, 55
Malthus, T. R. 74, 78, 188
March, Lionel 211
Markus, Thomas 132–33, 135, 138, 151
Masdar City, Abu Dhabi **234**, 235
Massey, Doreen 25
mass-production 166–67, 253
matter–energy flows 112
Maturana, Humberto 86, 88–91, 193, 197,
   215
Mead, George Herbert 268–70, 271
meanings 132–33, 135
mechanical age 236
Mees, Paul 233
meme complexes 105–6
memes 93, 93–112, 114–15, 119, 213,
   214, 259
   allomemes 110
   Aunger's interpretation 106–9, 114,
      147, 155
   Blackmore's interpretation 98–100, 101,
      105–6, 106, 147
   and coevolution 109–11, 112
   and cognitive extension 105–6
   competition 96–97
   Dawkins' theory of 96–97, 110–11, 114,
      155, 156, 195, 214
   De Landa's interpretation 109–11,
      111–12, 115, 158–59
   definition 2, 97–98, 98–100, 101,
      102, 110–11, 111, 114, 115,
      154–55, 214
   Dennett's interpretation of 97–98, 99,
      101, 106, 147, 157
   Distin's interpretation 100–104, 112,
      114, 147, 155
   Durham's interpretation 109–11, 112,
      115, 155
   genetic background 93–96
   holomemes 110
   Lamarckian character of 99, 100, 109
   location 101, 106–7
   and memory 107–8
   and natural selection 156
   neurological composition 106–9
   and niche construction 104–5, 157
   parasitic behaviour 97
   passive picture of human beings 157
   and personal possessions 106
   program 154–55
   propagation 4, 100, 112
   replication 99–100, 101–3, 107, 111,
      221–22
   and the self 105–6
   selfish characteristics 97
   Taylor on 144–45
   technical 119, 149, 154–57, 159,
      160–61, 161–62, 174, 219–20, 221
   transmission 100, 107, 108–9, 147,
      221–22
   viral analogy 221–22
memetic algorithms (MAs) 254, 256
memetic generations 100
memory 65, 66, 67, 70, 71, 107–8
Menara Mesiniaga tower, Kuala Lumpur
   206, **207**
Merleau-Ponty, Maurice 3, 26, 30–33, 35,
   36, 39, 40, 45, 47, 48–49, 51, 54,
   55–56, 90, 244, 261, 262, 266
Metzinger, Thomas 39–43, 45, 46–47, 51,
   56
Miletos, Greece **238**, 239
mind, the 48–49, 52–53
   Bateson's theory of 270–71
   and change 194–95
   Distin's model 103
mind–body dualism 3, 36–37, 245–47
mind–body synthesis, 3, 44, 45
Mingers, John 88–92, 120, 147, 148,
   161

mirror neurons 46–47, 48, 56
Mitchell, William 236–37, 239, 245, 256–57, 258, 260–61
Modern Times (film) 167
Molins Machine Company 251, **252**
monuments 141–42
Moore, Charles 29
Morgan, G. 230–31
morphological flexibility 153–54
morphology 127
  morphogenesis 254
  morphological flexibility 153–54
  morphological types 86–87
Moser, Edvard and May-Britt 44–45
motor vocabulary 45
movement space 28, 239–45, **243**, **244**, 261
movie genres 220–21
Mugerauer, Robert 29
Mullins, Justin 248–49
Mumford, Lewis 17, 62, 72, 169–70
Murcutt, Glenn 8, **8**, 20
musical technics 65–66

naïve functionalism 141
National Commercial Bank, Jeddah 205, **205**
natural drift 90–91, 113
natural history 82
natural resources 193
natural selection 2, 73–76, 86, 94, 97–99, 113, 129
  and change 195
  comparison with architecture 78–81, **79**, **80**
  Fodor and Piattelli-Palmarini's critique of 77–81, 81–82
  free-riders 78, 80, 81
  and genes 93–94
  and memes 156
  stabilization of phenotypic traits 77–81
natural technics 71
Nazi Germany 168
neo-Darwinism 75, 79–80, 110, 113, 155
neurology, body schema 42
New York 199, **200**, 201, **201**, **203**

New York World's Fair, 1939 168
Newman, Peter 232
niche construction 104–5, 105, 129, 157
Nimchinsky, Esther 47
Nolli, Giambattista 239, **241**
Norberg-Schulz, Christian 12–14, 14–15, 17, 18, 55, 139, 142
novel technologies, appearance of 192–94

objects, experience of 31
ocularcentrism 30
Odling-Smee, John 104–5, 105, 108, 129, 156
office towers 135–36
Ohain, Hans von 194
O'Keefe, John 44
Oliver, Paul 19–20, 55, 176
open systems 87–88
oppositional thinking 263
Oreskes, Naomi 227, 230
organizations, egocentric 230–31
Otis, Elisha Grave 198, **198**
out of body experiences (OBEs) 41–42
Ozenfant, Amédée 129

Paek, Joo Youn 257
palaeontology 125
Palazzo della Ragione, Padua 141
Palladio, Andrea 151–52, **152**, **154**, **184**, **186**
Pallasmaa, Juhani 30
parametric modeling techniques **255**
Paris 139, **140**, 237, **237**, 239
Pentonville Prison, 1842 **134**
Pepper, Simon 30
perception 18, 31–33, 46
peripersonal space 43, 56
permanent innovation 63
personas 159
Pevsner, Nikolaus 130, 132, 151
phallic symbolism 135
phantom limbs 41
phenomenology 2, 7, 12–13, 31, 48–49, 51, 56
phenotypes 76, 77–81, 81–82, 93–96, 100, 104, 157, 160
Piattelli-Palmarini, Massimo 77–81, 81–82, 86, 111, 113, 156, 221

place 7, 12–14, **14**, 21–25, 72
place cells 44–45
place-identity 2, 7, 7–14, 55
　　Australian Aborigines 15–16
　　and belonging 23–25
　　cultural relativism 19–20
　　and cyberspace 256
　　and self 21–23
　　and values 16–18, **18**
plan forms 176
Plato 146, 231, 245–46
Poëte, Marcel 141
Polanyi, Michael 3, 26, 31, 32–37, 39, 40,
　　42, 43, 45, 54, 55–56, 86–88, 195,
　　244, 261, 262, 263–64, 266–67
population thinking 146
possessions, personal 106
Post, George B. **200**
postmodernism 262–70
power relations 25, 132, 133, 135–36
primary forms 176
prime objects 144, 150, 191
prions 107
Proshansky, Harold 7–8
Proust, Marcel 12, 71
proxemics 7, 20–21, 55
psychological denial 229–30
public transport 231–33, 260
Pueblo Indians 19, 189
　　Pueblo methods of building 189, **190**
pure thought (*episteme*) 63

Queensland house, the 187, **187**

radar 192
radical design 195–97, **196,** 215
Raffles, Sir Stamford 184
Rapoport, Amos 14, 29–30, 55, 174, 177
rationality 37, 269–70
reading 71, 250
reciprocal relationships 88–89
reinforced concrete 195–97, **196**
relational concepts 19–20
replicas 144
Rizzolatti, Giacomo 45–46
Roberts, Ben 70
robots 248–49
Rome 17, 239, **241**

Rosch, Eleanor 48–51
Rossi, Aldo 139–42, 151, 152–53, 154
Rouse Hill Town Centre **137**, 233
Rowe, Colin 139, 151–52
Rykwert, John 30
Ryle, Gilbert 224

St Paul Building, New York **200**
Sapir, Edward 19–20
Sapir–Whorf hypothesis, the 19–20, 20
Saunders, P. 137, 138
Schon, Donald 188
Schwandbach Bridge 192, 195–97, **196**
Second Life (game) 249
Seidler, Harry 206, **206**
selective breeding 73–74, 78
self, the 1, 39–41, 43, 56, 224–25, 266
　　as aggregates of experience 48–50
　　Buddhist account 49–50, 51
　　Cartesian school 105
　　decentered 49–50
　　fields of being 53–54, 57
　　and the Internet 245–47
　　and memes 105–6
　　neurological basis for 48
　　paradox of 50–51
　　phenomenal self-model (PSM) 40
　　and place-identity 21–23
self-models 40–47
self-organization 86–88
self-producing systems 4, 88–92, 147–48,
　　161, 197, 214
semiotics 123
settlement patterns 177, **178**
shelter 72, 94–96
Sherman, David 231, 260
shopping malls 136–37, **137**, 161, 169
similitude, principle of 127–28
Sinan **80**, 81
Singapore 184
Sipe, Neil 225, 231–33
skeleton construction 126–27, **126**, 199
skyscrapers 125, 126, **126**, 151
　　evolution of 197–206, **198, 200, 201,**
　　　202, 203, 204, 205, 206, 207,
　　　215–16
　　exploration of type 207–12, **208, 209,**
　　　210, 211

extrusion principle 208
glass architecture 199, 201, **203**
internal structure 199, 203–4, **204**, 208
skygardens 205–6, **205**
spatial efficiency 211–12
vertical divisions 199, **200**
smart technology 257
Smith, Joseph Wayne 231, 260
snails 94–95
social consciousness 47
social Darwinism 129
social neurosciences 45–48
social relations, and building types 132–33, **134**, 135
social systems **90**, 148, 161–72, 215
sociality, and technics 69–72
space 19–20, 21, 42, 132, 243–45, **244**
space-mapping neurons 44–45
Spanish colonial architecture 189–91, **190**
spatial cognition 21, 29, 31, 41–45, 55–56
spatial dynamic, tacit knowing 34–36
spatial efficiency 211–12
spatial elements, housing 137–38
Special Modelling Group (SMG) 255, **256**
species, and types 64, 149–51
polytypic taxa 145
Sperber, Dan 154–55
sports utility vehicle (SUV) 221–22, **222**
Stea, David 17–18
Steadman, Philip 125–29, 129–30, 151
Stiegler, Bernard 2, 73, 82–83, 113, 115, 161, 192–93, 215, 228, 259
criticisms 61, 69, 70–71, 93
determinism 69–70, 71–72
epiphylogenesis 64–66
influence 68–69
and memory 70
and technics 61–68
and tools 65
Stone, Allucquere Rosanne 247–48
style 132, 151
subjective space 23
subsidiary awareness 33

suburbs, and suburban dwellings **8**, **9**, **10**, **11**, 12, 137–39, 161, 169–70, **171**
Sunstein, Cass 224, 229, 260
Swiss Re, London 206, **207**
Sydney **8**
symbolic animal, the 77
symbolic interactionism 268–70
symbolic systems 77, 103
symbolic values 15–16
symbolization 68
systemic effects 160
systems theory 87, 160

tacit knowing 26, 32, 33–37, 43, 56
taxonomies 2, 119–20, 123, 147–48, 213, 219
Taylor, Timothy 2, 82–86, 93, 113, 114, 144–47
technical memes 4, 119, 149, 154–57, 159, 160–61, 161–62, 174, 215, 219–20, 221
technics 61–72, 82–83, 113, 114
animal 68
anthropocentrism 67–68
apocalyptic aspects 72
and the body 70–71
and brain development 64–66
criticisms 93
deterministic 69–70, 71–72
development of 61–63
diffusion 64–65
duality 62–63
epiphylogenesis 64–66
musical 65–66
natural 71
and permanent innovation 63
and place 72
and sociality 69–70, 70–72
Stiegler and 67–68
transmission 69–70, 71–72
Vaccari and 68–70
and writing 65–66, 66, 69, 71
technology 2, 21, 61–62, 63, 72, 82, 191–95
territoriality 21
theatres 130, **131**
Thompson, D'Arcy Wentworth 124, 127, 150

Thompson, Evan 48–51
Thomson, David 220–21
Thoreau's man-alone vision 225
thought, conservatism of 222–25
three-dimensionality, sense of 29
Time magazine 239, **240**
tools
   animal tool use 61, 68, 113
   and brain development 65–66, 83
   early 69
   evolution 83
   exomatic organs 129
   found objects 71
   reproduction 120–21, **120**
   as spatial extensions 42
   Stiegler and 65
tower type *see* skyscrapers
transport 138–39, 231–33, 260
tribal thinking 4, 223–24, 227, 259
Tschumi, Bernard 22
Tuan, Yi-Fu 28
types 119–20, 213, 214, 219, 270–71
   boundaries 148
   and combinativity 120–23
   identifying 146–47
   and logic 144–47
   native classifications 122–23, **122**
   self-producing 147–48
   species 149–51
   Taylor on 144-147
   variations 146–47

United Architects 207–9, **208**
United States of America
   automobile dependency 139, 166
   interstate highways 167–70, **170**, 172
   shopping malls 137
urban dispersal 138–39
urban form 16–18
urban impacts, interstate highways 169–70,
   171, 172
urban planning 21
urban science 139
urban systems, computer modeling
   256–58
urban typologies 139–42
urban values 16–18
urbanization 2, 4, 232–33, 233, **234**, 235

Vaccari, Andrés 68–70, 70–72
Van Alen, William 199, **201**
Van Camp, Nathan 66–67, 70
van der Rohe, Mies 197, 199, 201, **203**
Varela, Francisco J. 48–51, 56, 86, 88–91,
   193, 197, 215
Venturi, Robert 17, 197
vernacular architecture 173, 174, 176
   the California Bungalow **9**, 10, **11**,
     187
   Chinese shop-houses 183, **185**, **186**
   houses-on-stilts 181
   the Malay house 181, **182**, 183, 187
   the Queensland house 187, **187**
   the Japanese house, 174, **175**, 177
vertical architecture 209
Vertical Architecture STudio (VAST) 209,
   210, **211**
Vesely, Dalibor 30
villas 151–54, **152**, **153**, **154**, **183**, **184**
Viollet-le-Duc, Eugène Emmanuel 125,
   154
virtual design 254, **255**, 256, 261
virtual selves 249–50, 261
virtual worlds 248–50, 260
Vitruvian Man 26, **27**, 30
Volti, Rudi 166–67, 169
von Economo neurons (VENS) 47–48

Wallace, Alfred 75
Wallace, Ken 102
Ward, Russel 20
Webber, Melvin 17, 256
wheels, spoked 162–63, 163–65, **163**, **165**,
   167, 215
Whitehead, Alfred North 262, 264, 265
Whorf, Benjamin Lee 19–20, 21, 189
Wilkins, John 146, 214
Williams, Caroline 47–48
Williams, G. C. 94
Williams, P. 137, 138
Williamson, D. T. N. 251
Williamson, June 233
Wise, Chris 254, 256, 258
Wittgenstein, Ludwig 36, 37, 159, 262,
   264–67, 268, 271
Wolf, Maryanne 71, 250
Wolfe, Maxine 7–8

Woolworth Building, New York 199, **201**
workhouse, 1835 **134**
World Trade Center competition, 2002
   207–9, **208**, **209**
Wright, Frank Lloyd 199, **202**, 203
writing 65–66, 66, 69, 71

Yeang, Ken 206, **207**, 211–12
Young, David 74, 75, 82, 124